OVER CLOCKED

The New Rules for Winning in the Kinetic Economy

MIKE WOKOSIN

Mike@OverClockedGear.com

Limited Distribution Beta Edition 2025

Overclocked *(adj.)*

A mindset and method for operating beyond convention, where performance is fluid, experimentation is constant, and evolution is intentional. To be Overclocked is to reject stagnation, embrace calibration, and accelerate value through the high-stakes harmony of speed, resilience, and self-awareness.

Table of Contents

SECTION III — THE TRANSMISSION

SECTION IV — THE FRONTIER

About the Author

Tuned by experience. Driven by velocity. Rebuilt to push the edge.

With over three decades in digital, I've never believed in default settings.

My digital journey began in the summer of 1995, when a chance conversation with a telecom strategist about the future of the Internet shifted my trajectory. From that moment on, I've been obsessed with the convergence of technology, human behavior, and business performance, not just watching it unfold, but helping to shape its evolution.

I've built systems that scaled, reinvented brands under pressure, and pushed organizations beyond what they thought possible. From helping digitize global media operations at Warner Bros., launching e-commerce brands before the "brick and click" concept became a buzzword, to architecting omnichannel ecosystems at Nautilus and American Eagle Outfitters, my work has always centered on collaboration, velocity, and value.

At Universal Studios, I led digital strategy for Home Entertainment, formed the Executive Digital Council, and helped unify over 150 million fans into a strategic engagement platform for TV, Film, and Games. At Redbox, I helped overclock the customer experience, architecting an AI-powered CRM core that connected real-time data across kiosks, apps, and campaigns to deliver personalized engagement at scale.

Along the way, I've experienced technology evolving from mainframes to AI accelerators, and business models mutating from distribution-first to data-native. I've seen what happens when organizations play it safe, and what's possible when they push the edge.

After seven years of teaching digital strategy at the University of Iowa's Tippie College of Business, I wrote Overclocked:.Business Reinvention as a tuning guide, a framework for navigating constant reinvention. It's built for those who know that strategy is not static. That performance isn't stable. And, to lead in digital, you must be willing to evolve under pressure.

This book is supported by a dynamic companion platform filled with evolving frameworks, diagnostics, and insights. Because digital strategy, like overclocking, isn't something you master once, it's a system you tune constantly.

Whether you're a founder, C-Suite Executive, consultant, or student, I hope this work provides you with the mindset and methods to unlock your potential and prototype the future.

— Mike Wokosin

Contributors and Collaborators

All my managers
Unnamed Forman — Corn Detasseling
Mike Winkelpleck — Hy-Vee
Chuck Cooley — Cimmarina
Student Work-study — University of Iowa
Brian Roberts — Lanier Dictation Equipment
Unnamed bar manager/Bouncer — The Bridge
Laura Gray — Midwest Real Estate Investment Co.
Ed Hanson — Jewel Foods
Karen Bruckner — Nestle
Sammy El Sadin — Nestle
Doreen Ida/Marie Queen — Nestle
Mark Hepp — Nestle
Mark Horak — Warner Bros
Jim Wuthrich — Warner Bros
Jim Newman — Acquity Group
Doug Textor — The Cannery
Mark Silva — Real Branding
Hilary Hofman — Universal Studios
David Armano — Edelman Digital
Kira Heinemann — Redbox
Galen Smith — Redbox
HNI
University of Iowa
Ya Ya Creations
Broken Earth Vineyard

Why Overclocked? Always-On as if Every Day Were Black Friday

While retail has operated in an "always-on" mode for decades through 24/7 stores and e-commerce, gaming provides the most comprehensive blueprint for high-intensity, always-on operations. Gaming companies don't just stay open; they operate at peak performance continuously, as if every day were Black Friday and every customer interaction were mission-critical.

The Intensity Difference

Traditional retail operates with predictable rhythms: busy periods (such as holidays and sales events) are followed by routine operations. Gaming companies have eliminated this distinction; they operate at Black Friday intensity continuously:

- **Millions of concurrent global users** requiring real-time response
- **Zero tolerance for downtime** during peak engagement periods
- **Instant deployment** of fixes and features without service interruption
- **Real-time personalization** for each user experience
- **Continuous content creation** to maintain engagement and prevent churn

Peak Performance as Standard Operating Procedure

While retailers prepare months in advance for Black Friday and experience website crashes or inventory shortages, gaming platforms like *Fortnite*, *Roblox*, and *World of Warcraft* handle their equivalent traffic volumes every day. When *Fortnite* hosts a virtual concert with 12 million concurrent viewers, or when *Roblox* manages 50+ million daily active users creating and playing simultaneously, they're demonstrating operational capabilities that most enterprises only attempt during their most significant sales events.

The Operational Excellence Standard

Gaming companies have solved the challenges that still plague other industries:

- **Dynamic load balancing** that automatically scales infrastructure based on real-time demand
- **Continuous deployment** without service interruption or user impact
- **Real-time customer support** integrated directly into the product experience
- **Instant personalization** that adapts to individual behavior patterns

- **Community-driven feedback loops** that inform product development in real-time

Why This Intensity Model Matters

In an AI-accelerated market, every interaction becomes potentially critical. Customer preferences shift in real-time. Competitive advantages emerge and disappear within market cycles measured in weeks, not quarters. Supply chain disruptions require immediate response. Revenue opportunities appear unexpectedly and vanish quickly.

Organizations that can operate in Black Friday mode continuously will capture value that others miss during their planning cycles. They'll respond to market shifts while competitors are still detecting them. They'll optimize customer experiences in real-time while others are scheduling A/B tests for next quarter.

The Gaming-to-Enterprise Translation

Gaming's "every day is Black Friday" model provides the operational blueprint for enterprises that want to compete in real-time markets:

- Infrastructure that scales automatically rather than requiring manual intervention
- Decision-making systems that operate in real-time rather than waiting for scheduled reviews
- Customer experience optimization that happens continuously rather than through periodic campaigns
- Product development that incorporates feedback immediately rather than through annual planning cycles

This isn't about making business more like entertainment; it's about adopting the operational intensity that enables companies to capture every opportunity, respond to every challenge, and optimize every interaction as if the stakes were always critical.

Because in an always-on world, they are.

How to Use This Platform

Overclocked isn't just a book. It's the front-end to a multi-modal learning platform designed for:

Students building a future-ready career

Managers and operators are optimizing their strategy in real time

Executives upgrading their thinking and digital literacy

Enterprises developing a shared language for reinvention

Overclocked is your initial boot sequence, where your character spawns into a new world.

This book was built on mastery learning principles, meaning you'll be exposed to essential ideas repeatedly, in different formats, and with increasing depth. Every chapter links strategic theory with tactical execution and contemporary business scenarios. Subsequent chapters will build upon and reintroduce those concepts with increasing complexity.

We meet you where you are and give you the tools to keep climbing.

Learning Mode	What You Unlock
The book	Ground yourself in the entire system, from strategy to execution.
Mastery Course	Go deeper with assessments, exercises, and guided application in an 8-week course.
Digital Fluency Self-Assessments	Diagnose where you or your organization are on the maturity curve.
Live sessions	Stay sharp as the tools and trends evolve.
Workshops	Hands-on experience for teams building real-world solutions.
Executive mentoring	Accelerate your leadership edge in 1:1 or group formats.

SECTION I

The Operating System

Build the core architecture that enables reinvention.

Strategy isn't in a binder; it's the operating system that runs your entire enterprise. This section rewires leadership, strategy, disruption, and infrastructure into a living system that senses, adapts, and compounds advantage. Without this foundation, everything else is just noise in the machine.

CHAPTER 1

The Next Gen Leader — Change Catalyst

Think Like a Digital Leader

Imagine your organization as a soccer club midway through the season. The league table is tight. A few bad matches, and you're flirting with relegation. A few decisive wins, and you could be in contention for a championship spot. The difference between moving up and dropping down isn't just the talent on the field; it's the leadership's ability to adapt the game plan, motivate the squad, and make bold substitutions at the right moment.

That's the reality of leading in the digital era. The "season" never really ends, the competition is global, and the rules change mid-match. You can have the most advanced tools, the biggest budget, and the flashiest tactics board, but if your team isn't aligned, confident, and adaptable, you'll be chasing the game instead of controlling it.

Here's the hard truth: 70% of digital transformation initiatives fail, and not because of the tech. They failed because leaders couldn't inspire confidence, break down silos, or adjust their strategy quickly enough when the market shifted.

In this chapter, we'll explore what it takes to be a digital-first leader who keeps the team in contention, whatever the conditions. You'll see how leaders like Satya Nadella didn't just rewrite Microsoft's playbook; they reshaped the culture, removed internal rivalries, and created an organization that could attack opportunities and defend against disruption in real time.

The best digital leaders are part strategist, part motivator, and part translator, able to see the whole pitch, adapt under pressure, and get every player moving toward the same goal. Because in the digital league, there's no guaranteed promotion, and the cost of relegation can be the end of the club.

MASTERY LEARNING OBJECTIVES

- Identify the key traits and competencies that distinguish effective digital-first leaders from traditional leadership approaches
- Recognize the need and apply the four building blocks of change to digital initiatives
- Evaluate organizational readiness for digital leadership challenges

Today's digital leaders operate at the intersection of technology, business strategy, and organizational development. They must simultaneously manage the acceleration of technological change, evolving customer expectations, and internal transformation challenges.

INDUSTRY INSIGHT

Satya Nadella — The Cloud-First Comeback

How Microsoft's CEO reframed a legacy tech giant around the cloud, transforming not just the product portfolio but the company's culture.

In 2014, Microsoft was viewed as a slow-moving giant, still defined by Windows and Office licenses in a world racing toward cloud and mobile. Enter Satya Nadella, who didn't just change the product roadmap; he rewired the company's mindset.

Challenge

Microsoft's culture had calcified; meanwhile, competitors like Amazon and Google were surging ahead in cloud services, while mobile had already slipped away to Apple and Android. The challenge: pivot from a product-centric, Windows-first strategy to a services-led, cloud-first enterprise, without breaking the machine that still printed billions in profit.

The Velocity Shift

Nadella declared a "mobile-first, cloud-first" vision, pushed Azure to the forefront, and embraced open source, a move unthinkable in the Ballmer era. He championed cross-platform compatibility, reoriented teams around growth markets, and placed collaboration and empathy at the center of Microsoft's leadership ethos. By treating Azure like a live-service platform, constantly patched, updated, and expanded, Microsoft competed with AWS on capability, not just price.

Results / Impact

Within five years, Microsoft's market cap tripled. Azure became the second-largest cloud platform globally, and the company's reputation shifted from that of a legacy software vendor to a leader in cloud innovation. Cultural scores improved, partnerships expanded, and Microsoft became a magnet for top talent once again.

STRATEGIC TAKEAWAYS

- **Lead with a Unifying Vision** — Nadella's clear "cloud-first" mantra aligned product, culture, and strategy.
- **Embrace Ecosystem Thinking** — Opening to rivals' platforms expanded reach and relevance.
- **Operate as a Live Service** — Continuous iteration kept Azure competitive in a rapidly evolving market.

REFLECTION

Before moving forward, take a moment to think about your own experiences with digital evolution.

- How has digital disrupted your industry or career? What were the signals?
- Are you leading digital transformation, or is your business reacting to change?
- What skills, knowledge, or perspectives do you need to elevate your digital leadership? How about your team?

No matter where you are in your journey, whether you are a seasoned digital veteran, an executive navigating transformation, or an entrepreneur scaling a business, this chapter will help you understand, adapt to, and lead in an increasingly digital world.

Digital Leadership as Change Management

At its core, digital leadership is fundamentally about creating a vision and navigating the inevitable change that accompanies it. As organizations navigate technological shifts, evolving consumer behaviors, and competitive disruption, the capacity to lead transformation becomes the defining characteristic of successful digital leaders.

Change management theory provides the intellectual framework for understanding how individuals, teams, and organizations adapt to new realities and challenges. Traditional models, such as Lewin's three-stage process (unfreeze-change-refreeze)[1] and Kotter's eight-step model for leading change, as well as the action research approach[2], provide insight into the various aspects of organizational transformation. These frameworks acknowledge that successful change requires both technical expertise and human-centered leadership.

Digital has amplified these challenges by accelerating the pace and scope of change. While traditional change management might focus on discrete initiatives with clear endpoints, digital leadership operates in an environment of continuous adaptation where the goal is not to complete transformation but to build organizational capacity for ongoing evolution.

Kurt Lewin 3 Stages Change Model

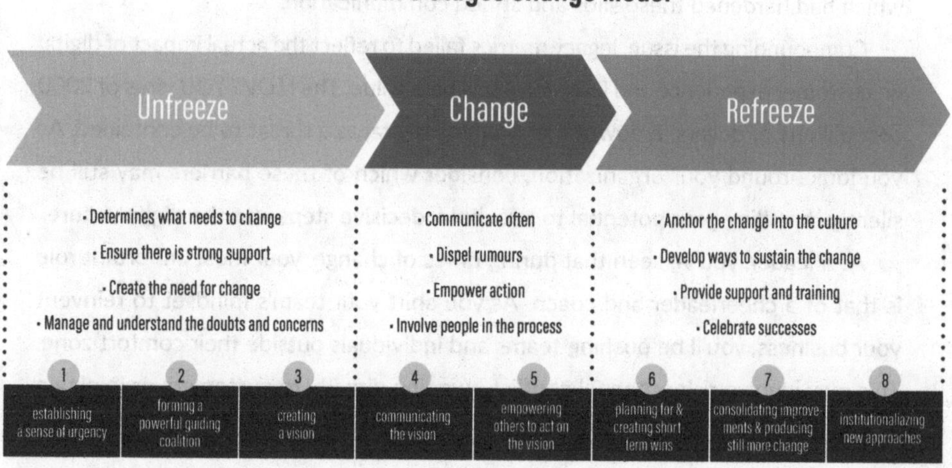

John Kotter 8 Steps Change Framework

The Evolution of Digital Strategy: From Experimental to Essential

When digital emerged, Fortune 1,000 firms hadn't seen a business catalyst like this since electricity or the steam engine. Outside of Silicon Valley, it was viewed skeptically as an experimental function, siloed from core business operations and treated as a specialized discipline. This early period was characterized by isolated initiatives, including the company's first website, initial email marketing campaigns, and experimental eCommerce platforms.

Digital is no longer a department or subject matter expert; it's a team sport and the backbone of modern business strategy. Those with a fully mature digital ecosystem are now adopting AI and Blockchain platforms beyond the experimental and pilot phases to reinvent themselves and outpace their competition.

From Skepticism to Integration

Digital evolution was stunted not by technology itself, but by deep-rooted organizational resistance. The collapse of the Internet Bubble in 2000[3] left boards of directors and executives gun-shy of digital initiatives, creating hesitancy about future investments. Internally, silos and territorial behavior created friction between traditional and digital teams, slowing collaboration and innovation. As it became clear that digital evolution was a revolution, every department, from PR to Sales, Operations, and Customer Service, battled the typical Marketing-IT ownership, which had hardened these silos and stifled communication.

Compounding the issue, legacy metrics failed to reflect the actual impact of digital on customer experience and long-term business value. The *I LOVE YOU* virus of 2000 cost billions of dollars in downtime[4], framing digital as a threat to be contained. As you look around your organization, consider which of these barriers may still be silently throttling your potential to take bold, decisive steps into the digital future.

As a leader, you've seen that during times of change, your most important role is that of a cheerleader and coach. As you shift your team's mindset to reinvent your business, you'll be pushing teams and individuals outside their comfort zone. This may involve risky channel conflict by going directly to customers or joining a cross-industry marketplace to capture untapped audiences.

The Optimization Catalyst: Data and Measurement

Digital hasn't just accelerated business; it has rewired how performance is measured, optimized, and leveraged. On the revenue generation side, leaders were flying blind, haunted by John Wanamaker's famous truth:

"Half the money I spend on advertising is wasted; the trouble is, I don't know which half."

Digital changed that. It didn't just offer visibility; it delivered real-time telemetry.

Multi-touch attribution connected every click to a customer and every campaign to the bottom line. Multi-variate, real-time testing replaced gut instinct with battle-tested decisions. Journey analytics exposed customer behaviors that had gone unnoticed. And real-time dashboards broke down the walls, putting insight into the hands of every operator, not just the analyst.

This wasn't just a measurement revolution; it was a mindset shift. Suddenly, CFOs weren't just tolerating digital, they were backing it. CEOs stopped asking *why digital* and started asking *what's next*. When performance became trackable, tunable, and transparent, digital transitioned from a nice-to-have to a growth engine that could be benchmarked, scaled, and optimized.

Five Essential Traits for Digital Leadership

Over the last 25 years, I've experienced both the highs of success and the lows of failure, and I've recognized a pattern for reducing risk and increasing positive outcomes. Successful digital leaders demonstrate distinctive characteristics that enable them to navigate complexity and drive sustainable personal and organizational transformation:

1. Translation

We. *Yes, you and I,* we're in this together for the next 18 chapters and beyond, and we can translate business objectives into technological possibilities with tangible business outcomes. Translating digital capabilities into competitive advantage.

2. Comfort with Ambiguity

We embrace ambiguity. Tech and processes are evolving as quickly in the AI & blockchain world as they did when Web 1.0 emerged. You must accept that there will be unknowns with multiple options to solve. Get intellectually curious, model continuous learning, and experiment with emerging technology. Recognize that expertise has a shorter half-life in digital domains and prioritize adaptability over rigid specialization.

"According to McKinsey, companies with digitally savvy leadership teams outperform their peers by 48% in revenue growth and 15% in margin improvement."

3. Cross-Functional Collaboration

Digital initiatives typically span traditional organizational boundaries. Successful leaders can speak the language of business functions, user experience design, and technology, creating shared understanding and aligning diverse stakeholders around common objectives.

4. Data-Informed Decision Making

Digital leaders understand that decision-making can be part art and part science, and leverage analytics to inform decision-making while recognizing data limitations. They balance quantitative insights with qualitative understanding, combining rigorous analysis with strategic intuition.

5. Customer-Centric Perspective

Effective digital leadership centers on developing strategies that meet customer needs. These leaders systematically gather and integrate customer feedback, empathize with pain points, and prioritize initiatives based on customer impact.

From Digital Expert to Transformation Catalyst

I'll never forget sitting in that Warner Bros conference room in 2003, staring at a whiteboard covered with org charts and process diagrams that looked more like archaeological diagrams than modern business structures. We had just completed our pilot, globalizing the B2B portal with a standard digital infrastructure that synced directly to product management operations, and it was working. Global, multi-lingual, and directly connected to our most important customers and sales teams. But as I looked around that room, I realized we were standing at the edge of something much bigger than portal optimization.

When I started my digital career, leadership meant being an expert who could navigate email campaigns, optimize website conversions, and manage banner ad buys across multiple markets. I was the go-to person for executives seeking someone who understood how to translate business objectives into tech delivery and tech infrastructure opportunities and limitations to the exec team. However, the success of our B2B platform has proven crucial: digital infrastructure can be the backbone for enterprise-wide transformation, not just marketing channel management.

We were ready to push the clock. Our 18-month global effort demonstrated that we could build scalable, global digital systems that integrated seamlessly with Warner Bros.' complex operations. Now we had the mandate to reinvent the studio's operations for digital cinema, the upcoming wave of streaming, and digital downloads, while driving massive efficiency gains by gutting traditional analog processes that had defined Hollywood for decades.

Working alongside David Wolf, Accenture's Media and Entertainment Managing Partner, and internal partner Darcy Antonellis, head of Technical Operations, we swung a wrecking ball through outdated workflows that were burning millions in analog expenses while constraining the organization's ability to adapt to digital distribution realities. But this wasn't destruction for its own sake; it was strategic demolition that freed Warner Bros. to focus on what it does best: creating and telling stories to the world, now delivered through digital channels that could reach global audiences instantly.

That transformation taught me that digital leadership had evolved far beyond channel expertise into something fundamentally different: becoming a catalyst who could help century-old entertainment companies rebuild themselves for a digital-native world. My role shifted from managing specific digital functions to architecting the technological and operational foundation that would enable the entire organization to reinvent itself for markets where digital wasn't a separate channel but the primary operating system for how content gets created, distributed, and monetized globally.

And this wasn't just a technology and process upgrade. More importantly, we were embarking on a dual transformation strategy that would repeat itself. We needed to make our core business of physical media as efficient as possible to capitalize on the massive margins and volume while building the digital streaming and download business, which would take years to scale.

One executive we interviewed for this book described it this way: "We no longer have a digital strategy. We have a business strategy for a digital world."

Digital Leadership through the Resource-Based View Lens

The essential traits of digital leadership identified above can be understood through Barney's (1991) Resource-Based View of competitive advantage[5]. Digital leadership capabilities represent valuable, rare, inimitable, and non-substitutable (VRIN) resources that create sustainable competitive advantage.

For example, cross-functional collaboration is valuable in creating integrated customer experiences, which are rare among traditionally siloed organizations. It is challenging to imitate due to its dependence on organizational culture and is non-substitutable, as digital integration increasingly becomes essential for delivering value.

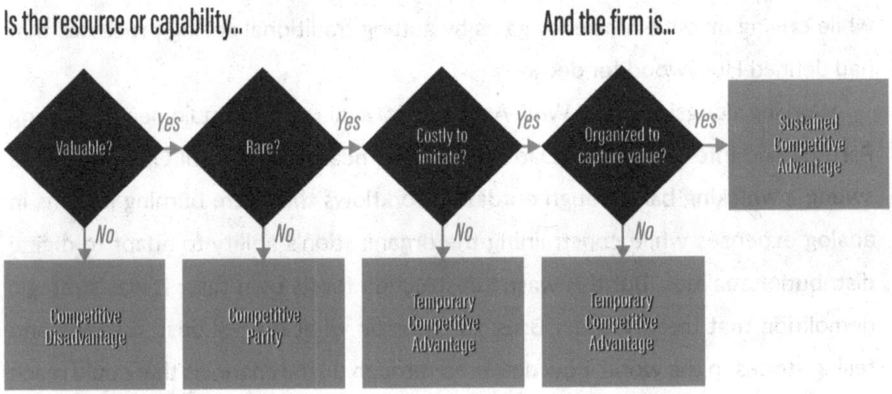

Organizations that develop these leadership capabilities effectively build what Teece et al. call "dynamic capabilities," which is the ability to integrate, build, and reconfigure internal and external competencies to address rapidly changing environments.

In the digital context, these dynamic capabilities enable organizations to sense new opportunities, seize them through organizational alignment, and transform operational capabilities in response to market evolution.

Leadership at Every Level: Load-Bearing Roles in a Digital System

Digital reinvention doesn't happen from the top down or bottom up; it propagates like a high-performance system. It needs tuned leaders at every layer, running aligned firmware, pushing in sync.

Individual digital leaders are the voltage regulators of change. They absorb the surge, direct the current, and stabilize the load when friction spikes. But, for transformation to hold at scale, leadership must be distributed from the C-suite to the shop floor, with each operating within a shared language, literacy, and cadence.

C-Suite: The Strategic Overclockers

Your job isn't just to approve the roadmap; it's to set the architecture.

C-level leaders don't just green-light digital initiatives; they architect the conditions for breakthrough performance. You fuel the system, ensure headroom, and permit teams to run hot when opportunities demand it.

High-impact digital leadership means crafting a vision that speaks to customers and spreadsheets equally, committing real capital instead of conference room enthusiasm, modeling the digital literacy you demand from teams through public learning and iteration, building cross-functional alliances that reward smart risks over safe bets, and defining KPIs that measure momentum rather than just stability.

The organizations that break away from the pack have leaders who understand that digital transformation isn't a project to manage, it's an operating system to architect. Your teams will move as fast as the infrastructure you build and the friction you remove. Design for speed, align for impact, and watch your organization leave competitors wondering what just happened.

If the execs overclock the CPU, middle managers manage the thermal flow.

Middle Management: The Translation Layer

Middle managers are the organizational glue that determines whether digital transformation occurs or merely gets discussed in meetings. They're translators converting C-suite vision into front-line action, motivators keeping teams focused during the messy middle of change, and the critical layer where change management theory collides with operational reality.

They make transformation real by translating executive strategy into actionable team objectives that people can carry out, motivating distributed teams through asynchronous communication and flexible work arrangements that demand new leadership skills, such as reading market signals and team dynamics simultaneously to identify when momentum is building or stalling, and leveraging their organizational tenure to navigate political landmines and cultural resistance that could impede progress.

In our remote-first, flex-hours world, middle managers rely on asynchronous team signals, real-time market alerts, and institutional knowledge to sense whether reinvention is accelerating or hitting organizational antibodies. They serve as an early warning system for executive blind spots and an amplification layer for frontline innovations. When middle management is aligned and empowered, transformation occurs at a rapid pace. When they're confused or resistant, even the best strategy dies in translation.

Front Line: The System Sensors

Front-line digital leaders are your organization's early warning system and acceleration engine rolled into one. These digital natives don't just adapt to change; they go *full send*[6] and anticipate what's next while everyone else is still processing what just happened.

They accelerate transformation by adopting cutting-edge tools, offering honest feedback that genuinely matters, and consistently advocating for what digital customers see and expect, rather than what internal processes assume. They also develop peer literacy through hands-on coaching during disruptions, catching small shifts that can lead to huge improvements before leadership even realizes they're happening.

Your front-line teams likely have the natural ability to innovate, create skunkworks projects, and either develop breakthrough solutions or dismantle ineffective processes.

CASE STUDY

e& — From Telco to Digital Conglomerate

How Hatem Dowidar rewired a legacy operator into a multi-sector digital powerhouse.

When Hatem Dowidar took the helm of Etisalat Group in 2020, he inherited one of the Middle East's largest telecom incumbents. By 2022, the company rebranded to e&, signaling a bold reinvention: from connectivity provider to diversified digital ecosystem spanning fintech, entertainment, AI, cybersecurity, and venture investment.

The Bottleneck

Telecom operators worldwide faced commoditization. Connectivity was a utility, ARPUs stagnated, and growth came from squeezing costs, not creating value. Over-the-top platforms (Netflix, WhatsApp, TikTok) captured consumer attention and margins, leaving telcos stuck as data pipes.

The Overclock

Dowidar reframed the business around "telecom as infrastructure, digital as growth."

- Fintech: Launched e& money to capture payments and financial inclusion opportunities across MENA and Asia.
- AI & Cybersecurity: Built platforms for enterprises, layering intelligence and protection on top of connectivity.
- Entertainment & Media: Expanded into streaming, gaming, and content, leveraging distribution scale.
- Global Ventures: Invested in adjacencies from mobility to healthtech, positioning e& as a regional venture catalyst.
- Brand Reset: The 2022 e& rebrand aligned internal culture with external ambition, telecom was now just one division in a larger digital conglomerate.

Results

e& now operates across 16 countries with 160M+ subscribers, diversified across digital services.

e& money became one of the region's fastest-growing fintech platforms.

Strategic partnerships with Microsoft, AWS, and regional governments embedded e& into national digital transformation agendas.

What It Means

Hatem Dowidar shows that the future of telecom isn't connectivity, it's ecosystem orchestration. By overclocking beyond the network, e& became not just a utility, but a digital catalyst for enterprises, governments, and consumers alike.

Digital Leadership Maturity Matrix

Digital transformation doesn't stall because the technology isn't ready. It stalls because leadership doesn't translate. You can buy cloud capacity, spin up AI pilots, and hire consultants, but if leadership is locked in the C-suite, change never escapes the boardroom.

Authentic digital leadership isn't about titles or org charts; it's a cultural operating system. The companies that win are those where every level of the organization feels empowered to sense change, act decisively, and lead forward. From frontline managers to mid-level operators to the executive suite, leadership becomes less about *who you are* and more about *what you do when the environment shifts.*

The **Digital Leadership Maturity Matrix** charts this evolution. It moves from title-dependent, top-down authority toward an environment where leadership is a shared mindset: distributed, data-driven, and reinforced by culture. At the highest level, leadership isn't a scarce resource; it's ambient, always-on, and built into the DNA of the enterprise.

Stage 1: Title-Dependent	Stage 2: Functional Champions	Stage 3: Cross-Functional Alignment	Stage 4: Enterprise Leadership System	Stage 5: Leadership at Every Level
Leadership is confined to formal roles (CEO, CIO, CMO). Digital is seen as "someone else's job."	A few digital advocates/champions emerge in pockets (marketing, IT, ops). Progress is uneven and fragile.	Cross-functional leadership forums and steering committees align around digital priorities. Still reliant on senior sponsorship.	Leadership becomes a system: distributed accountability, clear vision cascaded through objectives, and empowered middle management.	Leadership is a cultural operating system. Every employee sees themselves as a leader in digital reinvention, with permission to act, experiment, and adapt. "Leadership at every level."
Decision-making is a top-down, slow, and reactive process.	Decisions are made more quickly in silos, but coordination is often lacking.	Decisions are increasingly data-driven and integrated across functions.	Decisions are transparent, informed by data, and guided by shared digital KPIs.	Decisions flow at the edge of the org, powered by AI insights and cultural trust.
Talent strategy: leadership is positional.	Talent strategy: leadership = role or title.	Talent strategy: developing cross-functional leaders.	Talent strategy: building digital fluency as part of leadership development.	Talent strategy: leadership embedded in culture, AI-enabled coaching, continuous growth.
Change adoption: resisted, seen as a disruption.	Adoption of change is led by enthusiasts, with pockets of success.	Change adoption: coordinated but still top-heavy.	Change adoption: enterprise-wide, distributed, role-modeled by senior + mid-level leaders.	Adoption change: a natural and cultural reflex; innovation is everyone's mandate.

GLOBAL SIGNAL

Startups Born Overclocked

While incumbents often climb step by step through the digital maturity journey, startups in emerging markets frequently bypass the lower rungs entirely. They launch at the frontier, embedding adaptability and velocity from day one. Their operating environments, volatile, underdeveloped, and constraint-driven, demand this overclocked posture.

Signals

- Mikheil Lomtadze (Kaspi.kz, Kazakhstan): Transformed a struggling bank into Central Asia's dominant super-app, serving 75% of the population and generating $2B in annual net income. Kaspi exemplifies a platform that didn't climb maturity—it began as essential infrastructure disguised as convenience.
- Kamal Quadir (bKash, Bangladesh): Built Bangladesh's first unicorn by bringing 80 million citizens into the financial system. By treating "technology as the excuse, transformation as the goal," bKash skipped incremental maturity and went straight to ecosystem-scale impact.
- Oleg Gorokhovsky & Dmytro Dubilet (Monobank, Ukraine): Launched a branchless bank that captured 35% of Ukraine's mobile banking market in five years. With gamified UX and no physical branches, they show how a startup mindset can bypass legacy drag entirely.

Takeaway

Startups like these reveal how digital maturity isn't always a climb, it can be a leap. Tomorrow's digital leaders may not be those grinding through frameworks, but those born overclocked.

Leadership Cheat Code

Over index the time you spend with the staff that are on the front line, writing the code, shipping the emails & texts, merchandising the landing pages, and experimenting with AI and Blockchain. Provide them with support, resources, and permission to experiment. They will identify opportunities and solve problems that could take executive committees months to find and years to fix.

They don't just "operate" the system; they optimize it in motion.

Winning the Digital League

Leading in the digital era isn't a single match; it's a relentless season where the competition never rests, the rules evolve mid-game, and the scoreboard updates in real time. The difference between pushing for promotion and sliding toward relegation often comes down to how well you lead change, shape culture, and deploy the right leadership traits at the right moment.

Change management is your tactical system, the formations, substitutions, and set-piece plays that allow the team to adapt under pressure. Culture is your dressing room; if it's fractured, even the most talented squad will underperform. And leadership traits are your captain's armband, the qualities, such as vision, adaptability, and empathy, that inspire the team to play beyond individual limits.

As we saw in Microsoft's turnaround under Satya Nadella, winning the digital league means more than having the latest tech or a flashy playbook. It requires leaders who can sense shifting conditions, rally the squad behind a shared goal, and make decisive moves even when the pitch is muddy and the crowd is restless.

The takeaway? Your organization is always on the pitch, and the stakes are high. In the digital league, there's no room for playing to avoid losing; you must lead to win. Build a culture that believes in the mission, develop the traits that keep your team adaptable, and master the change management game plan that lets you shift tactics before the competition does.

Because in this league, there's no safe mid-table finish. You're either moving up or you're fighting to avoid the drop. And the team's position in the table? That starts and ends with the leader.

CHAPTER 2

Strategy Reimagined — Adapting versus Reacting

Think Like a Digital Strategist

What if the playbooks you were taught to analyze competition were built for a world that no longer exists? SWOT and Porter's Five Forces have served as managerial bedrock for decades, offering clean ways to assess internal strengths and weaknesses, industry rivalry, and competitive pressures. But those models assumed stable industries, long product cycles, and customers too invested to switch.

Today, those assumptions have collapsed. Industry lines are porous. Platforms and ecosystems dominate. Switching costs have evaporated primarily due to the advent of cloud computing, SaaS, and open APIs. Stablecoins and digital wallets enable borderless competition. And the pace of change is no longer measured in years but in weeks. In this environment, traditional frameworks feel like static maps in a world of live GPS.

What's needed is not an extension or quick fix, but an upgrade, a way to modernize strategy frameworks for the digital age. That means pivoting from the positional perspective of legacy models to the dynamics that truly drive competition today: Adaptability and Velocity.

This shift reframes strategy as a living diagnostic, not a static snapshot. It explains that, like Kodak, BlackBerry stumbled into agility deficits it couldn't escape. And it isn't confined to tech: even food supply chains are being reinvented through blockchain-enabled trust, transforming what was once a weakness into a source of advantage.

In this environment, traditional frameworks feel static.

MASTERY LEARNING OBJECTIVES

- Analyze how digital transformation has disrupted traditional strategic assumptions.
- Learn how to apply the dimensions of Adaptability and Velocity in the new era of Web 3.0.
- Evaluate the impact of compressed time horizons and consumer empowerment on strategic planning processes.
- Develop approaches for balancing long-term direction with agile-based adaptation.

INDUSTRY INSIGHT

Adobe — From Boxed Software to Creative Cloud

How Adobe abandoned the safety of packaged software for a subscription-first model that redefined its market leadership.

For decades, Adobe was a boxed software powerhouse — Photoshop, Illustrator, and Acrobat sat on retail shelves with hefty price tags. The model was profitable, but also vulnerable: piracy was rampant, and major version releases resulted in revenue that spiked and dipped unpredictably.

Challenge

By the early 2010s, creative work was progressing faster than Adobe's 18-to 24-month release cycles. Competitors were experimenting with SaaS models, while users demanded more frequent updates, cloud storage, and seamless cross-device functionality. Adobe faced a choice: stay in the comfort of packaged software or leap into subscriptions and constant delivery.

The Velocity Shift

In 2013, Adobe launched Creative Cloud, marking the end of perpetual licenses and the transition to a subscription model. Instead of major releases every couple of years, updates became continuous, with new features, patches, and integrations rolled out every month. Adobe layered in cloud storage, team collaboration tools, and cross-device syncing. The shift redefined customer relationships from one-off transactions to ongoing engagement.

Results / Impact

The transition was initially met with controversy, as users accustomed to one-time purchases expressed backlash. But within five years, Adobe's recurring revenue soared, piracy rates dropped, and its valuation tripled. By treating Creative Cloud as a live-service platform, much like a game with regular updates and expansions, Adobe has become indispensable to millions of creative professionals.

STRATEGIC TAKEAWAYS

- **Commit Fully to the Model** – Half measures would have diluted the transition; Adobe went all-in on subscriptions.
- **Deliver Continuous Value** – Frequent updates turned customers into engaged subscribers.
- **Bundle Ecosystem Benefits** – Cloud storage, collaboration, and integrations deepened stickiness.

REFLECTION

- Is your organization's strategy built for the speed of digital, or are you still relying on traditional 1 to 3-year planning cycles?
- What aspects of your business model leverage digital channels to create a competitive advantage?
- Are you prepared to pivot quickly based on customer data, market shifts, and emerging technology?

Regardless of where you are in your digital strategy journey, this chapter will help you adapt traditional frameworks for the digital age while developing the ability to respond to ongoing change.

Strategy Reimagined: The Death of Industrial Frameworks

We are living through a punctuated equilibrium moment in the history of competitive strategy. The traditional strategic playbook was built for a slower clock speed, an era when competitive cycles measured in years allowed for deliberate analysis and methodical response. Like computer processors operating at obsolete frequencies, Porter's 5 Forces and SWOT analysis now run too slowly for Web 3.0's overclocked business environment, where strategic windows compress from years to months and competitive advantage flows to those who can complete learning cycles the fastest. In our chapter on Disruption and Reinvention, we'll take a deeper dive into the corresponding relationships between business and technology in the Web 1.0 and 2.0 era that shaped our views of how to lead and manage through the emerging Web 3.0 era. To set the stage for our pivot in strategic models that follow, I'll provide a snapshot of how the rapidly evolving AI, Meta, and Decentralized tech landscape is impacting business.

Web3 is semantic on a technical level

The "Semantic Web" was a term first coined by Tim Berners-Lee[7] to describe a web of linked data that machines could understand.

A web of meaning: The core principle of a semantic web is that data is organized and connected in a way that provides context, allowing computers to process information more intelligently than simple keyword matching.

Web 3's semantic principles involve creating a web where machines can understand the meaning and context of data, enabling more intelligent, personalized, and efficient user experiences and interactions.

This is accomplished by using metadata and artificial intelligence to interpret information, linking data across different applications or Agents, and establishing a more connected and contextual understanding of digitized content.

Business responds to technology. While the underlying technology is semantic, the resulting business environment is "kinetic," meaning it is characterized by motion, energy, and constant change.

Below are the dimensions of the Semantic Web linked to related Kinetic business responses that facilitate higher velocity and demand greater adaptability to succeed.

Dimension	Semantic (Technical Layer)	Kinetic (Business Environment)
Ownership	Blockchain technology provides verifiable proof of ownership for digital assets, such as NFTs.[8]	This enables the creation of new and reinvented business models based on digital ownership, such as the buying and selling of virtual real estate or the perpetual resale of digital art.
Value creation	Smart contracts and tokenization enable the digital representation and exchange of value without the need for intermediaries.	This enables entirely new income streams and revenue models, such as token-based loyalty programs or revenue from secondary market sales.
Trust	Trust is built into the system through the cryptographic security of blockchain technology, which verifies transactions immutably.	This fundamental trust shifts customer relationships from a transactional basis to a partnership model, as brands and users become more tightly aligned through shared incentives and ownership.
Interaction	The semantic layer enables applications to understand context and intent through the use of AI and machine learning.	This creates more immersive and tailored user experiences, where the lines between the digital and physical worlds blur, leading to new forms of engagement.
Pace of change	Underlying decentralized and open-source protocols are the foundation of Web3 innovation. All of the above enable automation at a rate never seen before.	Adoption and development happen at an accelerated pace, often outpacing the traditional regulatory environment. Companies that can experiment and move quickly are best positioned to capitalize on the new market dynamics.

As a result, our assumptions on how to evaluate our businesses, the marketplaces they operate in, and the corresponding strategic options must be revisited and reinvented to compete in the Web 3.0 era.

We'll begin by reviewing the complications of relying on industrial era models.

The Porter Paradigm Collapse

Porter's framework rests on three foundational assumptions that Web 3.0 has obliterated. 1) Industry boundaries remain stable, 2) competitors consist of identifiable institutions, and 3) barriers to entry provide meaningful protection against disruption.

This logic crumbles when a solo developer in Estonia utilizes AI coding assistants to build enterprise-grade solutions, deploy them on blockchain infrastructure for pennies, and access global DeFi[9] capital markets, all while competing directly with Fortune 500 companies. The very concept of "industry" becomes meaningless when every customer interaction represents a potential disintermediation opportunity.

The framework's five forces reveal their obsolescence under examination. "Rivalry among existing competitors" assumes you can identify your competition, yet your most significant threat may come from someone who doesn't exist yet. The "threat of new entrants" becomes irrelevant when AI eliminates technical barriers and blockchain eliminates capital barriers, making everyone a potential entrant.

Most fundamentally, "bargaining power of suppliers and buyers" presumes stable relationships, but when every interaction occurs through smart contracts and AI agents, all relationships become algorithmic and infinitely liquid.

The SWOT Delusion

SWOT analysis suffers from equally fatal assumptions, presuming that internal capabilities and external environment can be analyzed separately and that strategic advantages persist long enough to justify building plans around them. In Web 3.0's accelerated reality, today's strengths become tomorrow's weaknesses when market conditions shift faster than organizational change cycles, while the most significant "opportunities" often require abandoning core competencies entirely.

Each SWOT category crumbles under the pressure of Web 3.0. The strengths category assumes durability, yet decades-old advantages can dissolve in months when new paradigms emerge. Weaknesses often presume they're fixable through traditional organizational development, when many now require complete restructuring. Opportunities assume you can pursue them with existing capabilities, yet most Web 3.0 opportunities demand entirely new organizational models.

Most critically, threats are often assumed to be external forces to defend against, when the most significant threats actually come from an internal inability to adapt quickly enough to changing competitive dynamics.

The Asset Ownership Trap

The most dangerous folklore from industrial strategy is the belief that asset ownership creates competitive advantage. Web 3.0 reveals the opposite: ownership often becomes a source of friction when access speed matters more than control depth.

Real estate transforms from a strategic advantage to a fixed cost liability when competitors operate fully remote with 60-80% lower operational costs.

Proprietary technology becomes technical debt when AI can replicate its functionality, and blockchain provides a superior, standardized infrastructure. Large employee bases create coordination complexity and decision-making bottlenecks, whereas AI-augmented small teams can deliver equivalent or superior output.

The most successful Web 3.0 companies demonstrate orchestration superiority over ownership accumulation. Netflix abandoned its DVD distribution assets to focus on building its streaming capabilities. Uber owns no cars but orchestrates a global transportation network. Airbnb owns no property but coordinates global accommodation. Stripe owns no banks but enables global payments. They recognized that in kinetic competitive environments, orchestration capability creates more value than ownership assets.

The Academic Validation

Thirty years of peer-reviewed research validate what Web 3.0 makes empirically evident. Clayton Christensen's disruption theory[10] explains why incumbents consistently lose to entrants operating under different competitive dynamics; they optimize for sustaining innovation, while markets reward disruptive innovation.

David Teece's dynamic capabilities framework[11] proves that organizational success comes from "the firm's ability to integrate, build, and reconfigure internal and external competences to address rapidly changing environments" rather than static resource accumulation.

McKinsey's research on agility, involving over 2,000 organizations, demonstrates that velocity and adaptability create multiplicative rather than additive performance advantages. Highly successful transformations achieve step-change improvements across multiple dimensions simultaneously.

The research convergence reveals a singular insight: competitive advantage has fundamentally shifted from static assets to kinetic capabilities, from positional defense to evolutionary capacity, from industry analysis to meta-capability optimization. For three decades, every foremost strategic management researcher has documented pieces of this transformation, while the business community continued to use frameworks designed for obsolete competitive physics.

The Retrofitting Fallacy

Despite overwhelming evidence that traditional frameworks mislead executives, the academic and consulting communities have failed to produce revolutionary alternatives. Instead, they've generated shallow modifications that preserve industrial-era assumptions while claiming innovation.

Porter's "improvements" introduce additional forces, such as complementors or government influence, while maintaining the same static competitive logic. SWOT "alternatives" like SOAR analysis[12], NOISE analysis[13], and PESTLE rearrange categories without addressing the fundamental problem of static analysis in dynamic environments.

The pattern reveals intellectual bankruptcy: every alternative modifies categories, adds dimensions, or changes terminology while retaining the core assumption that competitive advantage can be analyzed as static positioning. No alternative has recognized that competitive advantage itself has changed from positional to kinetic, from where you stand to how fast you evolve.

The Kinetic Breakthrough

Web 3.0's post-scarcity environment demands a strategy based on kinetic rather than potential energy. When information abundance eliminates intelligence advantages, capital abundance eliminates financial barriers, and technical capability abundance democratizes sophisticated development, competitive advantage flows to organizations that can sense and respond fastest to changing conditions.

Two meta-capabilities determine strategic survival when traditional barriers collapse: Velocity measures the speed of strategic response from market signal recognition to deployment completion. At the same time, Adaptability measures the capacity for strategic evolution and learning rate optimization.

The Adaptability axis, grounded in dynamic capabilities theory and strategic flexibility, measures an organization's capacity to sense, respond to, and reconfigure its resources to thrive during periods of change. The Velocity axis, rooted in time-based competition and the micro foundations of decision-making, assesses an organization's ability to learn, decide, and execute with a speed that outpaces its rivals.

These two vectors are sufficient because every other competitive advantage in Web 3.0 ultimately derives from the combination of velocity and adaptability. Innovation equals adaptability multiplied by velocity. Market position equals velocity multiplied by adaptive customer evolution. Competitive defense equals adaptability multiplied by the rapid deployment of countermeasures.

The mathematics of Web 3.0 competition follows increasing rather than diminishing returns. Velocity compounds because faster organizations complete more learning cycles, making them exponentially faster. In essence, they are becoming faster *at increasing their speed* with each innovation cycle.

Adaptability compounds because better-adapting organizations become superior at sensing what to adapt to, making them exponentially more adaptive.

Organizations strong in both dimensions don't add their advantages; they multiply them, creating an exponential competitive advantage that traditional competitors cannot match through incremental improvement.

The Strategic Revolution

The Kinetic Strategy Framework represents the first strategic model explicitly designed for post-scarcity, permissionless, AI-augmented competition. The market dynamics of the next era are driven by the convergence of decentralized technologies, new economic models, and the continued advancement of combined platforms of artificial intelligence and blockchain. This creates a new competitive landscape defined by the abundance of digital assets, open access, and AI-enhanced productivity.Unlike industrial frameworks that provide diagnostic photography of current positioning, kinetic strategy offers a prescriptive GPS that continuously optimizes strategic movement and recalculates routes as competitive conditions change.

The Kinetic Strategy Framework integrates the two foundational axes into a dynamic, two-dimensional strategic map. This framework surpasses the static, linear analysis of its predecessors, offering a more nuanced and actionable understanding of an organization's competitive posture and strategic imperatives. By plotting a firm's capabilities along both the Adaptability and Velocity axes, we can identify four distinct strategic archetypes, each with unique characteristics and challenges.

The vertical axis represents Adaptability, ranging from Low to High. A low score indicates an organization with rigid structures, static resources, and a limited capacity to sense or respond to environmental change. A high score signifies an organization with strong dynamic capabilities, high strategic flexibility, and an agile operating model. The horizontal axis represents Velocity, ranging from Low to High. A low score indicates slow learning cycles, bureaucratic decision-making, and inefficient execution. A high score reflects rapid insight generation, swift and empowered decision-making, and streamlined execution, all of which are managed within the constraints of time compression diseconomies.

This creates four quadrants that represent the dynamic between adaptability and velocity.

The Laggard (Low Adaptability, Low Velocity)

Organizations in this quadrant are very vulnerable. They tend to be slow, bureaucratic, and unable to make meaningful changes. Operating with outdated business models and often as incumbents in stable industries, they are unprepared for disruption. Their primary goal is survival, which necessitates a fundamental and immediate transformation of both their capacity to adapt and their operational speed.

The Stalwart (Low Adaptability, High Velocity)

This quadrant represents organizations that are highly efficient and fast at executing a fixed, established strategy. They may be cost leaders in mature industries, excelling at operational optimization. However, their high velocity is brittle; it is directed along a narrow path. While powerful in a stable environment, they are highly vulnerable to disruptive change because they lack the adaptability to pivot their efficient machinery in a new direction. Their strategic challenge is to build dynamic capabilities without sacrificing their execution excellence.

The Explorer (High Adaptability, Low Velocity)

These organizations are often innovative, creative, and excellent at sensing new opportunities. They may have strong R&D departments or a culture of experimentation. However, they struggle to translate their adaptive potential into market impact because they lack the velocity to make decisions and execute at scale. They are at risk of being outmaneuvered by faster competitors who can commercialize similar ideas more effectively. Their strategic imperative is to streamline decision-making and build the execution capabilities needed to capitalize on their insights.

The Architect (High Adaptability, High Velocity)

This is the ideal strategic position in the modern economy. Organizations in this quadrant combine the ability to sense and shape new opportunities with the speed to capture them. They are agile, innovative, and efficient. They can pivot their business models in response to market shifts and can scale new initiatives rapidly. These are the organizations that thrive on uncertainty and consistently outperform their rivals. Their strategic challenge is to sustain this dual capability, continuously renewing their dynamic capabilities and optimizing their velocity without succumbing to the penalties of excessive haste.

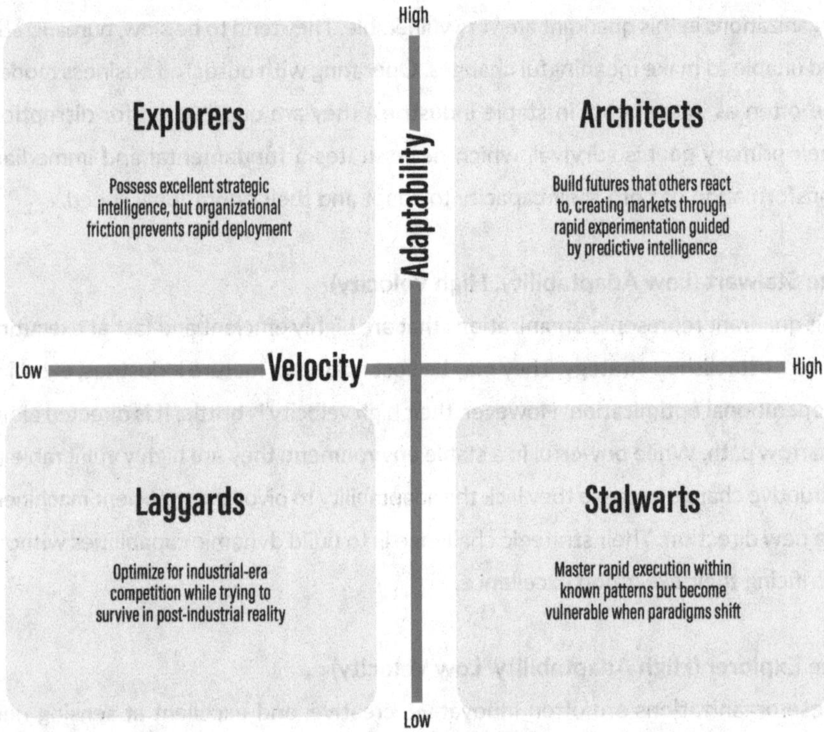

The strategic imperative becomes clear: organizations must migrate toward Architect positioning, building capabilities that strengthen through volatility while moving faster than competitors can copy or arbitrage their approaches.

In Web 3.0, your position on the Kinetic Strategy Framework matters more than your industry, size, or current market share. A Quadrant I individual developer can outmaneuver a Quadrant III Fortune 500 company because they operate with superior strategic positioning along both critical dimensions. In contrast, physical assets, layers of decision-making, and manual processes encumber the large corporation.

This construct evolves strategy from positional defense to kinetic optimization, from asking "What industry are we in?" to "What quadrant are we operating from?" The framework forces organizations to confront whether they're building for the world that was or the world that's emerging and provides the roadmap for those ready to abandon industrial nostalgia for post-industrial opportunity.

The Digital Business Model Canvas: Strategy in Motion

In an economy increasingly defined by platforms, marketplaces, and ecosystems, business models have become more dynamic, fluid, and interdependent. The traditional Business Model Canvas remains a powerful diagnostic and prescriptive tool; however, in the digital era, it functions best when reimagined as a translator, a live operating system that helps leaders make sense of shifting value creation logics and act on them with speed.

This evolution makes the Canvas an ideal companion to the Kinetic Strategy Model's Velocity and Adaptability dimensions. Where Kinetic Strategy identifies how fast and how flexibly an organization is, the Digital Business Model Canvas becomes the next step, mapping where to apply that movement and how to operationalize it across value, resources, customers, and ecosystems.

The value proposition shifts from selling products to delivering personalized, zero-friction, adaptive experiences where users co-create value and platforms evolve in real-time.

Customer Relationships move from CRM records to *AI-augmented intimacy*, self-service empowerment, community validation, and predictive loyalty that anticipates needs.

Channels evolve into *contextual access points*, transitioning from omnichannel and mobile-first to AR, wearables, and embedded commerce across platforms like TikTok, Slack, and Alexa.

Revenue Streams become *fluid and dynamic* through subscriptions, freemium funnels, ethical data monetization, and pricing that adapts instantly to demand and context.

Key Resources prioritize *data gravity, AI models, and cloud-native ecosystems* over physical assets, treating proprietary algorithms and API integration as defensible advantages.

Key Activities demand *continuous iteration*, sprint-based shipping, real-time data-to-action, and trust built through security — and privacy-by-design.

Key Partnerships emphasize *platform alliances, co-innovation, and API-first integration* that extend value at the ecosystem edge.

Customer Segments focus on *communities and niches* rather than demographics, blending B2B, B2C, and B2B2C around shared needs and identity.

The cost structure becomes *modular and performance-based*, leveraging cloud OPEX models, automation, and talent investment while eliminating legacy drag.

As you can see, the Business Canvas Model evolves from a *static planning tool* into a *living operating system*, one that orchestrates data, ecosystem feedback, and technological advancements, aligning directly with the demands of velocity and adaptability in Kinetic Strategy.

The Digital Horizon Planning Model: Three Speeds, One Engine

The original McKinsey Horizon Model, which involves expanding the core, building emerging businesses, and creating future options, was designed for an era when disruption occurred at slow, analog speeds. In today's digital world, disruption compresses timelines into a single, fast-paced cycle. Horizons no longer develop one after the other; they must be managed simultaneously. This calls for a dual transformation approach: optimizing and expanding the core (H1) while also pushing the enterprise toward bold reinvention (H2 and H3). In this way, the model serves as a straightforward path to the Kinetic Strategy's upper-right quadrant of Architects, where adaptability and speed come together to reshape entire industries.

Horizon 1

Digital Optimization enhances the core through advanced tools and AI-driven efficiencies, streamlining supply chains, personalizing customer journeys at scale, integrating physical and digital touchpoints, and deploying real-time pricing and inventory management powered by predictive analytics.

Horizon 2

Digital Extension expands current business models into adjacent areas, creating new digital products and services, launching marketplaces and platforms, monetizing data-driven insights, and leveraging APIs and partnerships that multiply reach without incurring proportional costs.

Horizon 3

Digital Transformation drives bold reinvention, designing business models that self-cannibalize before competitors can, by applying frontier technologies like blockchain, the metaverse, and spatial computing. It reconfigures value chains through digital-first design and launches AI-native businesses capable of learning and scaling faster than incumbents can respond.

Making Digital Horizons Work requires structural as well as cultural change:

1. Dedicated teams and budgets with autonomy to move at the right speed per horizon.
2. Distinct KPIs aligned to each horizon's risk-reward profile.
3. Parallel governance that balances H2 and H3 experimentation with H1 control.
4. Transition mechanisms that evolve H2 into new core businesses and graduate H3 moonshots without being rejected by legacy systems.

This is not a set of sequential rocket stages, but a multi-threaded growth engine, one that runs on live data, adaptive capabilities, and intentional reinvention. Organizations that master simultaneous horizons don't just defend their present; they compound competitive advantage in real time and accelerate their trajectory toward the Architect position in the Kinetic Strategy Model.

Organic Growth Strategy Framework

A strategy framework that lends itself well to a digital-first firm is the Organic Growth Strategy Framework.[14]

Organic Growth Strategy Overview

Organic growth is the process by which a company expands using its internal resources and capabilities, without relying on external funding, acquisitions, or mergers. This strategic approach focuses on increasing output, improving operational efficiency, boosting revenue, and enhancing cash flow through sustainable business practices.

Types and Benefits

Companies typically pursue three primary organic growth strategies: continually optimizing commercial activities (pricing, marketing, and sales), reallocating funds toward high-earning activities and products, and developing new operational models or innovative goods and services. While most companies focus on one strategy at a time due to resource constraints and the need for clarity of execution, top-tier organizations with substantial resources may implement multiple strategies simultaneously.

The benefits of organic growth include maintaining company independence, avoiding substantial debt, and building sustainable competitive advantages. Unlike inorganic growth, which relies on external resources and may enable faster expansion, organic growth creates lasting value through the development of internal capabilities and competencies.

The Organic Growth Framework (OGF)

The Organic Growth Framework below is adapted from the work of Bernard Jaworski and Robert Lurie.[15] It represents an advanced approach that prioritizes changing customer behavior over product differentiation. This methodology drives faster, more reliable sales growth by identifying and focusing on 1-2 high-yield customer behaviors, strategically shifting customers onto paths most favorable to your offering.

The OGF follows a systematic 5-phase process:

1. Map the Customer Journey[16]
2. Use Propensity-based Segmentation[17]
3. Identify Points of Leakage and Leverage

4. Develop a Behavior Change Value Proposition (BCVP)[18]
5. Invest Disproportionately and Sequentially

Success requires a deep understanding of target markets, achieved through consistent research into customer decision-making processes, which enables strategic investment allocation and the development of tailored marketing approaches. The following chapters and platform provide the insights and tools to execute the Organic Growth approach in practice.

CASE STUDY

Disney — Pivoting from Magic to Metrics

How a century-old entertainment icon rewrote its strategy around streaming and data.

In 2019, Disney launched Disney+, entering a streaming market already dominated by Netflix and Amazon. Within 16 months, it amassed 100M subscribers, an acceleration unmatched in media history. This wasn't just a distribution play; it was a strategic reinvention that put data, not box office receipts, at the heart of Disney's model.

The Bottleneck

Disney's traditional model depended on theatrical releases, linear TV advertising, and theme park experiences. Success was episodic, data was fragmented, and customer relationships were intermediated by theaters, broadcasters, and cable bundles. The company had limited direct knowledge of its global audience.

The Overclock

- Direct-to-Consumer: Disney+ created a first-party data engine spanning households, devices, and viewing behaviors.
- Personalization: Algorithms tailored recommendations, merchandising, and marketing campaigns to maximize retention.
- Content Feedback Loop: Streaming analytics informed creative and production decisions, closing the gap between audience signals and content investments.

- Ecosystem Leverage: Integration with Hulu, ESPN+, and Parks loyalty programs extended personalization across touchpoints.

Results

- 150M+ Disney+ subscribers by 2025, second only to Netflix in scale.
- Rich first-party data now informs marketing efficiency, franchise development, and park operations.
- Strategic shift created a platform to cross-sell merchandise, gaming, and travel.

What It Means

Disney's pivot shows that strategy in the digital era isn't just about entering new channels, it's about owning the customer signal. When companies reorganize around data, they don't just serve customers better; they redesign the business to anticipate them.

Strategy Maturity Matrix for Reinvention

It's often said that culture eats strategy for breakfast, but in the reinvention era, advantage comes from fusing the two. Strategy is no longer a static binder; it's a living operating system. This Maturity Matrix illustrates how organizations evolve from rigid, calendar-driven planning to always-on, AI-augmented orchestration, where leadership culture and strategic adaptability reinforce each other.

The progression mirrors the Kinetic Strategy Model: as organizations move rightward and upward in *velocity* and *adaptability*, they compound competitive advantage and advance toward the Architect archetype.

Stage	Mindset	Strategy Approach	Decision Cycle	AI / Digital Integration
Reactive	Defensive	Annual/multi-year plans locked in advance	Slow, retrospective	Minimal: dashboards, lagging metrics
Adaptive	Responsive	Updates triggered by shocks; firefighting mode	Episodic, project-based	Basic analytics, tactical pilots
Agile	Iterative	Horizon-based planning with quarterly recalibration	Faster, crossfunctional, team-driven	AI-assisted insights, scenario modeling
Anticipatory	Proactive	Dynamic playbooks informed by weak-signal and ecosystem scanning	Continuous sensing and pivoting	Predictive AI, foresight models, early-warning systems
Kinetic (Reinvention)	Cultural + Systemic	Strategy is ambient, *embedded into daily workflows, decisions, and ecosystems*; focused on velocity + adaptability.	Real-time, distributed, and networked decision-making	AI as co-strategist: generative foresight, automated simulations, adaptive orchestration across industries

GLOBAL SIGNAL

Strategy Born in the Storm

While incumbent strategies often evolve via scenario planning and risk buffers, in emerging markets strategy is forged in real-time turbulence. Startups there don't first map paths, they launch with strategic agility, constantly rewiring direction in response to shifting conditions.

Signals

- Reliance Jio (India): Jio entered a saturated telecom market in 2016 by building a greenfield, all-IP 4G network that leapfrogged legacy telecom infrastructures. Without dealing with prior base stations or legacy switching, they scaled rapidly and rewrote India's digital strategy playbook.
- TradeDepot (Nigeria & Africa): Originally a B2B FMCG distribution marketplace for informal retailers, TradeDepot has moved into embedded finance, credit, and even food manufacturing (launched brand "Mangrove" in 2025). By owning the supply, distribution, and financing edges, their strategic model keeps evolving on the fly.
- Chari (Morocco): A B2B2C FMCG + fintech startup providing credit and digital tools to merchants and consumers, setting up a strategy that simultaneously addresses demand and working capital gaps in underbanked contexts.

Takeaway

In volatile markets, the "plan then execute" doctrine often fails. Strategy emerges through continuous adaptation. The real strategic advantage may come from systems that can pivot, learn, and redeploy continuously, not from static five-year roadmaps.

From Maturity to Kinetics: Understanding the Trajectory

Most maturity models are built as linear progressions, ranging from Reactive to Anticipatory, with low to high levels. They're helpful as diagnostics, but digital reinvention doesn't happen in a straight line. Disruption compresses timeframes, collapses planning cycles, and forces organizations to evolve along two dimensions at once:

Velocity: how fast an organization can sense, decide, and act.

Adaptability: how flexibly it can shift direction, redesign models, and reconfigure resources.

The **Reinvention Strategy Maturity Matrix** maps these dimensions onto a single grid. Early stages (Reactive, Adaptive) cluster in the lower-left, where organizations move slowly and defensively. Mid-stages (Agile, Anticipatory) climb diagonally as they accelerate speed and expand flexibility. The destination is the **Kinetic stage**, an operating state where culture and strategy are fused, decision-making is distributed, and AI acts as a co-strategist.

In practice, this means that Maturity models help organizations benchmark their current state at a given point in time. At the same time, the **Kinetic Strategy Map** shows *what matters next:* the balance of adaptability and velocity that determines whether companies defend the status quo or advance into the Architect quadrant, reshaping industries rather than reacting to them. Seen together, the models provide both **diagnosis** and **direction**: maturity tells you where you stand; kinetics tells you how to move.

REINVENTION STRATEGY MATURITY MATRIX
(Adaptability × Velocity)

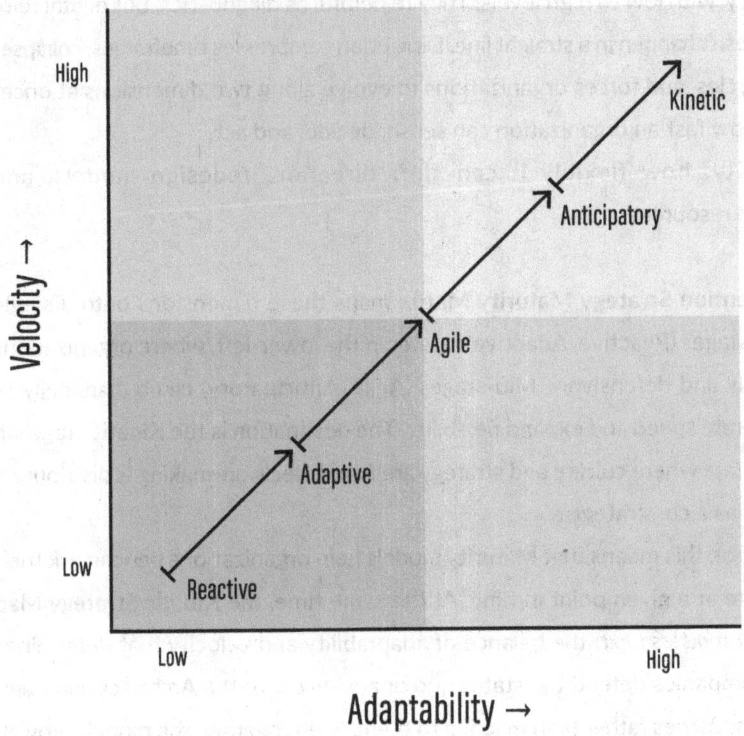

The Strategic Choice

We stand at a crossroads that will determine whether organizations survive the next century. The punctuated equilibrium moment of Web 3.0 has rendered industrial-era strategic frameworks not only outdated but also actively detrimental to competitive advantage. Organizations continuing to optimize through Porter's 5 Forces and SWOT analysis are playing yesterday's game with increasing precision, while competitors operate under entirely different competitive principles.

The evidence overwhelms denial. When individual developers can create AI agents to compete with Fortune 500 companies, when blockchain protocols eliminate traditional intermediaries overnight, and when asset ownership shifts from an advantage to a liability, we see the collapse of every assumption that supported traditional strategy. Research over the past three decades, from Christensen's disruption theory to McKinsey's agility studies, all point to a single insight: competitive advantage has fundamentally shifted from static assets to dynamic, kinetic capabilities.

The Kinetic Revolution

The Kinetic Strategy Framework emerges from this convergence as the first strategic model explicitly designed for post-scarcity, permissionless, AI-augmented competition. Based on the understanding that competitive advantage now stems from kinetic energy rather than potential energy, the framework categorizes organizations along two critical vectors that determine strategic survival when traditional barriers are no longer practical.

Velocity measures the speed of strategic response, from recognizing market signals to completing deployment, the organization's ability to finish learning cycles faster than market conditions change. Adaptability assesses the capacity for strategic evolution and predictive intelligence, the ability to detect weak signals and develop capabilities before competitors realize opportunities exist.

These meta-capabilities are sufficient because every competitive advantage in Web 3.0 ultimately stems from the combination of velocity and adaptability. Innovation equals adaptability times velocity. Market position equals velocity times adaptive customer evolution. The math follows increasing rather than diminishing returns, creating exponential advantages for organizations that master both dimensions at once.

The choice confronting every organization is fundamental: continue believing that what worked before will work again, or acknowledge that the rules of competitive advantage have fundamentally changed and require fundamentally different strategic capabilities. In this punctuated equilibrium moment, the organizations that choose correctly will not merely survive; they will define the competitive landscape for the next century.

Strategy has been reimagined. The remaining question is whether your organization will evolve fast enough to implement it.

CHAPTER 3

Digital Disruption and Reinvention

Think Like a Digital Disruptor

I've had the privilege, and the bruises, of living through every wave of the modern internet: Web 1.0, Web 2.0, and now Web 3.0. Along the way, I've watched entire industries get reshaped, old empires fade, and new giants emerge seemingly overnight. The best disruptors didn't just ride these waves; they reinvented themselves with each one.

Matt Wasserlauf embodies that mindset. We met during my Time Warner days, and even then, his instincts for spotting what was next were sharper than most. In the early 2000s, as online video was barely emerging from the buffering stage, Matt joined a first-generation streaming ad platform, fittingly named *The Platform*. While I was at Warner Bros., we became one of the first studios to buy ads on their network. For many in the media at the time, it was a curiosity; for Matt, it was the future.

That early leap into digital media became the launchpad for what came next. He founded multiple companies that blended his deep advertising knowledge, startup grit, and ability to see around corners. Three successful exits later, he's now reinventing ad sales again, this time with AI and blockchain, to tackle a billion-dollar industry problem: ad fraud. His latest venture, Blockboard, is not just another ad tech startup; it's a blueprint for how a career and a business can continually adapt to technological disruption while creating new value.

Matt's journey mirrors a larger truth: the companies and people who survive disruption don't just protect what they have, they build the capacity to let go, rethink, and reassemble their advantage for the next cycle.

In this chapter, we'll break down how disruption signals emerge, why timing is everything, and what organizational capabilities allow some to thrive while others vanish. We'll explore models like the innovation adoption curve to understand the pace of change and customer behavior. We'll examine how Netflix became the gold standard for self-disruption, pivoting from DVDs by mail to streaming dominance and now, global content production.

MASTERY LEARNING OBJECTIVES

- Analyze how digital disruption unfolds across industries, recognizing early warning signs, opportunity signals, and shifts in consumer or market behavior.
- Compare defensive and offensive approaches to disruption, assessing how different organizations adapt (or fail to adapt) based on posture, mindset, and timing.
- Use models like the technology adoption curve to interpret how innovations spread and what that means for customer behavior and competitive timing.
- Design strategies and structures that enable sustained adaptability, from agile operations to foresight systems and cultural resilience.

INDUSTRY INSIGHT

Shopify — Powering the Independent Seller Revolution

How Shopify built a commerce platform that turned small businesses into global retailers

In the mid-2000s, launching an online store meant wrestling with clunky software, expensive developers, and complex payment gateways. For most small businesses, going digital was more of a hassle than an opportunity. Shopify flipped that equation.

Context / Challenge

E-commerce was dominated by marketplaces like Amazon and eBay, which offered reach but little brand control for sellers. Independent merchants needed a way to create their digital storefronts without enterprise budgets or engineering teams, and to do it quickly enough to keep pace with shifting consumer behavior.

The Velocity Shift

Shopify launched in 2006 with a cloud-based platform that handled hosting, design templates, payments, and inventory out of the box. Over time, it evolved into a complete commerce operating system, integrating point-of-sale hardware, marketing automation, fulfillment networks, and a massive third-party app ecosystem. Crucially, Shopify empowered merchants to *own their brand and customer data*, while giving them enterprise-grade tools at a predictable subscription cost. Like a well-run live-service game, Shopify continually rolls out new "apps" on a similar marketplace platform to Roblox, ranging from AR shopping to TikTok integrations, all while maintaining competitive merchants in real-time.

Results / Impact

By 2022, Shopify powered millions of businesses in 175 countries, accounting for over $175 billion in global sales. It became the go-to choice for entrepreneurs and major brands alike, enabling businesses to scale from kitchen-table operations to multi-million-dollar enterprises without needing to change platforms.

STRATEGIC TAKEAWAYS

- Lower the Barrier to Entry – Make enterprise-grade tools accessible to small players.
- Build the Ecosystem, Not Just the Product – Apps, integrations, and partners drive network effects.
- Continuously Level Up – Frequent updates keep merchants ahead of shifting consumer and technology trends.

REFLECTION

- What was the last big bet your organization made that intentionally disrupted your core business?

- Have you built a culture that kills legacy ideas *before* the market does?
- Which part of your business is running on yesterday's playbook while tomorrow's competition is already deploying new rules?

Self-disruption is the competitive advantage. Predict. Cannibalize. Reinvent. Repeat.

The Foundation: Understanding Digital Disruption

The evolution of digital technology over the past three decades provides a living laboratory for understanding how innovations spread, transform industries, and create new competitive landscapes. At its theoretical core, digital transformation follows patterns described in Everett Rogers' "Diffusion of Innovations" theory.[19] This explains how, why, and at what rate new technologies spread through populations and organizations.

As a reminder, the theory identifies five adopter categories across the technology adoption curve:

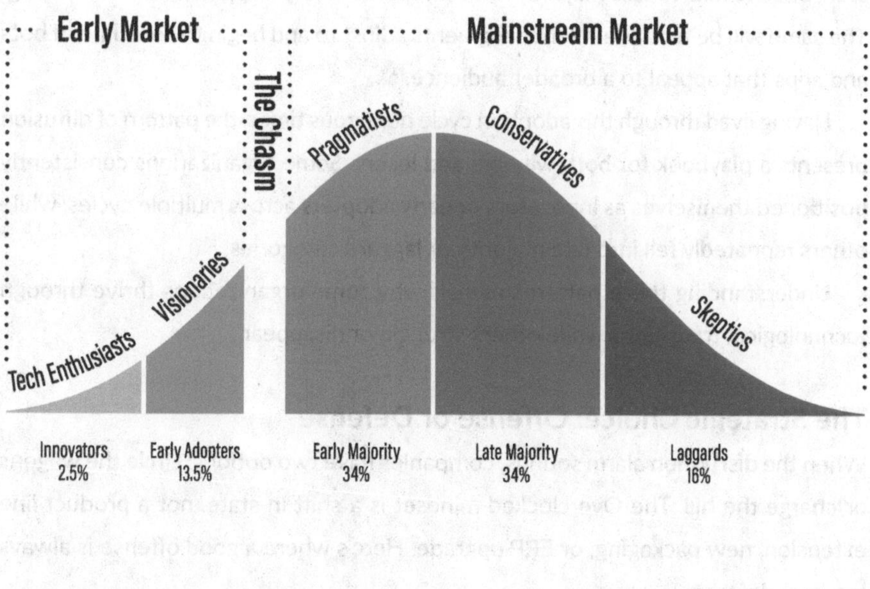

Innovators (2.5%)	Risk-tolerant pioneers who embrace new technologies before they are proven
Early Adopters (13.5%)	Visionaries who recognize strategic applications of emerging technologies
Early Majority (34%)	Pragmatists who adopt proven technologies with clear benefits
Late Majority (34%)	Conservatives who adopt only when technologies become standard
Laggards (16%)	Traditionalists who resist change until necessary

Rogers' work endures because we see this pattern emerge time and time again, but with a wrinkle that's been termed "Crossing the Chasm,[20]" which describes the phenomenon of the evolution from early adopters to mainstream market adopters and the unique characteristics that each of those audiences represents.

Anytime you're out for dinner with your parents or get together for the holidays, Roger's work shows up along with the chasm. Digital natives easily adapt to new tech, but the mid-to-late majority need a separate set of support and handholding. The same will be true as audience segments adjust to and begin to consume AI bots and apps that appeal to a broader audience.[21]

Having lived through this adoption cycle numerous times, the pattern of diffusion presents a playbook for both winners and losers. Some organizations consistently positioned themselves as innovators or early adopters across multiple cycles, while others repeatedly fell into late majority or laggard categories.

Understanding these patterns reveals why some organizations thrive through technological transitions while others struggle or disappear.

The Strategic Choice: Offense or Defense

When the disruption alarm sounds, companies have two options: circle the wagons or charge the hill. The Overclocked mindset is a shift in state, not a product line extension, new packaging, or ERP upgrade. Here's where a good offense is always the best defense.

Defensive Posture	Offensive Posture
Protecting legacy revenue streams and aging business models	Hunting for breakout plays within disruptive technologies
Downplaying disruptors as hype, fads, or "not our core"	Cannibalizing the cash cows *before* someone else does
Waiting until threats are too big to ignore	Spinning up skunkworks and rogue teams to test what's next
Making safe, incremental improvements	Placing bold bets on the edge, before they're mainstream

History has receipts: the companies that went on offense, such as Amazon, Apple, Siemens, and Walmart, didn't just survive disruption. They scaled it. They redefined their industries while their competitors defended yesterday's playbook.

Going defensive might buy time. Going offensive buys the future.

Digital Evolution – From dial-up[22] to Disruption

Web 1.0: The Foundation of Digital Business (1990s-2005)

Web 1.0 was the digital dawn, the static internet era, where businesses first showed up online, planted their digital flags, and hoped customers would find them. It was dial-up speeds and brochureware websites, but it changed everything.

As someone who lived and worked through the Web 1.0 era, I can tell you it was simultaneously primitive and revolutionary. The web was static, painfully slow by today's standards, but absolutely electric with possibility.

For the first time in human history, a world of information sat at your fingertips, accessible through dial-up connections that screeched their way to life at 56k speeds when you were lucky.

We could see and sense the massive trial and error happening not just on pixelated screens but in the daily headlines filled with IPO announcements, startup launch stories, tales of twentysomethings becoming millionaires through stock options, and the inevitable crash-and-burn stories of brilliant ideas that were ahead of their time. For those on the ground, it was both exciting and frustrating at times, marked by a mix of hype and self-destruction.

Digital was characterized by read-only websites that acted like digital storefronts where users could browse but not truly interact. It featured one-way communication, where brands talked at customers through static pages instead of engaging with them. Early e-commerce had basic shopping carts and clunky checkout processes that didn't convey trust.

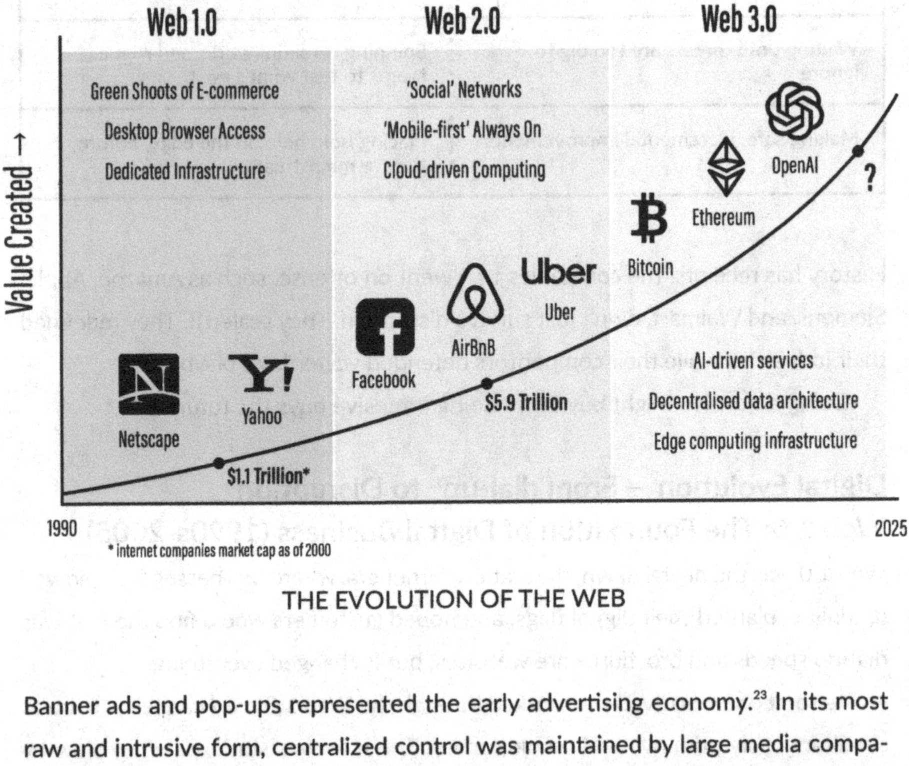

THE EVOLUTION OF THE WEB

Banner ads and pop-ups represented the early advertising economy.[23] In its most raw and intrusive form, centralized control was maintained by large media companies and major brands through top-down distribution, such as traditional channels.

But here's why it mattered: Web 1.0 laid the foundational infrastructure for everything that followed. Although it wasn't dynamic, social, or mobile, it fundamentally shifted how businesses thought about reach, visibility, and global scale. It put the entire world online, one URL at a time[24], creating the first digital commons where geography became irrelevant and 24/7 accessibility became the new normal.

The strategic moves that created lasting advantage were deceptively simple: being first online generated genuine competitive benefits because consumer attention was limited and search was primitive; SEO became the new version of storefront visibility where ranking high on early search engines like Yahoo and AltaVista could make or break a business; and email marketing began challenging direct mail by offering immediate delivery, measurable engagement, and practically zero marginal costs.

Amazon takes on the World

The most instructive study from this era remains Amazon versus traditional retail, because it perfectly illustrates how strategic vision mattered more than technological sophistication. In the 1990s, most established retailers viewed the internet as a digital flyer, essentially a glorified catalog slapped onto a screen with minimal functionality. Amazon saw something completely different: a new operating system for commerce that could fundamentally reshape how people discover, evaluate, and purchase products.

Jeff Bezos launched Amazon in 1994[25] As an online bookstore, the platform's DNA was baked in from day one. The company built its entire business model around scalability, customer obsession, and logistical precision rather than trying to replicate existing retail models online. Amazon treated its website as the core product, not a side project or marketing channel, investing early in personalization algorithms, user review systems, and real-time recommendation engines that made shopping feel intelligent rather than static.

Traditional retail's response was predictably cautious and ultimately catastrophic. Most established retailers treated digital as brochureware with no personalization, no frictionless checkout, and no integration with inventory management systems.

They were slow to adopt delivery logistics, data-driven pricing, and other customer experience innovations that Amazon was pioneering. Worst of all, e-commerce initiatives were typically siloed and built separately from core business operations, ensuring they would never achieve the integration necessary to compete effectively.

The result was inevitable: Amazon wasn't just first, it was fast, customer-centric, and relentlessly iterative in ways that traditional retailers couldn't match. Established retail chains remained slow, protective of their physical store networks, and consistently underestimated the speed of consumer behavioral shifts toward online shopping. The competitive gap wasn't just digital; it was fundamentally strategic, revealing which companies understood that technology was a growth engine rather than a cost center.

The Diffusion Pattern That Defines the Eras

The adoption pattern during Web 1.0 followed classic innovation diffusion curves but compressed into timeframes that caught most businesses unprepared. Innovators and early adopters included Amazon (1994), Yahoo (1994), eBay (1995), and Google (1998), companies that not only built websites but also reimagined entire business categories around digital capabilities. The early majority consisted of big-box retailers cautiously entering e-commerce, publishers testing paywalls and online subscription models, and banks introducing basic online banking portals that digitized existing services without fundamentally improving them.

The late majority and laggards told the real story of strategic blindness: brands stuck on static web pages that never evolved beyond digital brochures, companies avoiding online transactions due to overblown security fears, and executives still asking, "Do we really need a website?" well into the late 1990s when the answer had become painfully obvious to everyone except themselves.

Amazon didn't win Web 1.0 because it had a website; every company eventually got one of those. Amazon won because it reimagined what digital commerce could accomplish and weaponized early adoption advantages. At the same time, competitors debated implementation details and built scalable infrastructure. In contrast, others treated the web as an experiment and consistently treated technology as a strategic growth engine rather than a necessary risk to be managed.

The lesson that defined this entire era was simple yet profound: a first-mover advantage only matters if you move with conviction and continue to evolve. The companies that survived and thrived weren't just early adopters; they were strategic visionaries who understood that the web represented a fundamental shift in how business would operate, not just a new channel to bolt onto existing operations.

Web 2.0: Life's Operating System

The tail end of Web 1.0 was like an overclocked CPU; we pushed the early internet settings too far, too fast, and the whole system crashed spectacularly in 2000[26]. But like any good engineer knows, you don't abandon overclocking after the first failure; you rebuild with better cooling and voltage control. By 2005, the web had reached its tipping point and was ready for the next evolutionary leap into interactivity, video consumption, and user-generated creation that would fundamentally reshape human behavior.

I remember taking a step back that year and noticing patterns that would shape the next decade. Niche marketplaces were emerging from the most popular Craigslist categories; everything from apartment hunting to job searching was developing its dedicated platform with improved user experience and targeted features. Friendster and MySpace[27] Served as testing grounds for what social networking could become.

At the same time, Steve Jobs was beginning to explore consumer devices with the iPod, signaling the mobile revolution that would put the internet in everyone's pocket. Most importantly, the established Fortune 500 companies finally woke up from their digital slumber, realizing they could no longer treat the web as a side project.

Web 2.0 marked a significant shift where the internet stopped being just a destination you visited and instead became the fabric woven into everyday life. Suddenly, users weren't simply passive consumers clicking through static pages; they were creating content, connecting with communities, and expecting seamless experiences across every screen they encountered during their day.

This era was marked by social media's mainstream awareness, driven by platforms such as Facebook, Twitter, YouTube, and Instagram. Smartphones put the entire web in your pocket with 24/7 access, making digital engagement constant rather than episodic.

App ecosystems transformed every business into a software company, whether they realized it or not. Cloud computing[28] unlocked unprecedented scale, agility, and deployment speed for companies of all sizes. APIs enabled the plug-and-play innovation economy, where new services could be built by combining existing platforms instead of starting from scratch.

The strategic significance cannot be overstated: this was no longer just about being "online"; that had become a minimum standard. Success meant being everywhere your customers are, with relevant context, quick responses, and personalized experiences that felt natural on each platform and device.

Data became the new oil, fueling algorithmic decisions, as platforms grew into digital empires that controlled entire ecosystems. Digital strategy is finally aligned with core business goals, rather than being a separate IT effort.

Platforms and Marketplaces Jump off the 3rd Rope

The strategic moves that created lasting competitive advantages during Web 2.0 were fundamentally different from the Web 1.0 playbook. Platforms began systematically dominating entire verticals as Amazon expanded beyond books into everything; Google shifted from search to advertising and productivity tools; Apple built the app store ecosystem; and Facebook connected the world's social interactions.

Successful businesses shifted their focus from individual products to developing ecosystems where multiple services supported each other, thereby increasing the switching costs for customers. Growth strategies became tied to engineering network effects and viral loops that could scale exponentially rather than linearly.

The companies that not only survived but also dominated Web 2.0 weren't just digital opportunists riding market trends; they were digital operators who created the wave itself. They scaled faster than their competitors could respond, collected data more systematically than anyone had before, and built feedback loops that established strong competitive moats through ongoing improvement and customer retention.

This marked the rise of the winner-take-most economy, where platform effects, network externalities, and data advantages created natural monopolies that were nearly impossible to disrupt once established. The gap between winners and losers became exponentially larger than anything seen in traditional industries because digital platforms could scale without proportional increases in marginal costs.

Web 2.0 wasn't a feature upgrade; it was a full system reboot. As mobile, social, and cloud tech converged with wi-fi and broadband, entire industries were redefined. Looking back, it has shown us that in digital markets, being good enough is no longer enough; you must consistently outperform your competitors in learning, adapting, and scaling.

The companies that anticipated the changes created sustainable advantages that persist today, while those that viewed Web 2.0 as just another tech trend ultimately found themselves permanently relegated to secondary market roles or became completely irrelevant.

Today, it's happening again. It took three years for PCs to reach a 20% adoption rate, and two years for the internet to achieve the same level of adoption. Generative AI, particularly tools like ChatGPT, has achieved a 39.4% adoption rate among Americans aged 18-64 within two years.[29]

The insight that defined the era was simple but brutal: digital reinvention was the Darwinian mechanism. Companies that adopted systems for innovation, data-driven decision-making, and platform thinking would shape the future, while everyone else got disrupted, disintermediated, or dismantled.

The laggards? They were the NPCs[30] of the era. This chapter serves as a reminder for those who lived through the Web 1.0-2.0 eras to prepare the pipes and infrastructure of their organization for Web 3.0, and as a rallying cry for those who didn't step on the gas then, to push it to the floor now.

Uber's Platform Flywheel

Uber didn't just create a new transportation option; it rewired an entire industry by building a platform that scaled like code and moved like culture.

By 2011, I had moved from Los Angeles to Chicago and was working in the Loop at Edelman Digital; hailing a taxi was a competitive sport. If it were raining, you might as well give up and get soaked. While you can still enjoy the ritual of calling a taxi dispatch company and waiting in virtual darkness, never knowing if the ride would show up or when. The entire experience was an exercise in urban frustration that we just accepted as the cost of city living.

Then, rideshare companies like Lyft and Uber entered the scene, completely changing the game. Uber had launched in San Francisco a few years earlier, and I had downloaded the app and taken rides whenever I attended conferences there. The experience was so transformative that all I could talk about was Uber's upcoming arrival in Chicago that spring. The anticipation felt like waiting for the future to finally arrive in the Midwest.

Uber's genius wasn't just convenience; it was engineering a flywheel that made every interaction strengthen the entire platform. It quickly solved the cold start problem.[31] Of marketplaces. Instead of trying to launch in an entire city at once, Uber initially focused on smaller, specific geographic areas, which they called "atomic networks." This allowed them to concentrate on resources, build density, and create a positive experience for both riders and drivers within that smaller area.

As more drivers attracted more riders, the number of available drivers for faster pickups increased, reducing wait times and improving the overall user experience. This, in turn, drove better experiences, attracting even more riders in a positive feedback loop that triggered exponential growth.

Generating more rides resulted in more data for optimization, including dynamic pricing and route mapping intelligence. This additional data enabled a more innovative platform, powered by machine learning-driven matching algorithms, pricing optimization, and surge management, which made the service more efficient with every transaction.

This wasn't linear growth following traditional business expansion patterns; it was compounding momentum, where every single ride made the platform smarter, faster, and more competitively defensible. Uber had discovered how to turn individual transactions into a systematic advantage that accumulated over time rather than just generating immediate revenue.

The platform moves that changed the transportation game forever included turning underutilized assets like people's personal cars into a distributed global fleet without owning a single vehicle, using GPS technology, mobile payments, and user review systems as trust mechanisms that replaced traditional taxi medallion systems, building APIs and technical infrastructure that enabled expansion into adjacent markets like Uber Eats and Uber Freight, and designing a global expansion playbook rooted in understanding local liquidity dynamics rather than one-size-fits-all approaches.

Traditional taxi companies missed the transformation entirely because they remained focused on fleet ownership and dispatch optimization rather than user experience innovation, saw technology as a helpful tool rather than a platform foundation, and moved at annual planning speeds. At the same time, Uber operated at algorithm speeds that enabled real-time optimization and rapid market adaptation.

Uber didn't "do mobile" as an add-on feature; it was mobile-native by necessity. It didn't digitize an existing business model by putting taxis on smartphones; it completely rebuilt transportation around real-time supply and demand matching with transparent feedback loops that eliminated the frustration of calling dispatch companies and wondering if your ride would ever arrive. Uber scaled globally because it understood that in the platform economy, speed, data accumulation, and market liquidity create winner-take-most dynamics that are nearly impossible to disrupt once established.

The overclocked insight that defined Uber's dominance was recognizing that platforms aren't built through feature accumulation; they're engineered through feedback loops that create compounding value. Uber made every ride count, not just for immediate transportation but for improving the next million rides through better algorithms, more efficient matching, and superior user experiences that traditional competitors couldn't replicate without rebuilding their entire operational foundation.

This raises critical questions for every business:

- What parts of your operation could become platforms rather than just services?

- Are you feeding a flywheel that creates compounding advantages, or just running in operational circles that generate revenue without building systematic competitive moats?
- Do your customer interactions create compounding value that makes your business stronger over time, or do they remain isolated transactions that don't contribute to long-term competitive advantage?

Web 3.0: Digital Infrastructure Becomes Intelligent and Decentralized

Like the early internet, artificial intelligence, cryptography, and elements of blockchain technology have existed for decades; they just weren't commercially available in accessible SaaS models for both consumers and businesses. My early blockchain experience arrived from a call with longtime digital OG Matt Ballesteros, founder of 6 Foot Studios in Houston. He'd been running a digital agency and content studio since the early days of the web (hence the premium 6ft.com domain). He had evolved into indie films and games as part of their multi-modal service portfolio. Now, with NFTs, crypto marketplaces, and blockchain applications dominating industry conversations, he wanted to team up to navigate the transformation of the entertainment and media landscape.

That conversation launched an immersion into blockchain technology that's proven invaluable in understanding how distributed systems could reshape entire industries. The collaboration with Matt and his team opened my eyes to practical applications beyond cryptocurrency speculation. What became clear in my research of Fortune 150 companies was that they are investing time and resources in this space, and early proactive movers are already gaining market share and operational efficiency advantages.

Unlike Web 1.0 and 2.0, where individual companies pioneered new approaches, Web 3.0's early efforts have been characterized by industry consortia working together to solve common problems and build shared ecosystems that benefit all participants, thereby reducing risk while also mitigating the learning curve.

Web 3.0 represents more than a technological upgrade; it's a fundamental shift in power where control, computation, and creativity are migrating from centralized institutions to the decentralized edge. This era redefines how businesses learn from data, scale operations, and build trust with stakeholders through transparent, verifiable systems, rather than relying on institutional authority.

The key characteristics driving this transformation include artificial intelligence and machine learning, enabling real-time, adaptive decision-making at unprecedented scale; blockchain and distributed ledger technologies creating trust mechanisms that operate without traditional intermediaries; extended reality through AR, VR, and spatial computing, providing entirely new interfaces for human-computer interaction; and edge computing combined with IoT[32] moving intelligence from centralized data centers to distributed devices at the point of action.

The strategic implications are still being developed, creating unprecedented opportunities for organizations willing to experiment and learn rapidly. AI will automate insight generation while augmenting every business function from customer service to supply chain optimization.

Decentralization will systematically erode traditional gatekeepers who extract value without adding proportional benefit. Data sovereignty will shift value back to users who generate information rather than platforms that collect it. Most significantly, the distinction between digital and physical experiences will become increasingly blurred as spatial computing and IoT enable seamless integration between virtual and real-world interactions.

Building Tomorrow's Competitive Moats

Today's early adopters of AI, blockchain, and immersive technologies aren't just experimenting with new tools; they're building asymmetrical advantages that directly translate into revenue growth, improved customer retention, and expanded market reach. These companies represent the Amazon 1997s and Netflix 2007s of the Web 3.0 era, establishing dominant positions while competitors are still debating whether these technologies matter.

The diffusion pattern for Web 3.0 reveals a convergence of artificial intelligence, blockchain, decentralization, and spatial computing rather than a single breakthrough moment. Innovators and early adopters are building foundational infrastructure while others study theoretical implications.

Tesla and OpenAI are transforming AI into a foundational layer for real-world decision-making at scale. DeFi platforms are challenging traditional finance with transparent, composable alternatives that eliminate intermediary friction. Meta is betting on the long arc of embodied digital interaction through metaverse investments[33]. Enterprise blockchain consortia are redefining trust, provenance, and audit processes across entire value chains.

The early majority is beginning to emerge as mainstream adoption accelerates. Corporations are embedding generative AI[34] into core workflows and customer-facing products. Financial institutions are running serious pilots on tokenized assets and blockchain-based settlement systems. Retailers are experimenting with AR and VR technologies to create immersive shopping experiences that seamlessly blend digital and physical commerce. Manufacturers are leveraging IoT devices for predictive maintenance and real-time operational optimization that reduces downtime and improves efficiency.

The critical insight about Web 3.0 adoption is that technology is maturing rapidly, but a significant mindset gap remains among business leaders. Many executives still frame these shifts as interesting technology experiments rather than existential questions about the viability of their fundamental business model. This creates massive opportunities for organizations that recognize Web 3.0 isn't a feature layer to bolt onto existing operations; it's a full-stack rethinking of how value is created, control is distributed, and interactions are designed.

If Web 2.0 gave businesses networks that connected people and information, Web 3.0 provides agency, allowing systems to think, adapt, and operate with minimal human intervention. This isn't about adding AI capabilities to existing processes; it's about redesigning entire business models to think, adapt, and trust at machine scale, where artificial intelligence becomes the new operating system rather than just another tool.

The winners in Web 3.0 will be organizations that rewire trust through transparent, verifiable systems; decentralize ownership to create more substantial stakeholder alignment; and use AI not merely to automate repetitive tasks but to augment human potential in ways that create entirely new categories of value creation. You're not too late for Web 3.0 unless you act like these technologies don't fundamentally matter to your industry's future competitive landscape.

CASE STUDY

Walmart — Blockchain and the Supply Chain Reset

How a mango pilot turned into a blueprint for trust at Web 3.0 speed.

In 2016, Walmart ran a simple test: trace a pack of sliced mangoes back to its farm of origin. The old way? Seven days of phone calls, paper trails, and dead ends. The new way? Blockchain. Time collapsed to 2.2 seconds—not an incremental improvement but a wholesale rewiring of food safety velocity.

The Bottleneck

Global food chains were built on analog glue: static invoices, siloed databases, and supplier trust. That lag meant regulators couldn't act fast enough, recalls dragged on, and brands carried the reputational risk. Walmart needed to digitize the chain of custody, not just monitor it.

The Overclock

With IBM, Walmart deployed a blockchain ledger that gave every actor—from farms to distributors to store shelves—an immutable, time-stamped entry. No more chasing data; every step was verified in real-time. From U.S. lettuce to Chinese pork, perishables became trackable from farm to checkout in seconds. Think of it as swapping a clogged supply pipe for a transparent, fiber-optic feed: zero latency, shared visibility, and trust built into the protocol itself.

Results

Recall speed: days → seconds, minimizing consumer exposure.

Network accountability: shared data enforced compliance upstream and downstream.

Smarter shelves: real-time insights tightened forecasting, reducing waste and boosting availability.

What It Means

Walmart treated blockchain as logistics infrastructure, not PR gloss. By embedding transparency and verification into its operatingsystem, the company redefined food safety for a Web 3.0 economy.

Strategic Signals

Trust as Code: bake transparency into core systems, not policies.

Shared Ledgers = Shared Accountability: decentralization as compliance enforcement.

Speed + Safety = Loyalty: faster recalls aren't just risk mitigation—they're a market advantage.

This raises critical questions: Are you treating AI and Web 3.0 technologies as valuable tools or as catalysts for fundamental business model reinvention? Where does your organization remain centralized when distributed approaches would create better outcomes? What does value creation look like when data sovereignty shifts to users and decision-making becomes shared rather than hierarchical?

The Five Catalysts of Disruption

Across every digital wave, the same four catalysts have lit the fuse. Ignore them at your peril:

Catalyst	Web 1.0	Web 2.0	Web 3.0 / AI era
Information Asymmetry	Brands held the facts, consumers guessed	Consumers gained transparancy via reviews and forums	AI tips the scales again — whoever controls the algorithm owns the narrative
Cost	E-commerce killed rent	Cloud vaporized infrastructure costs	AI eliminates white-collar overhead at scale
Convenience	24/7 online storefronts	Smartphones put power in your palm	Voice, vision, and predictive UX erase friction
Capability	SMB's got global reach	Remote teams ran in realtime	PAI agents automate, anticipate, and adapt faster
Connectivity	Static websites met curious visitors	Social platforms scaled connection	IoT and ambient computing blur digital and real

Overclocked Take: The disruptors don't wait for these catalysts to mature. They ride them early and shape the rules.

Winners don't play defense; they hot-swap their parts before the market fries them. Reinvented incumbents carve off skunk-works units (think Google X or AWS) with their clock speed, push CEOs into the trenches, and cheerfully cannibalize yesterday's cash cows (iPod → iPhone) while bleeding cash today to rent the future back to us tomorrow. They draft talent for velocity, not tenure. Start-ups arrive with the same firmware uncluttered: solve one searing pain, stay asset-light, code data feedback into every interaction, ship MVPs[35] weekly, and let network effects compound the win. Offense, always.

Where you sit on the adoption curve is a choice, not fate. Innovators gamble early and big; early adopters pilot, learn, and snag first-mover gains; the early majority scales proven playbooks; the late majority tags along for shrinking scraps; laggards cling to legacy, praying for patches. Pick your lane deliberately or drift into the obsolescence penalty box.

Quick diagnostic: Are you pre-empting disruption or just flinching? Does your org chart accelerate ideas or throttle them? Which catalyst will define the next 12 months? Identify the offensive play before a faster rival rewrites your scoreboard.

Diffusion – Disruption Grid

How Catalysts Fuel Each Stage of Technology Diffusion

When we combine the concepts of technology adoption and the catalysts of disruption, we see not just *who adopts when*, but *why that adoption accelerates or stalls.*

Catalyst of Disruption	Innovators (2.5%)	Early Adopters (13.5%)	Early Majority (34%)	Late Majority (34%)	Laggards (16%)
Information Asymmetry	Chase hidden signals, experiment on weak ties	Spot strategic edge early, evangelize value	Need proof points, credible case studies	Require mass visibility & social proof	Still skeptical even after broad visibility
Cost	Ignore high costs to test bleeding-edge	Pay a premium for a strategic advantage	Adopt as prices drop to ROI-positive	Wait until commoditized, discounts common	Only adopt when legacy becomes more expensive
Convenience	Tolerate friction, patch workarounds	Lean into early convenience breakthroughs	Expect user-friendly UX, reliable uptime	Need plug-and-play simplicity	Only switch when forced by peers or regulators
Capability	Tinker with raw potential	Frame capabilities as a business advantage	Adopt when tools are packaged + training available	Use when institutionalized in workflows	Adopt only when mandated
Connectivity	Build first networks, APIs, guilds	Expand ecosystems, attract complementary players	Join once the network is stable and interoperable	Demand standards and mainstream platforms	Forced into adoption when alternatives disappeared

GLOBAL SIGNAL

Leapfrogging the Curve

The Maturity Matrix shows how disruption pressures incumbents to adapt incrementally across capabilities. But in emerging markets, startups often bypass this process. They build high-maturity solutions to solve urgent human needs, leapfrogging traditional development curves.

Signals

- M-KOPA (East Africa): Started with pay-as-you-go solar and grew into a fintech ecosystem, providing credit, smartphones, loans, and insurance to 5M+ customers. By solving energy poverty, M-KOPA jumped straight into ecosystem-level maturity.
- Grameen Shakti (Bangladesh): Scaled 1.8M Solar Home Systems by training women technicians, proving that workforce development and trust networks are as transformative as the tech itself. A social maturity leap, not a technological crawl.
- Husk Power Systems (India & Nigeria): Rebuilt 200+ hybrid microgrids serving 1.5M people, combining solar, biomass, and batteries. By redesigning its business from scratch, Husk showed how reinvention can bypass legacy entirely.

Takeaway

Disruption doesn't always follow the staged path in the matrix. In necessity-driven markets, startups leap ahead, proving that maturity can be catalyzed by urgency rather than sequence.

How to Use the Diffusion — Disruption Grid

The Diffusion — Disruption grid fuses two powerful ideas.

- Technology Diffusion (how innovations spread from innovators to laggards) and
- Catalysts of Disruption (the forces that accelerate or stall adoption)

Instead of asking *when* adoption occurs, this model helps you understand why adoption accelerates, slows down, or skips stages altogether.

Step 1. Identify the Technology or Business Model

Define the product, platform, or capability under analysis.

Example: AI copilots, blockchain logistics, direct-to-avatar commerce.

Step 2. Map Against Adoption Segments

Place your technology along the classic diffusion curve:

Innovators (2.5%) → Early Adopters (13.5%) → Early Majority (34%) → Late Majority (34%) → Laggards (16%).

Ask: Where is current adoption clustered? Who is still hesitant?

Step 3. Diagnose the Catalysts

Use the five catalysts of disruption to analyze friction or momentum in each stage:

Catalyst	Ask This	Implication
Information Asymmetry	Are signals about value clear or still hidden?	Early movers thrive on weak signals; later adopters need case studies + visibility.
Cost	Is adoption affordable yet?	Innovators tolerate expense; later groups wait for commoditization.
Convenience	How smooth is the UX and integration?	Early adopters patch around friction; the mass market demands plug-and-play.
Capability	Do users know how to capture value?	Innovators tinker; mainstream users need training, packaging, and workflows.
Connectivity	Is there an ecosystem yet?	Innovators build networks; late adopters wait for standards and platforms.

Step 4. Spot the Stalls and Accelerants

Stalls: Where adoption hesitates, ask which catalyst is missing (e.g., cost too high, networks too immature).

Accelerants: Where adoption surges, identify which catalyst tipped the balance (e.g., price drop, ecosystem interoperability).

Step 5. Define the Migration Path

Forecast how technology might move from one adoption stage to the next.

Example: *Generative AI assistants are moving from Early Adopters (knowledge workers, startups) → Early Majority (enterprise workflows) as cost drops and enterprise-grade platforms (Microsoft, Salesforce) institutionalize capabilities.*

The Payoff:

By overlaying catalysts onto adoption stages, the Overclocked Grid helps you see not just *who* adopts and *when*, but *why adoption accelerates, stalls, or leapfrogs stages.*

Catalyst–Adopter Fit:

- *Innovators* thrive on information asymmetry + capability (they love hacking together what's possible before it's polished).
- *Early Adopters* lean heavily on strategic convenience + signaling edge.
- *Majorities* are cost and convenience driven.
- *Laggards* only move when cost + connectivity make resistance impossible.

Compression in Digital

Each digital wave has accelerated this entire curve; catalysts like cost drops and connectivity leaps have compressed timelines from Web 1 to Web 2, and now, in Web 3, generative AI has reached mass adoption in just two years, serving as the ultimate proof.

Strategic Use:

If you know which catalyst is strongest for your innovation, you can predict where you'll gain traction first. For example, AI copilots: *innovators* driven by capability; *early majority* hooked by convenience once integrated in Office/Slack.

Overclocked Disruption & Reinvention Maturity Matrix

Give yourself and your team a chance to provide an honest self-assessment of your business, its typical responses, and behaviors that can be changed. Are you a 'wait and see' organization or a 'let's start experimenting' lean-in group? The recent surge in blockchain and AI will give you a snapshot of how you respond.

Traits	Stage 1 Denial & Deflection	Stage 2 Defensive Adaptor	Stage 3 Fast Follower	Stage 4 Proactive Reinventor	Stage 5 Anticipatory Disruptor
Behavior	Skeptical, dismissive, risk-averse	Reactive, cautious, protective	Opportunistic, copycat, cautious scaler	Bold, experimental, willing to self-cannibalize	Visionary, scanning, shaping new rules
Org Mindset	"Not our core."	"We'll adapt when we must."	"Let's wait until it's safe."	"We'll reinvent ourselves before others do."	"We *are* the wave."
Playbook	Delay, protect core revenues	Patch and bolt-on updates	Copy proven winners	Cannibalize, spin up skunkworks	Prototype relentlessly, weaponize foresight
AI Layer	Ignore AI as hype	Siloed pilots, narrow scope	Basic automation when peers move	AI as reinvention catalyst	AI as a full-stack operating system + disruption radar

The Ride So Far, and the Road Ahead

Over the past three decades, digital disruption has been less of a single event and more of an ongoing ride, equal parts thrilling, jarring, and unpredictable. We opened with Matt Wasserlauf, whose career arc from Web 1.0 content sales to Web 3.0 ad fraud prevention embodies the mindset of reinvention.

We looked at Shopify, which started as a way to sell snowboards and ultimately rewrote the rules for how anyone can sell anything, anywhere. We nodded to Uber, a marketplace and platform that didn't just change how we hail a ride but redefined the value proposition of transparency and trust in service delivery.

We saw how even the biggest incumbents, such as Walmart, can utilize emerging technologies like blockchain to break down information silos and drive supply chain visibility.

Threaded through all these stories are the same four catalysts of disruption:

- Information Asymmetry – When you can see something your competitors or customers can't (yet), you gain the first-mover edge.
- Cost – When technology drives down price without sacrificing value, the market shifts in your favor.
- Convenience – When you make things easier, faster, and more accessible, adoption accelerates.
- Capability – When new tools expand what's possible, they open entire categories that didn't exist before.
- Connectivity – When accessibility ranges from dial-up to the autonomous internet of things (IoT).

These forces rarely operate alone. When they converge, when cost drops as convenience rises, when new capabilities eliminate information gaps, markets don't just evolve, they *tilt*. Players who recognize the tilt and act decisively ride the wave upward. Those who don't often find themselves watching from the shore as the tide moves on without them.

The last thirty years have shown us that disruption isn't a one-off crisis to survive; it's a continuous environment that requires adaptation. The most resilient organizations aren't just reacting to the next wave; they're scanning for it, preparing for it, and positioning themselves to catch it before others even see it coming. The ride isn't slowing down. The only question is whether you'll be on the surfboard or in the water when the next swell arrives.

CHAPTER 4

Digital Infrastructure — Competitive Advantage

Think Like a Digital Architect

For too long, infrastructure has been treated like wiring or plumbing in a building, necessary but invisible. If the lights turned on and the servers didn't crash, most leaders checked the box and moved on. That mindset worked in the early days of the web, when digital storefronts were little more than brochures. However, in Web 1.0 and Web 2.0, companies without the proper infrastructure weren't only inconvenient but also sidelined.

Most readers may only know AOL because of their grandparents' email address, but back in the day, AOL[36] was the 800-lb digital gorilla. But this Web 1.0 leader learned the infrastructure lesson the hard way. Its entire experience revolved around proprietary templates and keyword navigation, an approach that couldn't keep pace with Yahoo's customizable portals, Microsoft's expanding content networks, or Google's lightning-fast search. A lack of brand or users didn't sink AOL; it was sunk by an inflexible, outdated foundation that couldn't adapt as the web evolved.

We're at a similar inflection point now. According to the latest forecast by Gartner, 90% of organizations will adopt a hybrid cloud approach through 2027[37], up from just 30% in 2021. That's not just a technology adoption stat; it's a structural tipping point. Infrastructure is no longer "IT's problem" in the basement. It's the competitive surface where milliseconds matter, resilience is engineered, and every other layer of your digital strategy, data, AI, and customer experience either accelerates or stalls.

Think of AI and blockchain readiness like building a world-class stadium. You can hire the best players (utilizing AI algorithms), design brilliant plays (employing business strategies), and even sell out the seats (meeting customer demand). Still, if the field is cracked, the lighting is unreliable, and the scoreboard lags, the game won't go your way. Infrastructure is the turf, the lights, the scoreboard, and the locker room all at once. Get it wrong, and nothing else performs at its best.

In this chapter, we'll map the five layers of the technology stack and show how the strongest performers treat infrastructure as a living, evolving asset, not a sunk cost. You'll learn how to audit stack maturity, identify throughput bottlenecks, and align each layer with your horizon-based growth objectives. When the leadership vision from Chapter 1 meets the adaptive strategy of Chapter 2, infrastructure determines whether that vision moves at market speed or grinds to a halt.

MASTERY LEARNING OBJECTIVES

- Assess the strategic role of digital infrastructure as a foundation for business agility, innovation, and long-term value creation, not just as a technical asset.
- Apply the Technology–Organization–Environment (TOE) framework to diagnose internal readiness, environmental fit, and organizational alignment in infrastructure decisions.
- Design integrated, modular tech stacks that can scale, adapt, and support real-time business needs, balancing composability with governance.
- Evaluate infrastructure maturity and governance models to create upgrade roadmaps that balance flexibility, standardization, and enterprise-wide acceleration.

INDUSTRY INSIGHT

Capital One, From Bank Vaults to Cloud-Native Launchpads

How a top U.S. bank turned compliance constraints into a cloud-powered competitive advantage.

In banking, mainframes were considered the "safe choice" because they were immovable, compliant, and proven. Capital One decided they were also anchors. Starting in 2010, the bank began dismantling its legacy stack in favor of a public cloud architecture that few in the industry dared to attempt.

Context / Challenge

Most financial institutions avoided large-scale cloud adoption due to regulatory pressure, security concerns, and cultural inertia. Innovation cycles stretched for quarters or years, while fintech startups launched new features in weeks. Capital One faced a strategic crossroads: maintain the status quo and risk irrelevance or take the leap into cloud-native banking.

The Velocity Shift

Led by CIO Rob Alexander, Capital One rebuilt its core infrastructure on a public cloud foundation, embracing microservices, DevOps, and in-house AI development. The transformation turned infrastructure from a bottleneck into a launchpad, cutting deployment cycles from months to weeks and enabling real-time experimentation. Critically, they embedded compliance and resilience into the architecture itself, turning regulatory requirements into a competitive moat rather than a constraint. On the blockchain front, while Capital One hasn't emerged as a headline member of public blockchain consortia, signs point to exploratory involvement.

For instance, Capital One is part of broader payment consortia, such as Zelle, which includes major banks exploring joint stablecoin initiatives.[38] Additionally, Capital One has filed patents related to secure decentralized computing systems, suggesting deeper investment in blockchain infrastructure.[39]

Results / Impact

By 2020, Capital One no longer resembled a traditional bank; it had evolved into a tech company with a banking license. Its cloud-first approach enabled the rapid deployment of AI-driven fraud detection, personalized offers, and digital services, outpacing both incumbents and fintech disruptors. The infrastructure now serves as a ready-made platform for next-gen innovations, from blockchain settlement layers to generative AI-powered customer service.

STRATEGIC TAKEAWAYS

- **Transform the Core to Unlock the Edge** — True digital agility starts with modern infrastructure.
- **Bake Compliance into the Build** — Security and regulation can become accelerators, not anchors.
- **Invest in Platforms, Not Just Projects** — A future-proof foundation multiplies innovation options.

REFLECTION

- Is your infrastructure helping you move faster or slowing you down?
- Are you investing in tech like it's a cost center or a growth engine?
- What will your future require that your current stack can't deliver?

Stay tuned. This chapter goes under the hood of digital infrastructure, the real power move for next-gen strategy.

Understanding Digital Infrastructure: A Strategic Framework

Digital infrastructure is more than routers and servers; it's the backbone of your agility, innovation, and growth. In a world where speed wins and complexity compounds, infrastructure isn't just technical plumbing. It's strategic fuel. And, if you're like Capital One, it sets your business up for future scalability into Web 3.0.

To build it right, you need more than specs and spending. You need context. That's where the TOE framework comes in.[40] Short for Technology-Organization-Environment, this model helps leaders evaluate and organize their strategy around infrastructure, not just in terms of what it does, but also how it fits, flexes, and fuels the business.

Context	Key Elements	Strategic Considerations
Technology	· Current technological assets · Emerging technological opportunities · Technical compatibility · Perceived benefits and risks	· How well do our systems work together? · What new technologies could enhance our capabilities? · What are the technical risks of our infrastructure choices?
Organization	· Leadership and governance · Structure and culture · Resource availability · Technical capabilities	· How are technology decisions made? · Do we have the right skills to leverage modern infrastructure? · Does our culture support technical innovation?
Environment	· Industry dynamics · Regulatory landscape · Market demands · Ecosystem relationships	· What infrastructure do our competitors use? · How do regulations affect our technology choices? · What do our customers expect from our digital capabilities?

This three-dimensional framework enables digital leaders to move beyond purely technical considerations, building infrastructure that aligns with organizational capabilities and responds to external pressures and opportunities.

Digital Infrastructure:
From Cost Center to Competitive Weapon

Let's rewind.

For decades, infrastructure lived in the basement, literally and metaphorically. It was a cost center and had a cost center containment mentality. Heavy, expensive, and slow. On-prem servers. Multi-year depreciation cycles. IT teams that existed to keep the lights on, not light the way. The goal? Stability, standardization, and as little disruption as possible.

Then cloud crashed the party. Infrastructure shifted from hardware to hybrid, from static to elastic. Capital expenses gave way to subscriptions in software as a service (SaaS) models. Suddenly, agility and scalability weren't just IT buzzwords; they were survival traits. The most innovative companies didn't just modernize; they rethought the role of infrastructure entirely.

Today, modern infrastructure isn't about racks and wires. It's about enabling speed, unlocking innovation, and creating resilience. It's not just a support function;

it's a strategic asset. Cloud-native architecture, microservices, APIs, real-time data pipelines — these aren't just technical details; they're growth levers.

The payoff? Infrastructure now drives:

- Operational excellence through automation, speed, and integration.
- Customer experience via personalization, self-service, and seamless omnichannel journeys.
- Innovation velocity with modern dev environments, AI engines, and open ecosystems.
- Agility and insights at scale thanks to modular design, distributed systems, and cloud-native platforms.

The companies that win the next decade won't just *use* infrastructure. They'll weaponize it.

The Integrated Tech Stack: A Straightforward Breakdown for Executives, Teams, and Operators

In the Overclocked era, digital infrastructure isn't just a collection of parts; it's a tightly integrated, high-performance system. And every layer matters.

Let's demystify the modern tech stack with a five-layer model. Whether you're a C-suite exec, department lead, or boots-on-the-ground builder, knowing how these layers connect gives you leverage.

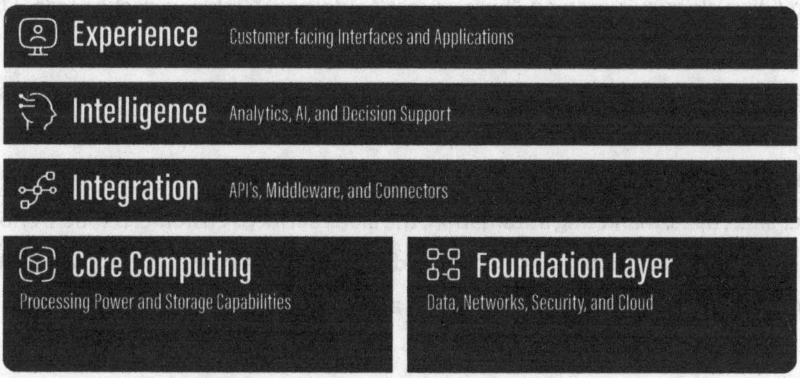

INFRASTRUCTURE REFERENCE MODEL

The Overclocked Stack — Plain-English Edition

A company's tech stack refers to the collection of technologies, including programming languages, frameworks, databases, and tools, that a company utilizes to develop and operate its applications and systems. It's essentially the foundation upon which a company's digital infrastructure is built.

Digital Utilities (Infrastructure)

Think of this as your building's electricity and plumbing, cloud servers, fast pipes, and iron-clad security. When it's rock-solid (AWS, Azure, zero-trust firewalls), everything hums. When it hiccups, the whole floor goes dark.

Source of Truth (Core Systems)

ERP, CRM, and supply-chain platforms keep the ledgers straight and the inventory real. SAP, Oracle, Salesforce: not flashy, but they're the heartbeat that keeps cash, customers, and widgets in sync.

Connective Tissue (Integration)

APIs, middleware, and data hubs are the wiring loom that lets parts talk instead of yell across the room. MuleSoft, Boomi, Snowflake links, this is where "we bought the tool" becomes "we built a platform."

The Brain (Intelligence)

Warehouses, analytics, and AI models transform raw logs into actionable insights, providing clear guidance on "here's what to do next." Tableau dashboards, Databricks pipelines, OpenAI copilots, insight at machine speed, delivered before the meeting starts.

The Handshake (Experience)

Websites, apps, marketing automation, the sleek surfaces customer's touch. Shopify checkouts, Adobe Experience sites, and HubSpot journeys. All the magic above funnels here to make or break loyalty in a click.

Overclocked Takeaway: Competitive edge isn't in a single layer; it's in how friction-free they snap together. Ask yourself:

- Are we wired for speed or tripping over silos?
- Can data sprint from back-end to front-end without a pit stop?
- Are we building tech that scales with our ambition or survives this quarter?

CASE STUDY

Maersk — Building the Digital Arteries of Global Trade

How a shipping giant turned container logistics into a data-driven platform.

For over a century, Maersk was synonymous with containers and cargo ships. But by the 2010s, its core business was under siege: freight rates were volatile, supply chains fragmented, and customers demanded transparency that analog paperwork couldn't deliver. The pivot? Redefining digital infrastructure for global trade.

The Bottleneck

Logistics was stuck in the dark ages: siloed databases, manual customs clearance, and disconnected carriers. Customers had little visibility into where goods were, while Maersk relied on slow, costly communication chains. Competitors raced to commoditize shipping capacity, eroding margins.

The Overclock

- TradeLens: In partnership with IBM, Maersk launched a blockchain-enabled platform that gave shippers, ports, customs, and carriers a single, immutable source of truth.
- End-to-End Visibility: IoT-enabled containers and predictive analytics turned guesswork into real-time tracking.
- Digital Marketplace: Maersk Spot allowed customers to book guaranteed capacity online, as easily as buying an airline ticket.
- Platformization: By offering APIs and ecosystem integration, Maersk

shifted from asset-heavy operator to digital orchestrator of global supply chains.

Results

- Reduced documentation processing times by up to 80% through TradeLens.
- Improved forecast accuracy and lowered logistics costs for global shippers.
- Grew digital revenue streams, moving Maersk from commodity shipping to a platform model embedded in global commerce.

What It Means

Digital infrastructure isn't just cloud servers and networks, it's the connective tissue that makes industries move faster, smarter, and with less friction. Maersk proved that even in the oldest of industries, infrastructure reinvention can transform you from carrier of goods to custodian of trust and data.

Digital Infrastructure Maturity Matrix

Infrastructure isn't wiring; it's the playing field. AOL didn't lose due to brand or demand; it lost because its digital foundation couldn't keep pace with the internet's rapid evolution. In today's hybrid-cloud era, infrastructure has become the competitive surface: milliseconds, resilience, and composability decide whether your strategy accelerates or stalls.

Dimension	Reactive	Standardized	Integrated	Intelligent	Orchestrated
Data Architecture	Fragmented silos, batch uploads, and manual reporting	Centralized systems, scheduled updates	Unified data lake/warehouse, governed schemas	Real-time pipelines, API-first access	Autonomous data fabric with AI-driven optimization
Customer Centricity	Digital channels are treated separately	Basic CRM, campaign-centric	Omnichannel, unified profiles	Dynamic personalization, contextual engagement	Anticipatory, predictive experiences across all touchpoints
Agility & Delivery	Waterfall IT projects, quarterly releases	Agile in pockets, slow cross-team alignment	Cross-functional DevOps, CI/CD pipelines	Automated deployments, AI-driven testing	Autonomous, adaptive infrastructure that evolves at market speed
Leadership & Culture	IT as a cost center	Business/IT alignment projects	Shared KPIs, IT + business co-leadership	Tech leaders drive growth strategy	Infrastructure leadership embedded as a cultural mindset
Security & Compliance	Reactive audits, bolt-on controls	Baseline security standards	Integrated identity + access management	Proactive risk modeling, real-time monitoring	DevSecOps-native, resilience engineered into every layer

GLOBAL SIGNAL

Infrastructure as a Platform Jumpstart

The Infrastructure Maturity Matrix guides incumbents from digital enablement to platform orchestration. But in many emerging markets, startups begin life not as users of platforms, but as their architects, creating core infrastructure to support entire ecosystems.

Signals

- Reliance Jio (India): Jio's greenfield 4G network allowed it to bypass legacy telco baggage. They architected their infrastructure to be cloud-native, software-defined, and scalable, enabling a fast rollout and ecosystem support.
- Beyond telecom: in many African markets, M-KOPA and solar-grid startups build infrastructure (energy, connectivity) as a foundation, which then enables fintech, data, and upstream services. (This ties to disruption but also to infrastructure leverage.)
- TradeDepot (Africa): Though more on commerce, their logistics + delivery infrastructure is deeply integrated with their distribution platform, giving them control over how goods move through fragmented markets.

Takeaway

Some of tomorrow's most powerful digital battlegrounds will be fought at the infrastructure layer, in connectivity, logistics, energy, and platform fabrics. Startups that build infrastructure first don't just compete, they enable entire ecosystems, and incumbents may have little choice but to plug into them.

Industry Groupings: Shared Patterns, Distinct Priorities

While every sector has its dynamics, industries often move in packs, adopting similar technologies to solve comparable problems. By clustering adjacent sectors together, leaders can benchmark themselves more broadly, seeing not only how direct competitors are evolving, but also how adjacent industries with shared challenges are leveraging digital transformation. This perspective widens the aperture for innovation, allowing executives to borrow, adapt, and accelerate lessons from beyond their walls.

Consumer + Retail + Hospitality

Consumer-facing sectors, such as retail/e-commerce, CPG, and hospitality, share a relentless focus on personalization, operational agility, and channel integration. These industries benchmark well against each other because they face similar challenges in omnichannel orchestration and customer-driven growth. Data-driven personalization and recommendation engines

- E-commerce platforms, omnichannel systems, and supply chain visibility
- Loyalty ecosystems and digital wallets
- Immersive experiences via AR/VR and connected IoT environments

Media + Entertainment + Gaming + Sports + Tech

Media, Gaming, and Technology companies are bound by content velocity, platform scale, and the economics of attention. Their reliance on data-driven personalization, immersive experiences, and creator ecosystems makes them instructive for one another, and increasingly, for other industries learning how to monetize engagement.

- Streaming platforms and cloud distribution
- AI-driven content recommendation and curation
- Creator economy tools and monetization engines
- Real-time fan engagement platforms, fantasy sports, and betting integrations

Healthcare + Education

Healthcare and Education both sit at the intersection of public need and private innovation. Their shared challenges include accessibility, personalization, and outcomes-based measurement, making them natural comparisons in digital maturity benchmarking.

- Telemedicine, remote learning, and digital health platforms
- AI-driven diagnostics, tutoring, and personalization
- Data integration across EMRs, student records, and wellness apps
- Wearables and IoT for continuous engagement and monitoring

Financial Services + Insurance + Real Estate

Banks, fintechs, and insurers are united by regulatory oversight, trust, and risk management. They benchmark across each other in digitizing legacy systems, enabling real-time transactions, and building data-driven, secure ecosystems. Blockchain for payments, provenance, and smart contracts

- AI for risk scoring, underwriting, and fraud detection
- Digital-first banks, wallets, and trading platforms
- PropTech platforms integrating data, transactions, and smart building systems

Manufacturing + Logistics + Automotive + Energy

Heavy industries such as Manufacturing, Construction, and Energy are united by large-scale infrastructure, asset intensity, and safety imperatives. They increasingly benchmark against each other through digital twins, IoT, and predictive analytics to optimize efficiency and resilience. IoT sensors and connected supply chains

- Robotics, AI-driven predictive maintenance, and Industry 4.0
- Digital twins for systems and infrastructure
- Smart grids, renewable integration, and electrification platforms

The Path Forward: Strategic Infrastructure Development

Modern infrastructure isn't just about uptime and storage; it's the foundation for innovation, speed, and scale. Here's how to future-proof your infrastructure in a world that won't stop changing.

1. Wire Infrastructure to Strategy

Infrastructure decisions aren't technical side quests anymore; they're central to your growth story. Map every infrastructure investment to business outcomes. Make sure your tech leaders have a seat at the strategy table. Foster a shared language between IT and business teams, and develop visible methods to demonstrate how infrastructure drives value. If your roadmap isn't aligned to customer needs or business goals, it's not a roadmap, it's a detour.

2. Balance Stability with Speed

Yes, uptime still matters. But so does shipping fast and learning faster. Adopt modern architecture that allows you to evolve incrementally, rather than in big, risky leaps. Use sandbox environments to test bold ideas without breaking production. Build governance that manages risk without throttling experimentation. The goal? Reliability without rigidity.

3. Build for Connection, Not Isolation

In a platform world, integration is king. APIs, data governance, and interoperability are the glue that binds your stack and your ecosystem. Invest in integration capabilities that let systems talk to each other, share data, and support partnerships. Ensure data flows seamlessly from source to insight to experience, eliminating black boxes and brittle workarounds.

4. Design for Resilience and Defense

Security isn't a bolt-on; it's built in. Resilience isn't optional; it's expected. Architect for failover, monitor like a hawk, and rehearse your recovery plans. Bake DevSecOps[41] Into your pipelines so you're securing as you build. Infrastructure must be your frontline and your fallback.

5. Upgrade Without the Overhaul

Not everything needs to be ripped and replaced. Identify the most constraining components, then modernize in modular steps, introducing new capabilities in parallel while maintaining stability in core systems. Test early, learn fast, migrate smart. Infrastructure evolution is a rhythm, not a revolution.

As we enter the post-experimental AI era, digital infrastructure serves as the nervous system that dictates how quickly you can sense, decide, and act. In industries where milliseconds mean market share, and in regulated sectors where compliance can slow change to a crawl, your infrastructure is either a launchpad or a leash.

That's why Capital One's journey stands out. In a space where regulation, much like healthcare or finance, often reinforces legacy systems, Capital One rewired its foundation. Instead of letting compliance be the reason not to change, they built for agility inside the guardrails: a complete public-cloud migration, microservices, and a DevOps culture.

The payoff? They didn't just modernize, they made infrastructure a competitive weapon, positioning themselves for AI scale and quietly exploring blockchain patents and payment consortia. It's a reminder that "regulated" doesn't have to mean "static."

Across industries

Similarities: All sectors share the same base layers, compute, storage, integration, intelligence, and experience. Every winner treats these as interconnected assets rather than siloed expenses.

Differences: The "what" and "how fast" are dictated by industry DNA, manufacturing integrates shop-floor sensors, retail obsesses over real-time personalization, finance and healthcare hardwire compliance into every layer, media builds for bandwidth and burst traffic, logistics optimizes for visibility and routing, and travel/hospitality for trust and seamless service recovery.

Your technology must align with your organizational capabilities and adapt to your environmental context, whether that means meeting HIPAA requirements, enabling open banking APIs, or streaming content to millions simultaneously. The rulebook for infrastructure is universal; the playbook is local.

The Capital One story drives the closing point home: modern infrastructure, when treated as a strategic asset rather than a cost center, gives you optionality, whether that's launching AI copilots, joining blockchain ecosystems, or scaling into new markets.

Infrastructure is no longer background. It's the lever that can accelerate or anchor your strategy. Build it with intent, wire it to your goals, and never let "we're regulated" become "we can't evolve." Because in every industry, speed plus compliance isn't just possible, it's the new competitive advantage.

CHAPTER 5

Digital Business Models — Value Creation

Think Like a Business Model Architect

I couldn't come up with a better opener for our business models chapter than Nvidia CEO Jensen Huang, who stated, "AI will create more millionaires in 5 years than the internet did in 20 years". Furthermore, he said that AI serves as the "greatest equalizer," equipping everyone with technical skills and enabling small teams to develop complex products, resulting in an unprecedented wave of wealth creation.

He also emphasized that those who don't use AI risk being replaced by those who do, and that future companies will have two "factories", one physical and one digital AI factory. These factories won't just be tech; they will also encompass the business models that depend on them. What once centered on the product as the primary unit of value is now expanding into a broader arena where the entire customer journey becomes the value exchange. Every interaction, from pre-purchase discovery to point-of-sale, post-purchase enablement, and community engagement, is an opportunity to create, capture, and compound value.

This requires more than bolt-on digital fixes. It demands a reimagined strategy that fuses resilience with reinvention, and an optimized infrastructure that enables businesses to operate with speed, flexibility, and responsiveness. In this world, value is not limited to products sold or services delivered; it flows across relationships with customers, their stakeholders, and even competitors through ecosystems, partnerships, and shared platforms.

The businesses that thrive are those that treat strategy as dynamic, infrastructure as adaptive, and the customer journey as monetizable beyond the transaction. In this model, disruption isn't just a threat; it's the catalyst for reinvention.

MASTERY LEARNING OBJECTIVES

- Examine how digital technologies enable fundamentally new business models and evaluate key archetypes, including platform-based approaches, their application contexts, and the strategic trade-offs they entail.
- Develop frameworks for creating, delivering, and capturing value in digital contexts, leveraging network effects, personalization, and data-driven capabilities to optimize outcomes.
- Formulate and execute practical approaches to evolve or transform business models, achieving sustainable advantages in the digital economy.

INDUSTRY INSIGHT

Peloton — The Power of the Platform

How a connected bike became a recurring revenue engine and redefined the fitness industry.

In competitive cycling, brands like Trek and Specialized shave grams off frames to chase marginal gains. Peloton took a different path, transforming the bike from a finely tuned machine into a fully connected platform blending media, community, and commerce.

Context / Challenge

For over a century, the bicycle saw incremental innovation but little disruption. The fitness equipment market was crowded, seasonal, and largely transactional in nature. Peloton faced the challenge of creating something that would engage customers daily, drive recurring revenue, and foster deep brand loyalty in a space where most products gathered dust after purchase.

The Velocity Shift

Peloton fused hardware, software, media content, and financing into a subscription-based ecosystem. Live and on-demand classes, leaderboard competitions, and community features gamified workouts, turning customers into competitive participants in an ongoing experience. By 2024, subscriptions accounted for ~63% of revenue, compared to 37% from hardware, thereby flipping the traditional fitness model. Financing options expanded the addressable market, while the platform's social hooks encouraged daily engagement and retention.

Results / Impact

- Rapid growth to over 500,000 paying subscribers by 2019 and ~$4B in revenue at its 2021 peak.
- Subscription revenue is overtaking on-premises hardware as the primary driver of profitability.
- A return to profitability in Q2 2025 under a wellness-focused strategy, with improving margins and a renewed growth plan.
- Peloton proved that in fitness, the actual asset isn't the machine, it's the network effect of engaged, paying members.

STRATEGIC TAKEAWAYS

- **Engineer for Recurrence, Not One-Offs** – Recurring revenue is the ultimate stability driver.
- **Gamify to Retain** – Competition, community, and content keep customers coming back.
- **Integrate the Stack** – Hardware plus software plus media equals a platform with defensible margins

REFLECTION

- Is your business model optimized for the digital era or anchored in pre-digital assumptions?
- How have digital technologies changed the fundamental economics of your industry?
- What opportunities exist using digital capabilities to transform your value proposition, delivery mechanisms, or revenue models?

Why the Old Business Models are Cooked

A digital business model isn't a web-skin on yesterday's engine; it's a wholesale refit that trades carburetors for AI-turbochargers. Four traits separate genuine transformers from tech-washed pretenders:

1. **Strategic Intent with Teeth** – Every move starts with a clear "why": disrupt, defend, or expand. Leaders wire that intent from the C-suite to the call center, so priorities survive budget meetings and board swaps.
2. **Non-Trivial Transformation** – Swapping paper for PDFs is housekeeping, not reinvention. True players re-code the value prop (subscriptions, usage pricing, network effects of community) and rebuild the customer journey from the silicon up.
3. **Dynamic Evolution** – The model breathes. Real-time data flows into feedback loops that sense shifts and auto-tune the enterprise while rivals are still loading last night's batch report.
4. **Full-Spectrum Digitization** – Data, products, interactions, and decisions all go digital. Sensors feed warehouses; AI augments judgment; physical goods morph into services. Anything less is a paint job.

Layer those traits onto the four macro shifts that rewired value creation:

Old World	Digital World	Why It Wins
Owning assets (factories, fleets)	Orchestrating platforms (Airbnb, Uber)	Low capital, hyper-scaling, defensible ecosystems
Linear pipelines (supplier→customer)	Networked ecosystems (Shopify, YouTube)	Co-creation, multiple revenue nodes, connection tolls
Ownership economics (buy once)	Access economics (Netflix subs, AWS pay-as-you-go)	Recurring revenue, wider funnels, predictable cash
Mass markets (one size fits most)	Mass personalization (Spotify mixes, Amazon feeds)	Higher relevance, conversion, and lifetime value

Put it together:

Intent + transformation + evolution + full-stack digital + the four structural shifts = a business model that compounds faster than incumbents can draft a response memo.

Punchline:

If your model still smells like 2005, asset-heavy, one-way, sell-and-forget, average-for-all, you're not just behind, you're buffering while the game streams past. Hit *refresh* or prepare for obsolescence.

The Agentic Marketplace: Business Models Beyond the Product

The next era of business models isn't about selling more products; it's about designing living economies where value flows across nodes, tokens, and trust loops. Products themselves are becoming table stakes; the real competitive advantage lies in the ecosystem that surrounds them.

Take wine as an example. In the old model, you bought a bottle. In the new model, as a wine enthusiast, you might take a stake in the next harvest through a tokenized asset. That token guarantees provenance, from the certified grape clone to the soil, weather, harvest, and vinification, all the way through shipment to your cellar. It also provides liquidity on the resale market and transparency that builds trust across every transaction. This isn't just a new way of selling wine, it's a new way of structuring value itself: shared ownership, blockchain-backed trust, and AI-enabled orchestration.

This is the fundamental shift: the center of value is no longer the product. The model, the ecosystem of flows, provenance, and networks, becomes the differentiator.

Amazon doesn't sell goods; it orchestrates trust and speed at scale.

Duolingo doesn't sell language apps; it gamifies persistence and a sense of belonging.

Shein doesn't just sell clothes; it monetizes supply chain agility as real-time intelligence.

And increasingly, the new marketplace logic is generative: AI, blockchain, and human trust loops create self-propelling economies that span digital, physical, and social surfaces simultaneously.

Five Shifts in the Business Model Lens

1. From Fixed DNA to Generative Engines

Old View: Products and services designed, shipped, and sold.

New View: Marketplaces that co-create, tokenize, and evolve with their communities.

Implication: Revenue emerges through flows, tokens, credits, and smart contracts, not just transactions.

2. From Channels to Surfaces

Old View: Linear funnels of distribution (websites, stores, ad channels).

New View: Every surface, from TikTok and Discord to Roblox and on-chain wallets, as well as IRL events, becomes a transaction and provenance point.

Implication: The boundary between marketing, sales, and service becomes increasingly blurred.

3. From Pipelines to Orchestration

Old View: Firms push value through linear supply-demand chains.

New View: Humans, AI, and blockchain function as nodes in a mesh. AI allocates, blockchain arbitrates, and humans validate.

Implication: Strategy shifts from efficiency to trust, coordination, and adaptability.

4. From Execution to Curation

Old View: Employees and managers "run the system."

New View: Teams curate experiences, design incentive loops, and orchestrate interactions between humans and machines.

Implication: Skills in design, systems thinking, and token economies become increasingly valuable.

5. From Enablement to Generative Economies

Old View: Digital layers added on top of physical products.

New View: Entire business models built as living economies that thrive on disruption.

Implication: Success depends not on how well the product sells, but on how the model compounds over time.

Business Model Maturity

The Business Model Maturity model integrates the agentic marketplace, blockchain provenance, and co-ownership concepts, while providing a clear and actionable progression.

From Left to Right = Evolution Path → from bolt-on digital presence to self-sustaining ecosystems.

Each Column = Strategic Position → with its strengths, traps, and transition challenges.

Top-Right (Control Tower) = where agentic marketplaces, blockchain provenance, and tokenized co-ownership converge to create living business models.

The progression is not inevitable; many firms stall in the middle, mistaking subscriptions or marketplaces for the finish line. But the frontier belongs to those who design **generative economies**[42] where customers, partners, and even competitors participate in value creation. These businesses don't just adapt to disruption; they thrive on it because every transaction strengthens the ecosystem itself.

Dimension	Supplier / Freemium (Commodity Corner)	Subscription / Owned CX (The Lockbox)	Marketplace with Gaps (The Crossroads)	Ecosystem / Generative Economy (The Control Tower)
Value Proposition	Sell products or basic digital access. Minimal differentiation.	Own customer experience, deliver personalization, and predictable value.	Connect buyers and sellers, but with limited orchestration or trust layers.	Orchestrate co-created experiences, tokenized assets, and ecosystem-wide flows.
Revenue Model	One-off transactions, low-margin freemium upsells.	Recurring revenue, subscriptions, tiered pricing.	Multi-sided fees or commissions, but fragile liquidity.	Token flows, asset appreciation, smart contracts, brand credits convertible to fiat/crypto.
Channels / Surfaces	Basic e-commerce, app store listing, or physical retail.	Owned apps, websites, loyalty programs, and curated digital CX.	The platform interface connects multiple sides, but is siloed.	Distributed surfaces: social platforms, on-chain wallets, DApps, IRL activations. Every interaction is a provenance checkpoint.
Customer Role	Passive buyer, price-driven, low switching costs.	An engaged subscriber, loyal but confined to brand walls.	Marketplace participant, but with limited influence.	Active co-creator, validator, investor, and marketplace node with tokenized ownership.
Trust Mechanism	Brand reputation, customer service.	First-party data, personalization, direct relationships.	Platform rules, ratings/ reviews, escrow-style protections.	Blockchain provenance, community governance, and AI-mediated trust scores.
Workforce Model	Employees execute, digital bolt-ons managed separately.	Employees + data-driven teams deliver owned experiences.	Marketplace ops teams manage supply-demand balance.	Hybrid orchestration: humans curate meaning, AI optimizes flows, blockchain secures provenance. Skills in UX, systems, and tokenomics.
Scale & Defensibility	Linear growth, commoditized competition, and low barriers.	Defensible within a niche or category, stronger retention via data.	Scalable but vulnerable until liquidity + trust are achieved.	Exponential network effects, self-reinforcing ecosystems, compounding advantage from shared participation.

GLOBAL SIGNAL

Born at the Frontier

The Business Model Maturity Matrix charts how incumbents progress from siloed digital plays to ecosystem orchestration. Emerging market startups, however, are often born at the far end of this spectrum, ecosystem-native from inception.

Signals

- Kaspi.kz (Kazakhstan): Bundled payments, commerce, and lifestyle into a national super-app serving 75% of the population. Kaspi wasn't a bank becoming digital; it was a platform economy from day one.
- Monobank (Ukraine): Captured 35% mobile banking market share in five years by making delight the competitive moat. Monobank demonstrates how skipping legacy integration enables instant UX-driven maturity.
- Sun Finance (Pan-Regional): Expanded across Europe, Asia, and Latin America with mobile-first lending and alternative credit scoring. Their borderless model reflects maturity at inception, not an endpoint.

Takeaway

In business models, the greatest competitive risk comes not from incumbents climbing maturity, but from startups already standing at the top. What looks like a 10-year transformation journey for you may be someone else's starting point.

Strategic Capabilities and Value Creation

This matrix helps you identify your organization's current business model and explore potential evolution paths based on your strategic digital capabilities and value creation approach. Although my research for the matrix is still in progress, I am sharing it here to provide a framework not only for evaluating your firm but also for conducting a competitive analysis. It draws on established concepts in digital business strategy, capability frameworks, and value creation models.

The principles and quadrants outlined align with common strategic considerations and evolutionary paths discussed in the context of digital business model transformation.

The Commodity Corner in the lower-left quadrant, Supplier / Freemium models operate with limited digital capabilities and a simple value proposition. These businesses, whether traditional retailers with basic e-commerce sites or software companies offering a minimal freemium tier, focus on transactions rather than building deep relationships. With minimal differentiation, limited customer data, and low switching costs, they are easily commoditized.

The Lockbox in the upper-left quadrant, Subscription / Owned Customer Experience players have built stronger digital capabilities but apply them within a relatively simple model. Think of brands like Netflix, Spotify, or Adobe Creative Cloud, which own the customer relationship end-to-end, leverage personalization, and generate predictable, recurring revenue. Rich first-party data deepens engagement and boosts retention, making the model defensible even without complex multi-sided dynamics.

The Crossroads in the lower-right quadrant, Marketplace with Gaps models, aspire to platform status but lack the full capabilities to sustain it. Early-stage marketplaces or niche platforms fit here, connecting multiple sides of a market but offering limited value-added services. Growth is often constrained by the "chicken-and-egg" problem, struggling to attract both supply and demand, and defensibility remains weak until capabilities mature.

The Control Tower, situated in the upper-right quadrant, houses the leaders of the Ecosystem/Data Platform, including companies such as Apple, Amazon, and Salesforce. These are high-capability, advanced-model operators that orchestrate complete digital ecosystems. They thrive on network effects, encourage complementary innovation from partners, and harness data advantages at scale. Their models are self-reinforcing, building high switching costs and fueling continuous innovation that keeps competitors on the defensive.

While the quadrants describe distinct strategic positions, they can also be read as an evolutionary path, from basic digital presence to advanced, self-reinforcing ecosystems. Each step up in capability and complexity opens new revenue models, strengthens customer relationships, and improves defensibility, but it also demands new infrastructure, talent, and cultural agility.

Common Sticking Points:

Just as technology adoption has its "chasm," business model evolution has its trapdoors:

- Freemium-to-Subscription Stall — Companies fail to deepen capabilities, relying on upselling rather than investing in personalization, data infrastructure, and owned channels.
- Subscription-to-Marketplace Leap — Many underestimate the operational complexity of multi-sided networks, hitting a growth wall when supply or demand fails to scale in sync.
- Marketplace-to-Ecosystem Gap — The hardest jump, requiring not just scale but trust, interoperability, and incentives for partners to co-create value rather than defect to competitors.
- Capability Complacency — Even leaders can stagnate if they treat their quadrant position as permanent; ecosystems decay without continuous reinvestment and adaptation.

CASE STUDY

Web3 Gaming — Play-to-Earn as a Business Model Reset

How blockchain rewired the economics of gaming from publishers to players.

In 2021, Axie Infinity went viral in the Philippines. By 2025, the Web3 gaming sector had matured into a multi-billion dollar test bed for new digital business models, with venture capital, publishers, and guilds converging on one radical premise: the players are also the owners.

The Bottleneck

Traditional video games operated on a closed economy. Players spent billions on skins, characters, and assets that lived only inside publisher-controlled ecosystems. Value stopped at the game's edge. Publishers captured all monetization, while players carried sunk costs.

The Overclock

- Tokenized Economies: Web3 games introduced cryptocurrencies and NFTs that let players own, trade, and monetize in-game assets.
- Guild Models: Player collectives like Yield Guild Games pooled resources, recruited new players, and shared earnings, turning gaming into employment in emerging markets.
- Interoperability: Assets became portable across games and marketplaces, creating open economies instead of walled gardens.
- Resurgence 2023–2025: After the initial crash, the strongest projects focused on sustainable tokenomics, hybrid free-to-play + earn mechanics, and mainstream partnerships (e.g., Square Enix, Ubisoft exploring blockchain integrations).

Results

- Axie Infinity distributed over $1B in rewards to players at its peak.
- By 2025, Web3 gaming attracted $4B+ in venture funding with new models focusing on retention, fun-first design, and regulated asset trading.
- Player ownership created grassroots evangelism, blurring the line between community and company.

What It Means

Web3 gaming illustrates the next frontier of business models: platforms where customers are also shareholders, producers, and marketers. While sustainability challenges remain, the resurgence proves that digital business models of the future may not just monetize engagement, they may share it.

The Evolution of Business Models in the Digital Era

Peloton's rise, and its challenges, show what happens when a familiar product is plugged into a different kind of business engine. For over 200 years, bicycles have barely changed in their basic form. Then Peloton didn't just improve the bike; it redefined what it was. The hardware became the on-ramp, the subscription became the fuel, and the community became the accelerator. That progression is exactly what the Business Model Evolution framework captures:

Supplier/Freemium stage – Companies rely on one-off sales or a basic digital presence, such as selling a bike in a store.

Subscription / Owned C – Firms add richer capabilities, recurring revenue, and deeper relationships. Peloton's core leap occurred when it tied a product to ongoing classes and content.

Marketplace with Gaps – Businesses open up participation to others, including riders, instructors, and apparel partners.

Ecosystem/Generative Economy – Where AI, blockchain, and network effects combine to create a self-reinforcing system; every new user, partner, or signal increases the model's value.

Think of it like a neighborhood coffee shop that has evolved into a global franchise. Initially, you sell coffee by the cup (Supplier). Then you add a loyalty program and subscription beans (Subscription). Next, you create a local marketplace for pastries, live music, and art shows (Marketplace). Eventually, you transform the shop into a global community platform, where cafés worldwide share recipes, customer data, provenance records, and tokenized ownership of the brand itself (Ecosystem).

This is where the Agentic Ecosystem emerges. AI agents[43] don't just help customers transact; they orchestrate matching, pricing, and personalization. Blockchain doesn't just store provenance; it guarantees transparency, enables tokenized co-ownership, and provides liquidity for participants. Customers don't just consume, they validate, invest, and co-create.

Peloton may still be climbing, but its journey reveals a bigger truth: the higher a company moves in this maturity model, the more defensible, adaptable, and customer-powered it becomes. The lesson for any business, whether you're selling bikes, coffee, or software, is to look past the product and design for the flows, nodes, and trust loops that surround it. In the next era, competitive advantage won't come from the thing you sell, but from the ecosystem you build and the economy you sustain.

SECTION II

The Engines

Fuel the system with insights, customer connection, and content power.

Engines don't run on good intentions; they run on fuel. In the digital era, that fuel is data, customer insight, and content designed to cut through infinite noise. Here you'll learn how to ignite growth across B2C and B2B, transforming every interaction into torque that accelerates your brand.

CHAPTER 6

Digital Insights — Weaponizing Data

Think Like a Data Strategist

The fastest-growing companies don't have more data; they have less dark data.

In today's AI arms race, it's not more data that separates the leaders from the laggards; it's how much of your data is illuminating your decisions. That's because somewhere between 60% and 73% of enterprise data goes dark, stored in logs and lakes, but never analyzed or acted on, resulting in data that remains untapped[44]. That idle data quietly becomes the most significant efficiency drain and lost opportunity in modern business, not to mention a potential security liability.

This chapter is about reversing that. We'll introduce the **Insight Value Chain**, a six-step process that converts raw, multi-source data into real-time, decision-ready intelligence. You'll learn how to audit your organization's data-to-decision flow, identify where insights stall, and craft interventions, across technology, culture, and structure, that turn your dark data into strategic fuel. In the 3.0 era, shadow data isn't a byproduct: it's an edge waiting to be claimed.

MASTERY LEARNING OBJECTIVES

- Construct end-to-end frameworks that convert enterprise-wide data into actionable insights using the insight value chain.
- Design cross-functional activation systems that connect insights to measurable business outcomes across marketing, product, and operations.

- Evaluate and improve your data ecosystem by assessing how well qualitative and quantitative inputs are integrated, accessible, and aligned across teams.
- Apply insight-generation models to real-world challenges in your organization, ensuring insight velocity, signal clarity, and strategic relevance.

INDUSTRY INSIGHT

Stitch Fix, Data as the Fabric of the Business

Stitch Fix Teaches Us About Data as a Moat

Most brands treat customer data as a byproduct of their sales efforts. Stitch Fix flipped that script, making data the primary product, and clothes simply the delivery mechanism.

Context / Challenge

Digitally native vertical brands (DNVBs) control their entire value chain, from product creation to direct customer sales, allowing them to capture every interaction without intermediaries. This end-to-end visibility generates a depth of customer insight that legacy brands, which are often reliant on distributors and third-party retailers, rarely achieve. The challenge: could personalization at scale become not just a feature but the entire business model?

The Velocity Shift

Stitch Fix embedded personalization into its DNA by collecting detailed data on every kept item, returned product, style note, and delivery change. Over 100 data scientists collaborated with human stylists, while algorithms made initial recommendations, optimized inventory, and forecasted demand. Stylists then refined selections with human judgment. This machine-human collaboration meant the company didn't guess at what customers wanted; it knew, and it knew before the customer did.

Results / Impact

- Achieved rapid scaling, leveraging one of the richest behavioral datasets in retail.
- Evolved from "a clothing retailer" to "a data company that sells clothes," strengthening defensibility.
- Competitors could copy surface-level offerings, but not the depth and predictive power of its data ecosystem.

STRATEGIC TAKEAWAYS

- **Own the Stack, Own the Data** — Controlling the whole value chain builds a high-resolution customer picture.
- **Integrate, Don't Bolt On** — Embedding data into the business model creates sustainable differentiation.
- **Pair Machine + Human** — Hybrid intelligence delivers both scale and personal touch.

REFLECTION

No matter where you are on your data maturity curve, early-stage scrapper or analytics powerhouse, ask yourself:

- Are you just collecting data, or turning it into *decisions*?
- Are your insights coming from every corner of the org or just the loudest teams?
- Is your data driving business model innovation, or stuck in dashboards nobody reads?

The hard truth: insight isn't deliverable. It's a capability. And it separates the leaders from the obsolete.

The Organizational Insight Ecosystem

When I took the helm of digital at Redbox, analytics had already grown into a mature team with skills, models, and infrastructure. Judy Ransford (now CEO at Hickory Farms) and Steve Olson (now VP, Data Science at Razorfish) had already wired a monster data rig, 30 million app downloads, tens of millions of identified buyers, and email/SMS lists any retailer would ransom. We referred to it as an *embarrassment of riches*, but riches turn to rust if they sit in silos. My job was to orchestrate the insights throughout the enterprise and continue to evolve every click, kiosk rental, support ticket, and supply-chain ping into one Insight Value Chain that could predict, not just report.

We started with capture, creating data hooks into every workflow so nothing escaped. Then came integration: reconciling five "John Smiths" into one and allowing finance to see the same truth that marketing did. With a unified view, our data scientists conducted multidimensional analyses that linked late-night horror rentals to next-day game rentals and identified regional spikes before inventory ran out.

Those patterns were translated into narratives the C-suite, board and investors cared about: "Add zombie title inventory in the Midwest this Friday or lose 200 bps in market share." Cross-functional squads turned those insights into action plans, operations were executed, and marketing tracked lift in real-time, allocating extra budget to the winners. Finally, every outcome, good or bad, looped back as fuel for the next sprint, tightening the chain.

The payoff? We moved from reacting to potential out-of-stocks to shaping Friday-night demand like clockwork. Support calls became product tweaks; kiosk stockouts became triggers for dynamic supply; marketing impressions evolved into market signals. We refused to become another Craigslist, sitting on gold while upstart platforms were platforming their best niches, because our insight engine kept spinning faster with every loop.

Seven links, minimal friction: Capture → Integrate → Analyze → Synthesize → Plan → Execute → Measure (see below). Break one and the system stutters; reinforce all and the organization hums at a higher clock speed than the competition can match.

That's the **Insight Value Chain**, noise in, strategic velocity out. Strengthen each link, shorten the distance from signal to action, and keep overclocking before someone else loots your data vault.

Dashboards show the score; full-spectrum insight explains the play that set it up and the turf conditions that made it possible. At Redbox, we learned that raw behavior, human motivation, and situational context must mesh like gears in an overclocked rig; otherwise, your "data-driven" strategy will throttle down at the first spike.

Start with behavioral intelligence, *the what*. Clickstreams, rental logs, support-ticket clusters, and service KPIs revealed exactly where customers hesitated, churned, or binge-watched zombie flicks. At scale, those patterns power reliable forecasts, but on their own, they're just a rear-view mirror.

Layer in attitudinal insight, *the why*. Customer interviews, sales-floor anecdotes, and the emotional subtext in social threads exposed the real drivers: parents grabbing a Friday-night film to keep kids quiet, gamers chasing new releases, or bargain hunters reacting to price nudges. Empathy transformed numeric blips into causal levers that we could pull with messaging, UX tweaks, or promotional timing.

Finally, weave in contextual intelligence, *the how and when*. Field visits revealed kiosks coated in Midwestern slush that froze card readers, while journey maps showed Wi-Fi dead zones that hindered app conversions on commuter trains. Economic signals and regional quirks flagged rollout hazards before they blew up the scale plan.

When those three streams converge, you unlock an insight multiplier. Behavioral data identifies the spike, attitudinal insight deciphers the motive, and contextual intelligence tests the tactic against real-world friction. Then, you fire the feedback into the roadmap before competitors even notice the signal. That's how full-spectrum insight stops being a buzzword and becomes strategic velocity.

GLOBAL SIGNAL

Insight-Driven by Default

Where mature firms ascend from descriptive reporting to predictive analytics, emerging market startups often begin at predictive, because actionable insights are survival tools, not luxuries. They embed data in every decision from Day 1.

Signals

- Tala (Mexico & Kenya): Automatically processes 10,000+

smartphone data points per credit applicant to make underwriting decisions in seconds. Their predictive models drive acquisition, pricing, and risk—no legacy credit systems involved.

- Mercado Pago (LatAm): Mining transaction and behavioral data from the broader Mercado Libre ecosystem, it builds credit scoring and lending models that incumbents cannot replicate.
- Chari (Morocco): Uses merchant transacting data to build credit profiles and financing offers, closing the feedback loop between usage and underwriting.

Takeaway

In emerging markets, data is not an afterthought, it's the oxygen. When you can't rely on existing credit systems or deep historical records, you build insights from usage. The winners will be those with data architectures built-in from Day 0, not those trying to retrofit analytics later.

From Raw Data to Enterprise Reflexes

The true power of digital insight isn't in collecting more data; it's in transforming that data into reflexive decision-making at every level of the enterprise. The Insight Value Chain illustrates how raw inputs are transformed into measurable business impact. But maturity matters: the same chain that drives innovation in one organization may barely function in another.

This matrix reframes the journey by mapping the seven stages of insight value against four levels of digital maturity. It shows not only how far you've come, but what the next step looks like, whether that's moving from gut-driven decisions to data-informed planning, or from siloed dashboards to self-optimizing, AI-augmented execution.

Insight Value Point	Reactive Ad hoc, siloed	Enabled Basic tools & standards	Integrated Enterprise-wide coherence	Optimized Continuous, AI-driven
Capture	Manual collection, inconsistent sources	Standardized data feeds	Real-time APIs & IoT capture	Edge processing & automated quality checks
Integrate	Department-level merges	Centralized warehouse	Hybrid data architecture, 360° entity views	Entirely governed, privacy-by-design integration
Analyze	Descriptive only	Basic predictive models	Prescriptive analytics embedded in workflows	Self-learning, AI-augmented analytics
Synthesize	Insights in isolation	Cross-team sharing	Multi-source fusion & collaborative tools	Dynamic, cross-domain intelligence
Plan	Gut-driven	Data-informed, periodic	Continuous planning linked to real-time insights	Predictive scenario planning & simulation
Execute	Manual process changes	Automated in pockets	AI-guided execution across functions	Self-optimizing, human-AI orchestration
Measure	Occasional KPI tracking	Regular performance dashboards	Linked to strategic goals	Real-time impact loops feeding the entire value chain

Integration and Maturity

In digitally mature organizations, the Insight Value Chain functions as an interconnected system, rather than a linear process, with continuous feedback loops between its stages. Success requires cultural transformation, embedding data-driven decision-making throughout the organization, a sophisticated technology infrastructure that supports real-time processing and AI capabilities, and an organizational design that breaks down silos through shared platforms, cross-functional teams, and collaborative processes. The result is a dynamic capability that continuously learns and improves its ability to generate competitive advantage through superior insight generation and application.

Enterprise Insights in Action:

How top performers win with data is that they know insight isn't a single spark; it's a current that races through every circuit of the enterprise, lighting up choices before rivals even see the flash. Here's how top performers convert raw data into edge, sector by sector, and why their playbooks matter no matter what you sell.

Retail & consumer brands win when they see the aisle *and* the algorithm in one frame. Target fused store-scanner data, Drive-Up patterns, and loyalty IDs into a "guest archetype" engine that identifies and eliminates out-of-stocks and optimizes local assortments. When every basket throws a signal, markdowns become exceptions, not habits.

Financial services leaders read life events faster than customers post them. USAA integrates deposits, claims, and geolocation pings into a detection model that identifies deployments, new babies, or PCS moves, and then pushes just-in-time offers. This is one reason its Net Promoter Score is nearly twice as high as that of direct-bank runners-up in Forrester's benchmarks. Risk models and relationship models now share the same data bus.

Healthcare systems translate bedside whispers into population-level change. The Cleveland Clinic integrated patient feedback text with clinical outcomes and revamped physician communication protocols. State-of-the-art reporting shows that experience and readmission metrics meet or exceed traditional benchmarks after the rollout. Empathy at scale is a data problem first.

B2B SaaS players weaponize telemetry long before churn tickets surface. Gainsight links feature-use drop-offs to health scores, enabling customer-success reps to intervene while the account is still expanding and turning "surprise churn" into upsell headroom. In the same arena, Slack's freemium pipeline converts roughly 30% of users to paid tiers, triple the SaaS norm, by mining in-app behavior and nudging teams inside the product.

Education proves insight saves lives *and* semesters. Georgia State University's predictive analytics cockpit monitors over 800 behavioral markers per student. Real-time nudges have increased graduation rates by 35% over the past fifteen years, while also narrowing racial equity gaps. When advising becomes data-driven, retention is no longer a retrospective KPI.

Travel & hospitality treat personalization as the new passport stamp. Marriott Bonvoy analyzes mobile check-in clicks, on-property spend, and preference toggles across 237 million members. Loyalty guests now book half of all occupied room nights and out-spend non-members, driving a disproportionate share of fee revenue for Marriott.

Across every case, the pattern repeats: behavioral *what* flags the opportunity, attitudinal *why* explains the motive, and contextual *how* tests the tactic against real-world friction. Feed those streams into a single insight bus, with no heat silos, a cloud infrastructure, and you get a strategy that runs at cycles while competitors throttle on legacy constraints. Fail to connect them, and you become the next Craigslist, watching niche after niche platformed by someone else.

The lesson is universal: fuse signals to decisions fast or work around your data while the market moves on.

Bridging the Insight-Action Gap

This section addresses the critical challenge of ensuring insights drive organizational decisions and actions across functions.

Data alone won't win the race; it's merely the high-octane fuel. Your advantage comes from how fast that fuel ignites, races through the enterprise, and turns into motion. Yet most organizations bolt shiny dashboards onto legacy habits and wonder why the business still crawls.

Before we delve into the playbooks for building "insight muscle," we need to identify the four hidden friction points — bias, silos, sluggish decision-making loops, and cultural drag. that dilute intelligence on its way to execution. Break those bottlenecks and your insight engine finally fires at full throttle; ignore them and you're just watching gauges while competitors lap you.

First comes cognitive bias, the silent governor that keeps RPMs low. At its best, intuition is a powerful form of pattern recognition, something human brains are wired to do. But when not managed well, pattern recognition and trusting one's gut may lead to bias and incomplete or overly simplistic thinking, both of which are detrimental to making sound decisions. The fix is procedural, not technical: pre-commit to act on the metrics before you know whether they flatter your pet project, strip labels from analyses so turf wars can't hijack conclusions, and make top brass model "data humility" in every meeting.

Next is the silo wall, where insight stops at the border of Marketing, Sales, or Ops. When signals can't flow, local teams optimize while the enterprise underperforms. Cross-functional insight squads, shared cloud workspaces, and a weekly "intel drop" via Slack or Teams transform private hunches into shared map coordinates.

Barrier three is decision velocity. MIT CISR's 2024 study of "real-time businesses" showed top-quartile firms, those that empower employees to act on live data, generate more than 50 percent higher revenue growth and net margins than the laggards[45]. Front-line guardrails, pre-approved playbooks, and insight-ops teams convert discovery into sprints while the competition is still scheduling the steering-committee review.

Finally, there's cultural drag: the "we've always done it this way" reflex. Executives who override metrics with HiPPO (highest-paid person's opinion) logic teach the org that evidence is optional. Flip the script, celebrate every insight-led win, make learning velocity a KPI, and tie bonuses to proof, not folklore.

Do that, and the culture starts treating new data like energy drinks.

In the introduction, we saw how digitally native vertical brands, such as Stitch Fix, flipped the script, turning data from a byproduct into the fabric of their business. That same principle lives at the heart of the **Insight Value Chain**: Capture → Integrate → Analyze → Synthesize → Plan → Execute → Measure. In the best organizations, this isn't a linear sequence you march through once a quarter; it's a continuous feedback loop woven into the enterprise's operational DNA.

The sequence is universal, but the tempo and tuning change by industry. In retail, speed-to-insight can mean adjusting inventory mid-season. With healthcare, latency matters less than precision and regulatory compliance. For finance, integration is the uphill battle, and in manufacturing, synthesis is the missing link between machine telemetry and market demand. The choreography shifts, but the dance is the same: data only creates value when every stage flows into the next without stalls or silos.

Building that activation muscle is pure gym science:

- **Protocols** – clear playbooks tied to specific signals, so no one hesitates when the data pings.
- **Democratized Access** – self-serve portals, org-wide data bootcamps, and permissions that treat insight as a shared resource, not a privilege.
- **Implementation Support** – insight coaches embedded with delivery teams to ensure follow-through.
- **Cultural Wiring** – rituals and rewards that value decisive action over "interesting analysis."

Train those four muscle groups, and your enterprise starts to behave like an over-clocked CPU, heat managed, cores synchronized, cycles spent on computation instead of waiting for permission.

Winning with data isn't about hoarding terabytes; it's about wiring a system that converts faint signals into decisive moves before your rivals even know there's a signal to hear. That means:

1. Treating information as strategic currency, with a cross-functional data council setting one taxonomy, one master record, and one integration architecture so marketing, ops, and finance finally speak the same dialect.
2. Making insight a team sport, with analysts rotating across business lines, data scientists paired with strategists, and "translators" who turn regressions into roadmaps.
3. Recoding planning cycles so every big bet starts with an insight review, OKRs anchor to live data, and scenario plans refresh when the market shifts, not when the calendar says so.
4. Closing the loop with measurement, using shared KPI frameworks, multi-

touch attribution, and real-time dashboards that link today's lift to next year's growth.

Then comes belief, the intangible yet critical final step. Executives model evidence-first decisions, celebrate fast pivots born from fresh insight, and embed activation over discovery into performance reviews. Wins become stories, stories become habits, and habits compound into a competitive advantage that's hard to catch.

Break one link and you're back to dashboards gathering dust. Lock them all, and you're running an overclocked insight engine, fast, precise, and relentless. Overclocked organizations don't just know more. They do more with what they know, faster, sharper, and together.

CASE STUDY

Spotify — Insights as the Operating System

How real-time data turned a streaming service into a cultural barometer.

Spotify isn't just a music app, it's an insights engine. Its architecture ingests billions of streams, skips, searches, and playlists every day, translating them into signals that drive personalization, marketing, and even the global music industry itself.

The Bottleneck

Before streaming, music consumption data was lagging and fragmented. Labels relied on sales charts updated weekly, radio spins logged manually, and focus groups that couldn't capture behavior at scale. Artists lacked visibility into who their fans were and how they engaged. Decisions moved slowly.

The Overclock

- Real-Time Architecture: Every stream, skip, and share becomes an input into a unified insights fabric. This powers "Discover Weekly," "Wrapped," and personalized playlists that feel custom-built for each user.
- Adaptive Feedback Loops: Insights flow back to creators, labels, and advertisers, turning data into strategy within days instead of quarters.

- Velocity + Adaptability: Spotify tests, launches, and refines features rapidly (e.g., social listening, podcast integrations) based on usage signals. Marketing pivots dynamically by geography, genre, or trend.
- External Impact: Spotify insights now shape the Billboard charts, influence touring schedules, and even forecast cultural shifts before they're mainstream.

Results

- Over 600M monthly active users in 2024.
- Personalized playlists drive the majority of listening hours.
- Spotify Wrapped campaigns became a global earned media phenomenon, with millions sharing individualized insights each December.

What It Means

Spotify proves that insights aren't a reporting function, they're a strategic core. With velocity and adaptability hardwired into its architecture, Spotify turned data into culture, and culture into growth.

CHAPTER 7

The Digital Consumer — Empowered & Always On

Think Like a Digital Anthropologist

The Digital Consumer: From ZMOT to Agentic Empowerment

In 2011, Google coined the term Zero Moment of Truth (ZMOT)[46] to describe the instant a consumer begins researching a purchase, often long before they encounter your marketing. Back then, ZMOT typically meant a Google search, a brand's website, or perhaps a glance at Amazon reviews.

Fast forward to today: the starting line has shifted again. For millions of consumers, especially Millennials and Gen Z, ZMOT now occurs in social feeds, AI chats, and marketplace search bars, rather than on your homepage. TikTok has become the new Google for product discovery. Reddit threads surpass brand brochures in trust. Even in high-consideration categories like financial services or healthcare, the journey begins with peer-driven validation, not a brand-crafted pitch.

The data confirms the shift: Deloitte's 2025 *Digital Media Trends* survey shows Gen Z spends 54% more time on social platforms and user-generated video than the average consumer, nearly an extra 50 minutes per day, while watching 26% less traditional TV and film. McKinsey's "attention equation" research finds that a 10% lift in consumer focus can trigger a 17% jump in spending. The algorithmic battlefield where that focus is won or lost is now the real front line of commerce.

But the future won't stop here. The next ZMOT won't belong to search engines or social feeds. It may belong to autonomous, agentic bots acting on behalf of consumers. Imagine AI-driven agents researching, negotiating, and transacting based on the parameters you set, while your identity remains cloaked by blockchain protocols. Ownership itself may evolve into a hybrid state: sometimes personal, sometimes pooled, tokenized into co-ownership models. A wine enthusiast may not only buy a bottle but also own a fractional stake in the next harvest, with provenance traced from the grape clone to the soil, weather, and vinification, all recorded transparently on-chain.

This represents a significant step in consumer empowerment. The consumer is already more informed, connected, and influential than ever before in history. Still, in the world of AI and blockchain, they may become anonymous investors, cloaked participants, and co-owners of the ecosystem. They will be harder to reach, yet more powerful in shaping the very rules of engagement.

This shift has massive implications for both the MBA student preparing to lead and the C-Suite executive steering a global brand. It's no longer enough to have a polished strategy (Chapter 2) or an insight-rich data engine (Chapter 6). You need a customer-centric operating system, one capable of detecting, interpreting, and acting on signals not just in feeds and searches, but in autonomous networks where consumers transact through their proxies.

In this chapter, we'll decode the digital consumer's decision loop, from ZMOT to post-purchase advocacy in an agentive economy. You'll learn how always-on data streams have rewritten the funnel, why mobile and social are the new front doors to commerce, and how to design journeys that feel native to nano-screens and, increasingly, invisible AI intermediaries while being powered by enterprise-class insight engines.

Buckle up. The consumer is closer, more cloaked, and more empowered than ever. Your job is to cut through, connect, and create value in ways that resonate with both the human behind the screen and the autonomous agent acting in their place.

MASTERY LEARNING OBJECTIVES

- Decode the digital decision journey by analyzing how technology, platforms, and connected behaviors have reshaped how consumers discover, evaluate, and buy.
- Apply behavioral science and psychology to design experiences that align with attention patterns, heuristics, and cognitive biases in digital environments.
- Evaluate the influence of social dynamics, from reviews and influencers to groupthink and algorithmic amplification, on

consumer behavior and trust formation.

- Design consumer research strategies that blend qualitative and quantitative approaches to surface real-time, signal-rich insights from empowered, always-on audiences.

INDUSTRY INSIGHT

McDonald's — Turning Loyalty into a Global Data Engine

How the Golden Arches Built a Golden Data Pipeline in a Franchise-First Model.

Forget flipping burgers, McDonald's is flipping the script on customer intelligence, using its loyalty app to turn every order into enterprise-grade insight.

Context / Challenge

With 93% of its 41,000+ global locations franchised, McDonald's has historically maintained a one-step removal from direct customer relationships. The challenge: how to unify customer data, influence demand, and optimize operations without owning most of the retail footprint.

The Velocity Shift

The launch and rapid expansion of MyMcDonald's Rewards changed the game. With 185 million active users in 90 days (aiming for 250 million by 2027), the app reestablished a direct data connection between the company and customers. Loyalty members visit 26 times a year, compared to 10.5 visits for non-members, providing a steady stream of first-party data, purchase habits, basket makeup, and promotional responses, which are fed directly into corporate systems. This is powered by edge computing with Google Cloud, enabling near-real-time innovations like AI-driven drive-thrus, geofenced "Ready on Arrival" orders, and instant maintenance alerts that can reduce wait times by more than half.

Results / Impact

- Strategic control in a franchise-heavy model through unified data visibility.
- Higher visit frequency among loyalty members is driving incremental revenue.
- Operational intelligence for staffing, menu optimization, and demand forecasting.
- Platform for future AI and personalization initiatives on a global scale.

STRATEGIC TAKEAWAYS

- **Loyalty = Leverage** — In franchise systems, digital engagement can re-centralize influence and intelligence.
- **Edge + Cloud = Real-Time Ops** — Processing data in-restaurant unlocks speed and responsiveness.
- **First-Party Data as a Moat** — A massive, unified customer dataset enables personalization, supplier negotiations, and predictive analytics that competitors can't easily match.

REFLECTION

- How has your purchase journey changed over the past five years?
- What role do social media, reviews, and digital content play in your buying decisions?
- How have your expectations for convenience, speed, and personalization shifted?

Regardless of your role, whether leading a marketing team, developing a digital strategy, or building customer experiences, understanding how technology has fundamentally reshaped consumer psychology and behavior is crucial for creating meaningful digital connections.

From Linear to Looped — The Reinvention of the Consumer Journey

The classic consumer journey, which involves research, comparison, and a single purchase, has traditionally been viewed as a checklist: simple, sequential, and relatively predictable. However, digital didn't just add steps; it completely transformed the entire model. What was once linear is now fluid, dynamic, and constantly looping. Consumers no longer move step-by-step. They jump stages, repeat behaviors, switch channels midstream, and often engage with a brand before they're even aware they have a need. It's always on, constantly evolving, and it's no longer just a marketing problem.

Every department, from product and IT to finance, operations, and customer service, must adapt to a looped journey that never truly ends.

Need recognition has evolved into personalized *trigger moments* no longer sparked solely by ads or in-store displays, but often algorithmically generated by voice assistants, social feeds, or even connected devices like smart fridges. For marketing, this means orchestrating hyper-targeted micro-moments. Product and IT mean that they're embedding offerings into broader digital ecosystems, which is now essential. Even finance must rethink CAC and ROI in the context of 24/7 trigger potential.

Information search used to be limited to catalogs or a neighbor's advice. Today, it's an endless stream of TikToks, Google results, Reddit threads, and influencer breakdowns, accessible instantly and continuously. Marketing must meet this moment with content that's discoverable, shareable, and trustworthy. Sales must move beyond repetitive pitching to deliver genuine consultative value. Customer service must intercept pain points before they become negative reviews, while product teams must ensure that every claim withstands public scrutiny in real-time.

Evaluation of alternatives once meant narrowing down a few options, maybe even using a spreadsheet. Now, consumers conduct real-time, side-by-side showdowns using smart filters, AR try-ons, "also viewed" lists, and AI-powered recommendations.

Success stems from design clarity, transparent pricing, and a standout user experience. Product and IT teams must deliver fast, differentiable experiences, while marketing needs to surface competitive value instantly.

Purchase decisions have shifted from one-channel checkouts to multi-touch journeys, involving research online, in-store trials, app-based ordering, Klarna payments, and tracking through chatbots. This complexity spans across operations, which must function seamlessly across all touchpoints; finance, which now manages subscriptions, partial payments, and digital wallets; and IT, which oversees system integrations, payment rails, and fraud prevention.

Customer service, meanwhile, must have visibility into the entire journey to resolve issues holistically.

Post-purchase experiences are no longer quiet and contained. Feedback is public, permanent, and can shape perception faster than a brand campaign. Software updates, usage nudges, loyalty incentives, and community forums extend the experience long after the sale.

Marketing must activate advocates. Product teams must consider the entire life cycle. IT supports these moments through app-based engagement and live support, while customer service operates on a stage where every win or failure can go viral.

Ultimately, the shift from linear to looped means your strategy, systems, and teams must evolve. Strategy can no longer rely on discrete phases; it must support continuous feedback and adaptive response. Marketing attribution becomes increasingly complex, requiring tools that track across multiple touchpoints. Sales teams transition from closers to coaches. And operations must align with the reality that the customer journey is not just extended, it's rewired. Navigating it isn't impossible, but it does require precision tuning across the enterprise.

Leadership Insight

Digital leaders can't afford to manage departments in silos while consumers move like free radicals across platforms and phases. Winning means syncing your data, people, platforms, and processes to match this nonlinear reality. The future belongs to the orchestrators, not the order-takers.

How Digital Rewired the Consumer Mind

Digital didn't just change where consumers shop. It rewired how they think, decide, and define value. From single-channel transactions to continuous engagement loops, here's how yesterday's rules collapsed, and what that means for your business playbook.

Before the digital era, customers followed a single path: catalog, store, phone, one channel at a time. Now, they're everywhere, all at once. Omnichannel isn't a strategy; it's the default setting. A massive 73% of consumers use multiple channels during their journey, and 90% bounce between devices. If checkout isn't frictionless, they're gone. 87% of customers abandon their carts when the checkout process is too slow[47].

The strategic hit: your data needs to be connected, your identity systems unified, and your touchpoints seamless. Governance must move beyond isolated channel managers to true journey orchestration teams. And attribution models? They need to evolve because coherence across touchpoints consistently outperforms channel KPIs.

Built for the Loop — Architecting Behavior-Led Business Models

Digital consumers don't just expect more; they operate differently. They subscribe instead of buy, trust peers over ads, demand hyper-personalized experiences, and abandon brands that create friction. Winning organizations don't simply react to these shifts; they hardwire them into the very architecture of their business models. As we enter the next era, leaders must prepare for an even more profound transformation, one where AI agents transact on behalf of consumers, blockchain ensures provenance, and ownership itself becomes tokenized or obscured.

Here are four critical behavioral pivots, and the structural evolutions they demand today, with a view toward what comes next.

1. From One-Time Buyers → Subscribers → Tokenized Co-Owners

Consumers prioritize access over ownership, from entertainment to essentials. Subscriptions are the norm. But the next leap is tokenized participation: customers won't just subscribe, they'll hold fractional stakes in products, services, or harvests through blockchain-backed assets.

Today's shift

Build subscription engines with churn-prevention, predictive analytics, and engagement pipelines.

Tomorrow's shift

Design tokenized models where customers invest in the future of what they consume (wine harvests, limited runs, community-owned assets), creating loyalty through co-ownership and resale liquidity.

2. From Trust in Ads → Advocacy → Blockchain-Verified Provenance

People trust people more than brands. Peer validation has replaced polished campaigns. The next layer will be trustless trust, verification encoded on-chain, where authenticity, origin, and fairness are indisputable.

Today's shift

Empower community-driven platforms, UGC systems, and creator economies.

Tomorrow's shift

Use blockchain provenance and community governance to let customers validate the story of what they buy, from grape clone to soil conditions, or from sustainable sourcing to ethical labor.

3. From Friction → Fluidity → Invisible Orchestration by Agents

Convenience is no longer a perk; it's the price of entry. The next frontier is agentic fluidity: AI agents will handle price matching, fulfillment, and renewals seamlessly in the background, often without direct brand touchpoints.

Today's shift

Deploy APIs, orchestration layers, and automation for unified customer journeys.

Tomorrow's shift

Build systems that are agent-friendly, where your value surfaces not through checkout pages but through being the preferred node in autonomous agent ecosystems.

4. From Generic → Hyper-Personal → Cloaked Identity & Preference Sovereignty

Consumers demand personalization, and they will share data if the value is clear. The next level is cloaked identity: consumers will toggle what data they reveal, when, and to whom, sometimes monetizing access to their preferences, sometimes remaining invisible.

Today's shift

Build privacy-first, AI-driven personalization with adaptive UX.

Tomorrow's shift

Create sovereign data models where customers control, cloak, or trade their identity layers, and personalization flows through consent-based, tokenized interactions.

Takeaway

The business model loop is evolving from selling products to selling relationships, and ultimately, designing ecosystems where customers act as co-owners, validators, and nodes in a larger agentic economy. The winners will be those who prepare now: embedding AI, blockchain, and community mechanics into their core infrastructure so that when consumers (or their agents) step into this new reality, your brand is already a trusted node in the network.

Strategic Insight

These behavioral shifts are not UX tweaks; they're business model disruptors. Each one forces a cross-functional reckoning:

- IT can't just build features; it must power fluid identity and session continuity
- Ops must deliver consistency across nonlinear paths
- Finance must account for complexity: returns, subscriptions, re-attribution
- Marketing must move from control to coordination
- Product must stop thinking in SKUs and start thinking in systems and flows

CASE STUDY

Sephora – Designing a Seamless Digital Consumer Journey

How a beauty retailer became a benchmark for omnichannel experience.

Sephora turned a fragmented beauty shopping journey into a seamless, personalized ecosystem where the app, store, and loyalty program all reinforce one another. It shows how an investment in digital UX can build not just convenience, but loyalty at scale.

The Bottleneck

Traditional retail separated online and offline. Consumers couldn't test products digitally, inventory visibility was patchy, and loyalty programs were generic. Beauty purchases—highly personal by nature, were treated transactionally, leaving gaps in experience and retention.

The Overclock

- Personalized UX: The Sephora app uses AR (Virtual Artist) to let consumers "try on" makeup virtually, backed by AI recommendations from skin tone, history, and trends.
- Integrated Ecosystem: Loyalty (Beauty Insider) links every touchpoint: app, website, and in-store. Customers can scan in-store products for reviews and tutorials, or buy online and pick up curbside.
- Data-Driven Personalization: Insights from digital interactions shape targeted promotions, tailored samples, and product launches.
- Community Layer: User-generated reviews and Sephora's Beauty Community provide trusted social proof at scale.

Results

- Sephora's app is consistently rated among the top retail apps globally.
- Digital channels drive over 40% of revenue, with loyalty penetration above 80%.
- Personalization engines fuel higher conversion and repeat rates than retail peers.

What It Means

Sephora proves that the digital consumer doesn't distinguish between online and offline, they expect one unified experience. Excellence in digital UX is no longer a differentiator; it's the price of admission for consumer loyalty.

Digital Consumer Archetypes

While each consumer is unique, consistent behavioral patterns emerge in digital environments. Understanding these archetypes enables organizations to design experiences that align with the distinct behaviors of different consumer groups.

Digital consumer archetypes, also known as customer archetypes, represent distinct groups of consumers with unique characteristics and behaviors within the digital landscape. These archetypes are influenced by a variety of factors, resulting in their variation across different industries and product or service types.

Below is a baseline of archetypes that can be tweaked and adapted for your business and industry.

The Signal Seeker

Alex won't add anything to the cart until the numbers align with a launch checklist. On Tuesday night, she has six tabs open: Wirecutter, Reddit, and three spec-comparison tools, because 81% of shoppers now research products online before making a purchase[48]. She screenshots a data sheet, drops it into a group chat for a second opinion, and only clicks "Buy" once every claim is cross-verified.

Strategic responses →

- Publish complete specs and third-party test data.
- Offer side-by-side comparison tools and downloadable PDFs.
- Train support to handle "why is this number different?" interrogations.

The Vibe Validator

Maya scrolls before she searches. If the product isn't in an influencer's reel, it doesn't exist. Nearly half of consumers make at least one purchase a month simply because a creator recommended it. investors.sproutsocial.com, and Maya is that statistic in motion, posting an unboxing TikTok before the tape is off the box, DM-ing screenshots to friends for instant approval.

Strategic responses →

- Hand the narrative to creators; supply assets, not scripts.
- Embed friction-free share buttons in the purchase flow.
- Nurture brand tribes with behind-the-scenes content and community drops.

The Friction Slayer

Jordan's thumb hovers over the back button the moment a page stutters. Google reports that 53 % of visits are abandoned if mobile load times exceed three seconds, and Jordan embodies that impatience: they voice-search the product, autofill payment, and expect a "Your order has shipped" ping before closing the app.

Strategic responses →

- Strip checkout to the absolute minimum; auto-reorder where possible.

- Monitor site speed like revenue depends on it, because it does.
- Lead messaging with "fast," "simplest," and "set-it-and-forget-it."

The Algorithm Assassin

Priya treats retail like day-trading. She sets Honey alerts, tracks price graphs, and knows your promo calendar better than your CMO. Sixty-five percent of consumers now visit comparison sites to hunt deals, but Priya stacks coupons and loyalty points for the dopamine rush of a perfectly timed pounce.

Strategic responses →

- Make discounts real, no fake strikethroughs.
- Use dynamic bundles and limited-time drops to channel the chase.
- Stress-test your servers for flash-sale stampedes.

The Meaning Maker

Luis buys the story first and the product second. He watches the brand's purpose video, checks its sustainability reports, and only then clicks 'add to cart.' Seven in ten U.S. adults say they favor brands that mirror their values. Marketing Charts, Luis makes the conviction visible with every tag and testimonial.

Strategic responses →

- Put mission and proof upfront, sourcing, impact metrics, and founder voice.
- Create forums where customers co-create content and cause campaigns.
- Treat post-purchase follow-ups as relationship moments, not receipts.

Why the stories matter

Each archetype is a living signal cluster. Map your data to these narratives, and you'll know which levers, proof, community, speed, price, or purpose will move which customer. Then, wire those levers into targeted product, UX, and marketing plays.

These five personas aren't static, nor are they the endpoint; they flow across devices, days, and decisions. But if your team doesn't calibrate each mode of behavior based on the response loop from your customers, you're playing analog in a digital arena.

Digital Behavior Rewires Every Sector in Its Way

Consumers may shop, bank, study, travel, or receive healthcare in different contexts, but their digital behaviors are consistent across industries. Mobile-first discovery, peer validation, instant fulfillment, and seamless loops of engagement are the baseline. What differs is how each sector builds infrastructure around those behaviors and how fast they can adapt when expectations reset.

Retail & Consumer Products

Shopping has migrated from aisles to thumbs. Nearly 60% of all e-commerce sales already flow through phones, making mobile the front door of commerce, not a side channel. Shoppers now hop across three or more touchpoints per trip, and 73% expect those hops to feel seamless. Discovery is visual and social. Pinterest Lens fields over 250M image searches per month, and patience is thin: one in four consumers will abandon a retailer that can't deliver within 3½ days. Target's Drive-Up service shows the model: phone-first ordering, curbside pickup in minutes, and inventory promises it can keep.

Financial Services

The mahogany desk has shrunk to a five-inch screen. More than half of Americans say a mobile app is their primary banking channel. Trust polarizes by generation: only 16% of Gen Z place "a lot of trust" in legacy banks, while 41% view digital-only players as more transparent. Relationship-building must flex from branch to bot. Bank of America's AI assistant *Erica* embodies this shift, blending fraud alerts, budgeting tips, and account management into a daily, AI-powered coach.

Healthcare & Wellness

Care now begins with Dr. Google: 80% of adults research symptoms online before consulting a clinic, and 94% read reviews before selecting a provider. Telehealth has stabilized at 38% of its pre-pandemic volume, while wearables stream continuous vitals into patient portals. Cleveland Clinic demonstrates what's possible: education, scheduling, test results, and virtual visits unified in a single app so the "first opinion" and "second opinion" coexist on the same screen.

Travel & Hospitality

Inspiration begins with a swipe: three-quarters of leisure travelers say Instagram, TikTok, or Pinterest sparked their last trip idea. Eighty-one percent read reviews before booking, and 40% complete transactions on mobile. Millennials then broadcast the journey, sharing 97% of moments online, turning every vacation into unpaid media. Marriott Bonvoy closes the loop with an app that spans booking, room selection, keyless entry, and loyalty offers, while encouraging guests to feed their content back into the brand's discovery engine.

Education

Prospective students now begin their search on social media and video platforms long before visiting a college's homepage. Once enrolled, 70% say mobile tools make coursework easier to access. Degrees are unbundling: 82% of institutions plan to offer micro-credentials within five years. Learners toggle between LMS portals, YouTube tutorials, and AI copilots to stack skills into résumés. Arizona State University meets them across multiple surfaces, offering courses on YouTube and Coursera, tagging each module to career outcomes, and treating education more like Netflix for careers than a rigid semester model.

GLOBAL SIGNAL

Consumers Born Mobile-First

In western, digitally established markets, there are patterns to behavior based on digital tenure within industries that are reflected in the archetypes. But, in many emerging markets, consumers leap directly to the high end, skipping desktop, skipping cards, and embracing mobile-first finance and commerce from day one while a the same time, may still be getting acclimated to what many of the western 'digital' basics.

Signals

- bKash (Bangladesh): With 80M+ users, bKash became national infrastructure by embedding mobile transfers so deeply that "bKash me" entered daily language. This isn't just adoption; it's cultural codification of digital behavior.

- PalmPay (Nigeria): With 35M users and 1.2M agents, PalmPay bridged cash-to-digital through hybrid networks, processing 15M transactions daily. It demonstrates how embedding finance in hardware distribution creates mass-scale inclusion.
- Momo (Vietnam): A $2B+ fintech unicorn serving 31M users, Momo built a lifestyle super-app by prioritizing trust and tier-2/3 city expansion. This illustrates how inclusive growth beats elite-only adoption.

Takeaway

In emerging markets, consumers don't evolve through digital maturity stages—they build new behaviors in a single leap. Tomorrow's consumer strategies must prepare for cultural shifts that embed digital as habit, not novelty.

Empowered & Always-On

If the last decade taught us anything, it's that the first click or swipe is rarely on your homepage. The Zero Moment of Truth has moved upstream into TikTok feeds, Amazon searches, AI chat windows, and private group chats. By the time customers land in your owned channel, they've already built a story about you, stitched from creators they follow, peers they trust, and algorithms you don't control.

McDonald's illustrates how to regain visibility. With 93% of its 41,000+ restaurants run by franchisees, the brand long had a fragmented view of its customers. But with *MyMcDonald's Rewards*, 185 million active members reconnect the dots[49]. Real-time data now powers not only promotions but also staffing patterns, menu design, supply chain timing, and even AI-driven drive-thru flows.

The Lesson Across Industries

The specifics differ: retail runs on omnichannel orchestration, finance on AI assistants, healthcare on integrated patient portals, travel on socially fueled discovery, and education on unbundled, mobile-first learning. But the common thread is clear: the brands that win are those that embed behavioral insight directly into their operating system. They design for the loop, not the funnel, recognizing that discovery, evaluation, purchase, and advocacy are non-linear, always-on, and often agent-mediated.

Because in the 3.0 era, your next growth curve doesn't start when the customer finds you; the digital consumer has moved from search-driven ZMOT to an always-on, socially validated, algorithmically filtered, and increasingly agentic marketplace. Discovery happens on TikTok and Reddit before a homepage visit ever occurs, and tomorrow it may happen through autonomous AI proxies negotiating on a consumer's behalf.

For leaders, this means that strategy can't stop at crafting messages or optimizing funnels. It requires building a customer-centric operating system that detects signals across platforms, responds in real-time, and creates value whether the engagement comes from a person or an AI agent.

The McDonald's case shows how even a franchise-first giant can turn loyalty into intelligence — transforming millions of everyday orders into an engine of data, personalization, and recurring connection.

The framework is clear

Attention as the front line — compete in feeds, chats, and nano-screens.

Empowerment as the baseline — consumers (and their proxies) hold the power.

Data as the advantage — loyalty and interaction streams become the raw material for personalization and reinvention.

The digital consumer is both closer than ever and harder to reach than ever. Winning requires cutting through noise, connecting authentically, and designing systems that can thrive in a future where the *human behind the screen* and the *agent acting for them* both shape the rules of the game.

CHAPTER 8

Platforming B2B

Think Like a B2B Digital Strategist

B2B Platform Evolution: From Handshakes to Hyperloops

B2B commerce has evolved significantly from its origins in analog commerce. Once, business development lived on golf courses, in boardrooms, and across trade show booths. Relationships were brokered face-to-face, awareness was built through conferences and catalogs, and transactions were facilitated through slow-moving paperwork.

The first digital detour came in the 1960s with Electronic Data Interchange (EDI)[50]. It was clunky but revolutionary: a two-lane road where machines could exchange purchase orders and invoices without human hands. For decades, EDI formed the backbone of B2B trade.

Fast forward six decades, and that two-lane road has become a hyperloop of platforms, ecosystems, and autonomous marketplaces. AI doesn't just record orders; it predicts them, suggesting quantities, timing, and even dynamic prices based on demand signals. Blockchain doesn't just keep receipts; it creates transparent, immutable supply chains, offering X-ray vision from raw material to delivery dock. Automated auction systems match buyers and suppliers in real time, while specialized vertical platforms pool demand and capacity with unprecedented efficiency.

These arenas haven't just changed how transactions happen; they've redrawn Business Model Canvas itself. In a platform world, your key partners may also be your key customers. And someone else's digital infrastructure might control your channels. Your revenue streams could come from fees, data monetization, embedded financial services, or even tokenized assets.

The B2B value chain isn't linear anymore; it's a network of nodes, each capable of creating, capturing, or redistributing value.

And while B2C often gets attention for digital disruption, B2B has been quietly running some of the most advanced playbooks. From blockchain-ledgers deployed in Fortune 100 supply chains to AI-driven sourcing, pricing, and risk assessment, B2B is undergoing a structural rewiring, turning products into services, transactions into integrations, and suppliers into co-innovators.

In this chapter, we'll decode that rewiring. You'll learn how to map buyer and supplier flywheels, diagnose ecosystem health, and know when to pivot from selling a product to embedding yourself in your customer's business model. In the next generation B2B era, the winners won't just be driving on the digital road; they'll be the ones laying new tracks for everyone else.

MASTERY LEARNING OBJECTIVES

- Analyze what sets B2B digital transformation apart from B2C, longer cycles, layered decision-makers, and legacy systems, and how digital platforms flip the buyer-seller dynamic from transaction to integration.
- Apply ecosystem thinking to modern B2B value chains by analyzing scalable, multi-stakeholder experiences that merge digital self-service with human trust and turn products into embedded services.
- Develop strategies for navigating hybrid B2B models, where digital and traditional must coexist, by aligning platforms, partnerships, and performance metrics to deliver value at every stage of the enterprise customer journey.

INDUSTRY INSIGHT

Honeywell Forge — From Product Supplier to Industry Operating System

How Honeywell transformed a traditional hardware business into an operating system for industrial performance, and why the data layer is the next competitive moat.

In the 1960s, Electronic Data Interchange (EDI) was the telegraph of B2B, slow by today's standards but revolutionary, replacing faxes and paper POs with structured digital documents. For decades, that one-to-one digital handshake was the gold standard.

Challenge

Fast-forward to today, and B2B supply chains are no longer point-to-point conversations; they're multiplayer ecosystems. Dozens of suppliers, integrators, service providers, regulators, and even competitors must operate off the same live data, not siloed spreadsheets. The challenge is to build a platform that unifies this complexity without forcing everyone onto the same hardware.

The Velocity Shift

Honeywell didn't just digitize workflows; they created Honeywell Forge, a shared industrial performance management platform that ingests data from *any* manufacturer's equipment. Whether you're running Caterpillar trucks, Siemens turbines, or Honeywell safety systems, Forge lets you manage all assets from a single dashboard. The true advantage: cross-vendor insights. Forge can benchmark performance across brands, turning competitors into data contributors and customers into ecosystem members.

Results / Impact

By controlling the data layer, Honeywell positioned itself as the de facto operating system for industrial performance. This shift enabled recurring revenue through subscriptions, analytics-as-a-service, and third-party apps, expanding value far beyond one-time hardware sales.

STRATEGIC TAKEAWAYS

- **Control the Data Layer** — When you own the unified view, you set the KPIs and decision frameworks.
- **Turn Competitors into Data Contributors** — Normalizing rivals' data creates unmatched industry benchmarks.
- **Monetize the Ecosystem** — Layer recurring services and apps on top of your core product sales.

REFLECTION

- How has digital changed how your buyers research, evaluate, and negotiate?
- Which parts of your B2B process still live in the pre-cloud era?
- Has the power dynamic shifted toward buyers, and are you equipped to respond in real time?

Whether you're building the next-gen B2B platform or modernizing legacy operations, the message is clear: Adapt faster than your buyers change or get left behind.

Digital isn't the end of B2B relationships. It's their acceleration layer.

B2B vs. B2C: Strategic Contrasts in Digital Evolution

While both B2B and B2C organizations are undergoing profound digital reinvention, their pathways diverge due to fundamentally different stakeholder dynamics, relationship structures, and buying behaviors.

B2B environments involve multiple decision-makers operating within committee-driven approval processes, navigating diverse technical, operational, and financial priorities. In contrast, B2C journeys revolve around personal preferences, emotions, and immediacy drives decision-making.

Relationship depth also varies: B2B relationships are long-term and account-focused, demanding continuous support, service integration, and deep operational alignment, while B2C models favor episodic, transaction-based engagement at scale.

This leads to different sales cycles, with consultative and extended sales processes in B2B versus compressed and self-service sales in B2C. As a result, B2B digital experiences prioritize workflow integration, efficiency, and ROI justification, while B2C experiences center on convenience, speed, and emotional resonance.

Risk tolerance shapes strategy: B2B buyers face high stakes, organizational impact, reputation, and budget justification, whereas B2C consumers tend to experiment more freely, with lower switching costs and fewer long-term consequences. Trust-building in B2B relies on technical validation, case studies, and expertise, whereas social proof, peer reviews, and brand perception carry more weight in B2C.

From a platform and infrastructure perspective, B2B solutions require configurability, system integration, and collaboration tools, reflecting complex needs and cross-functional usage. At the same time, B2C platforms succeed through intuitive design, mobile-first UX, and built-in social engagement. Even in data strategy, B2B focuses on account-level analytics, usage optimization, and predictive service, while B2C leans into segmentation, personalization, and conversion optimization.

For digital strategists, this comparison highlights the importance of designing journeys, content, tools, and KPIs tailored to the behavioral context of each audience. B2B success stems from aligning with complexity, integration, and delivering business value. B2C wins by providing speed, delight, and frictionless engagement. Different paths, but both demand precision.

Platform Theory in B2B[51]: From Transactions to Integration Engines

B2B platforms aren't just marketplaces; they're infrastructure for shared value creation. In the platform economy, B2B models operate less like one-way pipelines and more like multi-sided networks, where every node is a participant in value exchange.

In contrast to consumer platforms, where scale and speed dominate, B2B platforms prioritize depth, specialization, and interoperability. These systems connect complex players, manufacturers, distributors, service providers, and enterprise buyers across a matrix of transactions, integrations, and long-term collaborations.

Network Effects, Rewired for B2B

While B2C platforms ride on user volume, B2B platforms thrive on quality and alignment. Network effects and platform flywheels are related concepts, but they are distinct from each other. Network effects describe how a product or service becomes more valuable as more users join it. A platform flywheel is a model that illustrates how a platform's various components (like users, features, and data) interact to create a self-sustaining cycle of growth and value creation.

While network effects are a core component of many flywheels, they are not the only factor driving a flywheel's momentum.

In the case of network effects, a new vendor doesn't just add volume; they enhance the collective value through capabilities, certifications, integrations, or data. Network effects in B2B are layered:

- Direct effects (more suppliers, more choice)
- Indirect effects (more integrations, better automation)
- Cumulative effects (standardization, trust, and data network value)

Governance at Scale

Successful B2B platforms enforce clarity and trust through protocols, APIs, SLAs, and compliance frameworks, while allowing modularity and customization for diverse partners. Governance isn't just control; it's what keeps ecosystems open, scalable, and secure.

Co-Creation, Not Just Coordination

According to Caporuscio et al,[52] B2B platforms function as "value sharing" mechanisms where participants co-create value through collaborative processes rather than simple transactions. In B2B, platforms power shared workflows and joint innovation. From procurement orchestration to predictive maintenance integrations, platform participants don't just transact; they plug in, sync up, and build together.

This is a platform strategy as infrastructure: scalable, extensible, and ecosystem ready.

Network Externalities: B2B platforms exhibit strong network effects, where the value to each participant increases as more organizations join the platform. However, these effects are often more complex than on B2C platforms, with the quality of participants sometimes mattering more than the quantity.

Ecosystem Governance: The governance of B2B platforms involves striking a balance between control and openness to support both stability and innovation. Successful B2B platforms establish clear rules, standards, and protocols while allowing customization and integration.

Understanding these theoretical foundations provides the basis for analyzing how digital capabilities and platform dynamics transform B2B environments.

The Evolving B2B Buyer: Self-Directed, Digitally Native, Ecosystem-Aware

Just as consumer journeys became fragmented and nonlinear, so too has the B2B path to purchase. The modern B2B buyer expects on-demand access, peer validation, and digital transparency, but within a framework that respects procurement cycles, compliance, and ROI.

Today's enterprise buyer:

- Research before reaching out (often completing 70%+ of the journey independently)
- Demands integration over just access, APIs, data feeds, and compatibility come first
- Seeks value beyond price, including service layers, ecosystem benefits, and innovation potential
- Pushes for alignment, not just product fit, across ESG, security, scalability, and partnership approach

What this means for your platform or enterprise business model:

- You're no longer selling a product, you're building connective infrastructure
- You're not winning deals, you're earning systemic trust
- You're not serving customers, you're enabling partners to win with you

From Pitch to Platform: How B2B Buying Has Been Reinvented

Today's B2B buyer journey is no longer a linear path controlled by sales reps; it's a self-driven, multi-threaded marathon.

According to Gartner, buyers now spend only 17% of their time engaging directly with suppliers. The remaining 83% is split across researching online (27%), validating with peers (22%), aligning internally (18%), and documenting needs (16%).[53]

In this environment, vendors face competition not only from one another but also from consensus-building, content noise, and information overload. Buyers typically begin their journey with Google, Reddit, and LinkedIn, rather than trade shows or cold calls. They expect data-backed proof, not polished promises. Speed, transparency, and self-service have replaced slow deals and gated PDFs. Sales teams must evolve from pitchers to consultants, from inbox chasers to workflow-integrated problem solvers. Success now hinges on building platforms that enable buyers to configure, quote, and test-drive your product before they even make a phone call.

The consumerization of B2B expectations fuels this shift. Every seamless Amazon checkout or Netflix recommendation raises the bar for what buyers expect in the workplace. Those expectations now include intuitive interfaces, transparent pricing, intelligent recommendations, and instant access to demos, documentation, and proof points.

These aren't nice-to-haves; they're carryovers from B2C behavior that define how B2B solutions are evaluated. Companies that bridge the gap between B2B rigidity and B2C fluidity will outpace their competitors, not by mimicking consumer brands, but by meeting decision-makers where they already live, digitally and emotionally.

Layer onto this the growing complexity of the buying committee. The average B2B deal now involves 6 to 10 stakeholders, ranging from procurement and IT to end users, security, and engineering. Each comes with unique criteria, ROI, compliance, UX, integration, and scalability, and they all want answers fast. The modern journey isn't a funnel; it's a maze of micro-decisions, each with its digital trigger point. Sellers who can equip stakeholders with the right message, in the correct format, at the right moment, earn faster trust and make the shortlist more often.

This evolution shows B2B shifting from smarter selling to becoming a platform. As discussed in Chapter 5, modern platforms encompass various types, including transaction, collaboration, knowledge, and integration, such as Grainger KeepStock, Siemens Teamcenter, Salesforce AppExchange, and Coupa.

The common thread? High-fit, high-impact tools that embed directly into the buyer's daily reality. These platforms don't win by doing everything; they win by solving meaningful friction and aligning with ecosystem incentives.

B2B is no longer slow, analog, or led by reps. Expectations are high, and speed is essential. Buyers are well informed. Platforms aren't optional; they're your next competitive advantage. If you're not rethinking your buyer journey through a B2C-inspired, digitally driven, multi-stakeholder, platform-first perspective, you're already falling behind the curve.

The Four B2B Platform Archetypes

Not all platforms are built the same. In the high-stakes world of B2B transformation, your platform strategy shapes everything, from monetization and integration to partner dynamics and innovation velocity. The choice isn't just about going digital; it's about aligning your platform DNA with your industry's rhythm, organizational ambitions, and value creation model.

Broadly, there are four dominant B2B platform types, each optimized for different types of complexity, collaboration, and control.

1. **Marketplace Platforms** (e.g., Amazon Business, Alibaba.com) are built to aggregate supply and demand. They reduce search costs, standardize transactions, and enhance transparency through features such as pricing visibility, ratings, and digital payments. Revenue typically comes from transaction fees, supplier subscriptions, and data products. These platforms work well for SMBs, indirect procurement, or broad-category suppliers where trust, volume, and visibility matter more than customization.

2. **Procurement Platforms** (e.g., SAP Ariba, Coupa) focus on automating enterprise purchasing workflows. Their strength lies in seamless integration with ERP systems, contract and approval automation, and spend analytics. These platforms are typically used by finance, procurement, and enterprise operations teams, generating revenue through SaaS subscriptions, onboarding services, and premium capabilities. Integration requirements are high, but so is operational ROI.

3. **Industry-Specific Exchanges** (e.g., Procore, RealPage, Xometry) serve highly specialized verticals where compliance, regulation, or complex product configurations are the norm. These platforms combine market expertise with tailored functionality and often charge transaction fees or membership fees, in addition to premium services. They thrive in industries where depth outweighs breadth, such as construction,

manufacturing, or real estate, where workflows are nuanced and stakes are high.

4. **Ecosystem Platforms** (e.g., Siemens MindSphere, Salesforce AppExchange) are designed for co-creation and innovation across organizations. They support data sharing, joint development, and cross-enterprise governance. With very high integration and purchase decision complexity, these platforms often serve as the digital backbone for ecosystems. Revenue comes from enterprise subscriptions, transformation services, and analytics products. The goal here isn't transactions alone, it's sustainable value creation, IP management, and long-term orchestration.

Choosing your platform type isn't about picking what's trending; it's about defining what you need to win. Fit beats flash. Depth beats scale. Integration beats interface. The right platform becomes more than a tool; it becomes your competitive architecture.

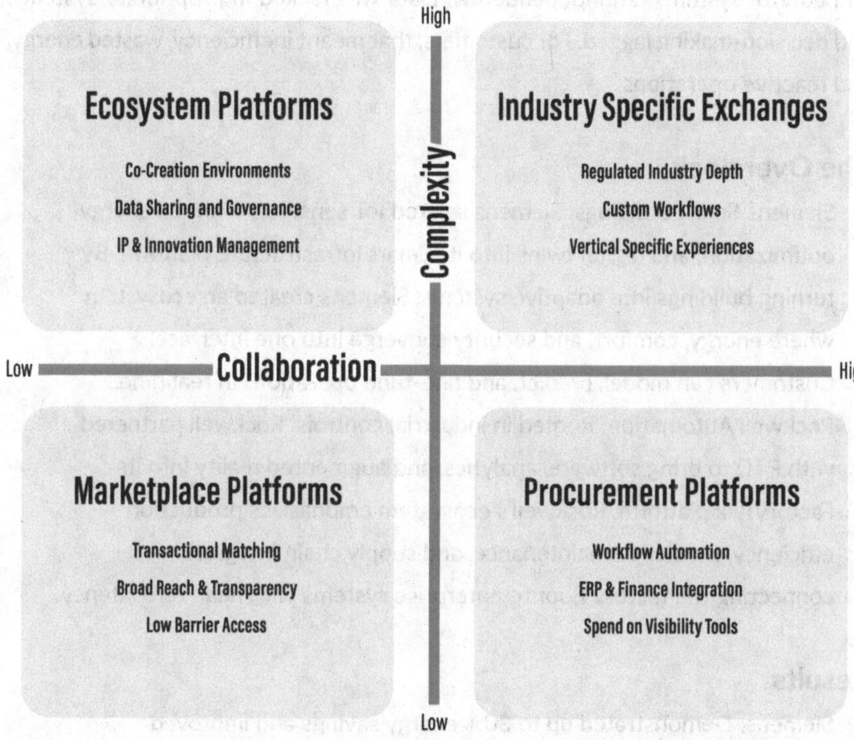

The Next Gen Tip: Choose platform architecture based on your industry friction, stakeholder density, and digital ambition, not by the tech stack.

CASE STUDY

Siemens vs. Rockwell — Competing Blueprints for the Connected Enterprise

How two industrial giants are overclocking B2B ecosystems through different plays.

In the age of Industry 4.0, buildings and factories are no longer static assets—they are data-rich, adaptive systems. Siemens and Rockwell Automation offer two lenses on the future of B2B platforms: one focused on smart infrastructure, the other on industrial automation.

The Bottleneck

Traditional industrial ecosystems were siloed: HVAC, lighting, security, robotics, and control systems ran independently. Data was locked in proprietary systems, and decision-making lagged. For customers, that meant inefficiency, wasted energy, and reactive operations.

The Overclock

- Siemens Smart Buildings: Siemens layered IoT sensors, AI-driven energy optimization, and digital twins into its Smart Infrastructure platform. By turning buildings into adaptive systems, Siemens created an ecosystem where energy, comfort, and security converge into one interface. Customers can model, predict, and fine-tune operations in real time.
- Rockwell Automation: Rooted in industrial controls, Rockwell partnered with PTC to bring software, analytics, and augmented reality into its FactoryTalk platform. Rockwell's ecosystem emphasizes production efficiency, predictive maintenance, and supply chain integration—connecting the factory floor to enterprise systems with near-zero latency.

Results

- Siemens: Demonstrated up to 30% energy savings and improved occupant comfort across global commercial real estate portfolios.
- Rockwell: Increased uptime and throughput for manufacturers, while

lowering total cost of ownership through predictive maintenance and integrated supply chain visibility.

- Both companies use platform strategies to embed themselves deeper in client operations, moving from vendors to long-term digital partners.

What It Means

The B2B platform race isn't about selling products, it's about owning ecosystems. Siemens bets on buildings as adaptive infrastructure; Rockwell bets on factories as intelligent organisms. Both approaches reveal that the future of industrial advantage comes from the same playbook: digitize the edge, unify the data, and orchestrate the ecosystem.

Matching Disruption with the Right Playbook

Organizations navigating digital disruption face a spectrum of strategic choices. The right approach depends on both the intensity of the disruption and the organization's posture, whether it is aggressive, cautious, or collaborative.

If your industry is experiencing significant platform disruption and your organization is willing to take bold action, a **Reconfiguration Strategy** may be the right move. After assessing your digital maturity, you'll know your company's capacity to reconfigure. A critical step given that this approach demands strong digital leadership, substantial investment, risk tolerance, and an influx of digital talent to support fundamental business model redesign.

If pressure from platforms is mounting but your posture is more cautious, consider a **Structural Transformation Strategy**. This involves balancing resources across legacy and digital initiatives, establishing clear transition timelines, educating customers, and building hybrid capabilities that gradually evolve your offering.

In more stable industries where disruption is only a future possibility, forward-thinking organizations may pursue a **Digital Incentivization Strategy**. This approach uses innovation budgets, adoption incentives, and pilot programs to test digital capabilities before fully committing, with an emphasis on metrics beyond short-term ROI.

Ultimately, in industries undergoing gradual digital evolution and exhibiting high potential for collective benefit, a Collaborative Strategy may be the most suitable approach. This strategy focuses on selecting the right partners, establishing clear participation boundaries, transferring knowledge, and scaling investments in line with opportunities.

Strategic Considerations Across Functions

Each of these strategies carries unique implications across leadership, investment, talent, technology, and risk:

- Leadership & Culture varies from requiring a digital-first, transformation-ready mindset (Reconfiguration) to fostering selective adaptation and partnership orientation (Collaborative).
- Investment Approaches range from bold bets on proprietary tech and platforms to low-risk, partner-leveraged digital exposure.
- Talent Strategy moves from aggressive acquisition and reskilling under Reconfiguration to interface-focused roles in Collaborative settings.
- Technology Focus aligns with the strategy, from developing platforms and APIs, to integrating CRM and e-signatures, to lightweight tools and partner APIs.
- Risk Profiles vary widely: Reconfiguration invites high potential gain and disruption, while Collaborative strategies aim to learn with minimal exposure.

In short, strategy must match both market conditions and internal capacity for change. Misalignment, whether due to overreaching or underinvesting, can stall momentum or cede an advantage. The goal is not to copy digital leaders, but to adopt a transformation strategy that aligns with your industry's velocity, organizational maturity, and long-term ambitions.

B2B Digital Maturity Matrix

B2B's journey from fax machines to AI-native ecosystems mirrors the broader arc of digital reinvention, but with higher stakes and longer cycles. The B2B Maturity Matrix shows how organizations evolve from analog transaction pipelines into platform orchestrators and ecosystem catalysts, where value creation comes not just from what you sell, but from *what you connect.*

Dimension	Stage 1 Faxers Analog & Reactive	Stage 2 Connectors Digital Basics	Stage 3 Integrators Platform-Ready	Stage 4 Orchestrators Ecosystem-Centric	Stage 5 Catalysts AI-Native, Ecosystem Builders
Commerce Infrastructure	Fax, phone, spreadsheets; EDI in silos	Web portals, basic e-procurement, and siloed CRMs	Unified ERP + CRM + APIs; marketplace pilots	Multi-sided platforms connecting suppliers & buyers	Ecosystem-as-a-Service; AI/Blockchain-native transaction rails
Buyer Journey	Manual RFQs, rep-driven, long cycles	Basic self-service catalogs, limited digital info	Hybrid journeys: configure, quote, order online	Predictive buyer journeys, integration into workflows	Anticipatory, AI-driven; buyers auto-provision services before need arises
Value Creation Model	One-time product sales	Product + service bundling	Subscriptions, predictive maintenance	Data monetization, shared benchmarks, partner services	Ecosystem monetization: apps, insights, co-created IP
Partnerships	Bilateral, transactional	Preferred vendor lists	Platform integrations, partner portals	Cross-vendor ecosystems, data-sharing agreements	Co-creation networks, competitor-as-partner models
Data & Intelligence	Historical reports, limited visibility	Customer/account-level analytics	Real-time dashboards across partners	Predictive analytics at ecosystem scale	Autonomous AI orchestration, blockchain-verified trust layer
Leadership & Culture	Sales-driven, IT as support	Digital curiosity, siloed teams	Digital strategy embedded across functions	Platform-first mindset, partnership as default	Leadership at every level; culture as ecosystem driver

GLOBAL SIGNAL

Platform Ecosystems Before Scale

The B2B Platform Maturity Matrix envisions a path from transactional marketplaces to full ecosystem orchestration. But in many emerging markets, startups are born as ecosystems, converging procurement, financing, logistics, and data from the outset.

Signals

- TradeDepot (Nigeria & Africa): Began as a digital distributor to informal retailers; then layered in credit, inventory financing, logistics, and consumer packaged goods branding (Mangrove). It acts as both a marketplace and supply backbone.
- OmniRetail / Wasoko (Africa): They embed OmniPay or similar fintech components into the B2B flows, increasing margins and creating stickiness across suppliers, retailers, and logistics.
- Udaan (India): A B2B e-commerce platform connecting small merchants with suppliers, offering credit and logistics to small towns and tier-2/3 areas.

Takeaway

The sharp edge in B2B is no longer just matchmaking, it's controlling the connective tissue of supply, payment, and fulfillment. Startups that stitch those wings early become essential infrastructure, not just intermediaries.

B2B Evolution by Industry

Manufacturing & Industrial — From Iron to Insight

Factories once sold metal; now they sell machine intelligence. Digital procurement exchanges like Xometry streamline sourcing, while IoT sensors feed continuous telemetry that powers Equipment-as-a-Service contracts. The result is a dual-mode model: revenue at install and recurring margin from predictive upkeep.

Siemens' MindSphere demonstrates the shift, connecting compressors, turbines, and robots into a single diagnostic cloud that enables customers to identify and fix faults before they occur, keeping Siemens at the center of every future upgrade.

Professional Services — Trust, Productized

Consultants used to parachute in, bill hours, then vanish. Today, they hard-wire themselves into the client's workflow with subscription platforms and AI-assisted toolkits. Deloitte's Greenhouse and Catalyst transform episodic advice into an always-on collaboration, leveraging dashboards, simulators, and curated knowledge feeds to scale expertise without compromising the human touch. The equation is simple: wrap scarce know-how in software, and you earn annuity revenue while deepening the advisory moat.

Distribution & Wholesale — Middleman to Mission Control

Price transparency and Amazon Business forced distributors to evolve from catalog flippers to supply-chain nerve centers. Leaders combine full-stack e-commerce, predictive inventory, and on-site vending into a seamless experience.

Grainger's KeepStock platform, for instance, doesn't just ship parts; it monitors bin levels, auto-reorders, and feeds procurement analytics straight to the plant floor, turning "what's the cheapest SKU?" into "who keeps my line running?"

Technology & Software — Platforms Building Platforms

This arena invents the playbook others follow. API-first products, open marketplaces, and X-as-a-Service wrappers enable core apps to grow entire partner ecosystems. Think Salesforce AppExchange or AWS Marketplace: each expands functionality while funneling data and dollars back to the hub.

The strategic tightrope is between openness and control. We invite developers to co-create, capture network effects, and guard the core, allowing the ecosystem to amplify rather than compete.

Success Example — Salesforce AppExchange:

Salesforce didn't stop at CRM; they became the OS for enterprise growth. AppExchange empowered thousands of developers and partners to build on its platform, unlocking a flywheel of value that no single product could match.

Winning B2B strategies don't chase trends; they translate platform theory into sector-specific systems of value. The edge comes from knowing how to match the mechanics of your market to the power of platforms, transforming industry constraints into competitive fuel.

From EDI to Ecosystem Dominance

With EDI, two companies could finally "talk" digitally, sending purchase orders and invoices without a single fax or phone call. It was clunky, costly, and closed, but it worked. For decades, that one-to-one connection was the gold standard of B2B digital sophistication.

Fast-forward to today, and that handshake has exploded into an always-on, many-to-many ecosystem. Platforms like Honeywell Forge don't just connect two trading partners; they connect entire industries, customers, suppliers, regulators, and even competitors into a single performance management layer. The rules of engagement have shifted: value no longer comes solely from what you sell, but from what you *connect*.

This shift isn't abstract; it's changing the very geometry of the business model canvas. Where relationships were once mapped as neat bilateral lines, they now resemble dense networks of data flows, integrations, and co-creation loops. Your "customer" might also be a supplier, developer, or competitor, depending on the workflow. Your moat isn't the product in the catalog; it's the platform that becomes indispensable infrastructure for everyone in the ecosystem.

For other B2B manufacturers, the lesson is both urgent and clear:

- If you make it, instrument it. Every connected asset is a node in your data network.
- If you measure it, share it. Benchmarking, even against competitors, creates stickiness and trust.
- If you connect it, monetize it. Once you own the data layer, you control the marketplace for add-on services, insights, and integrations.

Across manufacturing, services, distribution, and technology, the winning strategy is the same: stop thinking like a pipeline operator and start thinking like a platform orchestrator. The B2B buyer is now ecosystem-aware, digitally native, and impatient for value. They will reward the partners who can deliver speed, transparency, integration, and insight without friction.

The journey from EDI to ecosystem mirrors the digital reinvention arc we've traced throughout this book. In Chapter 4, we saw how infrastructure shifted from a back-office utility to a competitive surface, much like platforms like Honeywell Forge transform connected assets into strategic control points.

In Chapter 5, business models evolved into flywheels, where each new connection accelerated the creation of value. Today's multi-partner ecosystems operate on the same principle, compounding network effects with every integration. In Chapter 6, we explored how insight engines power decision speed; in the ecosystem era, that capability scales exponentially when data flows not only within your enterprise but also across customers, suppliers, and even competitors.

Together, these shifts redefine B2B from a pipeline of transactions into a living, data-rich network, one where the true competitive advantage lies in orchestrating the ecosystem. Now in Chapter 8, we see the same truth in B2B: the future belongs to those who can wire these pieces together into an open, extensible, and indispensable platform.

The bottom line? B2B is no longer the slow cousin of B2C. It's a high-speed, high-stakes, high-complexity arena where the companies that embrace platform thinking will not just survive, they'll set the terms of the entire industry's playbook.

The handshake has become the network. The network is the value. And the time to build yours is now.

CHAPTER 9

Content Strategy – Building Trust, Equity and Engagement

Think Like a Content Strategist

The average American is bombarded with 4,000 to 10,000 ads and brand messages every single day[54]. Most are instantly filtered out, unread, and unremembered in today's economy, which makes attention the most valuable yet elusive currency.

What's changed?

- The creator economy is already a $250 billion+ industry, and it's projected to soar to $480 billion by 2027[55]
- Global markets see explosive growth: forecasts suggest the creator economy could reach $1.35 trillion by 2033, expanding to 23.3% CAGR[56]
- Meanwhile, some media companies are flirting with bankruptcy, grappling with slow growth and structural decline, underscoring how fast the world has moved on.

Some brands adapted. Red Bull built a global media house. Nike transformed its apps and social media feeds into high-quality storytelling engines. Duolingo's TikTok is now a daily interaction point, full of the personality that fans crave.

Others? They're still buying primetime TV ad slots, playing Pong on an Atari while competitors run precision raids like pros in Call of Duty.

The old playbook is cracked. 66% of viewers don't actively watch TV ads, and 64% are scrolling on their phones during commercial breaks[57]. Traditional media has its moments, such as live sports and cultural events, but it's no longer the gravitational center. Without precision targeting, real-time insights, and a brand-owned content ecosystem that operates 24/7, brands risk wasting millions on silent airwaves.

In this chapter, we fuse the lessons from Chapter 4's competitive infrastructure, Chapter 5's business model flywheels, and Chapter 6's insight engines. You'll learn how to build a measurable, brand-owned content ecosystem that reaches the right audience, at the right time, with storytelling that sticks.

In 2025 and beyond, attention is the new currency. The thinkers and the winners aren't just buying media; they're building content marketplaces, owned platforms for attention, loyalty, and data supremacy.

MASTERY LEARNING OBJECTIVES

- Design and Operationalize Content Strategy to craft comprehensive strategies that align with business goals, brand voice, and customer needs, while building scalable content operations that balance quality, agility, and efficiency.
- Create High-Impact, Story-Driven Content and apply storytelling principles to develop compelling brand narratives that cut through noise and drive emotional connection.
- Build measurement frameworks that link content performance to business outcomes, because vanity metrics don't keep the lights on

INDUSTRY INSIGHT

Liquid Death — Punk Rock Meets Packaged Water

How a $1B disruptor turned content into a category takeover.

Liquid Death didn't just sell water; it staged a cultural coup. The name sounded like a metal band, the packaging looked like a dive bar tallboy, and the content strategy felt like a mash-up of Jackass and Mad Men.

Context / Challenge

The bottled water category was a creative desert, dominated by serene mountain imagery, pastel palettes, and calm wellness narratives. The challenge: break through a category where every brand "looked" and "sounded" the same.

The Velocity Shift

Liquid Death flipped the playbook by making the *brand* the entertainment. Its marketing arsenal included punk-rock irreverence, meme-fueled social skits, fake legal documents, YouTube Shorts, merchandise drops, and over-the-top videos that blurred the line between parody and persuasion. The brand didn't just go viral once; it engineered an always-on flywheel of content that kept fans talking, sharing, and buying.

Results / Impact

- $1B+ valuation and a rabid global fan base.
- Category disruption made water more culturally relevant than many beer brands.
- Omnichannel content dominates through TikTok, YouTube, and social platforms.

STRATEGIC TAKEAWAYS

- **Lead with identity, not just product** — Liquid Death sold belongings before hydration.
- **Engineer content flywheels** — Create interconnected assets that compound attention over time.
- **Make the technical human** — If actuaries and defense contractors can make data and torque specs engaging, so can you.
- **Stay alert to challengers** — In the platform era, the right voice can win mindshare before incumbents even know there's a fight.

REFLECTIONS

- With consumers filtering out thousands of daily brand messages, what unique elements of your organization's identity could become the foundation for a breakthrough content strategy?
- How can your business move beyond one-off campaigns to design a self-reinforcing content ecosystem that continuously

builds attention, loyalty, and data assets?

- Are your current content metrics tied directly to business outcomes, or are you still relying on vanity metrics that don't translate into growth or ROI?

Content Strategy in the Digital Ecosystem

Content strategy connects several dimensions of digital marketing, serving as the narrative layer that brings together insights, business models, and customer experiences. It is not merely a marketing function but a core element of digital strategy that requires executive alignment, cross-functional collaboration, and strategic resource allocation.

Content Is Currency: Lessons from the Studio Trenches

At Warner Bros. and Universal, content wasn't a slide in a deck; it was the strategy. Whether launching a blockbuster franchise or a niche thriller, we often begin seeding content a year in advance to build anticipation among superfans and new audiences alike.

It was a full-funnel, full-year commitment, built like a media plan, encompassing entertainment TV, high-traffic websites, niche fan communities, and genre-specific placements. The cast's social presence and legacy library outlets amplified our reach.

We considered content an engagement and insight tool; we tracked its every move. Website traffic, social sharing, and fan sentiment surveys revealed what resonated and what didn't. As the release date neared, we refined every element, including copy, tone, and audience segment, based on test screenings and research feedback. This evolved into agile marketing at scale.

The movie business had an edge: a surplus of content, an army of storytellers, and an audience hungry to engage and create. But it also had stakes; everyone's a critic, and with the advent of social media, a voice and a platform to spread their opinions. The real disruption catalyst was aggregator review sites like Rotten Tomatoes, which scored movies in real time. That forced us to be sharper, faster, and tuned in.

The same principles apply beyond Hollywood. Any brand, B2B or B2C, with a community, product, or service has stories worth telling. Whether you're launching a SaaS platform, a new service line, or a product refresh, your ecosystem, customers, partners, and suppliers all bring unique perspectives, emotions, and insights. It's your job to bring it to life.

The takeaway?

Content isn't filler. It's fuel. Delivered strategically, it earns attention, drives behavior, and builds long-tail brand equity. If your content isn't moving the business, it's noise.

Content is a strategy. And in a world where every click, share, and scroll can be tracked, it's your most powerful lever for learning, leading, and scaling.

But here's the truth: Content is what levels your brand up. It's your aftermarket components that boost performance, drive visual appeal, and unlock the power your base build could never reach. It's the custom setting that tunes your ecosystem to squeeze every ounce of competitive advantage.

Brands that treat content like a decorative add-on are stuck in stock mode. Those who tune it, test it, and let it drive strategy? They play at a higher frame rate, faster, sharper, and always ahead of the meta.

> Brands are using cloud-based design systems Tools like Figma, Canva, or Adobe Express, combined with automation tools like Zapier, can enhance their speed and agility in creative workflows.
>
> It enables multiple team members, including those in geographically dispersed teams, to work simultaneously on duplicate design files.
>
> This eliminates delays from back-and-forth email exchanges and ensures everyone is working with the latest version.

The Content Revolution: From Ads to Outcomes

Traditional ads are on life support. Over 70% of people don't trust them[58], and Gen Z isn't even looking. Linear TV is fading, and attention is scattered across streams, scrolls, and second screens. Meanwhile, the real power has shifted to peer discovery and social proof. Nearly 60% of Gen Z consumers now discover new products through social media[59], rather than search engines or commercials. Content isn't optional; it's the new path to trust.

Today's consumers don't want a transaction; they want trust and a sense of belonging to something bigger than themselves.

They seek:

- Story, not spin
- Help, not hype
- Community, not commercials

Content delivers all three.

And while paid media still matters, it's now the amplifier, not the anchor. Brands that lead with content and use paid to boost it, create flywheels: **Content → Engagement → Community → Advocacy.**

So, the real question isn't "Should we invest in content?"

It's "How fast can we build the engine?"

Because while your competitors are still running banner ads, your audience is already watching, sharing, and deciding, without them.

The Content Strategy Pyramid

This isn't content for content's sake; it's a high-performance framework wired for business impact. Each layer of the pyramid fuels the next, transforming scattered storytelling into a strategic growth engine:

This pyramid isn't a theory; it's a blueprint for scalable, purpose-built content that performs. In the following pages, we'll discuss how to take your content strategy from 0 to Reinvented.

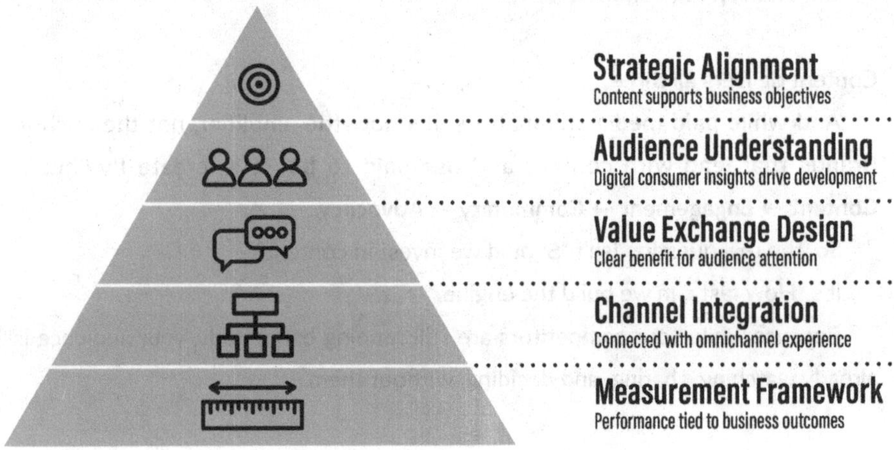

The Business Impact of Strategic Content

Content isn't a marketing accessory; it's the connective tissue powering brand, revenue, and ops. When deployed strategically, content becomes a full-funnel force multiplier:

Brand Equity That Sticks

Consistent, high-value content builds credibility, not clicks. It shapes perception, earns authority, and carves out brand distinctiveness that outlasts ad spend.

Engagement That Compounds

Strategic content fuels repeat interaction across the journey, driving deeper relationships, higher retention, and stronger LTV.

Demand That Converts

Content, in its various forms, is a key component of the whole customer journey. When integrated into demand generation, it warms leads, addresses objections, and accelerates pipeline velocity, resulting in a 3–5x boost in MQL-to-SQL conversion rates.

Efficiency That Scales

A smart content strategy reduces waste and multiplies impact. Reuse across channels, eliminate duplication, and scale production with lean governance, cutting costs by up to 40%.

Bottom line: Strategic content isn't an optional layer. It's a cross-functional growth engine that deserves the attention of the C-suite and operational rigor.

Scaling for Success: Enter the Content Hub

Once your content strategy is locked in, the real grind begins, scaling creation and managing complexity without sacrificing quality. This is where most teams stall out, but with the right operating model, content becomes a strategic engine, not a bottleneck.

To move fast without breaking brand, you need a centralized command center: the Content Hub. Think of it as mission control for content, overseeing creation, coordination, and deployment across the org. The hub keeps content aligned with business objectives, tightens editorial direction, and ensures every asset contributes to the broader customer experience.

Behind the scenes, the engine room manages calendars, deadlines, cross-team workflows, and quality control. It enforces brand standards, streamlines approvals, and ensures content is technically optimized across platforms. It also feeds the loop by tracking performance, flagging what works, and sharing learnings organization-wide to improve the overall game.

Hub Models: One Size Doesn't Scale

Depending on your org's size, speed, and specialization, the Content Hub takes one of three forms:

- **Centralized**: A single team drives all content creation. It's tight, consistent, and brand-safe, but can lack niche depth.

- **Distributed**: Functional teams create content with central oversight. Great for scale and subject-matter expertise but needs strong governance to avoid chaos.
- **Hybrid**: A core content squad handles high-stakes content and platform governance, while satellite creators across the org contribute on demand. It's the best of both models, offering control where it counts and flexibility where it matters.

Content Sourcing: Internal Brains, External Muscle

Smart content ops blend internal expertise with external scale. Your brand and product teams bring strategy, storytelling, and subject-matter expertise, including thought leadership, tutorials, updates, and brand campaigns. Sales and support teams offer frontline insight, testimonials, battlecards, FAQs, and content shaped by honest customer conversations.

But to go wide and fast, external partners amplify your reach. Agencies bring creative firepower and bandwidth. Industry sources inject relevance and credibility. Influencers and UGC add authenticity, social proof, and new distribution layers, all while reducing production overhead.

The winning formula isn't either/or. It's an agile content mix, one that's lean, smart, and built to adapt with your audience and sales funnel.

Governance: The Rules That Power Scale

Scaling content without standards is a recipe for noise. Governance is your invisible scaffolding, tight enough to ensure quality and compliance, yet loose enough to let creativity breathe.

At the core are editorial guidelines: tone, voice, quality criteria, and formatting. Wrapped around that are workflows: who creates, who approves, and how it moves from draft to distribution. Then there's rights and compliance, asset usage, privacy, accessibility, and regulatory guardrails. Finally, measurement standards keep everyone accountable by defining what good looks like, how it's tracked, and how it improves over time.

With the right infrastructure, content scales and compounds. The Content Hub, intelligent sourcing, and rock-solid governance transform content from a creative function into an operational powerhouse.

CASE STUDY

IKEA — Flat-Packs to Full-Funnel Storytelling

How a furniture giant turned content into a lifestyle operating system.

IKEA doesn't just sell furniture—it sells the idea of home. Its content strategy weaves storytelling into catalogs, showrooms, social feeds, AR apps, and sustainability reports, creating a brand voice that is simultaneously consistent and adaptive.

The Bottleneck

Furniture retail used to be transactional and episodic. Catalogs were expensive to print, websites were static, and campaigns spiked only around holidays. Consumers engaged at purchase moments but quickly drifted away.

The Overclock

- Evergreen Anchors: For decades, the IKEA catalog was the most widely distributed publication in the world. Today, IKEA pivots that authority into digital libraries of design inspiration, how-to guides, and modular lifestyle content.
- Real-Time Engagement: IKEA leans into social virality with witty, fast-response campaigns (e.g., "Place in Space" parody after NASA's Mars rover, viral AR filters).
- Omni-Presence: Showrooms double as content studios; the IKEA Place AR app lets users visualize furniture in their homes; sustainability initiatives become stories consumers share.
- Tone & Trust: Relatable, humorous, and democratic language makes content feel accessible rather than aspirational, ensuring engagement across demographics.

Results

- IKEA is one of the most-followed retail brands globally across platforms.
- AR and app-based experiences lifted conversion rates and reduced returns.

- "Evergreen + real-time" content cycle ensures the brand remains relevant year-round.

What It Means

IKEA proves that content strategy doesn't need Hollywood polish to win. By blending evergreen storytelling with real-time responsiveness, the brand turned content into its strongest piece of furniture: modular, adaptive, and built to last.

Real-Time Content: Agility in Action

In a world moving at algorithm speed, content has two publishing nodes: 1) calendarized to sync with consumer rhythms and marketplace seasonality, promotional cycles, and product usage, and 2) the agility to *pounce* on opportunities in real time. Look no further than @Wendys Twitter (X) handle for a history of quick wit, snark, and real-time. Overclocked organizations don't wait for quarterly calendars to catch up. They scan, sense, and strike, transforming cultural trends, breaking news, and performance spikes into high-impact content in real-time.

This isn't reactive. It's *responsive*. Agile content operations treat content like a live asset, not a static deliverable. That means your strategic scanning systems, initially built to detect digital disruption and shifts in consumer behavior, can now pull double duty. The same tools that spot business model threats can surface content opportunities. The same dashboards that track competitive moves can trigger creative sprints.

Trend response is table stakes. Great teams monitor cultural moments and industry chatter like radar operators, ready to ship content with speed and relevance. But speed without direction is chaos. That's why Web 3.0's Architect brands put guardrails in place: clear guidelines for real-time voice, streamlined approval pathways, and pre-approved playbooks for content drops.

Agility also extends to *on-the-fly optimization*. Real-time performance tracking lets you double down on what's working, pivot away from what's not, and remix winning themes in hours, not weeks. Live content adds another dimension. Whether it's streaming a product reveal, capturing the energy of an event, or pulling back the curtain on your people and processes, live formats drive interaction and build trust, especially when they feel genuine, not rehearsed.

Ultimately, real-time content is where planning meets instinct. It's a function of organizational readiness: the tools you use, the processes you trust, and the culture you build. Next-generation teams pivot to create content quickly, efficiently, and on mission.

B2B vs. B2C: Two Playbooks, One Core Engine

Content strategy runs on the same fuel in every industry: insight, intent, and impact, but the roadmaps diverge fast when you compare B2B and B2C. Here's how they stack up when you're playing in different arenas but aiming for maximum velocity.

Audience Mindset

B2B buyers operate in squads. Think procurement leads, technical evaluators, and finance gatekeepers, all with different needs, all watching risk. They're making high-consideration decisions, and they want proof, not poetry. Sales cycles are long, attention spans are short, and ROI is the universal language of business.

B2C consumers, by contrast, respond more quickly and emotionally. Peer influence, personal identity, and convenience matter more than spreadsheets. They're browsing during lunch breaks, scrolling at midnight, and converting in the moment. The stakes feel lower, but the emotional payoff must be high.

Content Strategy at Work

B2B content wins when it speaks to each role individually. You're not selling a solution; you're navigating a matrix of needs. That means building trust through thought leadership, mapping content to each stage of the buyer's journey, and arming sales teams with the necessary technical expertise. For major accounts, it's all about precision targeting and relevance at scale.

B2C content is a vibe. It draws people in with captivating stories, engaging entertainment, and inspiring aspirations. The goal? Build emotional resonance, encourage sharing, and make buying feel seamless. User-generated content is the social proof engine, and shoppable content removes friction from scroll to sale.

What Winning Looks Like

In B2B, you're tracking lead quality, engagement depth, and influence on deal velocity. Every white paper, webinar, and nurture sequence should be tracked in your CRM as having a revenue impact as well as reach and awareness.

In B2C, the scoreboard is lit up by shares, likes, conversion rates, and customer lifetime value. Engagement is a currency, and brand affinity is built by consistently delivering value across channels.

Success in Action

Salesforce nailed B2B content by playing the long game. Their *State of Marketing* reports position them as thought leaders, while Trailhead turns customers into power users. The result? 30% better lead quality and 23% faster sales cycles[60]. That's a flywheel, not a funnel.

Glossier flipped the B2C script by leading with content, not products. Their blog, Into The Gloss, built the community *before* the storefront was established. With growth from peer recs and UGC driving more engagement thank branded posts, they proved that trust scales when it's real.

Content Strategy Along the Customer Journey

A modern content strategy must meet your audience where they are, across channels, in real-time, and in the correct format. Whether that means a Reddit thread, a TikTok series, a deep-dive YouTube explainer, or a TMZ exclusive, your brand's message must show up in the proper context, at the right moment, and in the appropriate form, video, text, UGC, or live audio. By designing your content to track the evolving stages of the customer journey, you increase your ability to attract, nurture, convert, and retain your target audience across every touchpoint.

At the **Awareness stage**, content should focus on attracting new audiences by delivering thought leadership, category education, and brand storytelling that creates emotional resonance. This includes short, shareable formats designed for discovery and virality. Metrics should track reach, brand recall, and early-stage engagement.

As customers move into the Consideration stage, they need content that builds confidence and deepens interest. Case studies, problem-solution narratives, comparison guides, and interactive tools help audiences evaluate their options and develop preferences. Engagement depth, content flow progression, and nurturing velocity become critical measurement points.

In the **Decision stage**, content must remove friction and reinforce value. Prospects are seeking ROI validation, clarity on implementation, and reassurance regarding risk. This is where detailed product content, demos, and onboarding frameworks matter most, and where conversion influence and competitive win rate are tracked.

Once you earn the customer, the **Loyalty stage** demands content that strengthens the relationship. Onboarding guides, expert-level tutorials, community incentives, and user-generated content drive continued engagement, retention, and advocacy.

Each stage isn't a handoff; it's a signal for tuning your message. And in today's live-feed, algorithmic, and peer-driven world, content connects customers on the journey. It shapes it through closed-loop insights.

From Campaigns to Capabilities

Content used to be measured in assets shipped and campaigns launched. But in an orchestrated enterprise, content is not output; it's infrastructure. To compete, organizations must evolve from ad hoc production into a strategic, measurable, cross-functional, and future-ready system.

This matrix maps the journey, showing how five core capabilities, strategy alignment, measurement, operations, collaboration, and innovation, scale across four stages of maturity. It's not about making more content; it's about building the reflexes that make every piece smarter, faster, and more valuable.

Capability	**Stage 1** **Reactive** **Ad hoc, siloed**	**Stage 2** **Enabled** **Basic standards & tools**	**Stage 3** **Integrated** **Enterprise-wide alignment**	**Stage 4** **Optimized** **Adaptive, AI-augmented**	**Stage 5** **AI Orchestrated** **Autonomous, anticipatory**
Integrate Strategy into the Core	Content is campaign-driven, disconnected from business goals	Content aligned to marketing goals, but still tactical	Content embedded in business planning cycles	Content anticipates market shifts; the strategy-content loop is seamless	AI continuously senses signals (market, cultural, competitive) and dynamically adjusts content strategy in real time
Level Up Measurement	Clicks, views, vanity metrics dominate	Multi-touch attribution, but siloed	Revenue, pipeline, and retention are tied to content performance	Predictive analytics optimizes content in real time	Autonomous AI attribution connects content to lifetime value, competitive advantage, and brand equity
Operationalize with Precision	No governance; content fragmented	Basic style guides and CMS adoption	Modular content, governed taxonomies, unified stack	AI-driven content lifecycle management, personalization at scale	AI autonomously assembles, distributes, and retires content across channels; synthetic media and generative personalization at the individual level
Cross-Function Like a Pro	Content owned solely by marketing	Occasional cross-team coordination	Hybrid teams, content center of excellence, shared workflows	Fully networked teams co-creating content across silos	AI acts as connective tissue across functions, orchestrating workflows, compliance, and collaboration in real time
Bake in Innovation	Reactive to trends; no experimentation	Sporadic pilots, mostly opportunistic	Systematic experimentation, trend-tracking, and feedback loops	Continuous foresight + scenario planning fuel innovation cycles	AI scenario simulators generate, test, and scale new content formats and narratives before humans green-light them

GLOBAL SIGNAL

Content as Commerce Infrastructure

The Content Maturity Matrix tracks a shift from storytelling to integrated customer journeys. But in emerging markets, content doesn't evolve into commerce, it begins as commerce. Entertainment platforms double as storefronts from day one.

Signals

- TikTok Shop (Indonesia): Turned short videos into live shopping channels, driving billions in GMV and millions of seller accounts. It shows that when attention and trust collapse into one platform, commerce follows instantly.
- Shopee Live (Southeast Asia): Gamified livestream selling with millions in sales per hour. Parasocial trust between hosts and viewers creates conversion power traditional ads can't match.
- Rappi (LatAm): Bundled entertainment content into a delivery-fintech ecosystem spanning nine countries. By making attention a retention tool, Rappi turned content into a cost-saving growth engine.

Takeaway

In these markets, content isn't a campaign or a funnel, it's the store itself. Leaders who see content a s transaction-ready infrastructure will outpace those treating it as awareness-only media.

The journey from TiVo to TikTok

From Liquid Death's irreverent tallboys to Salesforce's thought-leadership flywheel proves one thing: content is no longer the side of lobster mac, it's the ribeye. The brands that win have built the infrastructure (Chapter 4) to deliver it at speed, the business model flywheels (Chapter 5) to make it compound, and the insight engines (Chapter 6) to tune it in real time.

Here's the real unlock: content strategy isn't powered by clever slogans, it's powered by signal-rich insights. The Voice of the Customer, captured through customer journeys, persona development, and continuous feedback loops, becomes the North Star. Quantitative data shows you what's happening; qualitative research tells you why. Together, they shape not just the topics you cover, but the tone, format, and platform mix. Without them, you're guessing. With them, you're building a content ecosystem that resonates with a heterogeneous audience whose needs, motivations, and decision triggers shift by segment.

The Content Strategy Pyramid still applies at its base, a deep understanding of brand voice and audience segments; in the middle, a precision mix of formats and distribution; at the top, performance measurement and iteration. AI now accelerates every tier, synthesizing journey insights into hyper-specific audience profiles, generating content variants for each persona, and even predicting the next topic before your competitors see it coming.

For anyone who's ever scrolled YouTube for a how-to instead of reading the manual, the shift is obvious: we trust what's relatable, what's human, and what feels like it belongs to us. Influencers scale word-of-mouth faster than any ad buy, and attention markets move at platform speed. Whether you're selling water, military vehicles, or SaaS, your story has to travel the way your audience does: across feeds, formats, and moments, in language they already speak.

For incumbents, this is also a "watch your six" moment; disruption no longer needs a factory, only a brand that can connect with an audience and feed the algorithm better than you can. In this environment, content strategy is not a marketing plan; it's your competitive architecture for earning attention, building trust, and creating a feedback loop that fuels the next cycle. Miss that, and you're racing in a stock car while your competitors are tuning for Formula 1. Build it right, and you're not just in the race, you're setting the pace.

CHAPTER 10

Owned Media – The Business Ecosystem

Think Like a Digital Ecosystem Architect

For the last two decades, omnichannel has been the leading operational model for retail and brands that leverage data, brand equity, and an integrated content strategy to engage customers at every touchpoint in the journey: websites and apps, search, social media, influencer feeds, and affiliate marketplaces, along with email, SMS, and push notifications. The idea was that attention and intent could be paid, persuaded, and guided.

But what happens when consumers no longer control the journey themselves? What if they outsource it to an autonomous artificial intelligence agent that understands personal preferences, consumption habits, seasonal changes, and interests, based on routine daily needs and lifestyle goals? An agent bot that scans, filters, negotiates, and makes purchases on their behalf.

Impulse buying diminishes. Upselling, cross-selling, and banner ads no longer affect them.

Promotions lose their impact, discounts and coupons become less convincing if the bot can calculate the actual cost of acquisition and ownership in milliseconds.

Identity cloaking becomes possible. Retailers and direct-to-consumer brands, accustomed to using customer data for segmentation, might find bots cloaking consumer identities, shielding them from tracking and effectively killing personalization.

The media landscape shifts. Instead of chasing consumers across various channels, brands will learn to compete in the *Agentic Marketplace*, where visibility depends on being recommended by a consumer's personal bot.

MASTERY LEARNING OBJECTIVES

- Design and optimize owned media environments that deliver connected, high-impact customer experiences across web, app, email, and in-product surfaces.
- Evaluate how owned media assets serve as strategic moats, driving retention, reducing CAC, and deepening brand control in a fragmented media landscape.
- Integrate content strategy, first-party data, and user experience design to create self-directed, measurable journeys that put the customer in control.

INDUSTRY INSIGHT

Marriott, Turning Owned Media Into a Moat

How one of the world's largest hotel brands rewired its growth engine by cutting out the middleman.

In a hospitality world dominated by third-party booking platforms, Marriott said no to the middleman and built a self-sustaining, owned media ecosystem that now serves as both a growth engine and a defensive moat.

Context / Challenge

OTAs, such as Expedia and Booking.com, were controlling customer relationships, taking commissions, and hoarding valuable traveler data. Marriott needed to reclaim direct engagement, deepen loyalty, and create a scalable, high-margin booking pipeline outside third-party control.

The Velocity Shift

- Marriott Bonvoy App: Evolved from a booking tool into a personalized concierge and loyalty driver, delivering tailored offers, upsells, and recommendations based on loyalty data, booking history, and in-stay behavior.

- Marriott Content Studio: Launched in 2015 under marketing leader Karin Timpone, producing destination guides, travel hacks, docuseries, and branded entertainment to attract and engage travelers before, during, and after their trips.
- Bonvoy TV & Social Channels: Original films, docuseries, and interactive content streams used not for pure promotion but for building community and direct engagement.

Results / Impact

- 140M+ Bonvoy members integrated into a unified content-commerce-personalization flywheel.
- Reduced dependency on OTAs by shifting bookings to direct channels.
- Proprietary first-party data powering precision marketing and upsells.
- Extended lifetime value by engaging travelers outside of traditional booking windows.

STRATEGIC TAKEAWAYS

- Own the channels, own the customer. Control over content, platforms, and data creates both margin and defensibility.
- Fuse content, commerce, and personalization. Each interaction fuels the next, creating compounding returns.
- Build brand media like a publisher. Treat owned platforms as an always-on storytelling engine, not just a transactional tool.

REFLECTIONS

- How much of your customer journey is still dependent on third-party platforms, and what steps could you take to shift that engagement into owned channels that strengthen loyalty and margins?
- If autonomous consumer agents become the gatekeepers of choice, how would your owned media ecosystem need to adapt

to remain discoverable, relevant, and recommended?

- Are your owned channels primarily transactional today—or are they evolving into holistic ecosystems that blend content, personalization, and community to deepen lifetime value?

From Brand Broadcast to Customer Control

The digital shift flipped the script; customers now run the show. They decide when, where, and how they engage. They comparison shop in seconds. They expect personalized experiences, not generic campaigns. And they won't give attention or data without a clear value exchange.

In this new reality, owned media is treated like an appreciating asset.

Your website, app, email, and loyalty ecosystem are now your direct line to the customer, beyond the noise of paid ads and the unpredictability of algorithms. Owned media enables:

- Consistent, brand-safe experiences across every touchpoint
- First-party data that fuels personalization and performance
- Lower acquisition costs and stronger long-term relationships

The mission is clear: If you don't own the connection, you don't own the future.

The Media Ecosystem Framework

Digital marketing operates within an interconnected ecosystem comprising three distinct media types.

Owned Media

Digital channels and content are brand controls (websites, apps, email, social profiles).

Paid Media

Advertising and promotional content that a brand pays to place on external platforms.

Earned Media

External coverage and engagement that a brand generates organically.

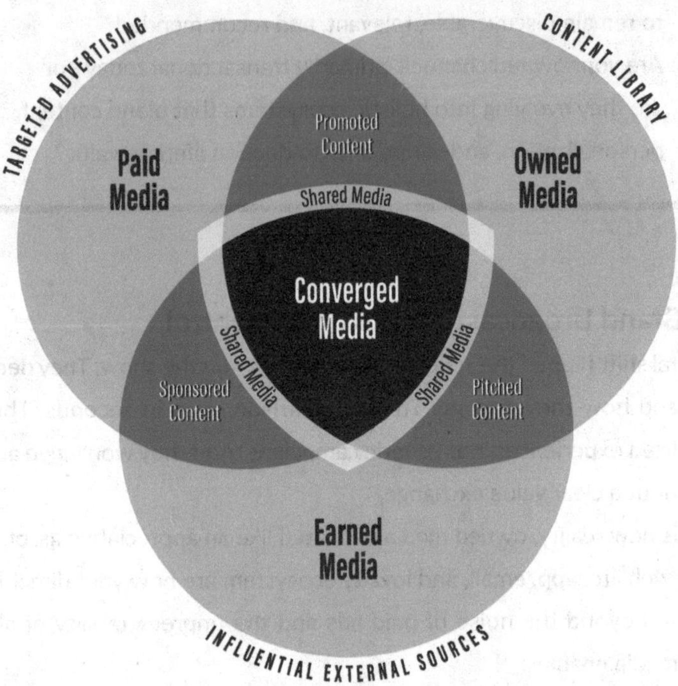

Regardless of the media source, anchoring Paid, Owned, and Earned[61] in the common denominator of impression creates a measurable starting point while allowing for nuanced evaluation based on quality, context, and intent.

While the table below is somewhat simplistic, it provides a directional perspective on each media pillar.

Media Type	Control	Cost	Credibility	Typical Impression Quality	Example
Paid	High	$$$	Low–Med	Highly targeted, but may be ignored	Sponsored Instagram post
Owned	Full	$	Medium	Relevant to loyal users, SEO dependent	Blog or branded website
Earned	None	Free-ish	High	Organic, but often uncontrollable	PR coverage or viral share

All Impressions Are Not Created Equal

In the world of digital media, whether Owned, Earned, or Paid, the one metric that cuts across all channels is the *impression*. On its surface, an impression is the baseline unit of attention: one moment of visibility, one chance to register. It's the common denominator that lets strategists compare impact across formats, frequencies, and platforms. And while it's tempting to treat all impressions as equally and tally them up, optimize for CPM[62], and call it a day, the truth is far more nuanced. Because in today's fragmented attention economy, *what counts as an impression isn't just a number; it's a multiplier of context, creativity, and behavior.*

An impression during a binge-scroll at 1:00 a.m. isn't the same as one delivered during a focused LinkedIn lunch break. A banner ad running as background noise on a blog doesn't hold the same weight as a TikTok video shared by a peer, or a product review embedded in a Reddit thread. Form factor, device, platform, time of day, placement, and, most importantly, intent, all significantly shift the value of that impression.

Research supports this asymmetry. According to AIS and Neuro-Insight, ads seen in contextually relevant environments yield a 36% higher recall[63]. Likewise, a study from IPG Media Lab and Sharethrough found that native ads, which blend seamlessly with content and format, generate more visual focus and achieve an 18% higher lift in brand affinity.[64] Beyond standard display, the format and context aren't just cosmetic; they reshape the brain's engagement.

This is why the strategist's job is dual purpose: to maximize impressions and *qualify* them. To treat media like a performance engine, not a volume play. The real work lies in mapping *which impressions* at *which stages* create lift. That's where form, story, and signal intersect, and where you earn ROI.

Reinvention Insight

Impressions are like pixels in a game; they only matter if they're rendered with clarity, timing, and relevance. Flooding the screen with low-quality touches won't level you up. Innovative brands don't chase impressions; they *engineer* them.

Your Platform. Your Rules. Your Edge.

Owned media is more than a channel; it's your digital moat. Unlike paid media, which shuts off the moment spending stops, owned media assets deliver compound returns over time. They build equity.

With owned media, you control the narrative, the data, and the experience. You engage customers directly, with no intermediaries or dilution. Every click, view, or swipe becomes a data point, giving you a privacy-compliant, high-resolution view of your audience. Unlike external platforms, you control the flow of the experience, ensuring it's on-brand, frictionless, and always on point.

Core Architecture of Owned Media: Your Brand's Digital Engine

High-performing owned media ecosystems run on four tightly integrated components:

1. Your primary digital destinations (websites, apps) serve as the control tower for your brand, driving discovery, conversion, service, and storytelling.
2. Through direct communication channels like email, SMS, and push notifications, you keep customers in the loop, reengage lapsed users, and deliver personalized moments that matter.
3. Physical-digital integration bridges online and offline experiences, connecting in-store technology, fulfillment, and location-based offers into a single, unified journey.
4. And your content ecosystem, blogs, resource hubs, communities, educates, entertains, and retains by solving real problems instead of pushing tired promotions.

These aren't siloed features. They form a connected system that gives you control of the message, the experience, and the data.

Data Is the Strategic Payload

Owned media's greatest unlock? First-party data[65], behavioral signals, preferences, and interactions captured directly from your audience. It's the gold standard: privacy-safe, high-fidelity, and proprietary.

Second-party data[66] adds fuel through trusted partners, such as co-branded campaign insights or shared distributor analytics. Third-party data[67], once dominant, is fading fast under tightening privacy laws and platform restrictions.

Cross-Functional Power Play

The value of first-party data compounds across the org:

- Marketing gets hyper-targeted personalization, smarter paid media, and attribution that makes sense.
- Customer Experience delivers seamless recognition, predictive service, and relevance without guesswork.
- Product Teams unlock usage patterns, prioritize features, and innovate based on what real users do, not what they say.

Owned Media = Long-Term Strategic Asset

While paid media throttles down as budgets decrease and ROAS limits are reached, owned media continues to compound its reach. You own the platform, the message, and the data, and that means lower acquisition costs, better margins, and a tighter feedback loop. You're not renting reach. You're building equity.

It also eliminates intermediaries. No gatekeepers. No algorithms are throttling your signal. Just direct, high-value connections with your audience, on your terms.

Content Strategy: The Power Multiplier

Owned media without engaging content that adds value to the audience is a static shell. The magic happens when strategic content and owned platforms work in lockstep.

Rather than chasing formats, start with narrative adaptability, core messages that flex across channels and formats. Match content to journey stages, deliver value-first interactions, and build journeys around customer intent, not org charts.

Leverage your owned media data to tune what you create continually. Identify what resonates, drop what doesn't, and focus not on volume, but on velocity, engagement, and lift. Adapt quickly to the shifts in audience behavior through active listening and responsive community management.

The Shift from SEO to AEO

For nearly two decades, Search Engine Optimization (SEO) has been one of the most efficient and valuable sources of digital traffic. Brands have invested heavily in websites, content hubs, analytics, and skill sets designed to help them rank higher in Google and other search engines. The payoff has been clear: organic traffic often delivers some of the highest-value conversions in digital marketing.

But in the kinetic economy of AI and blockchain, the discovery layer is shifting. Customers increasingly rely on AI agents and Agentic AI rather than search engines alone. Instead of delivering a page of ranked links, these agents provide a synthesized, context-aware answer and often act on it by booking, purchasing, or recommending. At the same time, blockchain adds verifiable trust signals that AI agents prefer when filtering misinformation and selecting reliable sources.

This evolution is redefining SEO as AEO — Agentic Experience Optimization.

- SEO was about ranking high for keywords.
- AEO is about being recognized, trusted, and actioned by AI agents.

For brands, this matters because the existing infrastructure of SEO cannot simply be abandoned. It must be adapted to ensure that owned media is:

- **Machine-readable** (structured data, schema, APIs).
- **Verifiable** (supported by blockchain-backed authenticity or trusted data feeds).
- **Contextual** (built around questions, intents, and entity relationships, not just keywords).

As with other aspects of the Web 2 → Web 3 transition, this is not an incremental tweak but a functional shift. Businesses that master AEO will continue to capture high-value organic traffic, but in this new reality, traffic flows through agents and answers, not search results pages.

SEO vs. AEO: From Ranking to Recommendation

Traditional SEO (Web 2)	Agentic Experience Optimization (AEO, Web 3)
· Optimizes for search engines (Google, Bing) · Focus on keywords & rankings · Success measured by SERP position & clicks · Relies on backlinks & authority signals · Content designed as pages & articles · Funnel: Rank → Click → Convert · Goal: Visibility in search results	· Optimizes for AI agents and Agentic AI · Focus on questions, intents & entity relationships · Success measured by agent recommendation & actions (book, buy, advise) · Relies on verifiable data & trust signals (blockchain proofs, verified credentials) · Content designed as structured, modular, machine-readable snippets · Funnel: Recommend → Act → Verify · Goal: Being the trusted source agents select & transact on

From Orchestration to Autonomy

For years, the holy grail of owned media has been omnichannel orchestration, where every touchpoint is connected, every customer is recognized, and every experience is seamless. But now there's a new ceiling. AI is transforming owned ecosystems into something qualitatively different: an intelligent operating system that adapts, optimizes, and even anticipates in real-time by leveraging in-house data and marrying it with geographic, cultural, and seasonal nuances that may affect your target audience.

The real leap is not from fragmentation to orchestration. It's from orchestration to autonomy. At this stage, owned media stops being managed and starts managing itself, freeing leaders to focus on strategy, creativity, and the next horizon. What began as marketing automation[68] has evolved into autonomous marketing action.

OWNED MEDIA MATURITY MATRIX

Value Dimension	**Stage 1 Initial Presence**	**Stage 2 Multichannel Coordination**	**Stage 3 Cross-Channel Integration**	**Stage 4 Omnichannel Orchestration**	**Stage 5 AI-Driven Operating System**
Marketing Impact	Basic website; disconnected campaigns	Coordinated channels; consistent but siloed messaging	Data sync enables more intelligent targeting; ROI visibility improves	Hyper-personalization at scale; unified attribution	AI continuously adapts creative offers and spending in real time across all touchpoints
Customer Experience	Customers restart every time	Slightly smoother, still fragmented	Recognized across some channels; intentional experiences	Seamless recognition; predictive service begins	AI anticipates customer needs before they act, providing proactive, context-aware engagement.
Product Insight	Minimal usage tracking	Basic analytics; limited feature feedback	Usage patterns inform roadmap	Deep behavioral insights drive agile product evolution	AI uncovers latent needs, auto-prioritizes features, and simulates adoption scenarios
Strategic Role	Owned media = brochure	Campaign amplifier	Integrated system	Relationship engine (HubSpot-style content, Duolingo communities, Mailchimp resources)	AI as invisible OS: owned media becomes a self-optimizing, always-on growth driver
Organizational Reflex	Reactive	Coordinated	Data-informed	Customer-centric	Autonomous + anticipatory (AI closes loops instantly, humans focus on strategy and storytelling)

GLOBAL SIGNAL

Content-Enabled Commerce as Core

The Owned Media Maturity Matrix moves from branded content to customer journey orchestration. In emerging markets, the leap is often reversed: content isn't a feeder, it is the commerce interface from Day 1.

Signals

- Jio (India): Jio's bundle of content apps (like JioTV, JioCinema, streaming) was integrated with its telco offering, turning content into a platform hook for subscriptions and engagement.
- Sea Group (Southeast Asia): Through Shopee and Garena, Sea converges gaming, content, and commerce into a single engagement stack, commerce is embedded in the content layer.
- Companies in African markets: Some e-commerce players now host mini-shows, product demonstrations, and live-selling content,blurring media and shopping.

Takeaway

In contexts where paid reach is expensive or fractured, commerce must be embedded in the owned content itself. The brand platform is not just a storytelling canvas but the primary engine for engagement, conversion, and community.

Nuance between B2B and B2C

B2B and B2C audiences may share the same broadband, but they play by very different rules. B2B buyers advance in committees, need proof before persuasion, and want tools that make their customers cheer; B2C buyers chase convenience, social validation, and the dopamine of a one-tap checkout. As Michael Brito[69], former Edelman Digital colleague and longtime B2B strategist, puts it, "Buyers today don't want to be sold. They want proof. They want perspective. And they want it fast."

B2B, enterprise cadence. Here, the content agenda prioritizes sales enablement first, then marketing. Account-based experiences tailor white-paper depth to each stakeholder's pain point and provide deal teams with targeted assets that accelerate consensus. Emerging B2B platforms, such as data-layer integrations or co-branded resource hubs, extend that value after the sale, transforming vendors into embedded partners rather than one-time suppliers. Success is measured by pipeline velocity, renewal rates, and the frequency with which customers reference your content in their own board discussions and decks.

B2C, consumer cadence. For everyday shoppers, the screen is the store. Mobile apps must feel instant, social commerce must feel native, and every swipe should offer a chance to buy, review, and broadcast. Here, innovation encompasses AR try-ons, one-click wallets, and partnerships with TikTok or Instagram APIs that seamlessly combine discovery and purchase into a single thumb motion. Trust comes from a seamless user experience and peers' reactions, not from a PDF case study.

CASE STUDY

Honeywell Forge — Turning Owned Media into Industrial Infrastructure

How a century-old manufacturer became a digital marketplace orchestrator.

Honeywell wasn't born digital. It built thermostats, avionics, and industrial systems. But with Honeywell Forge, it recast itself as a platform provider, an owned digital ecosystem where competitors, partners, and customers converge to transact, collaborate, and innovate.

The Bottleneck

Industrial buyers faced fragmented procurement, siloed data, and proprietary vendor lock-in. Software from one OEM rarely interoperated with another. For Honeywell, selling hardware meant episodic revenue and little visibility into ongoing customer operations.

The Overclock

- Unified Platform: Honeywell Forge centralizes IoT data from factories, aircraft, and buildings into one interface, giving customers holistic insights across assets.
- Marketplace Expansion: Beyond Honeywell tools, Forge opened its ecosystem to partner and competitor solutions, becoming a procurement facilitator rather than a closed shop.
- Community & Engagement: The Forge Community provides forums, best practices, and shared insights, creating peer-to-peer trust layered over corporate marketing.
- Recurring Value: By shifting from one-off sales to SaaS subscriptions and usage-based models, Forge built long-term customer stickiness.

Results

- Multi-industry adoption in aviation, energy, buildings, and manufacturing.
- Procurement platform with partner and competitor listings, increasing customer stickiness through ecosystem breadth.
- Positioning Honeywell less as a vendor and more as an operating partner for digital transformation.

What It Means

Owned media in B2B isn't just whitepapers and webinars, it can be the digital backbone of an industry. Honeywell Forge shows how incumbents can host communities, enable procurement, and even facilitate competitor offerings when the platform itself becomes indispensable.

Omnichannel vs. Agentic Commerce

To place a finer point on the shift from Omnichannel to Agentic Commerce, let's compare the two below:

	Human-Centered (Traditional Omnichannel)	Agent-Centered (Agentic Commerce)
Identity & Data	Consumers are visible and tracked across touchpoints via cookies, loyalty programs, and CRM systems.	Consumers masked by agents; bots transact anonymously or pseudonymously.
Discovery & Influence	Ads, promotions, influencers, and content shape awareness and impulse.	Bots filter out superfluous promotions; discovery is based on trusted data, provenance, and parameters set by the consumer.
Decision-Making	Human-driven; influenced by emotion, brand storytelling, promotions, and UX.	Bot-driven; optimized for cost, sustainability, convenience, or preferences defined by the consumer.
Transaction & Loyalty	Channels integrated (store, site, app, social, marketplace); loyalty programs tied to identity and rewards.	Bots execute purchases via APIs; loyalty shifts to **bot parameters** (e.g., "lowest carbon footprint," "highest value for money").

While this shift won't happen overnight, the dramatic changes in the user experience, value exchange, and consumer power will be undeniable.

From Omnichannel to the Agentic Marketplace: The New Upper-Right Quadrant

In the traditional maturity model, the "upper right-hand quadrant" of owned media referred to seamless omnichannel integration, where websites, apps, loyalty programs, social extensions, and marketplace storefronts are all connected into a unified ecosystem. For many brands, that was the ultimate goal: to build a self-sustaining, multi-sided platform where traffic could be captured, data owned, and experiences managed. However, that upper right is evolving.

The rise of Agentic AI[70], consumer-controlled bots that research, compare, negotiate, and transact, is pushing the frontier further. The agentic marketplace becomes the new horizon for maturity, where your owned ecosystem isn't just serving human users but also the autonomous agents acting on their behalf.

Examples in Action

Retail

Walmart has already begun prototyping AI shopping assistants that auto-generate carts for events like family dinners or birthday parties. These agents don't respond to ads; they parse availability, preferences, and sustainability data. Owned media feeds must be structured so these bots can ingest and transact seamlessly.

Financial Services

Visa is piloting AI-enabled payment flows where trusted bots can initiate purchases directly on behalf of consumers, within preset parameters. Here, the "owned channel" isn't a mobile app screen; it's a bot-readable infrastructure layer tied into blockchain-secured provenance.

Marketplaces & Platforms

Mirakl Nexus is building connective tissue for agentic commerce, allowing brands' product feeds, reviews, and data to flow directly into autonomous agent ecosystems. This demonstrates how owned media assets (product data, feeds, and provenance claims) will be increasingly repurposed as machine-parsable trust signals.

Consumer Products

LVMH experiments with agentic AI, not for front-end shopping, but for back-office intelligence, such as forecasting trends, monitoring sustainability claims, and ensuring brand trust data can flow into the discovery layer, where bots filter purchase options. Hospitality: Marriott Bonvoy has built an app that integrates booking, room access, loyalty, and UGC content loops. Today, it's optimized for humans, but tomorrow, bots may scan its APIs to price-match across loyalty tiers, carbon footprints, or experience add-ons. Owned media will need to support both.

The Implication

Omnichannel integration and multi-sided marketplaces were once the limit of owned media maturity. But in an era where bots serve as gatekeepers, that limit rises again.

The next competitive advantage comes from making your owned media bot-friendly, blockchain-verified, and provenance-rich.

In the agentic marketplace, the brand that wins isn't the one with the flashiest app or the deepest content library, but the one whose data, trust signals, and ecosystem hooks are most understandable to autonomous agents. That's the new upper-right: not just omnichannel control, but omni-agent fluency[71].

From Omnichannel to Omni-Agent

Over the last two decades, omnichannel integration has been a hallmark of mature owned media. Brands stitched together websites, apps, social outposts, loyalty ecosystems, and marketplaces into seamless journeys, leveraging data and brand equity to meet customers wherever they clicked, tapped, or swiped. The goal was orchestration across touchpoints, and for a time, that was the ceiling.

But the ceiling has been lifted. A new gatekeeper has arrived: the Agentic AI agent. Consumers are increasingly delegating decision-making to autonomous bots that negotiate, filter, and transact based on personal parameters, sustainability, budget, lifestyle goals, or total cost of ownership. In this world:

- **Impulse fades** – Bots strip away manipulation, optimizing for preference over persuasion.
- **Promotions weaken** – Discounts carry less weight if agents can instantly calculate long-term value.
- **Identity cloaks** – Bots may anonymize or filter consumer data, protecting privacy while reshaping personalization.

As you can see, the battleground shifts dramatically if your brand relies on any one of the above. Visibility no longer depends on consumer eyeballs but on trust signals that bots can read, such as provenance, ratings, data transparency, and alignment with values.

This is not the death of omnichannel. It's the rise of dual transformation. Leaders must master both:

Transformation 1 – Omnichannel orchestration for today's human-controlled journeys. Continued optimization of messaging, touchpoints, and conversion tactics to deliver customer experiences that drive loyalty.

Transformation 2 – Omni-agent fluency for tomorrow's agentic marketplaces, where autonomous systems transact and compete on behalf of consumers. The implications are profound. Your owned media isn't just a marketing channel anymore, it becomes:

- An API for agents as much as an interface for humans.
- A ledger of trust where blockchain provenance validates every claim.
- A growth engine that compounds through transparency, interoperability, and AI-driven adaptability.

The lesson is clear: the upper-right quadrant of owned media maturity no longer ends with omnichannel mastery. The new horizon is the agentic marketplace, where winning brands design ecosystems that are readable by bots, trusted by blockchain, and meaningful to humans.

The brands that thrive will be those that embrace this dual transformation path we discussed earlier, strengthening omnichannel performance while preparing for the agent-led future. In the era of revolution, where architects will dominate, owned media is not just your moat; it is your bridge to the next competitive frontier.

CHAPTER 11

Earned Media — Amplifying the Brand & Business

Think Like a Media Company

If the owned media ecosystem is your home field, earned media is what happens when the crowd takes the game outside the stadium. For centuries, word of mouth was a slow burn, an enthusiastic dinner-table recommendation, a letter to a friend, a movie review in the Sunday paper. Today, it's a detonation. A single TikTok post, a Reddit thread, or a LinkedIn comment can ripple to millions in hours, not months.

The scale is staggering: every day, over 4.9 billion people use social media[72], generating more than 500 million tweets, 95 million Instagram posts, and 720,000 hours of new YouTube videos[73]. Likes, shares, stitches, and user-generated content don't just pass along your message; they reframe it, remix it, and attach someone else's credibility to it.

This is one of the most significant payoff points for the integrated content strategy and owned media foundation you've built. When the value you create resonates with your audience, it doesn't stay confined to your website, app, or CRM channels. It jumps the fence, catches a ride on someone else's feed, and suddenly, your brand is being advocated for by voices you don't pay, can't fully control, but desperately need.

And here's where AI turns that detonation into precision firepower. AI-powered social listening tools scan millions of posts, reviews, and conversations in real-time, spotting sentiment shifts, identifying breakout advocates, and detecting micro-trends before they emerge. Generative AI can help craft context-specific responses, recap emerging themes for your internal teams, or even suggest which earned mentions to amplify based on audience fit and likelihood of further sharing. Predictive analytics can forecast which conversations are likely to become viral moments, letting you lean in at the exact right time instead of reacting after the wave has passed.

Word of mouth hasn't changed in principle; it's still about trust being transferred from one person to another, but physics has been rewritten. The time delay has collapsed from days to seconds, the network effect has expanded from a handful of acquaintances to global reach, and AI now serves as your early warning system, performance tuner, and amplification engine.

In the digital era, the scoreboard for brand health isn't just your NPS or brand tracker; it's the organic conversation happening in real time, far from your owned channels, in communities you may not even know exist. Earned media is the marketplace where your hard-won trust is bought, sold, and multiplied. And when the crowd is on your side, their amplification, augmented by AI's speed and precision, can outrun even the biggest paid campaign.

MASTERY LEARNING OBJECTIVES

- Analyze how earned media, encompassing press coverage, influencer advocacy, customer reviews, and social sharing, fuels brand credibility, extends reach, and reinforces authenticity in an increasingly skeptical digital landscape.
- Develop earned media approaches that align with brand objectives, mobilize internal advocates and external partners, and strategically complement paid and owned efforts across the customer journey.
- Implement frameworks to evaluate the effectiveness of earned media, tracking its influence on brand lift, traffic, engagement, and conversion, while transitioning from vanity metrics to genuine indicators of business value.

> ***"92% of consumers trust recommendations from friends and family over any form of advertising, highlighting the value of earned media strategies."***

INDUSTRY INSIGHT

Glossier — Turning Earned Media Into a Growth Engine

From side-hustle blog to billion-dollar brand, built almost entirely on community voices.

If the AI-enabled earned media flywheel is the theory, Glossier is the proof. Emily Weiss went from publishing candid beauty routines on *Into The Gloss* to building one of the most envied brands in beauty, without spending like a legacy giant.

Context / Challenge

In 2010, the beauty market was dominated by department store counters, celebrity endorsements, and glossy ad campaigns from L'Oréal and Estée Lauder. Social media was still a secondary channel, not the main stage, and legacy players weren't paying close attention to their audiences.

The Velocity Shift

Crowdsourced R&D: Every blog comment and reader suggestion became part of Glossier's product development roadmap.
Design for Participation: Products like Balm Dotcom and Perfecting Skin Tint featured minimalist packaging in soft pinks, made for the Instagram "shelfie" era.
Community as Media: Rather than rely on heavy ad spend, Glossier amplified customer content, seeded products to micro-influencers, and generated credibility through authentic user reviews.
Social-First Launches: The brand debuted products in the same places people were already talking about beauty, TikTok stories, YouTube hauls, and Reddit threads.

Results / Impact

- Achieved unicorn status in 2020 with $185M in funding, outpacing traditional beauty marketing efficiency.
- Built a highly engaged community that acted as both R&D lab and distribution network.
- Outperformed paid campaigns from competitors through trust-driven, community-led content.

STRATEGIC TAKEAWAYS

- Earned media can outcompete paid spend when it's designed for amplification.
- Customer voices are the most credible ads that engineer products and experiences that people *want* to share.
- Participation fuels loyalty when your audience feels like co-creators; they buy in emotionally as well as financially.

REFLECTION

- Are you treating earned media as a core growth driver, or a value-added bonus?
- Where are your strongest organic conversations happening, and how are you amplifying them?
- Is your content strategy designed for shareability and co-creation, or locked in broadcast mode?
- Are you building relationships with advocates that elevate brand equity?

From Content Value to Earned Trust

Content is the raw material; trust is the finished product; earned media is the market-place where that trust is exchanged. Chapter 9's Content-Trust-Value model outlines the chain reaction: deliver real value first, trust accrues almost automatically, and audiences respond by championing the brand on their own turf, through reviews, reposts, podcasts, and Slack channels.

Each step feeds the next: valuable insights or utilities spark confidence, confidence unlocks voluntary advocacy, and that advocacy widens reach and credibility, sending fresh prospects back to your content engine. Brands that treat content creation as a strategic discipline, not as periodic promotion, find the flywheel spins faster and cheaper than any paid campaign.

Digital dynamics have turbo-charged (and complicated) the equation. Trust has shifted from institutions to peers, meaning a single TikTok testimonial can now outweigh a hundred glossy ads. Audiences reward transparency over narrative control; the moment a company tries to stage-manage the script, screens light up with receipts and side-by-side fact-checks. One-way broadcasts have given way to rolling dialogues where brand voice matters less than brand responsiveness, and generic mass pushes now feel tone-deaf beside context-rich micro-stories inside niche communities.

Put: today's earned media is the scoreboard for a brand's relationship health. If the conversation about you isn't organic, plentiful, and positive, the problem isn't PR; it's that the content engine isn't generating enough value to earn trust in the first place. Build the value, nurture the dialogue, stay transparent, and advocacy will take care of itself.

Connecting Content Strategy to Earned Media

Your content engine, laid out in Chapter 9, was never meant to end at "publish." Its true payoff appears when owned ideas jump the fence, spark unsolicited advocacy, and echo back as earned media. That flywheel starts with a strict value-first mindset. Maria Dobrowski, long-time social media practitioner and consultant, calls this 'unbranding' your content. She states, "When I talk about unbranding, I'm really talking about the discipline of earning trust before you ever even try to sell. In fifteen years of building social strategies for large organizations, I've seen again and again that the brands that succeed in earned media are the ones that resist the urge to lead with logos, taglines, or quick asks. Instead, they create content that delivers real value first. Whether that's education, inspiration, or simply making someone's day a little easier...I tell clients all the time that you have to earn the right to promote, sell, or ask for anything. Social media makes that painfully clear. If your feed is only about you, people tune out. If it's about them; what they care about, what they aspire to, what they need, you then create a flywheel where owned ideas naturally jump the fence and spark advocacy. That is what unbranding is in action."[74]

If the article, video, or tool doesn't solve a real customer problem, educate or entertain them, no amount of outreach will coax the market into talking about it. So, every brief must begin with the audience's need, utility, insight, and entertainment, before a single brand message is introduced. Deliver that value consistently, and you establish a reputation that makes people comfortable attaching their name or handle to yours.

Once value exists, the next lever is strategic narrative integration. Earned mentions work hardest when they reinforce the same story your owned and paid channels tell. Craft a narrative spine, clear themes, distinctive language, and repeatable metaphors, then weave them through articles, webinars, and social snippets so that third-party voices can grab the thread and pull it forward without a brand guideline in sight.

The social web rewards a community-centric approach rather than a broadcast mentality. Stop. Re-read that sentence again. Put it on a sticky note and attach it to your screen. Instead of chasing eyeballs, identify the forums, Discords, LinkedIn groups, or sub-Reddits where your topic already lives. Show up with resources, invite co-creation, and spotlight the most insightful members on your owned channels. When the community feels seen, advocacy becomes self-propelling.

Because advocacy impacts decisions differently at each point, link your plan to journey alignment. Early-stage buyers require social proof and coverage of big ideas; late-stage committees, on the other hand, seek case studies in reputable trade journals or peer reviews on Gartner Peer Insights. Map which voices move which stage, then design content and outreach to ignite those touchpoints precisely when the prospect is listening.

Ultimately, you earn only compound interest when you master cross-channel integration. A podcast shout-out should surface on your site within hours, spark a LinkedIn thread the same day, and feed a paid-retargeting loop the next. Track it end-to-end so you can prove how a single organic mention nudged leads down the funnel or lifted search demand.

Tie these five disciplines back to the content framework you built earlier, and the scaffolding locks together: owned content creates value, earned media amplifies trust, and paid spend pours fuel only where the fire is already catching.

Your marketing operations team should set up process automation to connect the AI social listening to your planning platform and social publishing engine, with checkpoints for human approval based on exceptions.

An example of the tools that can facilitate this is platforms like Sprout Social or Sprinklr, or custom solutions that utilize APIs and language models to handle this.

Next, an automation tool, such as Zapier or Make.com, serves as the bridge between the social listening tool and Notion. The new Notion page contains all the relevant social listening data, and team members can collaborate, add creative briefs, and plan the response. It serves as the single source of truth for the content's status.

Example output: If the AI detects a major brand reputation crisis, an alert is sent to a senior manager. If the AI simply identifies a common topic for evergreen content, the process continues automatically. When the Notion page's status is changed to "Approved," a new action is triggered in Zapier or Make.com. It pulls the finalized copy and assets from Notion and sends them to a social media management tool, such as Sprout Social or Buffer.

Example output: A social post is automatically created and scheduled for publication based on the content in the Notion page. The publishing engine may use AI to further optimize the timing for maximum engagement.

While it's not completely autonomous, human intervention is additive for brand protection and voice integrity.

The Earned Media Ecosystem: Sources and Dynamics

Earned media spans various sources, each with unique characteristics and strategic implications. Understanding these sources helps digital leaders develop targeted approaches to connect content to customers in the moments that matter on the customer journey.

Customer Reviews and Ratings

Online reviews on platforms like Google Reviews, Yelp, Trustpilot, and Amazon provide powerful social proof[75] that directly impacts conversion rates. The credibility of these reviews stems from their perceived independence and specificity; consumers trust detailed accounts of actual customer experiences.

Strategic Connection to Content

Organizations with mature content strategies proactively develop content that addresses common customer questions and concerns, reducing friction points that might lead to negative reviews while encouraging positive experiences that motivate favorable ratings.

Social Media Conversations

Social platforms have become primary arenas for public discussion about brands, ranging from direct mentions to broader conversations where brands are referenced. The immediacy and visibility of these conversations make them particularly influential in shaping brand perception.

Strategic Connection to Content

Effective content strategies include developing "talk triggers[76]", distinctive elements designed to spark social conversation. These triggers provide audiences with compelling reasons to mention the brand authentically, rather than simply resharing branded content.

Influencer and Creator Relationships

The rise of social media has established new types of trusted authorities whose opinions greatly influence their audiences. While many influencer relationships involve paid elements, the most impactful results happen when influencers genuinely support brands, they truly believe in. More and more, it's not the influencer with millions of followers around the globe that makes the biggest impact; it's localized, peer-influencers that create a more meaningful connection. That said, if Oprah reaches out to you with an implied endorsement, don't pass it up.

Strategic Connection to Content

Advanced content strategies prioritize co-creating with influencers over simply paying for promotion. By collaborating with influential voices in content development, organizations foster more authentic advocacy opportunities. Imagine the power of co-creating not just content but products and services that are, in turn, amplified in your brand-owned media ecosystem.

Media Coverage and Expert Recognition

Traditional and digital media outlets continue to build credibility through their editorial coverage. Earned mentions in reputable publications provide third-party validation that paid advertising cannot match.

Strategic Connection to Content

Organizations with advanced content strategies create thought leadership programs that position key experts as valuable resources for media outlets, generating ongoing opportunities for earned coverage beyond traditional news events.

User-Generated Content

Consumer-created content featuring brands, ranging from unboxing videos to product demonstrations and creative interpretations of brand elements, represents one of the most potent forms of earned media, as it combines authentic testimony with creative expression.

Strategic Connection to Content

Mature content strategies include creating frameworks and platforms that inspire and showcase user-generated content, making it easier for customers to create and share brand-related content.

Community Discussions and Forums

Online communities organized around shared interests remain powerful channels for earned media. From Reddit threads to industry forums to private groups, these spaces host trusted discussions that significantly influence decisions. These are some of the most powerful tools for B2B brands in the technology space that support each other to solve problems while Salesforce and IBM's of the world parachute in and moderate, turn problems into relationships, and develop into new product features.

Strategic Connection to Content

Effective content strategies involve identifying and supporting relevant communities with genuinely valuable resources rather than promotional interruptions, building credibility that leads to organic advocacy.

By understanding these diverse earned media sources and their connection to content strategy, organizations can develop targeted approaches to cultivating advocacy across the ecosystem.

CASE STUDY

Patagonia vs. Duolingo — Two Paths to Earned Media Mastery

How activism and absurdity each built global reach without paid spend.

Earned media isn't one-size-fits-all. Patagonia and Duolingo show that radically different approaches—one rooted in values, the other in personality—can both generate disproportionate cultural impact.

The Bottleneck

- Patagonia: Outdoor apparel was commoditized, with every brand talking about performance and price. Paid advertising risked being lost in a sea of sameness.
- Duolingo: A language-learning app had little cultural cachet, struggling to compete for attention against entertainment-first platforms.

The Overclock

- Patagonia — Advocacy as Media: Patagonia leaned into activism. From "Don't Buy This Jacket" to suing the U.S. government over protected lands, the brand consistently turned values into headlines. Its "Earth is now our only shareholder" declaration in 2022 redefined purpose marketing.
- Duolingo — Personality as Media: Duolingo leaned into the absurd. On TikTok, its green owl Duo dances, trolls, and riffs on memes with chaotic humor. The owl became a character, not a mascot, turning the brand into an entertainment feed with language learning as the backdrop.

Results

- Patagonia: Billions in earned media value from bold campaigns. A reputation as the gold standard in purpose-driven branding, with loyalty that borders on activism.
- Duolingo: 10M+ TikTok followers, organic reach rivaling entertainment brands, and surging app downloads tied to social virality.

What It Means

Patagonia and Duolingo prove there is no single formula for earned media. One uses conviction to earn headlines and trust; the other uses humor to earn attention and love. Both approaches work because they are authentic to the brand's identity, and because in the digital age, earned media rewards the bold.

Success Signals & Watchouts for Earned Media

In a world where trust is earned, not bought, earned media becomes your credibility engine. But the engine only hums when the strategy is aligned across brand, audience, and intent. You'll know it's working when advocacy spreads authentically from trusted voices and your content gets amplified organically across the ecosystem. The strongest signals of success include increased organic sharing by credible third parties, community-driven amplification beyond your owned channels, and earned mentions that support business objectives such as growth, trust-building, or increased operational efficiency.

Measurement maturity is another tell, shifting away from channel-specific metrics to a more holistic view of strategic impact. And most importantly, optimization isn't reactive or episodic; it's always-on, adjusting for resonance and reach.

But what is as important as what to do is what to avoid. The biggest trap?

Forcing advocacy.

Brands that try to buy loyalty instead of earning it through consistency and relevance often fall flat. Another misstep is treating earned media as siloed or chasing vanity metrics, such as impressions, instead of tying success to measurable business value. Avoid reacting to coverage after it drops; instead, guide your narrative proactively. And remember, you can't control earned media, but you can cultivate the conditions for it to thrive.

The earned media playbook isn't about hype; it's about harnessing momentum that already exists and channeling it toward business impact. When done well, it drives organic growth, strengthens brand equity, and fuels the trust engine that paid and owned channels alone can't buy.

Reinvention Reminder: In today's noisy digital world, earned media is your system's natural heat signature. It's the residual performance signal that shows your message is resonating without needing artificial amplification.

GLOBAL SIGNAL

Hybrid Trust Models

The Earned Media Maturity Matrix highlights the journey from brand-controlled messaging to network-driven advocacy. In low-trust emerging markets, startups leap directly to hybrid models where digital convenience is validated through human relationships.

Signals

- TrueMoney (Cambodia/SEA): Grew into a regional super-app by leveraging 100,000+ local retailer-agents as community advocates. Brand equity came not from campaigns, but from trusted neighbors.
- 4G Capital (Kenya & Uganda): Blended digital finance with face-to-face advocacy for 100,000 SMEs. This "touch-tech" model shows that high-tech + high-touch is a maturity leap, not a contradiction.
- F88 (Vietnam): Combined mobile lending with 200+ branch locations, providing visible trust anchors for millions of loans. Their hybrid strategy shows how physical presence still matters in digital adoption curves.

Takeaway

Earned media in emerging markets thrives on community validation layered over digital. As global consumers grow more skeptical, these trust-first models may prove more scalable than ad-driven reputations.

EARNED MEDIA MATURITY MATRIX

Earned Media Source	Stage 1 Reactive	Stage 2 Organized
Customer Reviews & Ratings	Reviews happen passively; little response.	Basic monitoring, occasional replies.
Social Media Conversations	Respond only when tagged or a crisis emerges.	Social listening tools track mentions and reactive responses.
Influencer & Creator Relationships	Ad hoc, transactional sponsorships.	Paid influencer campaigns run with limited measurement.
Media Coverage & Expert Recognition	Earned mentions occur by chance or through a PR push.	Press releases + media lists; reactive journalist relationships.
User-Generated Content (UGC)	Sporadic, uncontrolled customer posts.	UGC is occasionally shared on brand channels.
Community Discussions & Forums	Absent or unaware of community chatter.	Basic monitoring of key forums (e.g., Reddit).

Stage 3 Integrated	Stage 4 Orchestrated	Stage 5 AI-Enabled Autonomy
Systematic review management; proactive outreach for feedback.	Integrated into CX loops; reviews shape product/content updates.	AI sentiment analysis detects risk/opportunity instantly; auto-personalized responses & product/service adjustments in real time.
Campaigns include designed "talk triggers."	Conversations are proactively seeded, and CX and marketing are integrated into response teams.	AI social listening identifies emerging narratives; generative AI crafts adaptive engagement across platforms in seconds.
Long-term partnerships with trusted voices; co-created campaigns.	Influencers embedded in product/brand storytelling cycles.	AI maps micro-communities; identifies rising voices before they peak and suggests optimal collaborations with authenticity scoring.
Thought leadership content is prepared and pitched systematically.	Dedicated UGC platforms/contests built into experience loops.	AI monitors editorial calendars, recommends expert placement, and generates briefing documents and angles tailored to journalists' interests.
Structured campaigns encourage creation; brand showcases best UGC.	Co-creation and resource sharing with communities; the brand is seen as a trusted participant.	AI curates, elevates, and personalizes UGC to user feeds in real time; detects and amplifies viral trends before they peak.
Community managers engage authentically with trusted groups.	Co-creation and resource sharing with communities; the brand is seen as a trusted participant.	AI detects emerging forums/threads, simulates authentic engagement scenarios, and provides advisors/community hosts with context about these scenarios.

The Future of Earned Media

Shifts in platform behavior, technological acceleration, and evolving consumer trust dynamics are reshaping the future of earned media. One of the most important developments is the convergence of commerce and earned media. Shoppable social posts[77], affiliate content from influencers, and community-led recommendations are increasingly driving awareness and measurable sales, as platforms like TikTok Shop, Instagram Checkout, and Amazon's influencer storefronts are narrowing the distance between recommendation and transaction. Earned media no longer fuels the funnel; it closes it.

AI is also playing a transformative role. Generative AI tools help identify emerging sentiment trends, summarize public opinion, and even craft rapid-response content that can be customized for specific markets or personas. Predictive analytics are enabling brands to anticipate which conversations are likely to gain traction and which voices might drive the next advocacy wave. And AI-powered social listening tools have evolved from binary sentiment analysis to recognizing emotions and context, enabling more accurate and faster calibration.

Verification and trust are also being reimagined. With deepfakes and misinformation on the rise, blockchain-based content verification is gaining traction. Projects like Content Authenticity Initiative[78] (Adobe, NYT, Twitter) and blockchain-enabled identity verification platforms aim to ensure that content comes from verifiable sources and has not been manipulated. This may prove critical as consumer skepticism increases and algorithms become less transparent.

Finally, community-led content creation continues to evolve. Brands are shifting from campaigns to movements, investing in co-creation platforms, shared storytelling frameworks, and fan communities that operate as decentralized brand amplifiers. Duolingo's TikTok success, for example, wasn't driven by top-down brand marketing; instead, a costume-clad owl and community memes led the way.

Turning Trust into Measurable Growth

Earned media is the proof point that your brand is resonating beyond your channels. It's where the value created by your owned media ecosystem (Chapter 10) and the trust it generates are put to the test in the open marketplace of public opinion. When aligned to a coherent brand narrative and supported by disciplined measurement, earned media becomes more than a halo effect; it's a strategic growth driver.

For B2C brands, the emphasis is often on scale, virality, and cultural relevance. The win comes when authentic advocacy breaks through algorithmic noise and creates brand moments that inspire participation, whether that's a trending hashtag, a community challenge, or a wave of UGC that feeds the conversion funnel.

For B2B brands, the levers are different. The most valuable earned media is targeted, credible, and tied to industry authority, such as analyst mentions, trade press coverage, peer-reviewed case studies, or expert endorsements within decision-maker networks. In these markets, reach matters less than influence over the right buying committees at the right point in the cycle.

Across both worlds, AI raises the ceiling. Trained AI models can act as real-time earned media copilots, detecting sentiment shifts, identifying breakout advocates, surfacing the most share-worthy content, and even crafting context-specific, brand-safe responses within minutes. Predictive AI extends that advantage, spotting early signals of advocacy waves or potential crises before they crest. When these systems are connected to your journey maps, they can trigger timely, relevant engagement that compounds trust rather than eroding it.

But speed is nothing without strategy. The earned media frameworks in this chapter, value-first content creation, narrative integration, community alignment, journey-stage targeting, and cross-channel amplification, serve as guardrails, ensuring real-time responses align with the brand voice and business objectives.

Measurement closes the loop. Tracking earned media isn't about counting mentions or likes; it's about linking advocacy to brand metrics (awareness, favorability, consideration, purchase intent) and downstream business outcomes (pipeline velocity, customer lifetime value, market share). In advanced organizations, earned media analytics feed directly into brand health dashboards, providing a living readout of reputation, trust, and cultural relevance.

When owned, earned, and paid media are fully integrated, and AI is deployed to amplify, anticipate, and protect, earned media shifts from a welcome byproduct to a deliberate, measurable driver of growth. It's where trust becomes influence, and influence becomes action.

CHAPTER 12

Paid Media — Strategic Amplification

Think Like a Paid Media Strategist

If owned media is your home field and earned media is the crowd carrying the story into the streets, paid media has always been the express lane, fast, direct, and able to get you exactly where you want to go, if you know how to steer.

But the highways have changed. In the 1980s, choices were simple: a few TV networks, a handful of magazines, maybe outdoor. Today's map is a multi-level interchange of search, social, CTV, retail media, in-game, and influencer networks, each re-routing in real time based on audience behavior, context, and even mood. What once was a billboard is now an adaptive control panel, with messages shifting before a prospect even scrolls.

That's the opportunity, and the pressure.

For the economics crowd, paid media is a case study in market efficiency, featuring auctions, targeting, and ROAS tracked to the decimal. For the C-Suite, portfolio management is under fire: balancing demand capture and brand equity, allocating dollars across volatile attention markets, and ensuring every impression proves its worth.

Next-gen marketing teams already see it differently. They're channel-agnostic, audience-obsessed, and treat paid as a live operating system: plugged into owned and earned media, fueled by customer data, and recalibrated on the fly by AI.

And here's the kicker: Professor Scott Galloway calls it out, traditional agencies are dead, they don't know it yet. The middleman layer of media buying, creative production, and campaign planning is dissolving.

AI doesn't need lunch meetings or 30-day cycles. It bids, swaps, and optimizes in real time.

MASTERY LEARNING OBJECTIVES

- Grasp the strategic role of paid media in your full digital arsenal. Understand how it fuels both short-term performance and long-term brand equity through the Paid Media Hierarchy of Needs.
- Design paid media strategies that align tightly with business goals, balancing precision targeting, creative execution, and seamless integration with content and earned media to accelerate the entire customer journey.
- Deploy advanced measurement systems that go beyond clicks and impressions. Learn to evaluate campaign performance across time horizons, navigate the impact of privacy shifts and AI, and optimize based on what moves the needle.

INDUSTRY INSIGHT

Procter & Gamble — Overclocking the Paid Media Engine

From the world's largest advertiser to a precision-built performance machine.

In 2025, digital video ad spend overtook traditional TV for the first time, capturing nearly 60% of all U.S. TV/video ad dollars. The dominance of the broadcast era is over. P&G saw this shift not as a threat, but as an opportunity to rewire its paid media model for real-time precision and cultural relevance.

Context / Challenge

Fragmented attention, rising acquisition costs, and declining broadcast ROI were eroding the reach and efficiency of traditional ad buys. Legacy campaign cycles couldn't keep pace with platform shifts, cultural trends, and audience micro-fragmentation.

The Velocity Shift

- Insourced Planning & Buying: Cut intermediaries to gain direct control, faster optimization, and unified visibility across campaigns.

- Scaled Programmatic Across Channels: Extended precision targeting beyond display into TV, social, and gaming, from culturally resonant work like Always' *Like a Girl* to immersive branded experiences like the Mr. Clean gaming map on Overwatch.
- Media Mix Recalibration: Shifted budget toward high-performance channels, even doubling down on "old" mediums like radio to reach niche but valuable audiences.
- Data-Driven Segmentation: Built a segmentation playbook to minimize brand cannibalization and ensure every ad dollar grows both market share and brand equity.

Results / Impact

- Increased speed-to-market and reduced inefficiency from fragmented agency/vendor models.
- Achieved cross-platform reach without sacrificing targeting precision.
- Strengthened cultural resonance and contextual fit of campaigns.

STRATEGIC TAKEAWAYS

- Treat paid media as an owned asset, not just a cost center.
- Collapse fragmentation for speed, visibility, and tighter feedback loops.
- Use data-driven segmentation to amplify both performance and brand health, avoiding short-term wins that erode long-term positioning.

REFLECTION

- Are your paid media dollars pulling double duty, capturing demand today and building brand equity for tomorrow?
- Is your paid media strategy integrated across the whole ecosystem, or running in isolation from your content and earned efforts?

- Do you measure what matters, tangible business outcomes in addition to clicks, impressions, or CTRs?
- How often do you optimize your creative, your audience targeting, your channel mix, or are you running on autopilot?

Whether you're shaping the strategy, managing the spend, or optimizing campaigns, mastering paid media isn't optional. In a fragmented, performance-pressured digital economy, it's the difference between linear returns and exponential lift.

Paid Media's Role in the Next Generation Media Engine

Paid media is no longer a megaphone; it's a control panel. It delivers precision at scale, enabling brands to reach the right audience with the right message at the right moment. Unlike earned (organic buzz) or owned (brand-controlled platforms), paid media offers predictable amplification, accelerated experimentation, and total control over narrative timing.

But that control only pays off when it's connected. Paid media is most potent when it amplifies strong content (Chapter 9) and extends organic momentum (Chapter 11). It turns strategy into velocity, fueling acquisition, boosting visibility, and reinforcing positioning at every stage of the journey.

Today's paid landscape is dynamic and multidimensional. Yes, it's still search or banners but now includes programmatic TV, in-game integration, AI-optimized creative, and privacy-first targeting. To stay ahead, marketers need to think like engineers, *building feedback loops, testing relentlessly, and scaling what works.*

Paid Media in the Attention Economy

At its core, paid media operates within what economist Herbert Simon first described as the "attention economy," a marketplace where consumer attention represents the scarce and valuable commodity brands compete to capture[79]. While traditional advertising relied primarily on interruption to gain attention, modern paid media strategies recognize the need to deliver genuine value to earn engagement in an environment where consumers have unprecedented control over their media consumption.

This shift has driven several fundamental changes in the conceptualization of paid media effectiveness.

The Evolution of Paid Media Theory: From Interruption to Value Exchange

Legacy advertising was built on interruption, breaking the flow of entertainment to deliver a message. But in the digital era, attention must be earned. The model has shifted to value exchange, where content, utility, or entertainment is offered in return for engagement. If the ad doesn't deliver value, it gets skipped, blocked, or ignored.

From Mass Messaging to Personalization

The old playbook blasted the same message to everyone. Today, paid media is about precision relevance. Behavioral insights and segmentation strategies power campaigns tailored to individual mindsets, triggers, and intent. The more personalized the experience, the greater the performance lift.

From Exposure to Journey Integration

Paid media can be more than reach and frequency anymore. With hyper-personalized targeting, it impacts the entire customer journey, from awareness to conversion to loyalty. Different formats and placements serve distinct functions at each stage, from discovery to decision.

From Channel Silos to Connected Ecosystems

Channels don't work in isolation; they amplify each other. This media multiplier effect means that integrated cross-channel campaigns (search + social + streaming, for example) deliver outsized returns. Strategy must be ecosystem-first, not channel-by-channel. Modern paid media isn't the evolution of advertising; it's a reinvention. It's engineered, data-powered, personalized, and integrated. And it doesn't interrupt, it adds value.

"Organizations with balanced paid media portfolios that allocate resources across performance and brand building achieve 60% higher long-term ROI compared to those focused solely on short-term metrics."

Navigating the Paid Media Landscape: Formats, Functions, and Fit

Paid media spans a diverse set of tools, each suited to different stages of the customer journey, from building awareness to driving conversions. Understanding how each format is planned, purchased, and optimized is key to unlocking performance.

Display Ads

Planned through media agencies or demand-side platforms (DSPs), display ads are typically purchased programmatically and optimized for impressions and click-through rate (CTR). Best suited for awareness.
Example: Google Display Network campaigns introducing new lifestyle products.

Search Engine Marketing (SEM)

Planned via keyword research, purchased on auction-based platforms like Google Ads, and continuously optimized via A/B testing and Quality Score. Ideal for high-intent phases, such as consideration and conversion.
Example: SaaS companies bidding on product-related search terms.

Social Media Ads

Planned based on audience personas and platform-specific behaviors, purchased through self-serve ad managers (e.g., Meta Ads Manager, LinkedIn Campaign Manager), and optimized using creative testing and lookalike audiences. Great for multi-stage engagement.
Example: Gen Z-targeted TikTok ads driving product discovery.

Influencer Marketing (Paid Partnerships)

Planned through influencer platforms or agencies, negotiated directly or via marketplaces, and optimized by tracking creator performance metrics and engagement quality. Effective during trust-building phases.
Example: Beauty brands using creators to introduce new launches.

Native Advertising

Strategically placed via native ad platforms (like Outbrain or Taboola), purchased programmatically or directly through publishers, and optimized based on time-on-page

and engagement. Strong for brand storytelling in mid-funnel stages.
Example: Sponsored content on financial publications explaining fintech trends.

Affiliate Marketing
Structured through networks (e.g., ShareASale, Rakuten), paid on a cost-per-action (CPA) basis, and optimized by recruiting top performers and refining commission structures. Focuses on conversions.
Example: Tech reviewers monetizing clicks to recommended products.

Video Advertising
Planned based on viewership trends, purchased on platforms like YouTube or programmatic video exchanges, and optimized by tracking view-through rates and audience retention. Strong for top and mid-funnel engagement.
Example: Movie studios promoting new releases with teaser trailers.

Programmatic Advertising
Managed through DSPs, purchased in real-time auctions, and optimized using machine learning for precision targeting and budget allocation. Versatile across the journey.
Example: Retailers retarget customers who abandoned their carts across multiple devices.

Audio Ads & Podcasts
Planned in alignment with listener demographics and content fit, purchased via podcast networks or platforms like Spotify Ads, and optimized by tracking listen-through rates and brand lift studies. Ideal for brand recall.
Example: Health and wellness products sponsoring fitness podcasts.

OOH (Out-of-Home) Digital Placements
Strategically located and timed via geotargeting and behavioral data, purchased through programmatic DOOH platforms, and optimized by layering in mobile retargeting or attribution models, and used for local and mass awareness.
Example: Streaming platforms using real-time artist streaming data to trigger city-specific billboard campaigns.

Reinvention Perspective: Think Beyond Media Spend. Precision planning, signal-rich optimization, and audience-aware placement are the actual levers. The most advanced paid strategies are efficient and engineered for velocity, tailored to the customer's actual journey.

Strategic Opportunity: Mastering the Paid Media Mix

In today's high-stakes digital economy, how you spend your paid media dollars is a marketing decision and a strategic bet on how you plan to grow.

Yet, too many brands approach media allocation as if they're throwing darts in the dark, chasing shiny platforms, copying last quarter's playbook, or spreading their spend across channels without a system. That's not a strategy. That's drift.

The price? Missed audiences. Wasted budget. Slower growth.

By contrast, Architect organizations treat paid media as an integrated performance engine, investing with intention, measuring with discipline, and optimizing with precision. According to recent benchmarks, brands with a strategic paid media allocation framework are twice as likely to outperform their peers in terms of ROI.

It begins by understanding the paid ecosystem not as a pile of disconnected tactics, but as a synchronized system. One must strike a balance between short-term wins and long-term growth.

Navigating the Paid Media Landscape: Formats, Functions, and Fit

While we downplayed the classic funnel in an earlier chapter as outdated, Awareness → Consideration → Conversion still offers a useful mental model. In today's landscape, it's less a straight line and more a network of touchpoints, triggers, and decision loops. Still, it provides a powerful organizing principle when planning your media mix.

Paid media spans a diverse set of tools, each suited to different stages of the customer journey, from building awareness to driving conversions. Understanding how each format is planned, purchased, and optimized is key to unlocking performance.

Integration with Owned and Earned Media

One of the keys to effective and efficient paid media is understanding the impressions already being generated by your owned and earned efforts. Paid doesn't exist in isolation; it amplifies earned and fills gaps in owned. When fueled by data-driven insights (see Chapter 6), paid media becomes a powerful tool for amplification and brand acceleration, targeting the right user at the right stage with the proper signal.

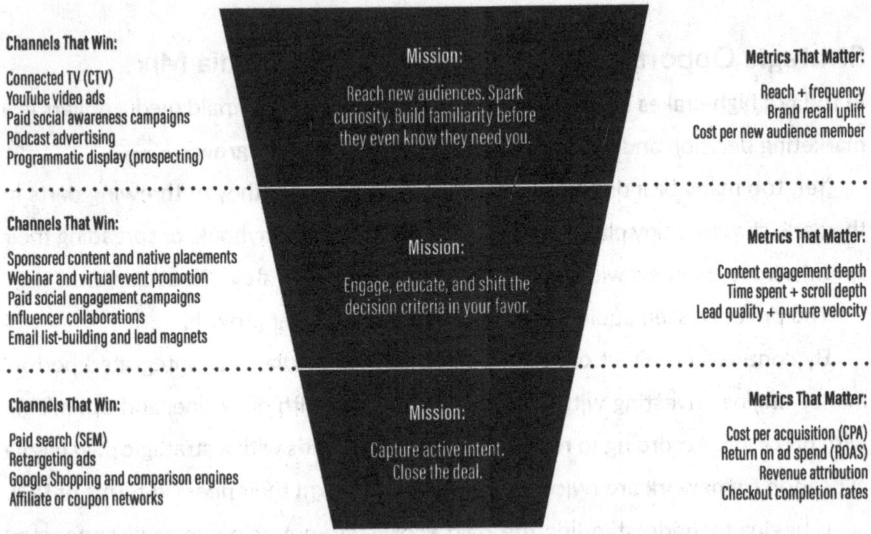

Reinvention Insight: The best-paid strategies aren't driven by spend; they're engineered like performance machines. Tuned to real signals, benchmarked across funnel stages, and constantly recalibrated using integrated analytics.

Beyond the Funnel: Avoiding the Two Biggest Mistakes

Let's be clear: modern buyers don't move neatly from top to bottom. They loop, bounce, research, ghost, reappear, and screenshot you. The funnel is a tool, not a truth. Flip it on its side, add the motives, media consumption, emotions, and actions, and you have the customer journey.

A paid-media plan isn't a static budget line; it's an audio mixing board you keep nudging as the music changes. Young brands still fighting for name recognition need the volume knob on reach and frequency cranked higher, while mature players can spend less on awareness and more on precision retargeting.

If you're launching into a new category, you buy broad, top-of-funnel impressions to frame the problem and claim the language; if you're defending share, the mix tilts toward conversion and loyalty ads that make rivals' offers look derivative.

Competitive intensity also warps the curve: a sleepy market lets you coast on efficient search and affiliate deals, but a hotly contested space demands premium placements and share-of-voice buys to stay visible.

Channel saturation also matters when audiences are inundated with lookalike ads on Instagram. Shifting the budget to emerging formats, such as retail media or podcast host-reads, can help restore cut-through.

Finally, media has to align with how your audience behaves: if decision-makers binge industry newsletters at dawn, that's where you anchor your spend; if they live on TikTok after work, short-form video becomes your prime real estate.

Calibration is the craft of continually re-tuning these dials so that every dollar chases current market physics, not last quarter's assumptions. But too many brands fall into one of two traps:

1 — The Performance Trap

Overloading the bottom of the funnel. Why? Because it's measurable. It "looks" good. However, in the long term, this creates brand erosion and diminishing returns. You're milking the cow but never feeding it.

2 — The Brand Trap

Pumping spend into awareness with no conversion engine behind it. Result? Attention with no outcome. Vanity metrics, no velocity.

The Hedge Fund Mindset

Think of every ad dollar as capital in a day-trading account. You spread it across the full customer-journey spectrum the way an investor balances short-term cash, growth stocks, and moon-shot options: awareness placements act as broad-market ETFs that compound reach, mid-funnel retargeting resembles dividend stocks that pay steady conversions, and experimental formats, say, shoppable livestreams or retail media, are the small-cap bets that could spike tomorrow.

Each slice carries a different risk-to-return profile, so you continually rebalance by pulling budget from under-performing channels, doubling down where cost-per-result is crashing, and keeping a sliver parked in emerging inventory to secure an early advantage.

Real-time optimization is the re-price ticker that runs under your buy, metrics tick, algorithms adjust, creative rotates, ensuring today's ad spend reflects today's market physics, not last quarter's plan. The net result is more than "buying ads"; it's architecting attention with the same discipline a portfolio manager uses to build wealth, diversified, risk-weighted, and constantly scanning for the next edge.

What Success Looks Like

The reinvented paid media system spends wisely and compounds performance by combining online and offline efforts[80], increasing awareness, engagement, and conversion. You'll know it's working when business results show up as more than vanity metrics. Campaigns should produce measurable lifts in revenue, retention, and brand consideration, not just spikes in clicks.

Think about Marriott, which increased ROAS by 25% and cut acquisition costs by 40% through attribution modeling and AI-optimized audience targeting.

But it's more than outcomes, it's about how you get there. Resonance is key. Are the right segments engaging, clicking, and coming back for more? If so, you're fueling flywheel momentum. Channel coordination matters as much: paid search should reinforce social; programmatic should retarget after CTV builds awareness. It's not multi-channel; it's one engine with many pistons.

True paid media maturity comes when your team lives in a test-and-learn mindset. Not quarterly audits, constant optimization. Creative variations, new formats, and tighter targeting are all measured and fed back into the system in real time to dynamically optimize CTA's visuals, product images, and promotional messaging. And while innovation is sexy, you can't sacrifice what's working. Mature programs know how to test new platforms without burning the base.

Mistakes That Drain Momentum (And Budget)

Even seasoned teams get tripped up. Silos are the first killer; running paid social without search insights or deploying display with zero CRM coordination leads to waste. Then there's metric myopia, where teams chase ROAS and overlook long-term brand lift, or obsess over CTR without tying performance to revenue.

Creative is the most underrated multiplier. Even with perfect targeting, bad creative will tank your results. Many teams become stuck in static budgets, failing to reallocate spending in response to real-time signal shifts. Perhaps most damaging: performance tunnel vision. When all your money chases bottom-funnel clicks, you starve your future pipeline.

How to Measure and Optimize Like a Pro

Marriott offers a roadmap. Its media engine utilizes multi-touch attribution to link CTV to both bookings and gross views. Incrementality testing (A/B holdouts) measures real contribution, while lifetime value modeling ensures each acquisition adds to long-term growth. The payoff? Higher conversion rates, better ROAS, and rising brand preference scores.

Across industries, the shift is toward full-funnel metrics, in addition to channel KPIs. It's about understanding how awareness fuels engagement, and how engagement primes intent. Every campaign should be aligned with the customer journey and measured accordingly.

Paid Media 3.0 – Build a Paid Engine, Not a Media Plan

Professor Scott Galloway argues that traditional agencies are already dead; they don't know it yet. The executional layers they once owned—media buying, creative production, and campaign optimization—are collapsing under the weight of automation. The real "nail in the coffin" may come from the rise of Agentic AI: autonomous marketing agents trained on brand data that buy, optimize, and iterate at a cadence that no human team can match.

In this world, paid media isn't just evolving; it's colliding with the Agentic Marketplace, where consumer-side bots filter, negotiate, and transact on behalf of individuals.

The result is a new media battlefield: brand agents pushing optimized offers, consumer AI agents filtering them out, and platforms serving as the infrastructure layer where these invisible negotiations take place.

Here's how that future could look:

Plug-In Marketing Agents

- Brands deploy AI agents trained on proprietary products, performance, and audience data.
- These bots plug directly into exchanges, as well as Google, Meta, Amazon DSP, TikTok, and retail media networks.
- Instead of static campaigns, they continuously rebalance their media mix in real-time.

Auction-Level Advantage

- AI replaces planners negotiating rates.
- Bids are placed in real-time at the lowest possible price that meets the ROI thresholds.
- Efficiency shifts from "buying reach" to precision at the auction scale.

Dynamic Creative Optimization 2.0

- Creative assets (images, CTAs, offers) are generated and swapped instantly, tailored to micro-contexts.
- Pricing, delivery options, and bundles are updated in real-time.
- Guardrails come from dynamic brand guidelines encoded as machine-readable rules.

Closed-Loop Feedback

- Agents continuously monitor impressions, clicks, conversions, and lifetime value, rather than quarterly.
- Underperforming assets vanish automatically; top-performers scale instantly.
- Optimization loops run without human delay.

Decentralized Marketplace of Platforms

- No more "media plans." Agents negotiate across multiple exchanges simultaneously.
- The edge shifts to who has the most sophisticated agent training, not who has the best planner.

CASE STUDY

Nike, Netflix, and Liquid Death — Paid Media Beyond the Feed

How integrated media strategies fuse digital precision with cultural presence.

Paid media used to mean buying GRPs and banner ads. Today's leaders integrate online and offline, influencers and outdoor, sponsorship and promotion into a seamless playbook. Nike, Netflix, and Liquid Death demonstrate three distinct but effective ways to fuse paid with cultural resonance.

The Bottleneck

- Nike: Needed to maintain cultural dominance as digital fragmented and younger audiences tuned out traditional media.
- Netflix: Global streaming growth required awareness beyond algorithms, especially in new markets where the brand wasn't yet household.
- Liquid Death: A challenger brand had no budget for mass media dominance, but needed outsized impact to break into commoditized categories.

The Overclock

- Nike — Full-Spectrum Integration: Nike invests in online video, influencers, outdoor billboards, athlete sponsorships, and retail activations. Paid amplifies organic campaigns like "Dream Crazy" (Colin Kaepernick), with spend spanning from Instagram stories to Times Square takeovers.
- Netflix — Stunts + Sponsorships: Netflix integrates outdoor spectacle (e.g., Stranger Things projections on landmarks), influencer tie-ins, and traditional promotions. Paid spend reinforces binge moments with cultural billboards that double as social content.
- Liquid Death — Paid as Provocation: Instead of broad campaigns, Liquid Death buys strategic placements (sponsorships in extreme sports, irreverent outdoor boards) designed to be photographed, memed, and shared—making every dollar multiply as earned.

Results

- Nike: Consistently ranks among the most effective advertisers globally, blending paid with owned and earned.
- Netflix: Shows routinely dominate cultural conversations thanks to launch-time media blitzes that bridge offline stunts with online buzz.
- Liquid Death: Reached unicorn valuation in under 5 years, with paid stunts driving massive organic spillover.

What It Means

Paid media is no longer siloed, it's the amplifier in a larger ecosystem. Nike proves integration at scale, Netflix shows how spectacle and sponsorship fuel streaming, and Liquid Death demonstrates that even startups can use paid strategically to engineer outsized cultural impact.

The Creative Shift – The Big Idea is Dead

The rapid automation and AI integration in paid digital media mark a fundamental shift in how creative campaigns are conceived, developed, and executed. While traditional methods relied on creating a single, big idea that would take months of production before being launched across various placements, the new approach revolves around generative systems capable of producing thousands of creative variations that are constantly optimized by AI algorithms. This change ensures brand consistency by embedding brand DNA in code, encompassing tone, color, and typography, rather than relying on manual oversight and production controls.

This transformation has significant implications for the entire media ecosystem. For brands, competitive advantage will increasingly come from owning and managing their AI systems and data training processes, thereby raising the strategic importance of AI media buyers to levels comparable to those of chief marketing officers. Successful platforms will be those that create the most agent-friendly buying environments, essentially building "DSPs for bots" that enable smooth automated transactions. Agencies face perhaps the most significant disruption, as their traditional middle-layer roles in execution and media buying become automated.

Those that survive will need to shift either upstream toward brand strategy, data ethics, and growth planning, or downstream toward AI oversight, compliance, and creative innovation. For consumers, this evolution promises more advanced filtering through their own agent bots, which will block manipulative offers and demand more genuine, value-driven brand interactions. This merging of AI and automation in paid media thus changes not just how advertising is created and distributed but fundamentally transforms the power dynamics and value creation throughout the entire marketing landscape.

The Collision Point

Paid media and the agentic marketplace are converging. Brands' agents push optimized content into exchanges. Consumers' agents filter ruthlessly, allowing through only what matches the user's values. The battlefield is no longer a Super Bowl ad or a search results page; its agents are negotiating in real time, invisible to humans, but decisive for commerce.

GLOBAL SIGNAL

Advertising Disrupted by Platform Gravity

The Paid Media Maturity Matrix shows firms evolving from channel stacking to audience orchestration. In emerging markets, the leap is often into platform gravity, where platforms themselves become media channels, bypassing traditional ad networks.

Signals

- TikTok Shop / Shopee Live (Southeast Asia): These commerce platforms are also ad channels. Brands advertise via live personas and short videos, bypassing external ad platforms entirely.
- ShareChat / MX TakaTak (India): Social platforms monetizing via integrated commerce and influencer-led commerce, paid media is native to attention channels.
- JioGames (India): Bundles access with connectivity and content, making platform inventory itself the ad medium.

Takeaway

Paid media in emerging contexts often skips external DSPs and search ads. Instead, marketing is baked into platform operations, placement, content, and conversion happen in the same fabric. Your next ad spend may live inside someone else's ecosystem.

PAID MEDIA MATURITY MATRIX

Domain	Stage 1 Reactive	Stage 2 Organized
Targeting & Audience Intelligence	Basic demographic targeting; reliance on third-party cookies.	Segmented targeting by channel; early contextual ads.
Measurement & Attribution	Last-click metrics dominate.	Multi-touch attribution dashboards; siloed MMM.
Creative & Ad Formats	Static display, banner, and basic video ads.	A/B tested creatives across a few formats.
Channels & Inventory	Linear TV, print, and early digital buys.	Programmatic display/ social with basic targeting.
Next-Gen Immersive	Experimental AR/VR pilots; low adoption.	Occasional branded experiences in AR filters, VR worlds.
Commerce & Shoppable Media	Links to product pages; basic affiliate programs.	Social commerce pilots; influencer integrations.
Data, Privacy & Trust	Minimal compliance; reliance on third-party data.	GDPR/CCPA-compliant processes bolted on.

Stage 3 Integrated	Stage 4 Orchestrated	Stage 5 AI/Autonomous OS
Cross-channel ID graphs unify reach; privacy-first targeting emerges.	Real-time predictive intent signals integrated into campaigns.	AI predicts not just intent but emotional context; edge compute personalizes across devices instantly.
Unified measurement across platforms; incrementality testing.	Attention metrics and edge analytics drive optimization in near real-time.	AI agents automate MMM, fraud detection, and creative rotation; blockchain secures transparency.
Dynamic creative optimization across web, social, and CTV.	Conversational and shoppable ad units orchestrated across ecosystems.	Generative AI produces and optimizes creative content in real-time, tailoring it to micro-segments or individuals.
Expansion to CTV, DOOH, and retail media with closed-loop reporting.	Interactive in-game ads, immersive CTV, and retail off-site expansion.	AI dynamically allocates spend across all channels, generating new inventory in XR/metaverse environments.
Persistent immersive campaigns; virtual placements in games and worlds.	Co-designed 3D spaces with influencers, creators, and brands.	Synthetic influencers, agentic ambassadors, and AI-generated worlds are integrated into persistent metaverse economies.
Shoppable video and CTV; livestream commerce.	Seamless omni-checkout across retail media, social, and CTV.	AI anticipates consumer demand, generates shoppable experiences on the fly, and embeds commerce into any digital surface.
Clean rooms, federated learning, and zero-party data strategies.	Transparent value exchange; authenticated identity graphs.	Decentralized data ownership: blockchain/ Web3 protocols give users control and enable them to monetize their data.

The Precision Engine for Market Momentum

Paid media, done right, is no longer a blunt instrument for blasting messages into the void; it's a precision-tuned growth engine. Whether you're Procter & Gamble moving billions with military-grade efficiency or a local coffee truck turning an influencer spike into a sustained sales surge, the principles are the same: target with intent, adapt in real time, and measure impact against the brand metrics that matter — awareness, engagement, and purchase intent.

The lines between paid, owned, and earned have blurred. Your ad isn't just an impression; it's a trigger for a customer journey touchpoint that can connect directly to owned channels, activate community advocacy, or convert in the moment. AI is accelerating this shift, transforming what used to be quarterly media optimizations into real-time decision-making engines that continuously learn and redeploy budgets toward what's working, before competitors even notice the trendline.

For B2B, this means outflanking bigger incumbents by owning your niche conversations on LinkedIn or targeting precise buyer-intent keywords. For B2C, it's about combining cultural relevance with algorithmic reach, so every dollar works harder than the last. And for everyone, it's about building media agility into your organizational muscle so you can pivot as platforms, formats, and audience behaviors shift.

Paid media isn't just a lever, it's a signal. It shows the market that you're not waiting for demand, you're creating and capturing it in the same breath. And that's the bridge to our next chapter: how to embed this responsiveness into your entire go-to-market strategy, so your campaigns, channels, and sales motions operate like a living system, adaptive, integrated, and always in pursuit of the next growth edge.

SECTION III

The Transmission

Shift gears to apply power to the market at speed.

Power without control burns out the system. This section shows you how to channel intelligence into action, through go-to-market precision, measurement that matters, and agile workflows built for constant adaptation. The goal isn't just to move, it's to shift gears faster than your competition can even find the clutch.

CHAPTER 13

Predictive Go-to-Market Strategy

Think Like a Strategic Digital Leader

Predictive Go-to-Market: The New Leadership Test

The leaders who thrive in today's market aren't just visionaries, they're dynamic sensors. They treat every market signal, customer behavior shift, and competitive move as a data point in a living, breathing strategy. In the *Strategy Reimagined* chapter, we explored how sensing and responding are no longer sequential; instead, they are simultaneous. In GTM, that means designing a system where insights flow directly into execution, and AI accelerates the feedback loop, allowing you to adapt in hours, not quarters.

Imagine if Kodak, instead of defining itself as a "film company," had embraced its broader role as a *capturing memory for life* for consumers and *connecting products to customers* for an industry platform. That single strategic shift could have completely changed its GTM approach:

- Detecting the emerging digital habits of younger customers as early signals rather than fringe behavior.
- Using those insights to pilot new products and services that blurred the line between hardware, software, and cloud storage.
- Building the partnerships, channels, and messaging to compete not just with Fuji, but with the likes of Apple, Google, and Adobe.

Adobe made that leap. It evolved from a static box of software to a living, subscription-based ecosystem, Creative Cloud, which evolves in real-time with customer needs. It didn't just change what it sold; it changed how it went to market, bundling continuous updates, community learning, and AI-powered creation tools into a system that makes switching almost unthinkable.

That's the mindset of a digital-driven, AI-informed GTM.

- Leadership sets the frame, defining the business by the problem it solves, not the product it sells.
- Digital insights map the terrain, quantitative and qualitative signals that uncover where audiences are heading, not just where they've been.
- AI sharpens the response, turning raw data into adaptive campaigns, tailored offers, and optimized resource allocation at speed and scale.

The result? A go-to-market engine that's not just built to launch, it's built to evolve, anticipating the next inflection before your competitors even see it coming.

MASTERY LEARNING OBJECTIVES

- Design go-to-market strategies that unify digital and traditional channels, combining audience insight, platform strengths, and real-world execution into one integrated plan.
- Utilize data-driven segmentation to target the right audiences with the most relevant offers, and link those actions to tangible business outcomes through modern measurement frameworks.
- Create dynamic, continuously improving GTM systems by embedding iterative processes and choosing organizational structures that support speed, alignment, and agility.

INDUSTRY INSIGHT

Oatly — Pouring AI Into an Adaptive GTM Strategy

From oat milk to a $10B IPO by reimagining go-to-market as an always-on growth engine.

Oatly didn't just sell oat milk; it sold a mindset. In a market ruled by dairy giants and soy incumbents, Oatly reframed the game: it wasn't competing in "milk" at all, but in the fast-moving arena of lifestyle alignment, where climate impact, dietary choice, and brand personality mattered as much as taste.

Context / Challenge

Legacy beverage GTM models were static, characterized by significant launches, extensive media coverage, and lengthy shelf reset cycles. That playbook couldn't keep pace with rapidly shifting consumer values, fragmented channels, and supply chain volatility.

The Velocity Shift

- Integrated Experience Design: Blended social storytelling, supermarket sampling, barista partnerships, and outdoor ads into a unified brand presence.
- AI-Powered Targeting: Used predictive audience modeling to identify high-probability conversion zones at the neighborhood level, matching climate-forward messaging to the right people at the right time.
- Real-Time Message Optimization: Combined social listening with retail scan data to fuel AI-driven sentiment analysis, testing copy variants across micro-segments, playful irreverence for urban coffee enthusiasts, and sustainability stats for eco-conscious suburban shoppers.
- Adaptive Operations: Applied AI forecasting to reroute inventory and adjust promotions before stockouts, turning scarcity into a storytelling asset.

Results / Impact

- Scaled from niche Swedish upstart to $10B IPO by 2021.
- Maintained cultural relevance while navigating category competition and operational constraints.
- Built a GTM feedback loop where awareness, trial, and purchase intent were continuously monitored via AI-enhanced marketing mix models.

STRATEGIC TAKEAWAYS

- Reframe the category to compete on lifestyle and values, not just product attributes.
- Connect marketing, sales, and operations into a single adaptive GTM system.
- Treat AI as the central nervous system of your go-to-market, not an add-on tool.

REFLECTION

- How effectively does your organization detect and act on early market signals, are you adapting in real time, or still operating on quarterly or annual cycles?
- Are you defining your business too narrowly around products, or are you framing it around customer problems and lifestyle values that could open new go-to-market pathways?
- Is AI currently an add-on tool in your GTM playbook, or have you embedded it as the central nervous system that links insights, execution, and adaptation at scale?

The Evolution of Go-to-Market Strategy in the Digital Age

Throughout this book, we've explored the components of a comprehensive digital strategy, from digital leadership and business models to content strategy, earned media, and paid amplification. In this final chapter, we combine these elements into an integrated, adaptive go-to-market (GTM) framework that enables organizations to launch effectively and sustain competitive advantage in an increasingly complex digital landscape.

The concept of go-to-market strategy has evolved dramatically in the digital era. What was once a relatively straightforward process of developing a product, establishing distribution channels, and creating marketing campaigns has transformed into a multidimensional, data-driven discipline that requires continuous adaptation. Today's most successful organizations recognize that GTM strategy is not a one-time plan but an ongoing learning, optimization, and evolution system.

As Harvard Business School Professor Thomas Eisenmann notes in his Diamond-Square framework,[81] GTM strategy represents a crucial component within the broader business model, integrally connected to customer value proposition, profit formula, and operational capabilities. But in the digital-first economy, these connections have become more dynamic and interdependent than ever before.

This chapter presents a comprehensive framework for developing, implementing, and continuously evolving a digital-first go-to-market strategy. By integrating the principles and practices explored throughout this book, we provide a roadmap for organizations seeking to build sustainable competitive advantage through intelligent, adaptive approaches to reaching and engaging customers.

Go-to-Market Strategy in Strategic Context

At its core, a go-to-market strategy addresses a fundamental business question: How will we efficiently and effectively reach, engage, and convert our target customers? Meanwhile, the theoretical foundations of modern GTM approaches have undergone significant evolution with the advent of digital transformation.

From Linear to Dynamic Models

Traditional GTM models often followed a linear path from product development through launch and into scaled operations. This approach assumed relatively stable market conditions and customer behaviors, with well-defined product lifecycles and predictable competitive dynamics.

Digital transformation has fundamentally disrupted this model, replacing it with more dynamic frameworks that recognize the continuous nature of market evolution, product development, and customer engagement. Modern GTM strategy operates as Jeffrey Bussgang calls an "experimentation machine,[82]" continuously testing hypotheses, gathering data, and adapting based on real-time insights.

From Channel-First to Customer-First

Old-school GTM began with the channel: How do we get this product out *into the world?* But digital flipped the script. Today, the most effective go-to-market strategies start with one question: How does the customer want to engage?

Power has shifted. As covered in our chapters on earned media and content strategy, customers now have control over how they discover, research, and make decisions. GTM strategy must align with customer-defined journeys, not legacy pipelines or org charts. The growth path begins by understanding those journeys, then reverse-engineering the right touchpoints, content, and channel mix for velocity and agility.

From Campaign-Based to Continuous Engagement

Launch campaigns used to be the main event, big pushes to build buzz, spike awareness, and (hopefully) convert. But in the digital ecosystem, campaigns are just one move in a longer game.

Modern GTM is about sustained engagement, not momentary attention. Customers don't buy on a schedule; they buy when they're ready. That means your strategy needs to be always-on, delivering value across the entire journey, not just during launch week. Think of nurture as flowing, adaptive content, smart retargeting, and owned channels that evolve with the buyer.

From Product Pitch to Value Ecosystem

Digital winners are selling products and building value ecosystems. The shift from selling a "thing" to delivering integrated solutions is at the heart of adaptive GTM. Nike's not only selling shoes, but also offering a community through Nike Run Club, training clubs, and the SNKRS app, along with a virtual coach.

Whether it's a SaaS suite, a connected hardware bundle, or a service layer riding on top of a platform, customers increasingly buy outcomes, not just features. Your

GTM strategy must reflect this, positioning your brand as a gateway to ongoing value rather than a one-time transaction.

What This Means for GTM

These shifts are more than trends; they're the foundation of modern go-to-market strategy:

- Customer-first thinking replaces top-down channel selection
- Continuous engagement trumps one-and-done campaigns
- *Ecosystem value beats standalone feature selling*

They're also the backbone of the adaptive GTM framework you'll build in this chapter.

The Six Pillars of Adaptive Go-to-Market Strategy

To win in a market shaped by constant change, GTM strategy can't be a static playbook; it must be a dynamic system. The Six Pillars of Adaptive Go-to-Market Strategy form the foundation of this system, providing organizations with a structured yet flexible approach for translating insights into execution. This digital-first framework enables teams to transition from reactive marketing to intelligent, orchestrated growth, one that adapts in real-time to shifting customer behavior, emerging technologies, and competitive disruptions.

Pillar 1: Market Intelligence & Audience Understanding

It all starts with knowing the field you're playing on. This pillar fosters a deep understanding of customers and competitors through the use of first-party data, behavioral analytics, digital listening, and contextual insights. Segmentation isn't static; it's continuously validated through engagement signals and decision-making patterns. The goal is to gain a 360-degree view of real customers in real-world conditions, including who they are, what they need, and what drives their purchasing decisions.

Pillar 2: Value Proposition & Messaging Strategy

Once you understand your audience, you must communicate with them. This pillar focuses on creating a differentiated value narrative, one that is scalable across channels, buyer types, and journey stages. Messaging isn't copy alone; it's part of a narrative architecture. It must resonate with decision-makers and influencers, remain flexible across touchpoints, and reinforce your brand voice while evolving through constant testing.

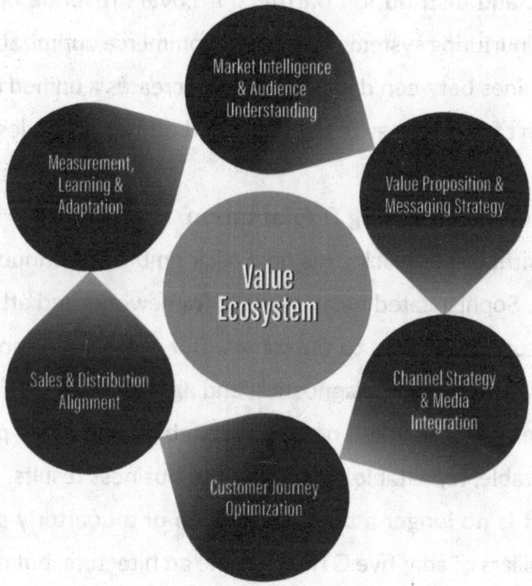

Pillar 3: Channel Strategy & Media Integration

No single channel wins alone. This pillar brings together paid, owned, and earned media into a connected system, each with a role in driving attention, consideration, and action. The strategy goes beyond individual channel tactics, emphasizing orchestration, sequencing, and spend optimization. Innovative GTM teams use this pillar to synchronize their media mix, ensure message coherence, and deliver seamless customer experiences.

Pillar 4: Customer Journey Optimization

Adaptive GTM means designing with the journey in mind, not just the transaction. This pillar maps the end-to-end customer experience, identifying friction points, content gaps, and opportunities for conversion. It includes personalization strategies, retention models, and advocacy activation.

The goal is to optimize both the buyer and the business, creating a seamless flow across acquisition, engagement, and loyalty.

Pillar 5: Sales & Distribution Alignment

Marketing doesn't go to market alone. This pillar ensures deep alignment between marketing, sales, and distribution partners. It covers revenue operations, sales enablement, lead nurturing systems, and digital commerce optimization. When done right, it blurs the lines between departments and creates a unified revenue engine, so customers don't feel like they're being handed off between silos.

Pillar 6: Measurement, Learning & Adaptation

Nothing scales without feedback. This final pillar embeds continuous learning into the GTM engine. Sophisticated measurement frameworks and attribution models allow teams to connect tactics to outcomes. But more importantly, they power experimentation, performance diagnostics, and agile optimization loops. Adaptive GTM strategies evolve in-market, not on a whiteboard, and this pillar makes that evolution measurable, repeatable, and aligned to business results.

Go-to-market is no longer a one-time launch or a quarterly plan; it's a living system. The six pillars of adaptive GTM form the architecture, but maturity is about how these pillars are wired together. At the highest stage, AI transforms GTM into an autonomous operating system[83], sensing markets, testing narratives, orchestrating channels, and optimizing journeys in real-time. This is where go-to-market transitions from being managed to managing itself.

GLOBAL SIGNAL

Data as Distribution

The GTM Maturity Matrix shows firms moving from static segmentation to predictive orchestration. In emerging markets, startups leap straight to predictive, using alternative data and AI as their only viable GTM infrastructure.

Signals

- Tala (Mexico & Kenya): Used 10,000+ smartphone data points per applicant to underwrite millions of unbanked consumers. GTM agility extended from product to hyperlocal targeting, neighborhood by neighborhood.
- Mercado Pago (LatAm): Turned e-commerce payments into credit scoring and lending loops. By embedding finance in Mercado Libre's ecosystem, it created a self-reinforcing GTM model at massive scale.
- Yape (Peru & Bolivia): Built an 80% penetration wallet among young adults, using viral adoption and QR-based micro-loans to become a cultural standard. Growth was powered by predictive peer-to-peer behavior, not campaigns.

Takeaway

In these markets, predictive GTM isn't an advanced stage—it's the starting point. Competitors who wait to evolve into predictive orchestration may find they've already lost the customer.

ADAPTIVE GO-TO-MARKET MATURITY MATRIX

GTM Pillar	Stage 1 Reactive	Stage 2 Organized
1. Market Intelligence & Audience Understanding	Basic demographic research; siloed surveys.	Persona libraries + channel analytics.
2. Value Proposition & Messaging Strategy	One-size-fits-all messaging; static brochures.	Segmented messaging by buyer type/journey stage.
3. Channel Strategy & Media Integration	Disconnected campaigns per channel.	Coordinated media plans; limited cross-channel.
4. Customer Journey Optimization	Transaction-focused; little post-sale engagement.	Journey maps exist, but with static, patchy personalization.
5. Sales & Distribution Alignment	Marketing and sales operate in silos, with handoffs being clunky.	Basic lead sharing, early RevOps.
6. Measurement, Learning & Adaptation	Vanity metrics (impressions, clicks).	Standardized dashboards; some attribution.

Stage 3 Integrated	Stage 4 Orchestrated	Stage 5 AI/Autonomous OS
360° view with unified first-party data; behavioral signals.	Real-time audience intelligence drives segmentation + targeting.	AI agents predict intent, context, and even emotional state across devices; systems adapt instantly.
Narrative architecture connected across touchpoints.	Dynamic testing + optimization of narrative at scale.	Generative AI co-develops messaging in real-time, hyper-personalized by micro-segmentation.
Paid, owned, and earned media synchronized.	Sequenced storytelling + spend optimization across ecosystem.	AI autonomously manages omnichannel spend and creates adaptive content across surfaces.
Integrated acquisition, engagement, retention flows.	Fully personalized journeys optimized with real-time data.	Predictive journeys: AI anticipates needs, intervenes preemptively, and automates loyalty loops.
Integrated revenue engine, shared KPIs.	Seamless digital commerce + unified customer view across partners.	AI dynamically aligns sales, marketing, and distribution, optimizing resource allocation in real-time.
Unified measurement + agile performance diagnostics.	Continuous experimentation + optimization loops.	AI creates self-improving GTM systems that autonomously close feedback loops.

Together, these six pillars enable companies to go beyond launch-day thinking. They provide a foundation for turning digital insight into sustained competitive advantage, aligning owned, earned, and paid efforts under one adaptive system. This framework equips leaders to set a clear direction while creating the conditions for constant refinement, where strategy is not locked in, but dialed in.

What Winning Looks Like: Success Signals for the Architect's GTM

You know your go-to-market engine is overclocked when it moves with the market, not behind it. Your team doesn't wait for trends to settle; it reads signals in real time and pivots quickly. Paid, owned, and earned media don't operate in silos; they work in harmony. The result? A unified customer journey that flows with precision, not friction. Data isn't wallpaper; it fuels action. High-velocity teams don't wait for quarterly reports; they test, learn, and adapt in cycles tight enough to feel like reflexes.

Operational agility is table stakes. Need to reallocate budget mid-month, shift messaging on the fly, or rework your channel mix after a competitor's surprise launch? No problem, momentum stays strong. And the business impact? Crystal clear. Customer acquisition costs decrease, conversions increase, and customer lifetime value extends. This isn't just better marketing; it's a faster, more innovative, and more resilient business.

What Holds Teams Back: Common Failure Modes

Even great strategies crash if execution lags. One of the biggest killers? The strategy execution gap. A perfect GTM deck means nothing if your team can't deploy it with confidence and speed.

Then there's the data deluge. Endless dashboards don't mean you're data-driven; unless you're extracting signal from noise, you're spinning in circles. Add siloed teams into the mix, and you've got a disjointed machine where paid doesn't talk to content, content doesn't sync with performance, and owned assets collect dust while paid media foots the bill.

And let's not forget rigid annual plans. In a market that shifts monthly (or even daily), static GTM frameworks can become a hindrance. Suppose your strategy can't flex, your relevance tanks. Lastly, chasing metrics without meaning, such as CTR, impressions, and ROAS, means nothing if you can't tie them to pipeline, revenue, or retention. Don't optimize noise. Tune for impact.

Overclock Your GTM

Your GTM strategy isn't a launchpad; it's a live system that demands tuning, testing, and torque. Success comes when you treat it like a machine built for adaptive performance. The faster you close the loop between insight and action, the harder it is for competitors to catch up. So make the engine. Wire it with intelligence. And punch it through the gears.

Overclocked Insight: Speed alone doesn't win. Adaptive precision does.

The playbook you're building isn't a one-time launch; it's a living system. When you implement these principles with discipline and speed, you unlock a go-to-market strategy that adapts more quickly, performs more effectively, and delivers a durable competitive edge. Ready to outmaneuver the status quo?

CASE STUDY

HubSpot – Adaptive GTM in Action

How an inbound playbook became a full-stack growth engine.

HubSpot didn't just market differently; they rewired how go-to-market (GTM) works. Starting as an inbound upstart, they scaled into a full-stack CRM by turning GTM from a set of tactics into an adaptive system that learned, compounded, and evolved in real time.

The Challenge

Small and midsize businesses were drowning in spam and cold calls. Legacy CRMs were clunky, sales-driven, and expensive. The market needed a GTM engine built on trust, education, and measurable outcomes.

The Overclock

HubSpot pulsed every move through six GTM pillars:

- **Market Intelligence**: Identified "spam fatigue" early through search data, founder empathy, and live user signals.
- **Value Proposition**: Flipped the funnel – "stop interrupting, start helping." Content became credibility.
- **Channels**: SEO, blogs, free tools, and automation stitched into orchestration long before "omnichannel" went mainstream.
- **Journey Optimization**: Free graders → personalized onboarding → evolving customer paths created a sticky funnel.

- **Sales Alignment**: Consultative, signal-driven selling scaled through freemium, resellers, and partnerships.
- **Measurement & Learning**: From engagement to lifecycle value, constant testing built a GTM flywheel that never slowed.

Think of it as taking a static GTM playbook and upgrading it into a living operating system: self-aware, feedback-fed, and fast enough to stay ahead of customer expectations.

Results

- **Inbound to CRM**: Expanded from a single marketing motion into a complete customer platform.
- **Community as Moat**: HubSpot Academy, INBOUND events, and certifications reinforced the ecosystem.
- **Scalable Trust**: Retention, advocacy, and growth moved in lockstep.

Strategic Signals

- **Education is Acquisition**: Authority built upstream of conversion pays long-term dividends.
- **Systems Beat Plays**: GTM as an adaptive engine compounds impact over time.
- **Community Is Infrastructure**: Users who learn together stay together — and spend together.
- **The Future of Go-to-Market Strategy**: Running Tuned, Not Default

Go-to-market (GTM) is no longer a static roadmap; it's a living system that runs hot, adapts in real-time, and evolves as quickly as customers do. In the high velocity AI era, advantage doesn't come from following playbooks; it comes from tuning precisely, optimizing relentlessly, and upgrading with intent.

The System Is Overheating: Why Your GTM Stack Needs a Complete Reboot

Something fundamental broke in go-to-market strategy around 2023, and most organizations are still running on legacy firmware. The old playbook, segmented campaigns, linear funnels, departmental handoffs, isn't just inefficient anymore; it's actively throttling growth. Meanwhile, a new class of companies has discovered what happens when you rebuild GTM from the ground up, treating it not as a collection of tactics but as an orchestrated operating system.

This isn't about adding more tools to your stack. It's about recognizing that we've entered an era where AI serves as overdrive rather than assistance, where personalization has evolved from segmentation and manual feeds to real-time prediction, and where customer journeys orchestrate themselves dynamically. Content generates and optimizes on the fly, interactions adapt in milliseconds, and what emerges is genuine one-to-one relationships at scale, not because AI was bolted onto existing processes, but because it became the core engine driving everything.

The most sophisticated GTM operations now treat the community as firmware, understanding that sustainable growth comes not from ad spend alone, but from creating experiences that behave like massively multiplayer game environments, where customers naturally co-create, problem-solve, advocate, and amplify. In this model, campaigns don't broadcast messages; they facilitate conversations that scale exponentially. The traditional funnel has flattened into an ecosystem battlefield where competition spans entire platform meshes, where APIs, partnerships, and developer ecosystems matter more than category dominance, and where winners orchestrate value across network nodes instead of trying to control them.

Trust has emerged as the cooling system that prevents the entire apparatus from overheating. Privacy-first design serves as the throughput limiter in an era of disappearing cookies and increasing regulation, making first-party relationships and transparent value exchanges the critical components that enable high-performance systems to run without compromising speed or effectiveness. The highest-velocity teams have discovered the power of unified revenue engines, erasing the walls between marketing, sales, and customer success through shared telemetry, aligned KPIs, and coordinated incentives that transform what was once a relay race into a synchronized operation where customers experience one seamless rhythm instead of three competing silos.

But here's where most organizations hit their thermal limits. Every GTM transformation functions like a system overclock, and the increased performance generates heat that reveals every weak spot in the organizational architecture. The shift from intuition to evidence-based decision-making threatens leaders who've built careers on gut instinct. Channel integration dissolves comfortable silos, triggering territorial conflicts as teams fight to preserve their domains. Faster iteration cycles stress legacy operations, while customer journey orientation cuts directly across established hierarchies. Creative teams fear that personalization at scale will force them to trade quality for quantity, creating resistance at the exact moment when agility becomes most critical.

The brutal reality is that roughly 70% of digital transformation initiatives stall not because the strategy is flawed, but because the organizational system cannot handle the upgrade. Self-interest, misunderstanding, competing value assessments, and change fatigue act like tripped circuit breakers, shutting down progress just when momentum becomes most crucial. The organizations that successfully navigate this transition treat GTM transformation like a complete systems reboot, designing for trust from the foundation up, building shared telemetry across all departments, creating protected spaces for experimentation, and most importantly, anticipating the emotional and cultural heat generated by change while installing the cooling mechanisms before the system overheats.

The ultimate differentiator in this new landscape isn't budget or technology stack, it's organizational capacity. Specifically, cognitive capacity to process complexity, cultural capacity to embrace continuous change, and feedback capacity to learn and adapt at the speed of market evolution. The companies that will dominate the next decade aren't those with the most sophisticated tools, but those that can run their systems hot while maintaining stability and adapting fluidly as the competitive environment shifts around them.

GTM as a Living, Learning System

As you've seen by the examples and frameworks above, in the digital-first era, a go-to-market strategy is no longer a one-time launch plan; it's a living, learning system that combines leadership vision, agile market sensing, and AI-powered precision into a single adaptive engine.

We've seen how brands like Oatly thrive by blending digital precision with real-world reach, activating with intelligence, and staying adaptive in the face of market shifts. These aren't static playbook steps; they're interconnected disciplines that feed one another, turning every campaign into a learning opportunity and every market signal into an action plan.

What separates winners from laggards isn't just creativity or channel mastery. It's the ability to sense change early, adapt in real time, and execute with cross-functional alignment. AI now accelerates that advantage, turning vast streams of customer, competitive, and operational data into insight fast enough to influence decisions *while the opportunity window is still open*.

But here's the truth: even the most elegant GTM strategy is only as good as its feedback loop. Without the right measurement systems in place, you're piloting without instruments and reacting to the surface symptoms instead of diagnosing the underlying drivers. If GTM is the engine, measurement is the dashboard, the system that tells you if you're accelerating toward market leadership or quietly bleeding momentum.

In the next chapter, we'll break down how to design a measurement architecture that goes beyond vanity metrics to track the signals that matter: brand awareness, engagement quality, purchase intent, and lifetime value. You'll see how high-performance organizations integrate AI into their analytics stack, closing the loop between execution, learning, and growth.

Because in the world of a dynamic marketplace, speed without measurement is just motion, and motion without direction won't win you the race.

CHAPTER 14

Measurement — Agile, Orchestrated Analytics

Think Like a Digital Measurement Strategist

In the digital era, the data exhaust from marketing, sales, operations, and supply chains has become the company's most underleveraged asset. Every ad click, loyalty program enrollment, email open, SMS opt-in, e-commerce checkout, and doorstep delivery leave behind a breadcrumb of intent and behavior. This isn't just marketing intelligence; it's the raw material for a fully integrated growth and efficiency engine.

On the front end, brands now have the unprecedented ability to close the loop between paid media, owned channels, and actual purchase behavior, tying campaign spend directly to first-party data streams from loyalty programs, customer profiles, and post-purchase feedback. On the back end, real-time logistics feeds, IoT sensors, and supplier data integrations create continuous visibility into inventory health, shipping performance, and production capacity.

The magic happens when these streams converge into a unified measurement system, supercharged by AI. Today, machine learning models can detect anomalies in ad performance within minutes, flag supply chain bottlenecks before they become crises, and recommend micro-adjustments to pricing, inventory allocation, or campaign targeting in real time. As these systems mature, they're evolving toward agentic autonomy, operational AI agents that don't just report the news, but take the wheel: shifting budgets between channels mid-campaign, re-routing deliveries to meet service-level agreements, or dynamically re-prioritizing product manufacturing based on live demand signals.

This is a measurement transformed, from a quarterly reporting ritual into a strategic nervous system that senses, decides, and acts before the competition even sees the change coming. The brands that master this shift won't just react faster; they'll operate at a higher frequency, where every decision compounds into advantage.

MASTERY LEARNING OBJECTIVES

- Learn how to design comprehensive frameworks that connect strategic objectives with KPIs, apply multi-touch attribution, and evaluate the effectiveness of marketing activities across the customer journey.
- Master the design and implementation of test-and-learn systems, including A/B testing and iterative feedback loops, to drive continuous improvement across channels, campaigns, and experiences.
- Gain the ability to communicate insights clearly via compelling data visualization while assessing and selecting the proper measurement technologies for your business model and operational context.

INDUSTRY INSIGHT

Domino's, Turning Data Into Dough

From "worst pizza ever" to the gold standard for digital transformation in QSR.

In 2009, Domino's was on life support. Customer reviews were brutal ("tastes like cardboard"), the stock hovered near $3, and analysts were preparing its obituary. Instead of hiding, Domino's did the unthinkable: it admitted the pizza was bad, publicly, and made fixing it the first chapter of a complete, data-fueled reinvention.

Context / Challenge

The brand's turnaround wasn't just about better dough or toppings. Dominoes realized it wasn't in the pizza business, but the convenience, technology, and data business. Every call, click, and cold delivery was a data point to capture, analyze, and act on.

The Velocity Shift

- Built a Real-Time Feedback Loop: Transformed every customer interaction into operational intelligence, from abandoned carts to delivery arrival times.
- Pizza Tracker as CX + Ops Engine: What looked like a simple progress bar doubled as a transparency play and a real-time process optimization tool.
- Predictive Logistics: Routing algorithms integrated traffic, weather, and historical performance to optimize delivery speed and staffing.
- Omni-Channel Ordering: Expanded ordering into voice assistants, smart TVs, and social platforms, each adding unique behavioral insights.
- Culture of Testing: Treated menu updates, store layouts, and promotions as live experiments with immediate data feedback.

Results / Impact

- By 2020, 70%+ of U.S. orders came through digital channels.
- Stock price surged from ~$3 to $400+.
- Moved from industry laggard to leader in customer satisfaction.
- Built a competitive moat through a self-improving operational system driven by measurement, not just marketing.

STRATEGIC TAKEAWAYS

- Treat measurement as a competitive weapon, not a quarterly report.
- Reframe your category, Domino's became a data company that sold pizza.
- Build feedback loops where every order, interaction, and delay makes the system smarter.
- Cultural shift is key: decisions driven by testing and insight, not hunches.

REFLECTION

- Are your attribution models providing insights or causing inertia?
- Do you understand your customer's entire journey, or just their last click?
- Are your teams working with real-time feedback, or only analyzing results after the campaign?
- Can you link marketing investments to incremental value, not just activity?

What Measurement Does (If You Let It)

High-performance measurement has one job: turn noise into knowledge, and knowledge into acceleration. That requires a unified approach across three dimensions:

1. Attribution & Causality: Decoding What Moves the Needle

The primary goal of any measurement system is attribution: determining which inputs lead to specific outcomes. However, modern teams don't only seek correlation; they want to establish causality.

Attribution models have evolved from simple single-touch approaches, which are quick and dirty first — or last-click models suitable for post-mortems but inadequate for multi-step journeys, into sophisticated multi-touch systems that assign credit across touchpoints using linear, time-decay, or U-shaped algorithms. These offer better fidelity but still stay surface-level.

The real breakthrough comes with algorithmic attribution, where machine learning builds influence models in real time, eliminating guesswork in favor of weighted impact based on actual conversion behavior. The holy grail is unified attribution, which combines online and offline, paid and organic, brand and behavioral data into a single, synchronized model.

But attribution without experimentation is like building a car and never taking it for a drive. That's where causal methods become critical. A/B testing isolates variables and compares cohorts to learn what works with surgical precision. Incrementality testing separates signal from background noise to discover the actual value behind your investment. Marketing Mix Modeling utilizes historical data to quantify the impact of various inputs on macro metrics, making it an ideal tool for long-range planning and budgeting.

The shift here is critical: stop measuring what's easy. Start proving what matters.

2. Customer Journey Intelligence: Mapping the GTM Flow in Real Time

The second dimension of measurement isn't about inputs; it's about the customer's path. Where did they come from? What slowed them down? What pushed them forward?

Legacy analytics view touchpoints as isolated events, but real journeys are multi-threaded and ongoing. Modern measurement captures the full complexity through journey analytics that follow decision paths across campaigns, channels, and devices while identifying drop-off points and revealing non-linear patterns.

Cross-channel and cross-device synchronization links behaviors across mobile, desktop, retail, and more, creating a single, unified view of each person, even if they use five devices. Instead of merely measuring conversion, lifetime value assesses the worth of long-term relationships, generating compounding returns rather than just tracking clicks. Momentum metrics monitor progress and spot where prospects stall, fuel content, offers, and user experience improvements that move them forward.

This isn't about tracking pixels. It's about understanding emotional motion across the funnel.

3. Operational Optimization: Speed, Precision, and Feedback at Scale

Measurement doesn't stop at the customer edge. It loops back into the org itself. Modern GTM teams need real-time system readouts to answer: Are we operating at full throttle? Or are we heat-locked by our processes?

Beyond standard efficiency metrics like ROI, CPA, ROAS, and CAC, you need to measure the cost of delays, misfires, and manual workarounds. Agility and cycle time matter. How fast can your team move from insight to action? Lag here kills growth. Execution requires auditing creative precision, tech delivery, and customer experience gaps, because good strategy dies on bad ops. Even capability development is measurable: track how well your team is evolving through training, tooling, and system maturity improvements.

Your GTM engine is only as good as the feedback loop that fuels it, the faster and more precise your loop, the more orchestrated your performance.

Build the Loop Before You Launch

Measurement isn't a post-mortem. It's not the report you make after the quarter ends. It's the guidance system you need before you hit scale.

Strategic GTM teams use measurement to test at the edge, tune in the middle, and translate outcomes into upgrades at every level. The future isn't about reporting what happened; it's about shaping what will happen. It's about staying informed about current events and knowing what to do next.

The Integrated Measurement Ecosystem

In a world where GTM speed is everything, measurement is your telemetry. It's not a dashboard; it's your decision engine. This high-performance framework has five interconnected modules designed to turn raw data into real acceleration:

1. Business Alignment + Strategic KPIs

Connect what you track to what you're trying to win. Measurement only matters when it drives outcomes, starting with a tight linkage between business goals and marketing KPIs.

First, define how marketing powers core business drivers, revenue, margin, and market share, then translate those into specific, trackable objectives with benchmarks based on past performance. Build a tiered KPI stack that encompasses growth metrics, including acquisition, LTV, and market penetration; efficiency measures, such as CAC, ROAS, and MER; experience indicators, like NPS, CSAT, and retention rates; and brand health, which tracks awareness, preference, and perception.

Cross-functional syncs are non-negotiable. Marketing, sales, product, and execs need shared definitions, unified reporting, and a rhythm of review that keeps KPIs aligned to strategy.

Insight: Metrics aren't the goal. Movement is.

2. Attribution + Journey Analytics

Figure out who touched what, and what moved the needle. Today's customer journey is multi-threaded and non-linear. Attribution isn't about credit, it's about clarity.

Start your attribution stack with rule-based models, such as first-click or last-click, and then evolve into machine-learned weighting. Layer in algorithmic and unified models to bridge online/offline connections and link real behavior to real value.

For journey analytics, map paths, identify drop-off points, and monitor velocity by segment, while leveraging identity resolution to build unified customer views across devices and channels. Track how different sequences and touchpoints influence both conversion and LTV. Attribution gives you correlation. Journey analytics adds the context.

3. Experimentation + Incrementality

Prove what works. Kill what doesn't. Fast.

Attribution tells you what happened. Testing tells you what matters. Together, they build a causality engine. Build a test-and-learn system with controlled A/B and multivariate tests backed by statistical rigor. Utilize geo – and audience-based holdouts to isolate incremental lift, track channel-level incrementality, and continually refresh your benchmarks. Leverage Marketing Mix Modeling when you need macro visibility for seasonal trends, offline media, and market forces, or when you're optimizing spend across multiple levers using historical data as your guide. Attribution is good. Incrementality is better.

A feedback loop that proves causality? That's next level.

4. Channel-Specific Analytics

Every channel has its own language. Speak it fluently. Integrated views are critical, but channels still need tailored diagnostics. Treat each like a subsystem in your GTM engine.

Owned Media requires tracking site pathing and conversions alongside UX drop-offs, app retention, cohort engagement, email open-to-click-to-convert flows, content consumption depth, and SEO lift. Paid Media requires monitoring of search CPC and quality scores, including intent density, display viewability, and attention metrics. Additionally, it involves tracking social engagement quality with assisted conversions, video completion rates, and lift metrics.

Earned Media involves tracking social buzz through mentions, sentiment, and share of voice; influencer reach, trust, and downstream action; review volume, tone, and impact; as well as PR coverage value and brand penetration. Sales Channels require e-commerce cart flow and AOV monitoring, including bounce analysis, retail store conversion, cross-channel effects, direct lead quality, win rates, partner activation, and revenue influence tracking. Channel data feeds tactical action. Roll-ups feed strategic vision.

5. Data Integration + Activation

If you can't act on the insight, you're just reporting noise. Data has no value unless it drives action. Integration and activation close the loop. Set up infrastructure with a CDP or data lake house to connect clean, high-quality inputs while enforcing governance and privacy compliance. Garbage in means throttle later.

Build an insight layer that transforms analytics into stories through visualizations, summaries, and relevance filters, prioritizing insights by impact rather than novelty and tracking who is using what. Create an activation engine that feeds insights directly into campaigns, customer experience tweaks, and operational shifts, automating where possible and monitoring implementation and results. Build a living knowledge base where insights don't get lost in decks. Reporting is in the past tense. Activation is where you create future wins.

The next-generation GTM system relies on measurement as telemetry, not reporting. It's how you sense turbulence, gauge performance, and decide where to accelerate. This matrix maps the progression from siloed dashboards to an autonomous measurement engine, one that not only tracks the business but also actively tunes it in real-time.

GLOBAL SIGNAL

Attribution Built for Which Didn't Exist

While mature firms climb from last-touch to multi-touch to AI-driven attribution, in many emerging markets, startups start with attribution built for environments where conventional tracking fails. They must design measurement systems that work across offline, mobile, and fragmented networks.

Signals

- AppsFlyer / Adjust / Singular (global but non-US origin): Though not "emerging market" startups per se, these attribution platforms were built for mobile-first, cross-device, cross-market complexity. Many product-led users in emerging markets embed these tools from Day 1.
- Local adtech players in India / Southeast Asia / Latin America: Some have built hybrid attribution models combining QR scans, SMS-based tracking, mobile signals, and offline validation to close attribution loops.
- Commerce platform-to-ad platform loops in Asia / Africa: Platforms that own both ad + commerce (e.g. TikTok Shop) can internally close attribution loops with zero reliance on external cookies or cross-site tracking.

Takeaway

In many markets, the first marketing measurement systems must anticipate imperfect connectivity, offline conversions, and identity gaps. The defensible measurement architecture will be the one that can stitch digital and physical signals before privacy restrictions bite.

Module	Stage 1 Basic Reporting	Stage 2 Functional Dashboards	Stage 3 Integrated Analytics	Stage 4 Predictive & Incremental	Stage 5 Autonomous Activation
1. Business Alignment + KPIs	Vanity metrics (clicks, impressions); limited link to business outcomes	Departmental KPIs (marketing vs. sales separate); basic revenue linkage	Cross-functional KPIs tied to growth + efficiency; shared dashboards	KPIs tied to lifecycle value, margin impact, and brand health	Self-adjusting KPI systems with AI benchmarking + exec-level telemetry
2. Attribution + Journey Analytics	Last click / siloed credit	Rule-based attribution (first click, time decay); basic funnel views	Algorithmic models + identity resolution; journey mapping across devices	Unified online/offline attribution + journey velocity tracking	AI-driven attribution weighting + real-time journey re-routing
3. Experimentation + Incrementality	Ad hoc A/B tests, often tactical	Structured A/B testing; limited lift studies	Test-and-learn culture with geo/ audience holdouts + MMM	Continuous incrementality tracking across channels + spend optimization	Always-on causality engine; AI designs and retires experiments automatically
4. Channel-Specific Analytics	Native platform reports (Google Ads, FB Ads, CRM exports)	Channel dashboards; tactical optimizations	Cross-channel visibility with tailored diagnostics per subsystem	Channel roll-ups tied to business impact + cross-channel synergy	Predictive, AI-driven optimization per channel + systemwide
5. Data Integration + Activation	Fragmented data sources; siloed spread-sheets	Partial integration; BI tools connect some sources	CDP/lakehouse with governance + unified views	Insights fed into GTM decision loops + automation triggers	Autonomous activation: AI pushes insights directly into campaigns, CX, and ops

Turn Measurement into Momentum

These five components above create a closed-loop measurement system that not only informs you of what happened but also enables you to move faster, make smarter decisions, and scale more smoothly.

The real breakthrough comes with actionable intelligence that doesn't sit in decks but sparks decisions, fuels playbooks, and prompts tactical pivots in real time. This fosters an optimization culture where testing, tuning, and tweaking are part of the routine, as if your team runs like a feedback loop rather than a reporting factory. At peak performance, measurement reaches strategic influence, shaping not only marketing but also product, CX, and even executive priorities, earning a seat at the table rather than just delivering side reports.

Don't Sub-Optimize Measurement Performance

Even innovative teams crash their telemetry. The most common measurement system killers start with metric overload; more isn't better, and if your team's tracking everything, they're focusing on nothing. Prioritize what moves the business.

Tool obsession follows close behind, where teams forget that tools are pipes, not strategy. It's not about the platform you use, but rather the insights you extract and how quickly you act on them.

Analysis paralysis leads to an endless stream of data with no decisions made. If you're staring at dashboards but not shipping improvements, your system's stuck in neutral. Channel silos exacerbate the problem by measuring in isolation, leading to GTM latency.

If you can't see cross-channel effects, you're flying blind in a multi-touch world. Finally, the perfect attribution chase becomes a trap where teams forget that attribution is a model, not a miracle.

Don't wait for 100% certainty to make 80% better moves.

CASE STUDY

Caesars vs. Fortnite — Measurement as the Game Itself

How two different gaming empires mastered real-time insights to drive growth.

Casinos and video games look worlds apart. But Caesars Entertainment and Epic Games' Fortnite share the same strategic engine: measurement. Both operate in high-velocity environments where real-time telemetry doesn't just inform decisions, it is the business model.

The Bottleneck

- Caesars: Casino loyalty once depended on blunt offers, comped buffets, generic coupons, or mailed promotions. Engagement lagged, and high-value players churned undetected.
- Fortnite: In traditional game development, new titles shipped every few years, with limited live feedback. Publishers risked investing hundreds of millions in features that missed cultural moments.

The Overclock

- Caesars — Always-On Loyalty:
- Caesars Rewards integrates data from hotel stays, slot play, dining, and its mobile app.
- Algorithms push real-time offers: a free drink, bonus chips, or show tickets the moment activity dips.
- Cross-channel measurement links digital gambling with in-property play, turning every interaction into a retention opportunity.
- Fortnite — Live Ops at Scale:
- Every action (kills, skins purchased, drop zones chosen) feeds into Epic's analytics fabric.
- Live events (Travis Scott concert, Star Wars tie-ins) are tested, optimized, and monetized in real time.
- Continuous A/B testing drives updates: underused weapons are retired, popular modes amplified, microtransactions promoted dynamically.

Results

- Caesars: Largest casino loyalty program globally (65M+ members), billions in incremental revenue through real-time personalization.
- Fortnite: Over 400M registered players, generating $6B+ lifetime revenue, with in-game measurement directly informing what stays, what goes, and what sells.

What It Means

Whether in Las Vegas or the metaverse, measurement is the heartbeat of modern business. Caesars proves it can turn bricks-and-mortar loyalty into an insights flywheel; Fortnite shows how digital-native platforms scale culture through constant telemetry. Together, they reveal that in an agile enterprise, measurement isn't reporting, it's the game itself.

The Future of Measurement

As we look toward the future, several key trends will shape the evolution of marketing measurements across organizations worldwide.

Privacy-First Measurement Approaches

The tightening of privacy regulations and evolving consumer expectations are driving fundamental changes in how organizations approach measurement. Modern measurement systems must develop consent-based analytics that function effectively within increasingly strict consent requirements, moving beyond traditional tracking methods to respect user privacy preferences. Organizations are creating sophisticated modeling approaches that derive meaningful insights from aggregate data rather than relying on individual-level tracking, which represents a significant shift in analytical methodology.

The emphasis on first-party data activation has become paramount, with measurement capabilities now centered around authenticated, permission-based customer relationships rather than third-party data sources. Advanced privacy-preserving technologies are being implemented across the industry, including federated learning, differential privacy, and data clean rooms that protect individual privacy while still enabling valuable analytics. Organizations that successfully develop these privacy-centric measurement capabilities will gain a significant competitive advantage as the regulatory landscape continues to evolve and consumer privacy expectations become more stringent.

AI-Powered Measurement and Optimization

Artificial intelligence is fundamentally transforming how organizations analyze data and generate actionable insights from their marketing efforts. AI systems now provide automated insight discovery, autonomously identifying significant patterns, anomalies, and opportunities without requiring analyst intervention, dramatically reducing the time between data collection and actionable insights. Predictive optimization through machine learning models enables organizations to forecast future performance and proactively optimize marketing investments, rather than simply reacting to historical results.

The development of natural language interfaces for analytics systems enables marketers to ask questions in their natural language rather than building complex queries, democratizing access to data insights across organizations. Prescriptive analytics represent the next evolution, with advanced systems that not only identify what is happening but also recommend specific actions to improve performance. These AI-powered capabilities democratize data access while dramatically accelerating the speed and sophistication of marketing optimization across all organizational levels.

Unified Measurement Across Physical and Digital

The boundaries between physical and digital experiences continue to blur, requiring increasingly sophisticated measurement approaches that span multiple touchpoints and environments. Online-to-offline integration has become essential, with comprehensive systems connecting digital marketing activities to physical world behaviors and transactions, providing a complete view of customer interactions.

Connected experience measurement now spans web, mobile, IoT, voice, and physical touchpoints to create unified customer journey views that reflect the true complexity of modern consumer behavior. Location analytics provide sophisticated approaches to understanding how physical movement and context influence marketing effectiveness, while new frameworks for measuring engagement and impact in augmented and virtual reality environments are emerging as these technologies become more prevalent. Organizations that successfully build unified measurement capabilities will gain significant advantages as customer journeys increasingly span multiple environments and touchpoints.

Real-Time Intelligence and Activation

The speed of measurement and optimization continues to increase rapidly across all marketing functions. Continuous measurement methods enable organizations to transition from periodic reporting to always-on analytics, providing real-time visibility into performance and facilitating faster decision-making and optimization. Automated optimization systems can now automatically adjust marketing parameters based on real-time performance signals, eliminating the need for human input and resulting in more responsive and efficient campaigns.

Instant testing platforms enable organizations to implement and evaluate tests in real-time, rather than waiting for complete campaign cycles, which significantly reduces the time required for optimization. Predictive alert systems provide proactive notifications that identify potential issues before they significantly impact performance, allowing for preventive rather than reactive management. This acceleration in measurement and response creates substantial advantages for organizations that can implement and act on insights faster than their competitors.

Ecosystem Measurement Beyond Owned Touchpoints

Modern measurement is expanding beyond controlled touchpoints to encompass broader digital and physical ecosystems that influence customer behavior. Partner experience analytics now measure how experiences delivered through partners and third parties influence overall customer perception and behavior, providing insights into the full ecosystem impact.

Community impact assessment evaluates how brand communities and user-generated content drive business outcomes beyond direct marketing activities, recognizing the increasing importance of organic brand advocacy.

Ecosystem influence modeling[84] enables organizations to understand how participation in broader digital ecosystems impacts the discovery, consideration, and conversion processes. Cross-brand journey analysis measures how customer experiences with complementary brands influence overall category behavior and brand preference, providing insights into the interconnected nature of modern consumer decision-making. This expanded measurement view offers a more comprehensive understanding of how customers make decisions in increasingly complex digital environments.

Attribution Models: Assigning Credit to Marketing Touchpoints

Attribution models serve as the foundation for understanding which channels, campaigns, and interactions truly drive conversions, helping marketers make informed decisions about resource allocation and optimization strategies.

First-click attribution is most effective for awareness campaigns and new customer acquisition efforts, as it credits the initial touchpoint that introduces a customer to the brand. However, this model has significant limitations as it completely ignores mid-funnel and bottom-funnel impacts that may be crucial for conversion.

Last-click attribution proves most effective for direct response campaigns and e-commerce tracking, as it gives full credit to the final interaction that precedes conversion. However, it tends to overemphasize final interactions while undervaluing the customer journey leading up to conversion.

Multi-touch attribution provides a more sophisticated approach for complex customer journeys, particularly in B2B environments and high-value sales processes, though it requires advanced attribution tools and technical implementation. View-through conversions offer valuable insights for display, video, connected TV, and brand awareness campaigns by tracking users who saw an ad but didn't immediately click. However, they provide no direct proof of causality between exposure and conversion.

Incrementality testing represents the gold standard for proving actual campaign impact by comparing exposed versus non-exposed audiences, though it requires carefully designed holdout groups and controlled testing environments. A/B testing excels at creative and conversion rate optimization by comparing different versions of marketing elements but typically provides only short-term insights rather than long-term strategic guidance.

Cross-media optimization proves essential for multi-channel campaigns that span online and offline touchpoints, although it requires sophisticated multi-source data integration capabilities. Marketing Mix Modeling offers valuable insights for long-term budgeting and understanding overall channel impact through historical data analysis. However, it tends to be data-intensive and provides fewer real-time actionable insights. The most effective approach typically involves a hybrid model that combines multiple methodologies to provide a holistic view of digital marketing's true impact.

Experimentation & Causal Testing: Evaluating Marketing Effectiveness

A/B testing, also known as split testing, compares two versions of marketing elements, such as ads, landing pages, emails, or calls-to-action, to determine which one performs better. This methodology is most effective for optimizing creative elements, messaging, landing pages, CTAs, and subject lines, with key performance indicators including conversion rate, click-through rate, and bounce rate.

Incrementality testing takes a more sophisticated approach by determining whether a campaign drives incremental conversions through careful comparison of exposed versus non-exposed audiences. This method proves particularly valuable for demonstrating the causal impact of paid media campaigns, with key metrics including incremental lift, conversion rate, and cost per incremental conversion.

Cross-media optimization assesses the interplay between various channels to drive overall campaign performance, making it particularly suitable for multi-channel campaigns that span television, digital, social, and out-of-home advertising. The key performance indicators for this approach include ROI by channel, media efficiency ratio, and blended return on ad spend.

Marketing Mix Modeling uses historical sales and marketing data to determine the long-term impact of various marketing channels, making it particularly valuable for budget allocation decisions across paid, organic, and offline media. This approach focuses on marketing ROI, contribution margin, and cost per sale as primary metrics of success.

Measurement Metrics & KPIs by Channel

Email Marketing Performance

Email marketing remains one of the most cost-effective digital marketing channels, making accurate performance measurements essential for maintaining high engagement and deliverability rates. Open rate measures the percentage of recipients who open an email, serving as a primary indicator of subject line effectiveness and initial audience engagement. Click-through rate tracks the percentage of users who click on links within an email, providing insights into content engagement and the effectiveness of calls to action.

Conversion rate represents the percentage of email recipients who complete a desired action, such as making a purchase or signing up for a service, directly measuring the email's effectiveness in driving business outcomes. The bounce rate indicates the percentage of emails that fail to reach recipients, serving as an essential indicator of email list health and potential delivery issues that need to be addressed. The unsubscribe rate measures the percentage of recipients who opt out of future communications, providing valuable feedback on the relevance of content and the impact of email frequency.

Revenue per email calculates the total revenue generated divided by the number of emails sent, offering a direct measure of campaign profitability and return on investment. For example, a fitness apparel brand successfully optimized its email strategy by conducting A/B tests on subject lines, ultimately increasing open rates from 18% to 26%. This demonstrates the significant impact of strategic testing on email performance.

SMS Marketing Effectiveness

SMS marketing delivers highly effective engagement for promotions, reminders, and urgent communications, though its performance requires careful measurement due to the direct and personal nature of the channel. Delivery rate measures the percentage of SMS messages that are successfully delivered to recipients, ensuring that messages reach their intended audience and identifying potential technical issues with carrier delivery.

The open rate for SMS indicates the percentage of recipients who open the message, although this metric can be challenging to track accurately compared to email. The click-through rate measures user engagement by tracking the percentage of recipients who click on links included in SMS messages, providing valuable insights into the effectiveness of messages and audience interest levels.

The conversion rate represents the percentage of SMS recipients who complete the desired action after receiving the message, directly demonstrating the campaign's effectiveness in driving business results. Opt-out rate tracks the percentage of recipients who unsubscribe from SMS communications, serving as an essential indicator of message relevance and frequency appropriateness. A retail brand demonstrated the effectiveness of SMS marketing by tracking a 15% conversion rate on abandoned cart SMS reminders, providing clear justification for continued investment in this channel.

Social Media Marketing Measurement

Social media marketing success depends on multiple factors, including engagement levels, reach effectiveness, and direct conversion impact. Engagement rate measures the total likes, shares, comments, and other interactions per post, providing insights into how well content resonates with the target audience and encourages active participation.

Reach quantifies the number of unique users who see a post, determining the extent of brand exposure and the effectiveness of content distribution strategies. Click-through rate on social media tracks clicks on both paid ads and organic posts, showing the effectiveness of calls-to-action and the audience's propensity to take further action.

Follower growth measures the net increase in followers over time, indicating brand appeal and growing audience interest in the content and messaging. Conversion rate tracks the percentage of users who complete desired actions directly from social media interactions, demonstrating the channel's direct impact on sales and business objectives. A sportswear brand exemplified social media's potential by achieving a 7x return on ad spend through TikTok Ads, clearly demonstrating the platform's effectiveness in driving measurable sales results.

Website & App Analytics Performance

Website and mobile app performance directly impact conversion rates and customer retention, making comprehensive analytics essential for digital success. Page load speed measures the time required for pages to load completely, directly affecting user experience and search engine optimization performance, as slower loading times typically correlate with higher bounce rates and lower conversion rates.

Bounce rate indicates the percentage of visitors who leave the website after viewing only one page, serving as an important indicator of content relevance and overall user experience quality. Pages per session tracks the average number of pages viewed during each visit, providing insights into the depth of engagement and the effectiveness of content in encouraging further exploration.

Average session duration measures the time visitors spend on the website per visit, indicating overall interest levels and the quality of content engagement. Cart abandonment rate represents the percentage of users who add items to their shopping cart but fail to complete the purchase, helping identify friction points in the checkout process that may be hindering conversions.

The app retention rate measures the percentage of users who return to use the app after initial installation, serving as a critical indicator of long-term user engagement and the delivery of app value. A luxury sneaker brand demonstrated the impact of user experience optimization by reducing cart abandonment from 68% to 45% through streamlined checkout processes, resulting in significant improvements in conversion rates and revenue generation.

Organizations can position their measurement capabilities for continued evolution and effectiveness by understanding and adapting to these emerging trends, ensuring they remain competitive in an increasingly data-driven marketing landscape.

Cultural and Organizational Dimensions of Measurement Transformation

Implementing the integrated measurement framework discussed earlier requires more than technical capabilities; it demands fundamental shifts in organizational culture, decision processes, and power dynamics. This section examines these organizational challenges to build a truly data-driven marketing organization.

The Organizational Politics of Measurement

Measurement systems inherently function as political systems within organizations by determining:

- What gets valued and rewarded
- Who controls access to critical information
- Which initiatives receive continued investment
- How success is defined and communicated

Research by Pfeffer and Sutton (2006) on evidence-based management highlights that resistance to data-driven approaches often stems from these political dimensions rather than technical limitations[85].

Three primary organizational barriers typically emerge when implementing advanced measurement systems:

1. Functional Measurement Silos

Traditional organizations develop channel-specific or function-specific measurement approaches that create competing views of performance:

- Sales teams focus on pipeline and revenue metrics
- Brand teams emphasize awareness and perception measures
- Digital teams prioritize engagement and conversion metrics
- Finance examines efficiency and ROI measures

This fragmentation creates "competing truths" where different functions draw contradictory conclusions from their isolated metrics, impeding unified decision-making.

2. Expertise and Authority Challenges

Advanced measurement approaches often shift authority from traditional decision-makers to data specialists, creating resistance from those whose experiential judgment is seemingly devalued. This manifests in behaviors such as:

- Questioning data validity when findings contradict intuition
- Selectively using metrics that support predetermined decisions
- Creating excessive approval requirements for data-driven changes
- Maintaining parallel "shadow" measurement systems

Accountability Resistance

Sophisticated measurement cuts through organizational BS like a hot knife through butter, creating transparency that makes some teams squirm. When you suddenly see who's driving results versus who's just talking a good game, resistance is inevitable. Teams that have thrived in ambiguous environments, where performance was difficult to measure, will push back firmly against systems that expose the truth.

In today's most advanced organizations, measurement isn't a rearview mirror; it's a satellite navigation system with real-time updates, constantly scanning for faster, more profitable routes. But here's the truth: most measurement transformations stall not because of tech, but because of people. You can build the most advanced analytics engine in the world, but if the tires, your people, processes, and priorities are flat, you're going nowhere.

Competing priorities, misaligned incentives, and low data literacy derail progress faster than insufficient data ever could. Successful transformation demands executive alignment on a weighted measurement framework, capability development that prioritizes practical application over theory, and a culture that values learning from experiments as much as hitting target numbers.

Digitally mature companies treat measurement as an always-on intelligence engine, powered by AI and embedded across the enterprise. Whether you're in marketing, logistics, product, or finance, insights become fuel for turning every department into a revenue center, just as Capital One did when it transformed its infrastructure into a growth driver.

Different organizational contexts require tailored tactics: augmenting judgment in intuition-led cultures, easing the transition to change for risk-averse teams, creating cross-functional analytics hubs for siloed organizations, and prioritizing high-impact use cases for resource-constrained teams. When these cultural and operational enablers are in place, the measurement frameworks presented in this chapter transition from theory to transformation.

Get these elements right, and your measurement system becomes more than a reporting function; it becomes the organizational nervous system, sensing opportunities, coordinating responses, and powering adaptive decision-making. Which is precisely where we'll go next: into the world of measurement-enabled, adaptive go-to-market execution.

CHAPTER 15

The Innovation Full Fly Wheel

Think Like an Innovation Strategist

Innovation has always been an act of creation, but the most enduring breakthroughs are rarely born in isolation. They emerge from a living ecosystem within your company, at the edges, with partners, in collaboration with customers, and increasingly, in symbiosis with AI. When done well, innovation is not a project or a department; it's a shared habit of mind, where ideas move fluidly across boundaries, are tested and refined in real-time, and are scaled with confidence.

Organic innovation comes in many forms:

- **Internal** — Employees spotting friction points, connecting dots across functions, and daring to reimagine "how it's always been done."
- **External-facing** — Directly engaging customers, not as research subjects, but as co-architects of the solution.
- **Partnership-driven** — Leveraging complementary capabilities, IP, and distribution to accelerate beyond what either party could achieve alone.
- **Co-creation ecosystems** — Communities that contribute ideas, validate concepts, and help carry innovations to market.

To understand the power of an innovation ecosystem, consider the gaming world, specifically Roblox. Roblox isn't just a game; it's a platform where players can become creators, and creators can become independent game developers. Roblox provides the physics engine, gamification hooks, customer identity, and rewards systems. It maintains the marketplace. And then it steps back, allowing millions of user-creators to design, launch, and monetize their own experiences.

The result? A compounding innovation engine. Roblox thrives because its creators thrive, and its creators thrive because Roblox has built the infrastructure, incentives, and distribution to make that possible.

Now, imagine your company in the same way. What if your infrastructure, manufacturing capacity, logistics, brand equity, data, or digital reach were a platform others could build upon? Could you enable customers to design a product that meets your specifications, slot it into your assembly line, and, if their audience (think social media following) pre-orders a minimum quantity, justify the retooling? Suddenly, your customers aren't just buyers; they're market-makers, leveraging your platform to co-create products that launch with built-in demand.

This isn't fantasy, it's the logical next step in customer-centric innovation. Now that AI can compress design cycles, optimize specs, and even predict market response, your "innovation platform" could empower a global community of co-creators to bring new products to life faster than any traditional R&D process could match.

In this chapter, we'll explore how to reimagine innovation as an always-on, multi-player platform, powered by creativity, disciplined execution, and AI-enhanced feedback loops, turning your company from a closed system into a thriving marketplace of ideas, with you at the center. The advantage doesn't go to the company with the biggest lab; it goes to the one that builds velocity and agility with the most connected loop from idea to value.

MASTERY LEARNING OBJECTIVES

- Learn to architect customer-centric innovation processes that turn ideas into impact, grounded in real needs, powered by agile workflows, and scalable across teams.
- Apply rapid testing, MVP design, and collaborative engagement to validate solutions early and often, with your customers in the loop, not just at the end.
- Assess the organizational design, talent models, and cultural conditions necessary to embed innovation as a repeatable and resilient function, rather than a one-off initiative.

INDUSTRY INSIGHT

How LEGO Rebuilt Its Future, One Digital Brick at a Time

From bankruptcy brink to a community-powered innovation engine.

In 2003, LEGO was in free fall, with sales down 30% in two years, debt mounting, and the board weighing a sell-off of its IP crown jewels. What happened next wasn't just a turnaround; it was a blueprint for how a traditional manufacturer can reinvent itself as a digital-first, innovation-at-scale platform.

Context / Challenge

LEGO's biggest threat wasn't losing kids to screens, it was its own slow, industrial-era product cycles. By the time a new set reached shelves, customer tastes had already shifted. The company needed speed, agility, and a way to fuse its physical product heritage with a digital-native mindset.

The Velocity Shift

- Embraced the Hackers: Instead of shutting down Mindstorms enthusiasts who reverse-engineered their robotics kits, LEGO invited them into co-creation, marking the start of a community-powered R&D model.
- Agile Transformation: Swapped multi-year waterfall development for agile sprints; a project estimated at 8,000 hours was completed in 800 hours, nearly 10x faster.
- Partnership Acceleration: Leveraged its new speed to secure and execute blockbuster IP deals (Star Wars, Marvel, Disney, Minecraft), moving from contract to launch in months.
- LEGO Ideas Platform: Crowdsourced product concepts, paying royalties to fan designers and moving winners from concept to retail in under a year.
- Digital Expansion: Treated games, apps, and online communities as core products, driving billions in incremental revenue and engagement between purchases.

Results / Impact

- Revenue hit a record DKK 73.1B and operating profit reached DKK 18.7B in 2024, outpacing a declining toy market.
- Portfolio doubled in pace, ~400 new products annually, half of the catalog refreshed each year.
- Built a co-creation community and agile infrastructure that competitors can't easily replicate.

STRATEGIC TAKEAWAYS

- Co-Creation as Core Capability: When customers help design your products, you build both relevance and loyalty.
- Agility at Enterprise Scale: Startup speed is possible in legacy manufacturing, if you rewire process and culture.
- Partnerships as Innovation Accelerators: The right IP deal can bring new audiences *and* sharpen internal capabilities.
- Physical + Digital as One Ecosystem: Don't treat digital as marketing; treat it as a revenue and insight engine.

REFLECTION

- How directly do your customers influence your innovation process? Are they passive subjects of research or active participants in creation?
- What percentage of your innovation initiatives begin with verified customer needs rather than internal assumptions about what customers might want?
- How quickly can your organization test a new concept with actual customers and gather meaningful feedback to inform next steps?
- To what extent have you integrated the experimental approaches pioneered by startups with the scale and resources of an established organization?

Reimagining Innovation in the Digital Era

In today's rapidly evolving digital landscape, innovation has expanded beyond Innovation Rewired, from R&D to Real-Time Value Loops[86].

Innovation used to live in a box, usually labeled "Product" or "R&D." It meant big ideas, long timelines, and even longer approval cycles. Not anymore.

In today's digital-first landscape, innovation has been uncaged, rewired, and distributed. It now spans the entire value creation system, from how you engage customers and generate insights to how you evolve your processes, business models, and experiences. And at the center of this new model? Customer-centricity, running on real-time feedback and digital infrastructure.

Digitally mature organizations no longer treat innovation as a side project. They treat it as a core operating system, powered by insight, scaled through tech, and refined through lean feedback loops. These are not one-and-done initiatives. They are always-on engines, tuned to learn faster, reduce risk, and generate value continuously.

"Companies that co-create with customers are 2.4x more likely to develop successful innovations and experience 32% faster time-to-market."

The transformation is structural. Innovation no longer occurs within isolated R&D labs; it emerges from dynamic ecosystems that encompass customers, partners, platforms, and even competitors. Digital has democratized innovation, turning customers from end users into co-creators, testers, and collaborators who actively shape products and models.

At the same time, lean methodologies, once exclusive to startups, are now embedded inside some of the world's largest enterprises. Why? Because they work. They let you test fast, learn early, and optimize before scaling. They replace assumption with validation, and rigidity with adaptability.

Why Traditional Innovation Models Are Breaking Down

For years, incumbent firms chased innovation by standing up labs, launching accelerators, and cutting checks through corporate venture capital arms. These moves were meant to future-proof the business. Too often, they just built silos, dashboards, and press releases.

Innovation Labs — Many operate like an innovation theater, with separate buildings, cultures, and KPIs. They excel at prototyping but are often disconnected from core operations. Ideas die on the handoff.

Corporate Venture Capital[87] — Sometimes, it's more about FOMO than foresight. Without strong integration mechanisms, CVCs struggle to bring startup innovation into the mother ship. Strategic alignment fades. Culture clashes flare up. And promising investments get stranded in pilot purgatory.

Accelerators and incubators — Useful for energy, signal detection, and scouting, but rarely deliver compounding returns unless tightly linked to product, marketing, and go-to-market execution.

The pattern is clear: these legacy innovation models optimize for exploration but fail at integration. They're BIOS-locked, running default startup playbooks inside systems built for scale, compliance, and quarterly reporting. Without rewiring how ideas move through the core business, even the best experiments stall.

You don't need more labs. You need a faster learning system, one that loops insights from the edge to the core, tests with real customers, and scales what works without losing velocity.

Innovation isn't a side hustle. It's an enterprise performance upgrade, and it only works when wired directly into how you engage, decide, and deliver.

Where Feedback Becomes Forward Motion

In traditional models, innovation was confined to a lab, tucked away in a separate building, driven by pitch decks and Post-its. But in leading organizations, innovation is no longer a department. It's an enterprise-wide performance system, one that fuses AI, feedback, infrastructure, and strategy into a closed loop of learning, testing, and scaling.

From Forcing Functions to Flow States: How Customer-Centric Velocity Killed Corporate Innovation Theater

The innovation lab is dead. So are the startup accelerators, the corporate venture arms, and the carefully orchestrated "innovation tours" of Silicon Valley. What killed them wasn't failure; it was irrelevance. While enterprises spent the last decade building elaborate external forcing functions to inject innovation into their organizations, a quiet revolution was happening: companies discovered that the most powerful innovation engine wasn't housed in a separate building or outsourced to consultants. It was embedded in the daily rhythm of customer obsession, operational velocity, and adaptive intelligence.

The shift represents a fundamental change in how breakthrough thinking emerges and scales. Where traditional approaches isolated innovation in controlled environments, accelerators, skunk works teams, and partnerships with startups, the new model recognizes that sustainable innovation flows from an organization's core capability to sense, respond, and evolve at customer speed. This isn't about managing innovation as a discrete function; it's about building organizational DNA that naturally produces breakthrough thinking as a byproduct of customer-centric velocity.

In high-velocity innovation systems, customers transform from research subjects into active co-creators, their real-time feedback and behavior patterns becoming the primary input for strategic direction. AI evolves from a tool into a strategy co-pilot, continuously analyzing patterns, predicting opportunities, and suggesting optimizations that human teams might never consider. Infrastructure scales automatically to handle experimental load, allowing teams to test bold ideas without worrying about system limitations or resource constraints.

Perhaps most critically, data flows bidirectionally rather than just up hierarchies; insights from customer interactions immediately influence product development, marketing strategies, and operational decisions, creating feedback loops that accelerate learning and adaptation. Content becomes part of the testing apparatus itself, with every piece of communication serving as both customer engagement and market research. Go-to-market strategies transform from annual planning exercises into dynamic proving grounds where hypotheses are tested, validated, and scaled in real-time.

What emerges is a strategy that adapts continuously rather than quarterly, responding to market signals with the agility that used to exist only in startups but is now powered by enterprise resources and reach. The entire organization becomes wired for signal detection, tuned for speed, and optimized for discovery, eliminating the artificial boundary between "innovation" and "operations" that has constrained so many traditional companies.

This customer-centric velocity model doesn't just produce better products or services; it creates competitive moats that are nearly impossible for slower-moving organizations to cross. When innovation becomes indistinguishable from customer obsession and operational excellence, it stops being a discrete corporate function and starts being the fundamental way the business breathes, thinks, and grows.

The Four Tiers of Strategic Alignment

The flywheel operates across four distinct but interconnected levels, each requiring different capabilities and generating various types of market intelligence.

1. Feature-Problem Fit represents the foundational tactical level where teams validate whether specific features solve genuine customer pain points. This is fundamentally about utility and usability. Can your solution solve a real problem in a way that users can adopt and benefit from? At this level, you're focused on the mechanics of problem-solving, ensuring that individual features deliver measurable value and remove friction from customer workflows. Success here means users can accomplish their goals more effectively with your feature than without it.

2. Product-Problem Fit expands the focus from individual features to the complete product package, validating whether your entire solution addresses the right problem in the most effective way possible. This is where value propositions begin to solidify and where you prove that you're solving problems that are significant enough to drive sustained customer engagement. You're moving beyond feature utility to demonstrate that your integrated solution consistently delivers value across a meaningful customer segment. Success at this level means that customers view your product as essential, rather than optional, for solving their core challenges.

3. Solution-Segment Fit shifts into business model territory, validating whether your solution approach matches the specific needs, preferences, and constraints of your target customer segment. This encompasses pricing strategies, distribution channels, onboarding processes, and market positioning. You're proving that you understand what problem to solve, but how your specific customer segment wants that problem solved. This includes validating that your go-to-market approach aligns with how your segment discovers, evaluates, and adopts new solutions. Success here means you've identified both the right solution and the right customers for that solution.

4. Product-Market Fit at the system level represents the tipping point where you've built the right solution for a market that's large enough, growing fast enough, and ready to scale adoption rapidly. This is where market pull begins to exceed your marketing push, where organic growth starts to compound, and where you're not just solving individual problems. Still, building sustained momentum across an entire market category. Success at this level means you've created something that the market actively wants to adopt and recommend to others.

The Flywheel Dynamic

The Full Fit Flywheel[88] transforms these four levels from sequential checkpoints into a continuous, self-reinforcing system. Your innovation engine operates simultaneously and repeatedly across all four levels, with success at each level providing the intelligence and momentum necessary to excel in others.

This dynamic is driven by continuous customer signal detection, which captures voice-of-customer feedback, journey analytics, and behavioral data in real-time, rather than relying on periodic surveys or focus groups. These signals feed into AI-powered feedback loops that deliver real-time pattern recognition, lifetime value modeling, and predictive insights about the most promising features, segments, and market opportunities.

The system operates through an agile experimentation infrastructure that enables rapid MVP development, continuous iteration, and sophisticated A/B testing across all four fit levels simultaneously. This isn't about testing individual features, but about testing entire solution approaches, segment strategies, and market positioning concepts in parallel.

Go-to-market telemetry provides continuous visibility into channel performance, retention cohorts, usage behavior patterns, and market response signals that inform decisions across all four fit levels. This creates a feedback loop where market success informs product development, which in turn enhances market success, yielding improved market intelligence.

Beyond the Milestone Mentality

Instead of treating fit as a one-time achievement, the Full Fit Flywheel recognizes that fit is a moving target in dynamic markets. Customer needs evolve, competitive landscapes shift, and new technologies create new possibilities for value creation. Your system must learn to track and hit these moving targets repeatedly, building the organizational capability to maintain and expand fit across multiple dimensions simultaneously.

This approach creates compound advantages because each level amplifies the others. A strong feature-problem fit makes it easier to achieve a product-problem fit. Precise product-problem fit provides the foundation for optimizing solution-segment fit. A validated solution-segment fit creates the conditions for gaining a sustainable product-market fit. A strong product-market fit generates the resources and market intelligence needed to continuously improve at all four levels.

The Full Fit Flywheel isn't a framework for achieving fit; it's a system for maintaining competitive advantage in markets where standing still means falling behind. It transforms innovation from a series of discrete projects into a continuous capability that gets stronger with every cycle.

Why It Matters

In legacy models, fitness is fragile. You find it once, and scaling breaks it. In next-generation innovation systems, fit is fluid. You re-validate, re-tune, and re-align as conditions shift, market signals change, platforms evolve, new technology emerges, and customer expectations shift.

The Full Fit Flywheel is what Digital Leaders build:

- Feature–Problem fit informs product updates
- Product–Problem fit drives roadmap prioritization
- Solution–Segment fit fuels GTM precision
- Market-level fit drives scale with agility

Aligning Innovation with Your Digital Business Model

You can't run a high-voltage innovation system on a legacy model. To drive tangible outcomes, innovation must align with your current digital business model configuration, then scale as your maturity grows. Innovation isn't one-size-fits-all. It's modular, adaptive, and strategically aligned to where you are and where you're going.

Organizations operate across a range of digital capabilities and transformation, requiring different innovation strategies depending on their current position. Knowing where your organization fits in this matrix determines which innovation model will generate the highest return on investment while developing systematic capabilities for future growth.

The flight path model shows innovation not as a box to sit in, but as a trajectory to climb.

Digital Defenders operate with low digital intensity and low transformation readiness, representing early-stage, analog-heavy organizations that remain protective of core systems while recognizing the need for digital evolution. These organizations benefit most from embedded cross-functional teams that act as lightweight squads within core operations, focusing on digitizing one customer journey at a time and developing customer-centric reflexes that don't threaten existing workflows.

Their main priorities are digitizing manual workflows, gathering baseline customer signals, and testing low-risk improvements that demonstrate value without disrupting operations. AI supports these efforts by automating feedback collection, enabling fundamental journey analysis, and providing lightweight voice-of-customer integration to build organizational confidence in data-driven approaches.

A regional insurance company demonstrated this strategy by launching micro-teams within claims and onboarding processes to digitize workflows, then using systematic feedback loops to reduce processing time by 30% without disrupting existing operations or requiring major system overhauls.

Digital Defenders should aim to achieve Feature-Problem Fit by starting with simple solutions rather than chasing disruptive innovation, thereby building credibility and organizational insight that lay the groundwork for future growth.

INNOVATION FLIGHT PATH: FROM DEFENDING TO LEADING

Stage	Innovation System Coherence	AI Leverage	Primary Innovation Mode	Innovation Fit	Strategic Focus	Example
Digital Defenders	Low, siloed, analog-heavy, fragmented processes	Low, basic automation, limited analytics	Embedded Teams	Feature–Problem Fit	Digitize one journey at a time, build confidence through visible wins	Regional insurer using micro-squads to digitize claims
Digital Explorers	Medium, infrastructure in place, culture lagging	Medium, AI for clustering, personalization tests	Networked Testing	Product–Problem Fit	Use digital reach for experimentation, and validate customer needs at scale.	A media brand is creating an AI-driven insights hub.
Digital Transformers	Medium–High, leadership alignment, rewiring readiness	High, AI for MVP simulation, scenario modeling	Dedicated Labs	Solution–Segment Fit	Launch new models in controlled labs, co-create with customers	Legacy manufacturer launching IoT lab
Digital Leaders	High, unified infrastructure, feedback loops, cross-functional orchestration	High, AI as the nervous system for orchestration and co-creation	Hybrid Embedded + X-Teams	Full Fit Flywheel (Feature, Product, Solution, Market)	Continuous innovation across core + frontier teams, systemic learning at scale	

Digital Explorers combine high digital intensity with low transformation readiness, representing organizations that are digitally equipped but still operate with legacy mindsets that limit their innovation potential. These companies have the technological infrastructure but lack the cultural operating system necessary to scale innovation across the organization.

They benefit from networked innovation, supported by shared signal layers that enable distributed experimentation and connect through unified data platforms. Their primary focus leverages existing digital reach to expand customer input collection and support decentralized testing across multiple business units simultaneously.

AI plays a more advanced role through signal clustering, behavioral trend detection, and rapid personalization testing, helping teams identify patterns across large customer bases. A digital-first media brand demonstrated this approach by creating an AI-driven insights hub that enabled content teams across different regions to test new formats in real-time using engagement telemetry, thereby speeding up learning cycles while maintaining brand consistency.

Digital Explorers should focus on achieving a Product-Problem Fit by leveraging their technological reach to identify what customers truly want, rather than relying solely on internal assumptions.

Digital Transformers operate with low digital intensity but high transformation readiness, representing legacy organizations where leadership is prepared to rewire operations fundamentally despite current technological limitations. These organizations need dedicated innovation labs that serve as controlled breakaway zones, providing space to rewire customer-centric, technology-enabled innovation without being constrained by core system limitations or organizational inertia.

Their primary focus involves launching entirely new business models, co-creating solutions with customers, and testing fundamental assumptions outside existing operational constraints. AI enables MVP simulation, early signal modeling, and testing digital capabilities in new contexts, informing broader organizational transformation.

A legacy manufacturer exemplified this approach by launching an IoT product lab focused on customer co-creation, validating prototypes through real-time usage data before integrating proven capabilities back into core operations.

Digital Transformers should prioritize Solution-Segment Fit by focusing on business model innovation rather than incremental product improvements, building new customer-model combinations that can eventually transform their entire market approach.

Digital Leaders attain both high digital intensity and high transformation readiness, representing fully optimized, multi-speed organizations that operate continuously across customer, technology, and strategy layers simultaneously. These organizations develop hybrid innovation systems that combine embedded experimentation across all business functions with dedicated frontier teams exploring breakthrough opportunities, unified by shared infrastructure and data platforms that support systematic learning and scaling.

Their primary focus includes continuous feedback integration, journey orchestration across multiple touchpoints, and radical adjacency exploration that opens new market opportunities. AI acts as the central nervous system by integrating cross-journey insights, predictive modeling, generative co-creation capabilities, and journey personalization at scale, adapting in real-time to individual customer needs.

A global fintech demonstrated this model by combining embedded innovation squads across customer experience and go-to-market functions with a dedicated frontier technology unit exploring AI-native financial products, both operating from the same customer data platform to ensure insights are combined across initiatives.

Digital Leaders achieve all four types of fit simultaneously: Feature-Problem, Product-Problem, Solution-Segment, and Product-Market, creating innovation engines that deliver individual results and build compounding systems that learn, test, and scale effectively amid changing market conditions and customer needs.

Strategic Insight: Scale the System with You

Innovation models don't stand alone; they're tuned to your infrastructure, leadership mindset, data maturity, and organizational velocity. This is why the reinvented enterprise doesn't default to a lab, Corporate VC, or accelerator. It builds the right loop for the current system, then scales it with every transformation milestone.

Full Fit Flywheel: The Innovation Fit Model

The Full Fit Flywheel represents the highest-performing state in an innovation fit model, where an organization continuously aligns, adapts, and accelerates innovation across all dimensions of product-market fit.

Most innovation models treat fit as a checkpoint, a static moment where teams ask whether they've achieved product-market fit or if their solution matches the intended segment. This binary approach fundamentally misunderstands how modern innovation works. The Full Fit Flywheel reframes fit as a dynamic system, a compounding loop of learning, validation, and scaling that operates across four interconnected tiers of alignment, each building momentum for the next.

This isn't about hitting a milestone and moving on. It's about creating a self-reinforcing system where success at one level amplifies your ability to succeed at the next, creating the kind of compound momentum that separates breakout innovations from incremental improvements.

CASE STUDY

Apple — The Services Flywheel

How a product company became a platform for perpetual innovation.

Apple's hardware dominance is well known. But over the past five years, its true innovation has been building a services flywheel that compounds with every new product launch, keeping users inside an ever-expanding ecosystem.

The Bottleneck

Hardware cycles are long, expensive, and vulnerable to saturation. As iPhone growth slowed, Apple needed a way to deepen relationships, drive recurring revenue, and monetize daily engagement without relying solely on device upgrades.

The Overclock

- Symbiotic Services: Apple TV+, Fitness+, Arcade, Pay, Card, and iCloud each drive incremental value—but also reinforce hardware adoption (watch workouts on your Apple Watch, finance via Apple Pay, stream content on Apple devices).
- Ecosystem Stickiness: Services share identity (Apple ID), billing, and cross-promotion. This reduces churn: the more services a user adopts, the harder it is to leave the ecosystem.

- Innovation Feedback Loops: Insights from one service shape others. For example, health data from Apple Watch informs Fitness+ content; Arcade adoption fuels chip innovation; Pay/Wallet expands Apple's role in fintech.
- Vision Pro as Catalyst: The 2024 launch of Apple Vision Pro wasn't an isolated moonshot, it leveraged decades of ecosystem infrastructure (apps, cloud, developer base) to instantly position spatial computing inside Apple's flywheel.

Results

Services revenue surpassed $90B annually by 2024, becoming Apple's second-largest segment.

Apple now counts 1B+ paid subscriptions across its ecosystem.

Cross-service engagement has raised ARPU and reinforced customer lifetime value.

What It Means

Apple demonstrates full flywheel fit: each innovation strengthens the next, creating compounding momentum. New services don't dilute the brand, they amplify it, pulling in symbiotic audiences and anchoring Apple as not just a hardware maker, but an innovation ecosystem in perpetual motion.

Closing Loop: Innovation as a Live System

You've already built the parts: strategy, infrastructure, insights, GTM, journeys, and content. The role of innovation is to connect, tune, and test what's next, at scale, with speed.

Innovation isn't about running the lab harder. It's about integrating the loop into your business model, so every insight becomes action, every experiment becomes intelligence, and every customer interaction becomes a signal.

This is how you build a company that continually reinvents itself from within.

Building the Lean, Customer-Centric System

Breakthrough innovation doesn't happen by chance or in silos. Organizations that build systemic innovation engines, converting customer insights into market impact with ruthless efficiency, will win the Web 3.0 race. These engines aren't brainstorm factories or creative workshops; they're full-stack systems engineered for velocity, evidence, and agility.

At the core lies a deceptively simple four-part loop that transforms how organizations create value:

But the magic happens in how these components interconnect and amplify each other, creating compound momentum that separates market leaders from everyone else playing catch-up.

1. Customer Engagement: From Listening to Co-Creation

Most companies are still stuck in the survey age, sending quarterly questionnaires and calling it customer research. Engagement evolves across four increasingly sophisticated levels, transforming customers from passive respondents into active innovation partners.

Passive observation begins by tracking customer behavior, clicks, sentiment patterns, and search intent, all without directly interrupting the customer experience. This creates a foundation of behavioral intelligence that reveals what customers do, rather than what they claim to do. Active listening expands this approach through surveys, interviews, and polls, but treats these as starting points rather than endpoints for understanding customers.

The transformation accelerates with facilitated participation, where customers become active collaborators in design sprints, prototype feedback sessions, and co-testing initiatives. This moves beyond asking customers what they want to involve them in creating solutions. Continuous co-creation represents the pinnacle, where communities, ambassador programs, and shared roadmap input turn your most engaged customers into extensions of your innovation team.

Glossier exemplifies this evolution perfectly. The beauty brand didn't just build products for customers; they built them *with* customers, transforming blog comments into a billion-dollar business. When customers complained about packaging, those complaints became input for redesign. When community discussions revealed skincare gaps, those conversations became bestselling product launches. Glossier built feedback systems that integrated customers directly into their development loop, creating innovations that felt inevitable because they emerged from genuine customer collaboration.

Additionally, the bonus is that co-creation with customers fosters a culture of customer centricity, an organic earned media loop, and product amplification.

2. Lean Experimentation: From Assumptions to Evidence

The riskiest thing any organization can do is build products and services based on executive opinions, industry best practices, or competitive assumptions. Lean experimentation flips this dangerous process by treating every idea as a hypothesis that must earn the right to exist through market validation.

The process begins with documenting assumptions explicitly, forcing teams to articulate what must be true for their ideas to succeed in the market. These assumptions form the foundation for designing micro tests, MVPs, landing pages, and teaser videos, enabling quick and cost-effective validation or invalidation of core hypotheses. The key is compressing learning cycles, moving through build-measure-learn-iterate loops as rapidly as possible to accumulate market intelligence faster than competitors.

Most importantly, decisions must be driven by data rather than politics, hunches, or organizational hierarchy. Evidence becomes the ultimate arbiter of what moves forward and what gets discarded, creating a culture where the best ideas prevail, regardless of their origin.

Dropbox provides a masterclass in this approach. Before writing a single line of code, co-founder Drew Houston created a simple three-minute explainer video demonstrating their file-syncing concept. The video generated 70,000 waitlist signups in 24 hours, providing irrefutable evidence of market demand that secured funding and validated their entire business model. This test-first, build-second mentality allowed them to prove product-market fit before investing in expensive development, dramatically reducing both risk and time to market.

3. Digital Infrastructure: The Backbone of Velocity

Modern innovation can't run on spreadsheets, email chains, and quarterly planning cycles. The organizations that consistently out-innovate their competitors have invested in digital infrastructure that enables real-time experimentation, collaboration, and decision-making at scale.

Customer Data Platforms[89] provide unified customer intelligence that fuels both insight generation and personalization at scale, ensuring that every team has access to the same customer truth rather than working from conflicting data sources.

Experimentation platforms enable sophisticated A/B testing, cohort analysis, and automation of statistical significance, democratizing testing capabilities across the organization rather than limiting them to specialized teams.

Collaboration tools like Asana, Figma, and Miro connect distributed teams and enable real-time customer participation in design and development processes. Insight management systems tag, cluster, and share what works and why, ensuring that learning compounds across projects rather than remaining trapped in individual team silos.

Booking.com demonstrates the competitive power of proper infrastructure by running over 1,000 concurrent A/B tests daily across its platform. Every team can test hypotheses independently, and every decision generates data that informs future experimentation. This is operational efficiency and institutionalized learning that turns optimization into sustainable competitive advantage. Their infrastructure enables them to learn faster and adapt quickly than any competitor operating with traditional planning cycles.

4. Commercializing What Works: From Test to Transformation

Validation without implementation is organizational waste. The most sophisticated customer insights and experimental results are worthless if they can't be translated into scaled business impact. Disruptive organizations close this loop with structured scaling mechanisms that ensure validated innovations transform business performance.

Stage-gated governance ensures that resource allocation matches validation levels, with small wins receiving appropriate small funding while big bets must earn larger investments through demonstrated market traction. Balanced portfolio management tracks core, adjacent, and radical innovation initiatives within a single system, ensuring that organizations maintain the right mix of incremental improvements and breakthrough opportunities.

Implementation pathways provide clear routes for bringing validated concepts into the business, eliminating the common problem of successful pilots that never scale beyond test environments. Knowledge transfer systems ensure that insights get codified, reused, and shared across the organization rather than remaining trapped within individual project teams.

Amazon exemplifies this systematic approach through its "working backwards" methodology and six-page memo culture[90]. Every innovation proposal must start with a mock press release and detailed customer FAQ, forcing teams to think through implementation and customer impact before beginning development. Small experiments receive rapid approval and resources, while larger initiatives face data-rich review processes that ensure only validated concepts receive significant investment. This system enables continuous launch velocity at enterprise scale, allowing Amazon to innovate across dozens of business lines simultaneously while maintaining operational discipline.

The System in Motion

Each component of this innovation engine delivers value independently, but its true power emerges through its interconnection and mutual reinforcement. Customer engagement generates a signal that experiments transform into proof. Infrastructure enables the velocity needed to run multiple experiments simultaneously. Scaling mechanisms ensure that proof becomes performance rather than remaining trapped in pilot projects.

Over time, this system creates compound advantages that become increasingly difficult for competitors to replicate. Every successful test builds organizational credibility for future experimentation. Every customer insight fuels more targeted hypothesis formation. Every scaled innovation generates resources for additional experimentation while building market intelligence that informs future innovation directions.

The result transforms innovation from a luck-dependent creative process into a repeatable momentum engine. Organizations stop hoping for breakthrough innovations and start systematically creating them, building the kind of sustainable competitive advantage that defines market leaders in every industry.

Success Indicators for Innovation

When your customer-centric innovation engine is tuned correctly and running smoothly, specific patterns appear in your organizational telemetry that indicate sustained competitive advantage. These aren't vanity metrics or feel-good indicators; they are complex performance signals that show your innovation system is producing compound returns.

Learning speed becomes immediately apparent as your organization shortens test cycles, validates hypotheses more quickly, and sharpens solutions with each sprint. Teams stop spending months debating possibilities and start delivering market-validated answers in weeks. Customer impact is visible through measurable improvements in user experience, with solutions that clearly reduce friction, boost value delivered and enhance retention rates across customer segments.

Organization-wide engagement shows that innovation has moved beyond the R&D lab and has become integrated across teams, functions, and levels. When customer service teams begin suggesting product improvements and operations teams propose experience enhancements, it's a sign that the innovation mindset is systemic rather than confined to departments. Implementation efficiency increases as more ideas successfully move from prototypes to market, withstand real-world constraints, and adapt to customer behaviors.

Most importantly, measurable business growth can be directly linked to innovation efforts, as reflected in revenue increases, improved retention rates, enhanced Net Promoter Score, and expanded customer metrics. This creates a financial feedback loop that supports ongoing innovation investment and boosts organizational confidence in systematic experimentation.

Nine Ways Your Innovation Pipeline Gets PWND[91]

Even the best-designed innovation systems can stall when predictable failure modes go unaddressed. Most stem from cultural resistance, short-term pressures, or process breakdowns that disrupt the loop between insight, experimentation, and scale. Recognizing these patterns early helps leaders maintain momentum and credibility.

1. **Signal-to-Nowhere** – Collecting rich customer insights but never turning them into testable hypotheses or experiments. Teams become data-rich but action-poor, drowning in feedback without a clear path to conversion.
2. **Overbuilt MVPs** – Shipping polished prototypes instead of quick, low-fidelity tests slows learning and drains resources. Rough sketches, demos, or landing pages often spark better feedback because customers feel freer to suggest changes.
3. **Innovation Theater** – Hackathons, idea contests, and flashy labs generate excitement but lack follow-through. When ideas vanish into organizational black holes, cynicism takes root and trust erodes.
4. **Premature Scaling** – Rushing solutions to market without validating customer needs, market size, or business model viability creates costly

rework, churn, and missed expectations, undermining confidence in innovation processes.

5. **Siloed Capability** – Great tools and talent scattered across disconnected systems can't amplify each other's impact. Without integration, capabilities remain underused and collaboration opportunities are lost.
6. **The Expertise Trap** – Internal experts reject external insights, favoring existing knowledge over fresh market feedback. The result: blind spots and solutions optimized for internal preferences rather than customer realities.
7. **Short-Termism** – Quarterly targets crush long-term bets before they can mature. Investor pressure forces teams to chase immediate returns, creating a cycle where innovation never has time to prove its value.
8. **Fragmented Ownership** – Without a single owner for the whole customer journey, departments optimize in silos. Disconnected efforts miss opportunities for systemic improvement.
9. **Middle Management Bottlenecks** – Frontline teams want to experiment, executives demand innovation, but middle managers, measured on efficiency, not learning, block risk-taking. Forward-thinking firms like 3M address this with dual career tracks that reward both operational excellence and innovation leadership.

Installing Customer-Centric Innovation: A Phased Build

Organizations can't create genuine innovation engines overnight without risking cultural rejection or operational disruption. Successful transformation requires the systematic development of capabilities across multiple phases, enabling teams to build competence and confidence gradually. The foundation phase emphasizes establishing signal systems that generate basic voice-of-customer and customer journey insights. Starting small but making these systems genuinely helpful builds organizational trust in data-driven decision making while providing the intelligence foundation that more sophisticated innovation activities require.

The experimentation phase deploys a lean testing infrastructure, an MVP development culture, and precise go/no-go decision-making rhythms that enable rapid hypothesis validation. This phase teaches teams how to design meaningful experiments, interpret results accurately, and make evidence-based decisions about continuing or killing initiatives.

The activation phase defines innovation pathways that specify how validated concepts move from experimental test benches to operational business units. This eliminates the common problem of successful pilots that never scale because no one knows how to integrate them into existing operations.

The unification phase connects all system components, allowing customer signals to flow into experimental hypotheses, validated experiments to inform scaling decisions, and scaled innovations to generate both business impact and additional customer intelligence. This is where the flywheel effect begins to emerge, with each component amplifying the others to create compound momentum.

GLOBAL SIGNAL

Necessity-Driven Ecosystems

Innovation has a range of incremental improvements to ecosystem-scale breakthroughs. In resource-constrained markets, startups leap directly to ecosystem innovation by necessity, merging digital, biotech, and climate-tech from inception.

Signals

- iFarm (Finland/Qatar): Automated vertical farms in arid regions, yielding 300x traditional output per square meter. By embedding AI and hydroponics, they bypassed traditional agriculture entirely.
- Boomitra (Global South): Used AI + satellites to help 300,000 farmers monetize regenerative practices. In doing so, it turned climate stewardship into an economic model.
- Nbryo (Australia): Compressed decades of cattle breeding into years with accelerated embryo transfer. A biotech leap that redefines agricultural productivity cycles.

Takeaway

Innovation flywheels in these markets show how convergence accelerates reinvention. Mature industries aren't safe—they're one cycle away from being remapped by necessity-born ecosystems.

Aligning Org Design for Innovation

Sustained innovation demands more than just better ideas or improved processes; it requires a fundamental structural realignment that hardwires innovation capabilities into an organization's DNA. This transformation begins with reprogramming resource allocation systems to fund uncertainty rather than just rewarding efficiency intentionally. Organizations must dedicate capital and headcount specifically to testing, learning, and pivoting activities that may not generate immediate returns but build long-term competitive advantages.

Key performance indicators must evolve beyond traditional throughput metrics to include validated learning rates and signal conversion effectiveness. When teams are measured on their ability to generate market intelligence and translate that intelligence into business improvements, innovation becomes a core competency rather than a side activity.

Customer-centricity must become embedded in every team's default operating system, from operations groups that optimize internal processes to product teams that design new capabilities to customer experience functions that manage touchpoint interactions. This isn't achieved through training programs or cultural initiatives alone; it requires systematic changes to hiring criteria, performance evaluation systems, and career advancement pathways.

The structural transformation activates embedded innovation squads within operational units, cross-functional pods that can move quickly on validated opportunities, and networked innovation models that reflect the organization's digital maturity level. These aren't cosmetic organizational changes or temporary pilot programs; they represent BIOS-level upgrades that change how the organization processes information, makes decisions, and allocates resources.

This full-stack realignment makes innovation everyone's responsibility rather than a specialized function, creating distributed capability that can identify and act on opportunities faster than centralized innovation departments. When properly implemented, this structural approach generates sustainable competitive advantage because it becomes increasingly complex for competitors to replicate the integrated system of capabilities, processes, and cultural patterns that enable consistent innovation success.

CASE STUDY

Roblox Innovation as Co-Creation

How a gaming platform turned customers into builders, sellers, and innovators.

Roblox didn't just make a game. It built a universe where the players are also the producers. By fusing social engagement, user-generated content, and monetization loops, Roblox created a multi-sided marketplace that continuously reinvents itself through customer participation.

The Bottleneck

Traditional gaming studios relied on top-down development: long cycles, expensive releases, and limited feedback loops. Players were consumers only, leaving creativity, and potential revenue, on the table.

The Overclock

Roblox flipped the model. It built an engine where users design games, monetize experiences, and trade virtual goods using Robux. The platform scaled not by producing content, but by enabling millions of micro-innovators. Roblox Studio gave customers the same tools the company used, creating a flywheel of creation → community → commerce.

Results

- Over 70M daily active users in 2024, with peak engagement among Gen Z.
- $680M+ paid out to developers in 2023, making customers into entrepreneurs.
- Network effects where the value of the platform compounds with every new game, avatar, and micro-transaction.

What It Means

Roblox demonstrates that customer-centric innovation isn't about listening harder, it's about handing over the tools. When customers become co-creators, innovation scales exponentially, and the company becomes the platform where culture itself is built.

From Co-Creation to Ownership: The Rise of the Agentic Orchestrated Innovation

Imagine a future state, where AI agents rule the day, filter our content, and gatekeep customer identity. How will we generate awareness, create engagement, and build relationships that lead to higher lifetime value? The answer will be that customer-centric innovation no longer stops at the transaction.

In the **Agentic Marketplace**[92], where AI agents transact on behalf of consumers, value creation shifts to ongoing participation. Brands that once rewarded loyalty with points or discounts must now design rewarded ecosystems where amplification and advocacy generate real, tradable value.

- **Autonomous Paid Media Meets Earned Media**: Brand-side AI optimizes spend and creative in real time, while consumer and influencer agents amplify messages. Every share, remix, or referral is logged, scored, and rewarded instantly.
- **Rewards as Currency**: Instead of static points, advocates earn tokens or credits that are convertible into crypto or fiat, are borderless, immediate, and global.
- **Gamified Participation**: Leaderboards, badges, and tiered access transform participation into a game, where social capital and economic capital intersect.
- **Key Shift**: Loyalty shifts from being transactional to equity-driven; customers and creators are incentivized to co-own the brand's success.
- **Influence as Equity**: NFT-Backed Advocacy

Traditional sponsorships paid influencers a flat fee. The next era introduces **Influence-Backed NFTs**, asset-backed tokens that appreciate as the influencer drives measurable engagement and advocacy.

- **NFT Issuance**: Brands assign NFTs to influencers (human or AI). Each token is tied to performance metrics, such as reach, velocity, or conversion.
- **Accrued Value**: The more an influencer successfully amplifies the brand, the greater the value of their NFT grows.
- **Redeem or Convert**: Tokens can be held as speculative assets, redeemed for exclusive brand benefits, or converted into cryptocurrency or fiat currency.
- **Skin in the Game**: Influencers aren't just advertisers; they become stakeholders. Their success is tied directly to the brand's growth.
- Key Shift: Influence evolves from *endorsement* into *equity participation*, aligning incentives between brands and advocates.

Customers as Co-Creators: Profit-Sharing Through NFTs

The ultimate form of customer-centric innovation is to bind customers not only to the product but also to its outcome. Enter the **Customer-Creation NFT**: tokens issued to customers who co-design, purchase, or promote a product, tied directly to the product's P&L.

- **Co-Creation & Issuance**: Customers who help ideate or beta-test products receive an NFT tied to that SKU or service.
- **On-chain engagement**: Purchases, referrals, and advocacy contribute to the NFT's value, recorded transparently on the blockchain.
- **Profit-Sharing**: As long as the product is profitable, NFT holders receive fractional payouts via smart contracts.
- **Dashboard Transparency**: Customers track their product's P&L, see how their advocacy impacts performance, and feel like true partners in the outcome.
- **Key Shift**: Customers transition from being consumers of value to co-owners of value, adopting a participatory innovation model that transforms loyalty into shared equity.

Just as this new era of velocity and adaptability will demand innovation in products and services, the process of GTM (Go-To-Market) will also require innovation. Here's one possible scenario: companies will need to develop a content strategy that attracts bots and anonymously adds value after purchase, so that either the customer reveals themselves because the value is sufficient or the product itself provides anonymized information on usage, durability, quality, and overall value.

Executive Team Dialogue: Competing in the Agentic Era

CEO: "We used to talk about winning the shelf, then the homepage, then the app icon. Now, it feels like the real battle is invisible; it's happening between our customers' bots and those trained by our competitors. In a world where discovery is bot-driven and customers are cloaked by default, how do we even see them, let alone serve them?

VP of Product: "The answer lies in what happens *after* purchase. If bots flatten pre-purchase choice into commodity filters, we need to make the post-purchase stage our differentiation frontier. Our products can't just work; they need to talk back. Imagine if every unit self-reported durability, efficiency, and usage patterns directly to the customer and to us. The catch? It's under their control. If they share only basic telemetry, they remain cloaked but still get predictive service alerts. If they reveal usage + context, they unlock extended warranties or community entry. If they uncloak fully, they receive an NFT tied to that product line, one that accrues value as the product is used, repaired, recycled, or resold."

VP of Technology: "Exactly. Think of it as cookies for objects but owned by users. IoT sensors generate anonymized insights by default, while smart contracts allow customers to set filters. Each filter transforms into a slider in its cloaked identity[93], offering options such as durability-only, durability plus environmental footprint, or full lifecycle usage. On-chain, their NFT records every lifecycle event, purchase, service, and recycling. That's proof-of-care for us, and a tradable, redeemable asset for them. We shift from ownership to stewardship."

VP of Marketing: "This flips loyalty upside down. Content isn't just for people anymore; it's for bots first. Bots don't buy into branding; they parse structured data, provenance, and trust signals.Now, our strategy has to operate in two layers:

1. **Human-facing storytelling** builds meaning and emotion.

2. **Bot-facing trust signals**: verified supply chain, standardized performance data, and sustainability scores.

But the incentives are what unlock the reveal. Not promo codes. Relationship accelerators:

Entry into a community of users, where ownership feels like membership. Predictive service loops that extend product life and usage feedback that help customers optimize performance.

And here's an innovation incentive. Co-creation rev share, equity in the very products they've helped to improve."

VP of Manufacturing: "This also changes how we price and produce. Pricing is normalized based on dynamic demand signals, as well as current and pipeline inventory, and target audience price elasticity, eliminating the need for a static MSRP. Bots will expect real-time value, and our entire supply chain has to support it.

Every price reflects logistics, inventory, labor, and even energy costs. If a batch was produced using renewables, its cost curve shifts. If we're overstocked, prices auto-correct downward. Customers or their bots will see those signals instantly."

VP of Logistics: "And if a port bottleneck or energy surge drives costs up, the blockchain record will show that too. Price becomes a live indicator of our operational resilience, not a hidden margin calculation."

CHRO (VP of HR): "This also changes the workforce model. Instead of fixed labor blocks, we'll rely on an on-demand human cloud.Remote specialists are activated worldwide when demand spikes occur. Micro-task teams spun up for predictive analytics, customer support, or content loops. Costs are integrated directly into the pricing algorithm, so we only pay for the capacity we need."

Chief Risk Officer / COO: "And it doubles as an early detection system. IoT + blockchain feedback loops will surface defects before they snowball into crises.

Imagine if product failures are flagged instantly, warranties are adjusted in real-time, and bots steer customers toward safer SKUs while we course-correct. Pricing becomes not just dynamic but self-healing."

CEO (closing): "So let's connect the dots. We stop thinking of GTM as a funnel and start treating it as a loop: Purchase (often cloaked) → Post-purchase value creation → Selective reveal → Incentives & community → Profit-sharing via NFTs → Dynamic pricing informed by real-world inputs → Stronger advocacy & stewardship. Our products aren't just SKUs anymore. They're living assets. Our customers aren't just buyers, they're partners with equity in the system. And our price tag? It's no longer a number. It serves as a living proxy for logistics, labor, sustainability, and resilience. This is the new GTM: design for the bot, earn the reveal, reward stewardship, and let dynamic pricing tell the story of our strength. That's how we win in the agentic era."

Customer-Centric Innovation

Customer-centric innovation is no longer about merely adding features or launching campaigns; it's about re-architecting the relationship itself. In the agentic era, where bots handle discovery and customers remain anonymous by default, the battlefield shifts to what happens after the purchase. Products become self-reporting assets, NFTs turn ownership into stewardship, incentives evolve into equity, and pricing reflects the real-time state of logistics, labor, and sustainability.

The companies that succeed will be those that treat identity as negotiable, consent as earned, and post-purchase value as the flywheel that compounds trust, loyalty, and revenue. Innovation is no longer limited to R&D labs; it's built into every product that interacts, every incentive that deepens relationships, and every transparent price that signals resilience.

The future belongs not to brands with the loudest campaigns, but to those that create ecosystems where customers choose to reveal themselves because the value is clear.

CHAPTER 16

Agile Marketing

Think Like an Agile Marketing Leader

In a world where agility has already redefined operations, with just-in-time inventory, blockchain-powered transparency for logistics, and agile/lean approaches for product and tech, marketing is still playing catch-up. Despite being the most variable line item in the enterprise (with 60–70% of budgets shifting quarter to quarter), too many Fortune 500 companies still run marketing like it's 1995: long planning cycles, static calendars, and "waterfall" campaign launches that are outdated the moment they hit the market.

Meanwhile, the rest of the organization is preparing for the coming wave of AI and blockchain. Marketing can't afford to be the last silo standing. With real-time behavioral signals, instant creative production, and agentic marketplaces already reshaping consumer choice, the teams that cling to rigid, top-down planning will find themselves not just behind but irrelevant.

Markets don't move in neat fiscal quarters. Competitors pivot in days. Customer sentiment can shift dramatically with a single viral post. And yet, too many organizations still run their marketing like it's 1999, with waterfall planning, fixed budgets, and media buys locked in long before reality sets in.

Digitally mature companies know better. They inject agility into marketing, enabling it to move at the same speed as their product cycles and customer feedback loops. Because marketing isn't a factory line, it's one of the most variable, market-sensitive levers you have.

Agile isn't a buzzword anymore. It's the next era of marketing.

MASTERY LEARNING OBJECTIVES

- Learn how to architect sprint-based, outcome-driven marketing operations that align with core business objectives while adapting rapidly to changing market conditions.
- Develop the capability to launch, measure, and refine campaigns through collaborative sprint planning, real-time performance tracking, and continuous optimization.
- Identify the tools and infrastructure, from martech stacks to AI agents, that empower agile marketing execution at scale across owned, earned, and paid channels.

INDUSTRY INSIGHT

How Kraft Heinz Went from Corporate Giant to Startup Speed

When 150 years of tradition met agile@scale.

In 2019, Kraft Heinz faced a harsh reality: in an era where startups could launch and iterate products in weeks, the food giant was still moving at a pace of years. Enter *Agile@Scale*, a transformation that would recode a heritage brand for market speed.

Context / Challenge

Legacy processes slowed down product development and marketing. Cross-department handoffs, rigid approval layers, and calendar-based planning meant opportunities passed before products even hit shelves. The mandate: keep the quality, lose the lag.

The Velocity Shift

- Pod Structure: Built small, cross-functional "pods" with all capabilities in one team, marketing, R&D, commercialization, analytics, and empowered to make decisions in real time.
- Parallel Development: Replaced sequential stage gates with concurrent workstreams, collapsing timelines from years to months.

- Tech Leverage: Repurposed existing 360Crisp food-tech to accelerate new launches instead of starting from scratch.
- Data-First Decisions: Began with customer insight (e.g., 95% of restaurant quesadilla fans lacked confidence to cook them at home) to drive product bets.
- 360° Launch Strategy: Integrated market entry, education, retail partnerships, feedback loops, from day one.

Proof Point: *Delimex Crispy Quesadillas* went from insight to shelf at startup speed, backed by real-time customer feedback and a multi-channel launch.

Results / Impact

- Increased share of sales from new products.
- Faster speed-to-market across categories.
- Improved marketing ROI via more personalized, adaptive campaigns.
- Efficiency gains through automation and streamlined labor allocation.

STRATEGIC TAKEAWAYS

- Agility ≠ Chaos: True agility applies discipline to *learning*, not prediction.
- Reuse Wins Time: Repurpose existing tech and capabilities to cut development cycles.
- Integrated Pods Drive Focus: Embed all functions in one decision-making unit to eliminate bottlenecks.
- Feedback Loops Compound Advantage: Products get better and faster when iteration is baked into the launch plan.

REFLECTION

- Where in your marketing operations are you still running "waterfall" processes, and what would it take to shift those areas into sprint-based, adaptive workflows?

- Do your teams operate in functional silos, or could cross-functional "pods" help you collapse timelines and make faster, data-driven decisions?
- How well does your marketing system capture and act on real-time customer feedback—are you iterating at the pace of your market, or at the pace of your calendar?

The Case for Agile Marketing Transformation

In previous chapters, we examined how digital transformation has profoundly affected business strategy, customer engagement, and go-to-market strategies. However, many organizations continue to operate with marketing processes that are outdated for today's era, characterized by annual planning cycles, siloed execution teams, and linear campaign development that can take months from conception to deployment. This traditional method presents significant challenges in a digital environment marked by rapid change, real-time customer feedback, and the need for continuous adaptation and optimization.

Agile marketing marks a total rethinking of how marketing teams operate in today's digital world. Inspired by the software development methods that revolutionized tech product creation, agile marketing applies these ideas to develop marketing practices that are flexible, data-focused, and continually improving. Instead of viewing marketing as fixed campaigns with set plans, agile methods consider it a continuous series of tests that can be quickly adjusted based on market reactions and performance data.

The benefits of this shift go well beyond a mantra of "moving faster." Proper agile marketing offers key competitive advantages through a deeper understanding of customers, more innovative use of resources, and the ability to seize opportunities that might be missed with traditional marketing cycles. For digitally mature organizations that are already advanced in data infrastructure, cross-channel integration, and customer-centric strategies, agile marketing becomes the operational model that unlocks the full value of these efforts.

This chapter examines how organizations can transform their marketing operations by applying agile principles, identifies the specific capabilities necessary for success, and outlines strategies for navigating the challenges of this transition. We examine how agile connects to the broader digital capabilities discussed throughout this book, creating an integrated marketing approach that reflects the demands of today's dynamic marketplace.

From Plans to Learning Systems

It is not just a process change; it is a change in how marketing *thinks, organizes, works, and learns.*

Each dimension of agile speaks to a shift from traditional outputs to agile outcomes:

- Mindset → Shifting from control to curiosity
- Structure → From departments to integrated pods
- Process → From campaigns to continuous delivery
- Measurement → From what we *did* to what we *learned and delivered*

Agile marketing is faster, brighter, and more connected to the customer, and better equipped for the speed of the digital era.

The Rise of Agile Marketing as a Performance System

Traditional marketing relied on timelines, approvals, and campaign calendars. But in a digital world where customers' needs change weekly and channels evolve daily, that model falls apart. Agile marketing flips the script: it treats marketing as a real-time learning engine rather than a broadcast machine. It operates on signals, adapts in cycles, and delivers value through iterative sprints, cross-functional collaboration, and data-driven decision loops.

Agile is more than a process tweak. It's a full-stack operating system for speed, relevance, and growth.

The Agile Marketing Operating System: Five Core Components

1. Cross-Functional Teams Built for Speed

Agile marketing begins with how teams are structured. Instead of isolating creative, media, and analytics functions, Agile teams form cross-functional pods aligned with customer journeys, product stages, or market segments. These groups have everything they need: design, data, content, and channel expertise to deliver outcomes from idea to launch.

Each pod is guided by a Marketing Owner, who sets priorities based on customer needs and business goals, supported by an Agile Lead (similar to a Scrum Master), who maintains the rhythm and removes obstacles. Whether co-located, remote, or hybrid, the goal remains the same: reduce friction and enhance flow.

Success relies on T-shaped talent, shared metrics, and the authority to act swiftly without waiting for approval from multiple levels above.

2. Iterative Planning & Sprint Execution

Agile marketing doesn't ditch strategy; it makes it adaptable. Quarterly objectives set the course, while weekly and daily cycles keep teams aligned with current realities. Work progresses in short, focused sprints (typically 1–3 weeks), each with its planning, stand-ups, reviews, and retrospectives.

Backlogs prioritize impact over bureaucracy. Visual tools, like Kanban boards[94], track progress, velocity, and blockers in real-time. This layered approach provides teams with long-term clarity while maintaining short-term agility, enabling quick pivots without losing sight of their goals.

3. Data as the Decider

In Agile marketing, data drives decisions. Each sprint is a test, and every test offers a learning opportunity. Teams utilize real-time dashboards, journey analytics, and feedback signals to guide decisions mid-flight.

A/B and multivariate testing are integrated into campaigns with clear hypotheses, outcome goals, and feedback loops. Customer insights, from journey tracking to social sentiment, are incorporated into backlogs and optimization cycles.

Every insight is shared, tagged, and reused, eliminating hoarded learnings and gut-driven decisions. Agile teams function like testing labs, moving fast and learning continuously.

4. Adaptive Resources, Rolling Budgets

Agile teams don't wait for Q1 budget approvals to pursue opportunities. Resourcing is flexible. Budgets roll over. Teams can expand or scale back based on the initiative's size and stage.

Underperforming programs are phased out early. High-performing initiatives scale rapidly. Shared talent pools and ecosystem partners enable rapid deployment of new capabilities without excessive bureaucracy.

MarTech platforms automate the creation, distribution, and optimization of marketing activities. Collaboration tools, such as Asana, Miro, Figma, Slack, and Teams, facilitate real-time, cross-functional work. Your resources move at market speed, or faster.

5. Alignment Without Bottlenecks

Agile isn't chaos; it's coordinated independence. Teams operate autonomously but stay aligned through shared goals, synchronized cycles, and open communication.

Frameworks like OKRs ensure everyone remains focused on strategic objectives. "Scrum of scrums" and planning retrospectives connect teams without slowing progress. Strategic narratives clarify the purpose behind work, while stakeholder feedback loops keep decision-makers informed without interference.

Agile also strengthens the connection between marketing and sales. Shared pipelines, joint metrics, and rapid feedback loops provide customers with a unified brand experience, rather than a fragmented organization chart.

Don't Run Marketing. Tune It.

Agile marketing is more than sprint cycles and standup meetings; it's about making adaptability work in practice. In a market that changes daily, the winners will be those who can sense, test, and respond quickly.

Think of it this way: if traditional marketing were a campaign calendar, Agile is a marketing engine that runs constantly, driven by data, supported by teams, and tuned to the customer.

Agile OS Component	Level 1 Traditional Ops	Level 2 Emerging Agility	Level 3 Advancing Agility	Level 4 Adaptive Excellence
Cross-Functional Teams	Rigid silos, sequential handoffs, long approval chains	Pilot pods formed for projects; early T-shaped skills; partial matrix reporting	Stable pods aligned to journeys with CoEs for expertise	Fully fluid, self-organizing pods with universal T-shaped talent
Iterative Planning & Sprint Execution	Annual plans, linear campaigns, and minor mid-course corrections	Quarterly reviews + basic sprint pilots; backlog emerging	Quarterly strategy + weekly sprints; retrospectives and continuous refinement	Rolling-wave planning, AI-assisted backlog optimization, real-time pivots
Data as the Decider	Intuition-driven, siloed metrics, post-campaign reports	Basic dashboards, early A/B testing, weekly reporting	Integrated cross-channel dashboards, systematic testing, shared learning repos	Predictive analytics + AI decision support, embedded real-time experimentation
Adaptive Resources & Budgets	Fixed annual budgets, rigid resourcing, static tech stack	Quarterly budget reviews, shared resource pools, and modular MarTech	Rolling budget allocation, performance-based resourcing, integrated partner ecosystems	Dynamic allocation with AI-driven optimization, just-in-time skills, automated delivery pipelines
Alignment Without Bottlenecks	Hierarchical approvals, channel-centric KPIs, and siloed goals	OKRs piloted, cross-team check-ins, limited transparency	Shared OKRs, synchronized sprint cadences, journey-based KPIs	Complete alignment through shared telemetry, "scrum of scrums," AI-augmented stakeholder sync

GLOBAL SIGNAL

Experimentation as Survival Mode

The Agile Marketing Matrix moves firms from rigid campaigns to iterative experiments. In volatile emerging markets, experimentation isn't a methodology, it's survival, marketing teams must test, pivot, and reallocate budgets daily.

Signals

- M-KOPA / solar-fintech hybrids: They constantly test tariffs, bundling of services, cross-sell propositions, and repayment schemes in different geographies to optimize adoption.
- Fintechs in Latin America (e.g., Nubank, Rappi): Use real-time A/B testing across credit offers, messaging, pricing, and loyalty incentives to adapt in volatile macro conditions.
- D2C brands in India / Southeast Asia: They run micro-experiments on chat-based commerce, influencer partnerships, and regional creative variations with high iteration speed.

Takeaway

In stable markets, you may phase experiments over quarters. In emerging markets, you live in continuous test mode. The advantage accrues not to perfect plans but to the teams that can test 100 ideas, kill 90, and scale the 10 that show signal.

Where Does Your Organization Stand?

The shift from traditional marketing to adaptive excellence isn't a flip of a switch; it's a climb. Most organizations fall into one of four maturity levels, each defined by how they structure teams, plan work, make decisions, and allocate resources. Knowing your current level is the first step to accelerating progress.

Level 1

Traditional Marketing Operations, *Channels, Not Journeys*

Siloed functions, hierarchical approvals, and annual campaign calendarsare the norm. Teams optimize channels in isolation, data is fragmented, and decisions lean on intuition and post-mortems. Results: slow time-to-market, missed cultural moments, and weak ROI visibility. Rigidity that once meant stability now creates drag.

Level 2

Emerging Agility, *Pilots, Not Systems*

Pilot pods and matrix reporting begin to break silos. Teams experiment with quarterly planning, sprint execution, and modular tech. Early dashboards, basic testing, and flexible budgets create pockets of momentum. Hybrid models deliver proof of concept but often stall against legacy processes and risk-averse governance.

Level 3

Advancing Agility, *Journeys, Not Silos*

Organizations rewire around journeys and outcomes, with pods taking end-to-end responsibility. Strategy is set quarterly, while tactics are executed every week. Unified data platforms and shared learning repositories fuel systematic testing and optimization. Rolling budgets and connected tech stacks enable responsiveness. Results include faster campaigns, clearer ROI, and tighter business alignment; however, scaling consistency across the enterprise remains a hurdle.

Level 4

Adaptive Excellence, Anticipation, *Not Reaction*

The operating system itself becomes fluid. Teams self-organize, roles are universally T-shaped, and resources are allocated in real-time. Planning is continuous, not episodic. AI augments everything, from backlog prioritization to predictive decision support, while integrated data ecosystems turn every action into a learning loop. Organizations at this level don't just adapt faster; they anticipate, seizing opportunities before competitors even register them.

Diagnostic Questions

To assess your organization's current maturity level, evaluate these key indicators across each dimension.

- Do your teams focus on customer outcomes or internal functions?
- How quickly can you test new ideas and implement successful ones?
- What percentage of your decisions depend on real-time data versus historical data or executive intuition?
- How adaptable are you in reallocating resources when new opportunities arise?

The honest answers to these questions reveal your current position and highlight the specific capabilities you need to develop to reach the next level of maturity. Keep in mind that sustainable transformation requires systematic growth across all dimensions, rather than progress in isolated areas, because true agility stems from integrating evolved capabilities rather than excelling in individual components.

A Digital Leader's Roadmap

In today's constantly connected market, the difference between leaders and laggards is no longer about brand equity; it's about speed of response. Agile marketing has become the digital leader's advantage: the ability to test, iterate, and scale campaigns quickly, faster than others can even prepare a PowerPoint presentation.

McKinsey summarizes it well: "If you're not agile all the way, you're not agile." Partial implementation delivers only partial results. However, full-stack agility has led to revenue increases of 20-40%, and in some product segments, up to four times growth.

As Mastercard's CMO Sarah Watson said, "When competitors took 12 weeks to test a campaign, we ran three versions in three weeks. That's not an operational edge; it's a strategic one."

Start with a System Check: Assess to Accelerate

Before you sprint, you scan. Use the Agile Marketing Maturity Matrix to:

- Map the current state across eight core agility dimensions
- Prioritize gaps that block performance

- Set phased targets that scale with impact
- Assign ownership and track progress like a product roadmap

As digital exec Jason Chen says, *"Most leaders skip the scan and jump to execution. That's why most transformations stall."*

24-Month Transformation Plan

Phase 1: Foundation Build (0–6 Months)

Start small, move fast. Launch one cross-functional "pod" with time released from day-to-day work. Run 1–2 week sprints, daily standups, and pilot high-impact areas with clear customer outcomes.

Key moves:

- Build a pod of 8–12 people
- Define sprint rituals and service-level agreements with legal, IT, and procurement
- Launch real-time dashboards and agile backlogs
- Set cultural expectations: speed, autonomy, data over opinion, customer at the core

Early wins:

- Campaign deployment shrinks from 4–6 months to <1
- Leadership sees proof, buy-in grows
- Adjacent teams start to pull the model

Gartner reports that orgs in this stage see 15–20% faster campaign cycles in just six months.

Phase 2: Scale with Control (6–12 Months)

Once the pilot works, scale with discipline. Add teams one by one. Don't outpace your learning curve.

Key moves:

- Launch pods aligned to journeys, segments, or products
- Stand up a "Control Tower" to standardize playbooks and share learnings
- Expand analytics depth and train up org-wide capability
- Bring agencies into the rhythm

Mid-stage outcomes:

- 2–3x increase in campaign velocity
- Test-and-learn culture spreads
- Cross-team collaboration strengthens
- Marketing ROI begins to climb

Phase 3: Enterprise Integration (12–24 Months)

Agility becomes the default operating system. Teams, tech, budget, and structure evolve around learning speed and customer feedback.

Key moves:

- Organize marketing around customer journeys, not silos
- Shift budgets dynamically based on performance
- Fully integrate partners into sprint cycles
- Deploy AI, automation, and predictive tools
- Launch agile career tracks and performance frameworks

System-wide impact:

- Continuous optimization embedded into every campaign
- Channel collaboration turns into journey orchestration
- Resilience under pressure improves
- Teams don't just move faster, they move smarter

From Process to Strategic Superpower

McKinsey's research[95] highlights the transformative impact of agile marketing through an 18-month journey of a North American retailer, yielding exceptional results: a 4x increase in campaign throughput, a 30% increase in customer satisfaction, and a 2x increase in digital sales growth.

These are not merely minor improvements; they offer a fundamental competitive advantage in markets where customer expectations are constantly evolving, and competitive opportunities are fleeting.

Agile marketing goes beyond process improvements to become a strategic operating model that fundamentally changes how organizations create and deliver customer value. Market leaders are those that ship, test, learn, and scale faster than market conditions change, turning adaptability into a sustainable competitive advantage.

The transformation requires more than just adopting new meeting formats or project management tools. It calls for systematic changes in leadership approaches, infrastructure investments, and cultural shifts throughout the organization. Success is defined by specific factors that high-performing transformations consistently implement, while stalled initiatives tend to overlook them.

CASE STUDY

Pepsi vs. Gucci — Agility Across the Spectrum

How a snack brand and a luxury house both learned to sprint.

Agile marketing looks different when you're selling chips versus couture, but the underlying principles are the same: listen faster, test smaller, and adapt continuously. Pepsi and Gucci show how agility scales across opposite ends of the consumer spectrum.

The Bottleneck

- Pepsi: Traditional CPG marketing ran on long cycles—TV spots, seasonal pushes, and fixed retail campaigns. That rhythm couldn't keep up with TikTok trends or snack-aisle fragmentation.
- Gucci: Luxury marketing thrived on exclusivity and seasonal shows, but this cadence clashed with Gen Z's appetite for always-on culture, digital experiences, and unexpected collaborations.

The Overclock

Pepsi — Agile at Scale:

- Built a global Digital Hub using AI + social listening to spot micro-trends in days.

- Agile pods launched snack-culture campaigns within 48 hours, localizing assets for markets from Mexico to Malaysia.
- Modular content libraries let Pepsi remix and deploy creative instantly across retailers and social channels.

Gucci – Agile in Luxury:

- Embedded "creative war rooms" that monitored memes and cultural moments, producing limited drops in weeks instead of seasons.
- Partnered with platforms like Roblox and Fortnite to experiment in digital fashion with real-time feedback loops.
- Used capsule collections and collabs (e.g., Gucci x Balenciaga) as agile tests before scaling to full runway shows.

Results

- Pepsi: Campaign cycles shrank from months to days, lifting share of voice with Gen Z and driving incremental growth across snack categories.
- Gucci: Roblox collab reached 20M+ players; limited drops routinely sold out; earned media spikes reinforced Gucci's position as a culturally relevant luxury brand.

What It Means

Agile isn't one-size-fits-all. For Pepsi, it's about volume and velocity—meeting consumers in snackable cultural moments. For Gucci, it's about exclusivity and experimentation—protecting luxury cues while adapting to new audiences. Together they prove agility isn't about category—it's about mindset.

Critical Success Factors for Sustainable Transformation

Executive sponsorship is the essential foundation for a successful agile marketing transformation. Without visible commitment and active support from CMOs and functional leaders, agile initiatives tend to stall in middle management, where operational pressures often override the incentives for experimentation. Leaders must model a test-and-learn mindset while actively removing organizational obstacles that hinder teams from operating with the necessary speed and autonomy.

Strategic focus helps prevent the common mistake of attempting enterprise-wide transformation before proving agile approaches in controlled environments. Organizations see better results by starting with a high-impact pilot team that can master the operational rhythm and demonstrate measurable results before expanding. Premature scaling that exceeds cultural readiness usually leads to superficial adoption without actual behavioral change.

Breaking down functional silos is crucial because agile teams succeed when marketing, legal, finance, and IT work as integrated units, rather than as sequential handoff systems. Cross-functional "war rooms" serve as the foundation for quick decision-making and smooth execution, eliminating delays and miscommunication often found in traditional campaign processes.

System standardization must strike a balance between cohesion and responsiveness through shared playbooks that ensure operational consistency while allowing team-level autonomy to foster adaptability. This balance helps organizations expand successful approaches across multiple teams while maintaining the flexibility to respond swiftly to unique opportunities or market shifts.

Performance visibility transforms decision-making through real-time dashboards that enable data-driven choices, rather than relying on intuition or historical precedent. Shared accountability through outcome-based metrics fosters alignment while mitigating the political dynamics that often hinder marketing execution in traditional organizational structures.

Team empowerment requires leaders to provide strategic clarity, access to necessary tools, and political support while avoiding micromanagement that undermines the purpose of agile autonomy. The most successful transformations occur when leadership focuses on removing obstacles rather than controlling execution details.

This transition has consequences for the staff. Empowerment, assumed authority, and the permission of dissent need to be communicated and demonstrated from the highest levels. A call to the CEO, two levels above your manager, can't ruffle feathers. Frontline employees will be welcome at executive commitment meetings to unblock outstanding issues in the way of adaptability and velocity.

The Strategic Imperative

Agile marketing is more than a process shift; it's a strategic rewiring of how organizations create and deliver customer value. The Kraft Heinz transformation proves that even legacy giants can move with startup speed when leadership commits to learning faster than the market changes. Their pod model, fueled by real-time insights and cross-functional execution, didn't just launch products faster; it built an engine for continuous innovation and market responsiveness.

The demand for this capability will only intensify. Customer expectations are evolving in weeks, not years. Channels, algorithms, and cultural moments shift daily. Competitors can appear from anywhere. In this environment, speed without focus is chaos, and focus without speed is irrelevant. Agile delivers both when it's built on bold leadership, the proper infrastructure, integrated data systems, and teams skilled in turning signals into action.

Think of agile marketing as a living operating system for growth:

- Bold leadership sets the vision and clears the obstacles.
- Robust infrastructure provides tools, data, and automation to operate at market speed.
- Skilled, cross-functional teams turn insights into outcomes in weeks, not quarters.

In the coming years, the winners won't be the ones with the most significant budgets or longest planning decks; they'll be the ones who can sense, decide, and act in real time, scaling what works before the window closes. Agile marketing isn't just about how you keep pace; it's about how you set it.

SECTION IV

The Frontier

Push beyond the red line into AI, enterprise intelligence, and new models of value.

The frontier is where the gauges turn red and the old rules no longer apply. This is where AI stops being a tool and becomes an operating layer, and where emerging models, from decentralized finance to platform ecosystems, rewrite the playbook entirely. For leaders ready to run past the limiter, this is where tomorrow's advantage is forged.

CHAPTER 17

AI & Enterprise — Agility with Intelligence

Think Like an AI Strategist

Let's face it, we're still in the early days of the AI revolution, and most enterprises are dabbling when they should be redesigning. The winners of the next decade will treat AI not as a bolt-on toolset but as the central nervous system of their business, sensing market shifts, predicting customer needs, and adapting operations before competitors even realize the game has changed. Right now, the gap between leaders and laggards is measured in months. Soon, it will be calculated in hours. The question for every C-suite is no longer if AI will transform your industry; it's whether your organization will be the one doing the transforming or the one struggling to keep up.

According to McKinsey's 2025 State of AI report[96], "the value of AI comes from rewiring how companies run, and the latest survey shows that, out of 25 attributes tested for organizations of all sizes, the redesign of workflows has the biggest effect on an organization's ability to see EBITDA impact from its use of gen AI."

You've built agile marketing capabilities that can sense market shifts and adapt campaigns in real-time. Your teams move from insight to execution in days, not quarters. Customer feedback loops drive continuous optimization. You're faster, more responsive, and more data-driven than ever before.

Now that you're agile, just in time, and process automated, how can you become more proactive, quicker, and more service-oriented?

What if the real competitive advantage comes not from human teams moving faster, but from intelligent systems that can sense, decide, and act faster than market conditions change? What if your subsequent campaign optimization happens in milliseconds, not sprint cycles? What if your customer insights come from real behavior, not reported preferences?

The most successful organizations are discovering that agile marketing is the bridge to something more powerful: AI-native enterprises that don't just respond to change, they anticipate it, shape it, and profit from it before competitors even detect the shift.

The gap between traditional agile and AI-accelerated agile isn't incremental. It's exponential. And it's widening every quarter.

Welcome to the intelligence layer of enterprise agility.

MASTERY LEARNING OBJECTIVES

- Explain how AI applications extend beyond marketing into sales, logistics, operations, product development, and IT.
- Analyze how organizations adopt and scale AI, comparing pilot programs, embedded applications, and enterprise-wide orchestration.
- Demonstrate understanding of how AI systems interconnect across functions, integrating marketing, operations, customer service, supply chain, HR, and IT, into a cohesive orchestration layer that drives enterprise-wide intelligence, agility, and strategic alignment.

INDUSTRY INSIGHT

How P&G Became an AI-Native Enterprise

Turning a 184-year-old consumer goods giant into a real-time intelligence system.

In 2017, Procter & Gamble's CIO, Vittorio Cretella, faced an uncomfortable truth from a connected toothbrush: people brushed for only 47 seconds on average, not the two minutes they claimed. That gap between *stated* and *actual* behavior wasn't just a dental insight; it was a mirror showing where decades of survey-based decision-making had been wrong.

Context / Challenge

Legacy research methods couldn't keep pace with the nuance of real-world behavior. P&G needed a way to see, sense, and adapt to consumer habits in real-time, across every category, geography, and function, without slowing down its massive operations.

The Velocity Shift

- Embedded Intelligence[97]. Integrated AI directly into products to create always-on feedback loops (e.g., Oral-B GENIUS X toothbrush analyzing thousands of brushing sessions).
- AI-First Operations: Partnered with Microsoft to digitize 100+ manufacturing sites, enabling predictive quality, touchless operations, and real-time analytics.
- Data Infrastructure: Built a multi-cloud architecture to unify insights from R&D, supply chain, marketing, and retail partners.
- Hyperlocal Decisions: Used AI-powered "Neighborhood Analytics" to tailor promotions, assortments, and pricing at market speed.
- Scale, Not Pilots: Moved beyond test projects to make AI the connective tissue of the enterprise.

Results / Impact

- Reduced manufacturing waste and improved yield through predictive analytics.
- Accelerated R&D cycles by feeding real-world usage data directly into design.
- Delivered hyper-personalized products and marketing at scale.
- Shifted from reactive adjustments to proactive, algorithm-driven decision-making across business units.

AI is evolving at a speed unlike anything we've seen before in business technology. Web 1.0, the era of static websites and early e-commerce, took more than a decade to reach maturity. Web 2.0, the social, mobile, and cloud wave, compressed that cycle to about seven years. Today's AI and Web 3.0 landscape is advancing in three to six-month sprints. Each leap brings entirely new capabilities, toolsets, and market expectations, and the competitive window for adoption is far narrower than it was

STRATEGIC TAKEAWAYS

- **Measure What's Real: AI reveals the truth in behavior, not just the story in surveys.**
- **Think Pervasive, Not Point Solution: Legacy transformation requires intelligence woven through every process, not bolted on.**
- **Operational + Customer Value: The strongest AI strategies improve both efficiency and experience.**
- **Build AI Fluency Enterprise-Wide: When everyone understands how to apply intelligence, innovation compounds.**

REFLECTION

- **Is your organization still relying on human-driven agility, or are you beginning to embed AI systems that can sense, decide, and act faster than your teams ever could?**
- **Have you moved past AI experiments and pilots into scaling intelligence across core functions, marketing, operations, supply chain, and customer service, or are you still treating AI as a side project?**
- **What would it take for every function in your business to speak a standard "AI language," turning intelligence into a unifying layer rather than a patchwork of disconnected tools?**

---

in past technology waves. Leaders who try to follow the same multi-year planning cycles used for earlier digital transformations will find themselves launching their "first" AI initiatives years after the competition has already completed their second or third generation of capability.

From a business perspective, AI can be understood on two levels. For a small business, it functions like a hyper-capable assistant that can read, write, and analyze in seconds. It digests a wide range of data, including customer inquiries, inventory spreadsheets, and sales emails, learns from the patterns, and predicts the most helpful next step.

This could involve answering a customer question, generating a piece of marketing content, or routing a support ticket. In this setting, AI often arrives as a feature embedded in tools companies already use, such as Microsoft Copilot, Shopify Magic, or HubSpot AI.

In a large enterprise, AI becomes an operating system for decision-making and process orchestration. Multiple AI models may be running simultaneously, including large language models for reasoning and generation, computer vision systems for image and video analysis, recommender engines for personalization, and specialized models for forecasting or anomaly detection.

These models are continuously fed by data pipelines that pull data from ERP, CRM, IoT devices, and third-party sources. An MLOps[98] or LMMOps layer governs how models are deployed, tested, updated, and monitored for drift, while compliance systems ensure outputs meet regulatory, security, and ethical standards.

Outputs are integrated directly into workflows so that AI doesn't just suggest an action but can also trigger processes in claims handling, supply chain optimization, product development, and more.

At the core of any AI system are its data sets and the process of "training the model." Models learn patterns, associations, and probabilities by analyzing large amounts of structured data (such as databases and spreadsheets) and unstructured data (including text documents, emails, audio transcripts, images, and videos).

Training involves providing the model with examples so it can infer rules and relationships, adjusting billions of internal parameters until it can make accurate predictions or produce coherent, relevant outputs.

A company can fine-tune an existing model using its proprietary data, such as past sales records, product specifications, or internal documents, to make the model more relevant to its operations. This fine-tuning doesn't require surrendering control of the data. Organizations can run models in private cloud or on-premises environments and incorporate privacy-preserving techniques to ensure proprietary information and personally identifiable information (PII) stay within the company's control.

With the right architecture, such as retrieval-augmented generation (RAG)[99] that keeps sensitive data in a secure internal store, businesses can comply with regulations like GDPR and still deploy powerful AI agents for internal-only tasks.

Industry adoption is uneven.

Technology, financial services, retail, and healthcare are moving fastest, leveraging AI for customer engagement, risk modeling, supply chain management, and clinical decision support.

Media and entertainment are rapidly experimenting with AI-assisted content creation. Manufacturing is adopting AI for predictive maintenance, quality control, and process automation.

The **public sector, construction, and specific aspects of education** are lagging, constrained by regulatory complexity, legacy infrastructure, and budget cycles. However, these slower-moving sectors often have high-impact opportunities once the foundational barriers are addressed.

A common question is whether organizations still stuck between Web 1.0 and a complete Web 2.0 capability can leapfrog directly into AI-driven Web 3.0. The short answer is yes, but it requires a deliberate and strategic approach. AI adoption is not exclusively sequential; companies can deploy modern AI platforms that come bundled with cloud infrastructure, collaborative workflows, and analytics, effectively "jumping" over intermediate stages.

For example, a manufacturer with a static brochure-style website and minimal e-commerce presence could deploy an AI-driven B2B ordering portal with integrated chat support, skipping a decade of incremental upgrades. The key is to choose platforms that provide both the AI capabilities and the digital foundations, modern data architecture, integration hooks, and governance tools, so the leap isn't just a tech showcase but a sustainable competitive advantage.

Governance and ethics must underpin every step of this acceleration. Rapid deployment without oversight risks bias, hallucinations, privacy violations, and reputational harm. Adopting frameworks like the NIST AI Risk Management Framework[100] or ISO AI standards helps define guardrails.

These include maintaining a human-in-the-loop for sensitive decisions, keeping audit logs for traceability, and conducting regular red teaming exercises to identify vulnerabilities. The speed of AI adoption in Web 3.0 makes these governance measures not an afterthought but a prerequisite, especially when the cost of a single misstep can be amplified across digital channels instantly.

A BRIEF HISTORY OF AI (BUSINESS-FOCUSED)

1950s–1970s
Foundations in symbolic logic and rule-based systems.

1980s
Expert systems in industry (e.g., medical diagnosis, credit scoring).

1990s–2000s
Machine learning emerges; statistical models replace hard-coded rules. Search engines, fraud detection, targeted ads.

2010s
Deep learning + massive data + cloud computing → image recognition, speech-to-text, translation at scale.

2020s
Foundation models & generative AI, Large Language Models (LLMs) and multi-modal systems that can understand, reason, and create across text, images, audio, and code.

A Guided Tour for the C-Suite

Picture this: it's Monday morning, and your executive committee has gathered in the strategy war room. But instead of thumbing through last quarter's slide decks, you're watching a live, unified intelligence feed, a panoramic view of your business in motion, augmented by AI. The data is not static; it's breathing, learning, and anticipating.

Your head of product begins. *"This weekend, our market sensing engine flagged a spike in forum chatter about battery anxiety in our newest wearable, not in reviews, but in the subtext of what customers are asking online. The system traced it to a growing microtrend in Europe: consumers want wearables that blend into formal clothing without sacrificing power. Our AI co-pilot has already modeled three design concepts and run simulated demand tests. Option B outperformed by 18% with the target segment."*

This is product and innovation intelligence at work, with no surveys months later and no guesswork. The system listens at the edge, identifies unarticulated needs, and tests solutions before competitors even realize the trend exists. Nike utilizes this method to identify style shifts from social media platforms and e-commerce reviews. At the same time, Dyson employs it to identify user frustrations with vacuum attachments that traditional research might overlook.

Your CMO takes the floor. *"We've moved beyond campaigns. Last week, we launched the dynamic app, which tailors content based on time of day, day of the week, past purchases, and geolocation. This means we're not just offering different products, but also a different sequence, tone, and offer. Our AI-generated creative tested ten variants overnight, auto-optimized, and doubled engagement in the 25–34 segment. Revenue lift from personalization last quarter? $42 million."*

This is content and experience intelligence, enabling the real-time orchestration of experiences, such as Netflix tailoring your watchlist or Spotify crafting a "Made for You" playlist on the fly. In your company, every touchpoint adapts instantly, informed by behavior, context, and predicted intent.

Your CRO jumps in. *"Our sales AI flagged a $3M deal in Asia-Pacific that looked healthy on paper but showed conversational fatigue in call transcripts. It suggested a targeted executive briefing, which we ran on Friday, and the deal's now projected to close two weeks early. Meanwhile, the system found six dormant accounts with expansion potential; two are already in negotiation."*

This is *sales and revenue intelligence*, the same logic ZoomInfo, Gong, and Clari use to spot risk and surface growth opportunities. It's no longer about managing a pipeline; it's about actively shaping it in real time.

The COO leans forward. *"Our logistics AI predicted a severe weather disruption in the Southeast three days out. We rerouted 12% of our deliveries before the storm even made the news, saving $1.4M in late penalties. The same system is now simulating warehouse layouts for peak season, early models suggest a 9% throughput increase."*

This is operational and supply chain intelligence, which UPS, Maersk, and Amazon have mastered. Instead of reacting to disruptions, your operations sense them early, reroute, and re-optimize.

Your CIO follows. *"Last Thursday, our infrastructure AI detected a pattern of anomalies in our ERP system that could have cascaded into a full outage. It self-corrected in 90 seconds. No downtime, no customer impact. It also flagged two emerging security threats before they reached our network perimeter."*

This is IT and infrastructure intelligence, the predictive, self-healing approach used by hyperscalers[101] like Microsoft Azure and Google Cloud to keep global systems always on.

Your CHRO adds. *"We're now matching employees to emerging roles before they open. Our AI mapped internal skills data to market trends, found 140 hidden candidates for high-demand roles, and recommended learning paths. It's reduced time-to-fill for strategic positions by 32%."*

This is HR and talent intelligence, the predictive workforce modeling that companies like Unilever use to spot future skills gaps and prepare talent pipelines years in advance.

Then your Overclocked fractional CDO chimes in with a wry grin. *"As you've probably seen in the US radar dashboard, it's hurricane season in Florida, and this one looks massive.*

Our AI CRM platform, which we've branded 'Pulse', was integrated with NOAA data feeds to obtain real-time weather intelligence. Pulse automatically shifted all outbound messaging in the anticipated impact zones: no August promo pushes, no product hype, just service and customer empathy during a rough time.

On the flip side, the exact triggers detect hyper-local weather events year-round. In Denver, we swap in 'Plan for Snow' offers; in Phoenix, Beat the Heat' campaigns. It's not just personalization; it's situational awareness at scale."

As the meeting ends, you realize something important: these aren't separate wins. They're connected, intelligence flowing from product insights to marketing personalization, into sales plays, through operations, supported by IT, and fueled by talent. Your AI operating system is not a set of pilots; it's a nervous system for the enterprise. It senses, decides, and acts across every function, with leadership, infrastructure, strategy, and insight all working in sync.

The companies that master this will do more than survive disruption; they'll set the pace of their industries. The question isn't whether AI will rewrite the rules. It's whether you'll be the author or just a reader.

The AI Stack Is Getting Simpler (And More Powerful): Why Your Business Needs to Think Like a Conductor, Not a Shopper

Remember when the internet evolved from simple websites to interactive platforms where users could create, share, and collaborate? We're witnessing a similar transformation in AI, but it's happening at business speed. The days of frantically evaluating individual AI tools, chatbots here, image generators there, are ending. What's emerging instead is something far more strategic: AI as the intelligent nervous system that runs through every part of your business.

Think of it like building a house. You don't just buy random tools and hope they work together. You need a foundation, a framework, and then specialized equipment for specific jobs. The AI landscape has organized itself into three essential layers that, when combined, create something much more powerful than their individual parts.

At the foundation level, you have massive AI brains, models like GPT, Claude, and others that provide the raw intelligence. These are like having access to a brilliant generalist who can understand language, analyze patterns, and generate ideas, but doesn't know the specifics of your industry or business. They're incredibly powerful, but they need guidance and context to be truly useful.

The middle layer consists of enterprise platforms that transform raw intelligence into actionable business insights. These platforms manage technical complexities, security, integration with existing systems, and user management, while providing the tools your teams need. Think of them as translators between the AI's capabilities and your business needs, ensuring everything operates smoothly with your current processes and fulfills compliance requirements.

At the top layer are specialized AI solutions built specifically for your industry or business function. These understand the unique language, regulations, and challenges of your sector. A healthcare AI solution knows about HIPAA compliance and medical terminology. A financial services AI understands risk management and regulatory requirements. These specialized tools leverage foundational intelligence and apply it with the precision and knowledge your specific business demands.

The magic happens when these three layers work together as a unified system. Your specialized tools leverage the enterprise platform's security and integration capabilities, which in turn tap into the foundational models' intelligence. Rather than managing dozens of disconnected AI experiments, you're orchestrating a coherent system that gets smarter and more valuable over time.

This isn't just about efficiency; it's about competitive advantage. Companies that understand how to combine these layers effectively will be able to innovate faster, serve customers better, and adapt to changes more quickly than those still thinking about AI as individual tools to purchase rather than an integrated capability to build.

What Platform Orchestration Means

Platform orchestration represents a fundamental shift from "best-of-breed" tool selection to "best-of-system" capability integration. Instead of choosing the single "winning" AI model or vendor, successful enterprises are building intelligent orchestration layers that combine multiple AI capabilities, data sources, and business systems into unified, adaptive platforms.

Think of it like conducting a symphony orchestra. The conductor doesn't replace the violins, brass, or percussion; they coordinate all instruments to create something more powerful than any individual section could achieve alone. Platform orchestration does the same thing with AI capabilities, business systems, and data flows.

The Infrastructure Strategy Connection

This evolution directly builds on the infrastructure principles we established in Chapter 4, where we defined infrastructure not as servers and storage, but as a strategic capability that enables scalable experimentation and cross-functional data flows. Platform orchestration is an infrastructure strategy evolved for the AI era.

Traditional Infrastructure Strategy: Build reliable, scalable systems that support business applications. AI-Era Platform Orchestration: Build intelligent, adaptive systems that coordinate AI capabilities across business ecosystems

The key insight: AI doesn't just run on infrastructure; it becomes part of the infrastructure layer itself, providing intelligence that makes the entire platform more adaptive and valuable.

From Infrastructure to AI Ecosystem to Agile Enterprise

Layer 1: Infrastructure Foundation

Your cloud-native platforms, unified data lakes, and API-first architecture become the foundation that enables AI orchestration. Without this layer, you're limited to isolated AI tools rather than coordinated intelligence.

Example

A global retailer's infrastructure enables real-time data flow between inventory systems, customer behavior analytics, and pricing engines, creating the foundation for AI orchestration across all touchpoints.

Layer 2: AI Ecosystem Orchestration

Multiple AI models, tools, and capabilities work together through intelligent coordination layers, enabling seamless integration and effective collaboration. Instead of choosing between GPT-4, Claude, or industry-specific models, you orchestrate them based on task requirements, cost optimization, and performance needs.

Example

The same retailer orchestrates:

- GPT-4 for customer service conversations requiring creativity
- Industry-specific models for demand forecasting and inventory optimization
- Computer vision models for quality control in fulfillment centers
- Recommendation engines for personalized shopping experiences

All coordinated through a unified platform that routes requests to optimal models while maintaining consistent security, governance, and performance monitoring.

Layer 3: Agile Enterprise Operations

The orchestrated AI ecosystem enables agile business operations that sense, decide, and act faster than traditional organizational structures. Teams work with intelligent systems that enhance human decision-making rather than replacing it.

Example

When the retailer's market sensing AI detects emerging trends in social media, it automatically triggers:

- Product development teams to evaluate opportunity fit
- Supply chain systems to model demand scenarios
- Marketing teams to develop campaign concepts
- Financial planning to assess investment requirements

All within hours, rather than quarters, because the AI ecosystem orchestrates the flow of information and initial analysis across functions.

Why Platform Orchestration Beats Tool Selection

As individual AI tools become more powerful, the value of integration increases. GPT-4 is impressive, but when combined with your customer data, integrated with your CRM, coordinated with your supply chain systems, and governed by your compliance frameworks, it becomes transformational.

The Flexibility Advantage

Platform orchestration enables you to:

- Swap AI models without rebuilding applications (when GPT-5 launches, you route to it seamlessly)
- Optimize costs by using expensive models only when necessary and cheaper ones for routine tasks
- Reduce vendor risk by avoiding lock-in to any single AI provider
- Scale capabilities by adding new AI tools without disrupting existing workflows

The Compound Learning Effect

Orchestrated platforms create learning loops that no single tool can achieve. Customer interactions inform product development, enhancing marketing personalization, which in turn improves customer satisfaction and generates better training data for all AI models in the ecosystem.

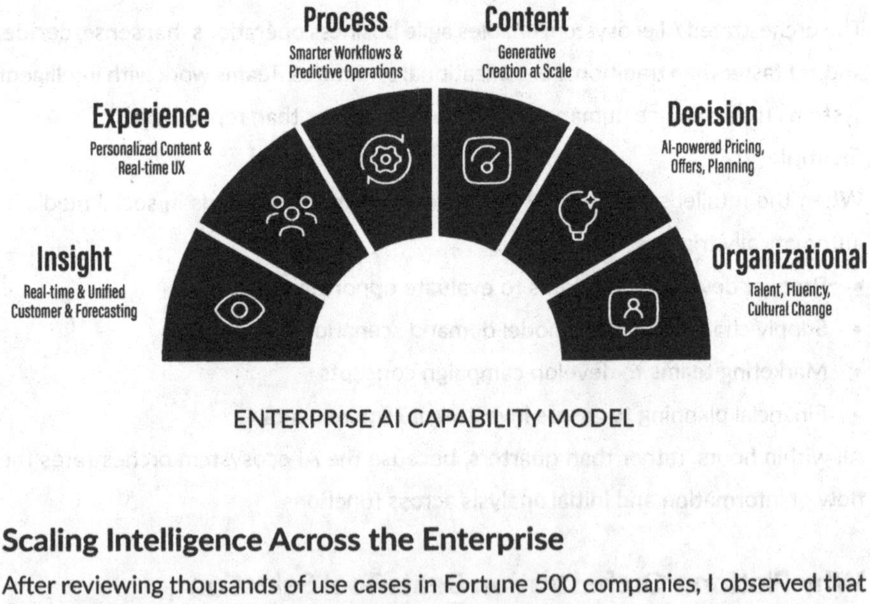

ENTERPRISE AI CAPABILITY MODEL

Scaling Intelligence Across the Enterprise

After reviewing thousands of use cases in Fortune 500 companies, I observed that operational patterns were emerging across the business, not just in isolated instances. Enterprises must build capability in six interconnected domains. Each one translates intelligence into velocity, adaptability, and value creation.

GLOBAL SIGNAL

AI as Core Infrastructure

The AI Maturity Matrix shows enterprises evolving from pilots to integrated orchestration. In emerging markets, some organizations skip experimentation entirely, embedding AI at the core of operations from inception.

Signals

- Ping An Good Doctor (China): AI-powered platform serving 190M users and 1B+ consultations. Healthcare AI here isn't a trial—it's population-scale infrastructure.
- Seha Virtual Hospital (Saudi Arabia): Linked 224 hospitals through AI-driven telemedicine and translation. By building a national health AI fabric, Seha bypassed incremental rollout.
- Cera Care (UK/EU): Applied predictive AI to home care at scale, shifting healthcare from reactive to preventive while optimizing caregiver logistics.

Takeaway

AI-native enterprises prove that maturity isn't a path—it's a posture. The competitive gap will widen not between adopters and laggards, but between those piloting AI and those already running on it.

THE FIVE STAGES OF AI MATURITY ACROSS ENTERPRISE CAPABILITIES

Capability	Stage 1 Basic ML / Predictive Models	Stage 2 Individual Experiments
Insight Intelligence From Data Swamps to Decision Engines	Descriptive dashboards, siloed BI, and some regression-based predictions.	Individual teams run churn or segmentation models in isolation.
Experience Intelligence Hyper-Personalization at Scale	Basic segmentation; static rules for offers (e.g., loyalty tiers).	Single-channel personalization pilots (email, app).
Process Intelligence Self-Tuning Operations	Rule-based automation, static ERP/forecasting.	Localized RPA bots or demand-forecast pilots.
Content Intelligence Creative Firepower, On-Demand	Manual campaign workflows; creative bottlenecks.	Early Generative Pilots: Copy, Image, and Video Experiments.
Decision Intelligence Smarter Systems, Faster Strategy	Rule-based pricing, fraud rules, static dashboards.	Pricing a Copilot or fraud ML experiment in a single market.
Organizational Intelligence Humans + Machines = Force Multiplier	AI is a tool for specialists with low organizational fluency.	Pockets of early adoption (marketing, IT).

Stage 3 Pilot Programs	Stage 4 Departmental Leverage	Stage 5 Enterprise AI OS
Cross-functional dashboards combining LTV + churn pilots.	Integrated data platforms (Snowflake, Databricks) fuel predictive + prescriptive analytics for multiple functions.	Real-time decision engines are embedded across the organization, enabling data → insight → action through fully automated and self-improving processes.
Multichannel pilots (adaptive homepage, app recommendations).	Hyper-personalization across digital touchpoints; behavioral clustering at scale.	Anticipatory experiences: context-aware personalization across every interaction; AI predicts needs before they are expressed.
AI forecasting & reordering in one supply chain unit.	Department-wide AI-driven ops: supply chain, finance, procurement rebalanced dynamically.	Fully autonomous operations: end-to-end sensing + rerouting across the enterprise ecosystem.
Generative A/B pilots with tone/visual variations.	AI-embedded creative pipelines; scaled localization + compliance guardrails.	Modular, real-time adaptive content engine; AI creates, optimizes, and distributes autonomously across channels.
Dynamic pricing pilot across product lines with guardrails in place.	AI-assisted decision-making across departments (pricing, risk, routing).	Autonomous decision loops: AI adjusts levers in real time; human oversight focuses on exceptions and ethics.
90-day AI fluency sprints; prompt playbooks for teams.	Org-wide AI literacy programs and new hybrid job archetypes have been formalized.	AI as organizational OS: every function AI-native, human + machine workflows the default.

Insight Intelligence

From Data Swamps to Decision Engines

A bank integrates structured, unstructured, and synthetic data to power real-time LTV modeling, churn prediction, and risk scoring. Lending teams now work from shared dashboards, rather than silos.

- Use cases: Customer segmentation, forecasting, credit risk, pricing optimization
- Tools: Snowflake, Databricks, H2O.ai, BBVA Valora, Tableau + GPT
- Pilot: Develop a real-time, cross-functional dashboard showing LTV tiers and churn risk by cohort

Experience Intelligence

Hyper-Personalization[102] at Scale

A QSR giant customizes menus on mobile and in-store screens based on loyalty tier, weather conditions, and the time of day. AI predicts the right offer before the customer even scrolls.

- Use cases: CX, digital commerce, loyalty, travel, banking
- Tools: Adobe AEP, Salesforce Genie, Dynamic Yield, Bloomreach
- Pilot: Launch an adaptive homepage in your mobile app tailored to engagement patterns and behavioral clustering

Process Intelligence

Self-Tuning Operations

A manufacturer integrates AI into its supply chain to forecast demand spikes, automatically reorder parts, and reroute deliveries in real time, reducing inventory slack by 15%.

- Use cases: Supply chain, finance operations, procurement, R&D
- Tools: SAP Business AI, Celonis, Palantir, o9 Solutions, Google Supply Chain AI
- Pilot: Implement AI for SKU-level demand forecasting to cut inventory buffers without risking stockouts

Content Intelligence

Creative Firepower, On-Demand

A healthcare system utilizes AI to automatically create patient education packets tailored to diagnosis, age, and language, allowing teams to focus on delivering care.

- Use cases: Marketing, HR, compliance-intensive industries, knowledge management
- Tools: Jasper, GPT-4, Synthesia, Runway, Canva Magic Studio
- Pilot: Conduct a generative A/B campaign with varied tone, visuals, and calls to action based on user behavior

Decision Intelligence

Smarter Systems, Faster Strategy

A global retailer implements dynamic pricing models that automatically adjust online prices based on margin limits and competitor actions, removing the need for human input.

- Use cases: Pricing, promotions, fraud detection, route planning, demand shaping
- Tools: Vertex AI, SageMaker, IBM WatsonX, TIBCO Spotfire
- Pilot: Launch a pricing copilot that dynamically adjusts offers using market signals and margin guardrails

Organizational Intelligence

Humans + Machines = Force Multiplier

An energy firm retools every department with AI fluency, prompt libraries, and new job archetypes for collaboration with AI agents.

- Use cases: Change management, L&D, HR, innovation culture
- Tools: Microsoft Copilot, Workday Skills Cloud, Degreed, Responsible AI kits
- Pilot: Deploy a 90-day AI fluency sprint with department-specific upskilling and prompt playbooks

CASE STUDY

UPS – AI as the Operating System of Logistics

How orchestration turned pilots into enterprise-wide agility.

UPS moves more than 20 million packages per day across 220 countries. In a business where minutes matter, the company's AI journey shows how orchestrated intelligence can shift from small-scale pilots to a system-wide operating model.

The Bottleneck

Logistics optimization was long dependent on heuristics, paper-based routing, and local dispatcher knowledge. Fuel costs, traffic congestion, and delivery windows created endless inefficiencies. Isolated AI pilots in routing or forecasting showed promise, but without orchestration, the impact was trapped in silos.

The Overclock

- ORION (On-Road Integrated Optimization & Navigation): An AI-driven routing engine that crunches billions of data points daily to optimize delivery routes in real time.
- AI Orchestration: UPS didn't stop at routing. AI now manages predictive maintenance for vehicles, customer demand forecasting, staffing schedules, and even sustainability initiatives.
- Agile Iteration (Konomi Code): Each pilot (routing, predictive analytics, digital twins) was deployed iteratively, tested in live markets, then scaled into the enterprise fabric. AI became an operating system layered across logistics, not just a tool for isolated tasks.

Results

- ORION saves 100 million miles driven per year and reduces fuel costs by $400M annually.
- Predictive maintenance extended fleet uptime, lowering capital costs.
- Integrated orchestration increased delivery reliability, enabling new growth in same-day and cross-border services.

What It Means

UPS demonstrates the future of enterprise AI: not pilots, but platforms. Orchestrated AI becomes the nervous system of the business, with agility as the code that allows scaling from experiment to operating model. The lesson: AI success isn't about the algorithm—it's about integration, orchestration, and iteration.

Building Enterprise Intelligence

AI implementation across enterprise functions is about building integrated intelligence networks that enhance each other's effects while addressing specific business challenges. Organizations that succeed in treating AI as the connective tissue between previously siloed capabilities, creating systematic advantages that grow across every operational area.

Organizations that are successful with enterprise AI share distinct characteristics, setting them apart from companies that are still struggling with pilot projects and vendor evaluations. These traits reflect systematic AI approaches rather than ad hoc adoption.

Strategic integration aligns AI with core business goals and digital transformation, embedding AI into planning and treating it as essential infrastructure. This means investments are evaluated for strategic impact.

Balanced value creation involves optimizing multiple objectives, including efficiency, innovation, customer experience, and beyond, to achieve cost reduction. Human-AI collaboration focuses on augmenting human decision-making and creativity, not replacing them.

Responsible AI deployment includes proactive governance to ensure fairness, privacy, security, and ethics, creating a competitive advantage through trustworthy AI. Learning capabilities foster continuous feedback and sharing across teams, enabling insights to inform and scale initiatives, creating organizational learning loops.

AI and Collaboration

What was once a 'soft skill' to be introduced and integrated into organizations, Collaboration will now become a hybrid skill-infrastructure component with agentic AI orchestration. Whether it is multi-agent internal-external or cross-departmental, humans and AI will lead the next evolution of collaboration, providing the backbone for adaptability and velocity to coexist.

The research supports this evolution. McKinsey identifies that agents shift from reactive tools to proactive, goal-driven virtual collaborators that automate complex business processes using general AI. At the same time, enterprises need to fundamentally rethink how they govern and collaborate with agents as they blur the lines between tools and teammates.

But there are structural challenges in this transformation:

While organizations need to expose APIs and become "enterprise-ready" for agent deployment, most lack the collaboration maturity to orchestrate human-AI workflows effectively. This creates a dependency problem; you can't successfully deploy multi-agent systems without first solving the issues of human collaboration and coordination. This involves asking and answering some of the tough questions of where and why bottlenecks, delays, and process breakdowns occur today. So, yes, AI presents the opportunities to gain velocity and adaptability, but the house needs to be in order before beginning.

Not doing so introduces risk into the business ecosystem. Gartner estimates that 40% of agentic AI projects will fail due to unclear business value or inadequate risk control in the coming years. While we can dismiss this as the growing pains of the learning curve, the challenge isn't technical capability, but rather organizational readiness to manage hybrid human-AI decision-making processes. In short, similar to getting your data in order, process, people, and culture shifts will make these failures preventable.

The Skills-Infrastructure Hybrid Model

Collaboration becomes simultaneously a human capability and a technological architecture requirement. This creates new organizational challenges.

Traditional collaboration skills (communication, consensus-building, conflict resolution) must now include agent orchestration, AI governance, and hybrid team leadership. Success may increasingly depend on "agent literacy," the ability to supervise, collaborate with, and strategically direct agent teams. Unlike traditional soft skills, which can be developed through training, this hybrid model requires the development of technological infrastructure, data architecture, and governance frameworks in parallel with the development of human capabilities.

AI Maturity: Leaders vs. Laggards

Accenture's global analysis of 1,200 companies found that only 12% are accurate "AI Achievers" firms that combine strategy, talent, and technology into a cohesive operating system. Meanwhile, 63% are still Experimenters, dabbling in pilots without scale or integration. The middle ground, represented by Innovators (13%) and Builders (12%), has pieces of the puzzle but lacks balance across strategy, culture, and execution.

This reality splits the enterprise landscape into two scenarios:

AI Leaders (Achievers)	AI Laggards (Experimenters)
Revenue Growth: Achievers enjoy 50% higher revenue growth than peers. AI-influenced revenues are 3.5x more likely to surpass 30% of total sales.	Growth Drag: Struggle to prove ROI from scattered pilots; AI initiatives remain stuck in experimentation without scaling.
Leadership & Culture: 83% have full CEO & senior sponsorship for AI strategies. Innovation culture is embedded, not ad hoc.	Leadership Gaps: Only 56% have senior sponsorship. Culture remains reactive, with AI projects competing for attention and resources.
Talent & Fluency: 78% of Achievers enforce mandatory AI training across functions; nearly half of employees demonstrate strong AI competencies.	Skill Deficits: Minimal training, siloed expertise, and resistance to adoption. Talent bottlenecks slow progress.
Industrialization: Achievers build strong AI cores (cloud + data + MLOps). They scale pilots into production 25% more often.	Pilot Paralysis: Proofs of concept remain isolated, without industrialization or integration into core systems.
Responsible AI: 53% more likely to design AI responsibly from the start, embedding trust and regulatory compliance.	Risk Exposure: Governance is weak or non-existent. Bias, privacy, and compliance risks remain high.
Investment Trajectory: Devoting ~34% of tech budgets to AI by 2024. Investments expand scope and compound advantage.	Underinvestment: AI budgets remain fragmented, under 10–15%, with limited alignment to strategy.
Stakeholder Outcomes: Achievers outperform on customer experience (+8%), sustainability, and workforce empowerment.	Stakeholder Gaps: Customer churn, workforce disengagement, and sustainability lag due to reactive practices.

COMPARATIVE LENS: AI LEADERS VERSUS LAGGARDS

What This Means

For Leaders

The mandate is to stay ahead. With only 12% in the Achievers category, the risk is complacency. The competitive moat is temporary, and Accenture estimates Achievers will more than double by 2024, raising the bar for all.

For Laggards

The opportunity is to catch up by leapfrogging. Just as many companies skipped Web 1.0 and jumped straight to cloud-native or mobile-first, laggards can bypass intermediate steps by adopting AI-native platforms that bundle infrastructure, orchestration, and governance.

AI Governance and Ethics: Building Sustainable Intelligence Systems

Whether a leader or a laggard, time spent on governance and ethics within your org is time and money well spent. You most likely already have governance in place for IT projects, social media, and communications, as well as finance and accounting. AI governance represents the comprehensive framework of policies, processes, and oversight mechanisms that ensure artificial intelligence systems operate safely, ethically, and in alignment with organizational values and regulatory requirements. Unlike traditional IT governance, AI governance must address the unique challenges of systems that learn, adapt, and make decisions with varying degrees of autonomy. This encompasses everything from data sourcing and model development to deployment monitoring and ongoing performance evaluation, creating accountability structures that can evolve in tandem with rapidly advancing AI capabilities.

The ethical dimension extends beyond compliance to encompass fundamental questions about fairness, transparency, and societal impact. Organizations must establish clear principles around bias prevention, algorithmic accountability, and human oversight, ensuring that AI systems don't perpetuate or amplify existing inequalities while maintaining explainability in high-stakes decisions. This requires cross-functional governance structures that bring together technical teams, legal counsel, ethics specialists, and business stakeholders to evaluate trade-offs between AI capabilities and responsible deployment.

The Critical Imperative of AI Maintenance and Model Health

Perhaps the most underestimated aspect of enterprise AI deployment is the ongoing maintenance required to keep systems performing reliably over time. AI models experience what researchers term "model drift" or "model fatigue", a gradual degradation in performance as the real-world conditions they encounter diverge from their training data. This isn't a minor technical issue but a fundamental challenge that can lead to increasingly inaccurate predictions, biased outcomes, and what appear to be "hallucinations" where models generate plausible-sounding but factually incorrect information.

Model fatigue manifests in several ways that directly impact business outcomes. Prediction accuracy declines as customer behaviors evolve, market conditions shift, or new product categories emerge that weren't represented in historical training data. Classification systems may begin misidentifying patterns as they encounter scenarios outside their original learning parameters. Language models may start generating responses that become less relevant or accurate as language usage patterns and domain knowledge evolve. Without systematic monitoring and retraining protocols, these performance degradations compound over time, ultimately undermining the business value that justified the AI investment.

Data Health: The Foundation of Sustained AI Performance

The quality of AI outputs is fundamentally determined by the quality of input data, making data health a critical component of AI governance. Data cleansing must be treated as an ongoing operational discipline rather than a one-time project, encompassing both technical accuracy and ethical considerations. Organizations need systematic processes for identifying and correcting data quality issues, removing outdated information, and ensuring that training datasets remain representative of current business contexts and customer populations.

Similar to the closed-loop components of the Insights Value Chain discussed in our Data Driven Insights chapter, a closed loop of clean, current data needs to refresh the internal AI data lake and undergo comprehensive validation testing before models are retrained and deployed. This process mirrors software regression testing, where new code changes are systematically validated to ensure they don't break existing functionality or introduce unexpected behaviors.

For AI systems, this validation protocol should include data distribution consistency checks to ensure new data maintains similar statistical properties to previous training sets, bias detection across demographic segments to prevent the introduction of unfair outcomes, and performance benchmarking against held-out test sets to verify that model accuracy isn't degraded by the data refresh. Just as software teams run unit tests, integration tests, and performance tests before releasing code to production, AI teams must validate data quality, model performance, and ethical compliance before deploying retrained models.

The models are then retrained and validated through systematic testing protocols before deployment, mirroring software release cycles where rigorous quality assurance prevents production failures. This disciplined approach treats AI model updates with the same operational rigor that organizations apply to mission-critical software releases, recognizing that poor data quality can compromise business decisions just as effectively as buggy code can crash applications.

This systematic data lifecycle management ensures that AI systems maintain reliability and trustworthiness over time, preventing the gradual performance degradation that occurs when models are trained on stale, biased, or incomplete data without proper validation protocols.

Data health extends beyond simple accuracy to include completeness, consistency, and bias detection. Missing or incomplete data can create blind spots in AI decision-making, while inconsistent data formats or definitions across different systems can introduce errors that propagate through model outputs. Perhaps most critically, data that reflects historical biases or unrepresentative samples can embed unfair outcomes directly into AI systems, making bias detection and mitigation an essential component of data governance.

Continuous Learning Systems and Retraining Protocols

Enterprise AI systems require structured approaches to continuous learning that strike a balance between model performance and operational stability. This involves establishing monitoring systems that track key performance indicators, detect drift patterns, and trigger retraining protocols before performance degradation becomes significant. Organizations must develop capabilities for evaluating when models need updating, what new data should be incorporated, and how to validate that updated models perform better than their predecessors without introducing new problems.

The most sophisticated organizations are implementing automated monitoring and retraining pipelines that can detect performance issues, curate new training data, and deploy updated models with minimal human intervention, while maintaining human oversight for critical decisions. This approach treats AI models as living systems that require ongoing care and feeding rather than static tools that can be deployed once and forgotten.

Effective AI governance ultimately recognizes that artificial intelligence systems are not traditional software applications but complex, evolving capabilities that require ongoing stewardship to remain valuable and trustworthy. Organizations that invest in comprehensive governance frameworks, systematic model maintenance, and robust data health practices position themselves to capture the long-term benefits of AI while avoiding the risks that can emerge when these systems operate without proper oversight and care.

AI Operationalization: From Centralized Bottlenecks to Distributed Intelligence

The operationalization of AI represents the strategic deployment of artificial intelligence capabilities throughout an organization's operational fabric, transforming it from an experimental technology into a fundamental business capability. Unlike traditional enterprise software implementations, which can be managed through centralized IT departments, AI operationalization requires a fundamentally different approach—one that recognizes AI as a capability multiplier that must be embedded directly into the workflows, decision-making processes, and domain expertise of every business function.

The Bottleneck Problem: Why Centralized AI Fails at Scale

When organizations treat AI as a traditional IT project, relegating it to centralized technology departments, they create structural bottlenecks that fundamentally limit its transformative potential. IT teams, regardless of their technical expertise, lack the deep domain knowledge necessary to identify the most valuable AI applications within marketing, sales, operations, finance, or customer service. This creates a dependency model where business teams must translate their needs into technical requirements, wait for IT resources to become available, and then iterate through development cycles that may not capture the nuances of their actual challenges.

More problematically, centralized AI governance often yields generic solutions that fail to capitalize on the specialized knowledge and workflows that make each department unique. A marketing team's need for dynamic content generation operates very differently from a finance team's requirement for anomaly detection in transaction data, and a supply chain team's demand forecasting challenges require different approaches than HR's talent acquisition optimization. When AI development is bottlenecked through a single department, these distinct needs get homogenized into one-size-fits-all solutions that miss the specific value creation opportunities that make AI transformational rather than merely incremental.

Distributed AI: Embedding Intelligence Where Decisions Happen

Effective AI operationalization distributes both the capability and the responsibility for AI implementation across the enterprise, positioning artificial intelligence as close as possible to the domain expertise and decision-making processes where it can create the most value. This doesn't mean abandoning governance or creating chaos; it means establishing frameworks that enable departments to develop and deploy AI solutions within their areas of expertise while maintaining consistency, security, and strategic alignment across the organization.

This distributed approach recognizes that the most valuable AI applications often emerge from the intersection of technical capability and deep domain knowledge. Sales teams understand customer interaction patterns that can inform conversation intelligence systems. Operations teams recognize workflow inefficiencies that AI can address. Customer service teams identify pattern recognition opportunities that can improve response quality and speed. When AI development happens within these departments, guided by appropriate governance frameworks, the resulting solutions are more targeted, more useful, and more likely to drive meaningful business outcomes.

AI Champions: Building Distributed Expertise and Advocacy

Here's where history repeats itself. Just as when the new ERP, document management system, or digital rights management systems were implemented, adoption depends on literacy, confidence, and encouragement. Here's where front-line leaders can really make a difference.

The linchpin of successful AI operationalization is the development of AI champions within each department, individuals who combine domain expertise with sufficient technical literacy to identify opportunities, guide implementation, and drive adoption within their functional areas. These champions serve as translators between technical possibilities and business needs, advocates for AI investment within their departments, and bridges between centralized governance and distributed implementation.

AI champions don't need to be data scientists or machine learning engineers, but they do need to understand AI capabilities well enough to recognize opportunities and communicate effectively with technical teams. More importantly, they need credibility within their departments to guide change management, address resistance, and demonstrate value through practical applications. These individuals become the organizational antibodies that prevent AI from being treated as an external imposition, instead positioning it as a natural evolution of how work gets done.

The champion model also creates feedback loops that improve AI effectiveness over time. Champions understand how AI systems perform in real-world conditions, can identify when models need retraining or adjustment, and can spot opportunities for expansion or optimization that centralized teams might miss. This distributed intelligence gathering ensures that AI systems remain aligned with evolving business needs and continue to deliver value as markets and operations change.

Training for Distributed AI Literacy

Successful AI operationalization requires systematic training programs that build AI literacy across the organization, rather than relying on generic awareness sessions that treat AI as an abstract concept. Instead, effective training focuses on practical applications within specific functional contexts, helping teams understand how AI can enhance their existing workflows rather than replace them. Marketing teams learn about content generation, personalization, and campaign optimization. Finance teams explore anomaly detection, forecasting, and risk assessment. Operations teams investigate predictive maintenance, supply chain optimization, and quality control applications.

This contextual training approach accelerates adoption by directly connecting AI capabilities to the immediate business challenges and opportunities that teams already understand. Rather than learning about AI in the abstract, teams discover how it can solve problems they face daily, making the technology feel accessible and relevant rather than intimidating or disconnected from their work.

The training must also address change management, helping teams understand not only what AI can do but also how it will impact their roles, workflows, and decision-making processes. This includes building comfort with human-AI collaboration, understanding when to trust AI recommendations and when to apply human judgment, and developing new working rhythms that incorporate AI insights into daily operations.

Governance Without Bottlenecks: Distributed Authority with Centralized Standards

Effective AI operationalization requires governance structures that enable distributed development while maintaining consistency, security, and strategic alignment. This entails establishing clear standards for data security, model validation, ethical guidelines, and performance monitoring, while granting departments the authority to implement AI solutions within their respective domains. Centralized teams provide platforms, tools, guidelines, and support, but decision-making authority for AI applications rests with the business functions that understand the context and can measure the impact.

This distributed authority model accelerates AI adoption because departments can move at their own pace, prioritize their own use cases, and iterate based on their own learning, while still benefiting from organizational standards and shared resources. It also ensures that AI development remains aligned with business strategy, as the people making implementation decisions are the same individuals responsible for business outcomes in each functional area.

The result is an organization where AI becomes embedded in the operational DNA rather than bolted onto existing processes, creating sustainable competitive advantages that compound over time as each department develops deeper AI capabilities and more sophisticated applications within their areas of expertise.

Cross-Functional Collaboration

As we mentioned in the leadership chapter in the beginning of the book, digital is a team sport. Formal and informal mechanisms to share use cases across departments, success and failure stories of adoption, efficiency, and growth will shorten learning cycles and improve processes to make your business more adaptable and improve velocity.

From Pilots to Flywheels — Closing the Loop

We began this chapter with a simple truth: AI is not a bolt-on feature; it's the central nervous system of the enterprise. The leaders of the next decade will not just move faster, they will sense, decide, and act in real time, compressing advantage into cycles of hours rather than quarters.

Through the Enterprise AI Maturity Model, we've seen the path from scattered pilots to the fully autonomous enterprise. Industry examples, such as P&G and Siemens, have proven that maturity compounds. The flywheels showed how advantage reinforces itself once AI is embedded in the loop.

For laggards, the opportunity is to leapfrog, not catch up. For leaders, the mandate is to widen the gap, not settle into complacency. Either way, the future of enterprise advantage will not be written in boardrooms or static plans. It will be written in living systems of intelligence, where AI is not a tool you use, but the operating model you run.

The takeaway is clear: in the next era, winning is about architecting an AI-native enterprise where every decision compounds into the next. The question is no longer *if* your enterprise will reinvent, but *how fast* you'll close the loop.

CHAPTER 18

Future Casting — From Adaptation to Anticipation

Think Like a Digital Futurist

Let's be honest about what just happened.

Over the past 17 chapters, Overclocked:.Business Reinvention has thrown a relentless stream of information, case studies, playbooks, and processes at you. We've reimagined leadership paradigms, deconstructed digital strategy, rewired business models, and rebuilt entire innovation engines from the ground up. We've explored agile marketing methodologies, enterprise AI implementations, and systematic transformation frameworks that could keep any organization busy for the next three years.

And now, as we turn toward the future, I know what you're thinking: *"I haven't even executed a fraction of the playbooks and concepts I've just read. How am I supposed to think about the next 5-10 years when I can barely wrap my head around next quarter?"*

In every era of reinvention, there's a moment when the fog parts just enough for the most curious leaders to glimpse what's next.

Right now, we're in that moment.

Financial systems are emerging without banks. Warehouses are going dark. Machines are teaching themselves to design medicines, buildings, and supply chains. This is not a trailer for the next science-fiction blockbuster; it's the scaffolding of the next economy, assembling itself in real time.

The question isn't *if* these shifts will arrive; it's whether you're building the capability to sense them, interpret them, and act on them before everyone else.

MASTERY LEARNING OBJECTIVES

By the end of this chapter, you will:

- Recognize the 11 future movements reshaping global markets and industries.
- Use sensing tools to turn weak signals into strategic advantages.
- Prioritize your future bets with the Scenario Grid and Complexity/Value filter.
- Build personal leadership readiness for a world where anticipation outruns adaptation.
- Turn foresight into a Future Action Map, a living portfolio of strategic experiments.

INDUSTRY INSIGHT

The Dark Warehouse

Somewhere in Japan, a warehouse hums in perfect silence.

No footsteps. No forklifts. No lighting at all. Just hundreds of autonomous robots gliding on magnetic tracks, pulling bins from high-density racks to AI-orchestrated loading bays.

This is the "dark warehouse," a fully automated fulfillment center that no longer requires human operation. Pioneers like Ocado, JD.com, and Amazon aren't simply testing the waters; they're proving that orders can be processed, picked, and packed with near-perfect uptime, no seasonal hiring spikes, and no disruptions from pandemics or labor disputes.

Dark warehouses alter the physics of logistics: they can be built closer to customers for faster delivery, deep in rural areas for lower real estate costs, or underground to protect against environmental risks. They're already live in pilots, Ocado's swarms process 50-item grocery orders in five minutes, while JD.com's facilities have been running dark since 2017.

Your local chain grocery store may very well be converted to a design not meant to increase impulse purchases on high-margin items, but a dark warehouse with ambient, cool, and freezer sections uniquely fit for automation that only accepts online orders, picks, packs, and ships curbside or to your home via autonomous vehicle from an orchestrated, autonomous loading bay.

When we look back, we may realize that the most significant supply chain leap wasn't the drones in the sky, but rather the day the lights went out on the warehouse & retail floors.

In this chapter, we'll explore how to:

- Read the weak signals at the edges of markets and technology before they break into the mainstream.
- Prototype customer workarounds, adjacencies, and blue ocean opportunities with fast, small experiments in spaces where the rules haven't been written yet.
- Scale what works with decisive speed, making the future part of your core business before competitors even recognize the opportunity.

The clock is already ticking. The next decade will reward those who can sense, shape, and commercialize before others even start. The rest will watch those moments pass, brilliant, transformative, and gone, like sparks in the dark.

STRATEGIC TAKEAWAYS

- Build Foresight Muscles: Treat sensing weak signals and market shifts as a core leadership discipline, not a side activity.
- Experiment Early, Scale Fast: Use small, rapid prototypes to test emerging opportunities before rivals even notice them.
- Shift from Adaptation to Anticipation: Don't just respond faster, design systems that predict and shape what's next.
- Institutionalize Future Readiness: Make scenario planning, horizon scanning, and Future Action Maps part of your ongoing operating model.

REFLECTION

- What if the crypto wallet, not the checking account, becomes the default identity layer for global consumers?
- Can your product work in a world where Web3 is the front door, not the edge case?
- How would you serve someone who has no credit score, but a blockchain reputation?
- Are we designing for the edges, or will the edges become the center?

Futureproofing You *and* Your Enterprise

Everything in this book has been built to this moment.

We began with leadership, not as a title, but as the mindset engine of reinvention. We reimagined strategy for a digital-first world, rewired business models for velocity and resilience, and reframed infrastructure as a competitive advantage rather than just an IT line item. We unlocked intelligence through data, insight, and human behavior to drive decisions that resonate across B2B and B2C ecosystems.

We didn't stop at insight.

We operated it through content strategies that connect across owned, earned, and paid media with a unified narrative arc. We adapted innovation for velocity by creating a full-system innovation engine, marketing that is turned agile by design. We stretched AI from a productivity tool to an enterprise-wide operating system.

Now comes the final shift: From adaptation to anticipation.

Each example isn't just a future signal; it's a testbed for applying everything we've covered: strategy, systems thinking, agile execution, content alignment, and enterprise AI fluency.

Because in this next era, the winners won't be the fastest adapters. They'll be the best anticipators, the ones bold enough to imagine, test, and build the future before the rest even see it coming.

Are you ready?

From Trend Spotting to Trend Systemization: How Foresight Creates Competitive Velocity

The most resilient organizations of the next decade won't be those that react faster to change; they'll be the ones that see it coming and position themselves advantageously before it arrives, transforming potential disruption into competitive acceleration. This represents a fundamental evolution from traditional strategic planning, where future-readiness was treated as an annual exercise or delegated to specialized innovation teams. Instead, leading companies are operationalizing foresight as a core business function, embedding it into their organizational DNA with the same rigor they apply to finance, operations, or customer service, because they understand that early signal detection is what separates proactive strategy from reactive scrambling.

This systematic approach to future-sensing begins with broad-spectrum scanning that extends far beyond immediate competitors and market research, creating the wide-angle vision necessary for strategic agility. Organizations are monitoring startup ecosystems for emerging business models, tracking regulatory developments that could reshape entire industries, observing research breakthroughs in academic and corporate labs, and studying adjacent industries where similar challenges might have already produced innovative solutions. This expanded field of vision enables companies to detect weak signals that could evolve into major market forces before they become apparent to others, providing the crucial lead time necessary to develop thoughtful responses rather than hasty reactions.

The real competitive advantage emerges through cross-functional interpretation, where diverse expertise from across the organization collaborates to understand what these signals might mean for the business and how to capitalize on them before competitors recognize the opportunity. Engineering teams may recognize the technical feasibility of an emerging technology, while marketing understands its potential for customer adoption, and finance can model its economic implications. This collaborative sense-making process transforms raw data about trends into actionable strategic insights that no single functional area could generate independently, enabling the organization to move with confidence rather than uncertainty when opportunities arise.

Rather than making large bets on uncertain futures or being forced into expensive pivots when change arrives unexpectedly, sophisticated organizations create strategic optionality through portfolios of low-cost, scalable experiments that position them to respond rapidly when trends crystallize. They design small-scale tests that can validate assumptions about emerging opportunities while limiting downside risk, building capabilities that can be quickly scaled if conditions prove favorable. This approach allows companies to develop muscle memory around new possibilities without committing resources they can't afford to lose, ensuring they can move decisively when market conditions shift rather than spending precious time and resources playing catch-up.

Learning acceleration occurs through embedded organizational structures, AI labs that explore technological possibilities, pilot teams that test new business models, and venture studios that incubate breakthrough ideas, all designed to compress the time between insight and action. These aren't isolated innovation theaters but integrated capabilities that feed insights back into core business operations, ensuring that experimental learning influences mainstream strategic decisions and operational improvements. When change does arrive, these organizations don't need to build new capabilities from scratch; they can immediately deploy and scale proven approaches that have already been tested and refined.

Most importantly, future-ready organizations make foresight a cultural rather than departmental endeavor, rewarding horizon thinking throughout the year rather than just during annual planning cycles, because they recognize that speed and adaptability emerge from collective awareness rather than centralized prediction. They create incentives for employees at all levels to contribute observations about changing customer behaviors, emerging technologies, and shifting market dynamics, recognizing that the most valuable insights often come from those closest to customers, operations, or technical developments. This cultural embedding transforms foresight from a specialized skill into a distributed organizational capability, dramatically increasing the company's ability to sense and respond to change before competitors recognize what's happening, turning market volatility from a threat into a source of sustainable competitive advantage.

Examples in Motion

- Blockchain & Tokenization[103] – From JPMorgan Onyx's tokenized funds to Audius rewarding artists directly, tokenization creates liquidity in illiquid markets, fractional asset access, and programmable value exchange. Winners focus on regulation, ecosystem design, and real-world problem solving.

- Autonomous Discovery Agents — AI systems that proactively surface opportunities and next-best actions across silos. Already used by Roche and Amazon, they extend strategic cognition, not replace it.

Three Core Mindsets for Future-Readiness

- Build for Access, Not Assumption — Design for mobile-first, low-bandwidth, and diverse digital literacy.
- Value Flows, Not Just Products — Shift from purchase models to participation models, where tokens and community drive engagement.
- Platform Thinking at the Edge — Enable others to innovate on your rails via APIs, embedded finance, and decentralized identity as if your business were a Roblox or Shopify platform.

GLOBAL SIGNAL

Frontier Tech, Rooted in Need

The Future Frontiers matrix points firms toward moonshots and speculative bets. But in emerging markets, tech like blockchain, DeFi, Web3, and token economies often arise not from novelty but from addressing deep structural gaps in finance, identity, and inclusion.

Signals

- Chipper Cash / Yellow Card (Africa / Latin America): Crypto-enabled cross-border remittances and payments fill gaps where banking rails are weak.
- Bitso (Latin America): Crypto exchange + payments + digital wallet bridging fiat and crypto—for users who previously had minimal access to global capital flows.
- Dapp / DeFi platforms in Southeast Asia / Latin America: Some projects are building tokenized credit, identity systems, and decentralized finance that leapfrog traditional institutions.

Takeaway

In many developing contexts, the frontier isn't speculative, it's necessary. When traditional institutions fail, users adopt radical tech earlier. The next wave of innovation will often arise not in Silicon Valley but in Lagos, Mexico City, or Manila, anchored in foundational need.

Future Frontier Compass

How far into the future can your organization sense, shape, and architect new realities?

Capability Dimension	Stage 1 Firefighting (weeks–months)	Stage 2 Probing (1–3 years)	Stage 3 Shaping (3–7 years)	Stage 4 Architecting (10+ years)
Signal Scanning	Ad hoc, reactive reviews of trends	Dedicated foresight unit scanning for 1–3 years out	Cross-functional horizon systems identifying early inflections	Systematic co-creation with partners, ecosystems, and even competitors to shape the future
Innovation Testing	Siloed pilots, one-offs, no scaling	Innovation labs running small-scale experiments	Business-unit prototypes aligned with strategy and shared learnings	Always-on test-and-learn loops embedded in core operations and ecosystem networks
Digital Infrastructure	Legacy, fragmented systems, and limited cloud	Modular cloud pilots, some automation	API-first integration across enterprise platforms	Frontier tech embedded: Web3, embedded finance, edge/quantum computing
Business Model Flexibility	Traditional product sales, linear revenue	Early experiments with ad-based or subsidized models	Participation-based ecosystems (tokens, memberships, co-ownership)	Modular, adaptive business models with micro-monetization and shared/distributed/ownership

The Strategic Imperative of Designing What Comes Next

Organizations that thrive in the next era of competitive advantage will not simply adapt to disruption; they will anticipate, shape, and design it. This requires building repeatable, institutional capabilities for sensing what is next, testing bold hypotheses, and scaling the ideas defining future value creation.

Why Early Movers Better Their Long Game Odds

Enterprises that systematically build foresight into strategy don't just see around corners; they buy themselves time, resilience, and market premiums. Accenture, McKinsey, and others demonstrate that "reinventors" consistently outperform their peers, capturing 15 percentage points more revenue growth and 5.6 points more profit margin than their competitors between 2019 and 2022. The signal is clear: markets reward those seen as innovation leaders.

But foresight isn't about prediction for prediction's sake. It's about translating global currents, AI everywhere, synthetic realities, decentralized economies, climate imperatives, demographic shifts, and geopolitical tech blocs into actionable systems that deliver speed and advantage. Reports like FTSG 2025[104] map these forces at a planetary scale, where education, health, supply chains, and energy grids are being rewired in real time. These aren't distant forecasts. They are strategic fault lines enterprises must navigate now.

The challenge: Knowing the currents isn't enough. The winners will be those who can operationalize foresight into reinvention, moving from passive observation to active playmaking. That's the role of the following 11 Trends: a framework that bridges megatrends with enterprise execution.

Each trend isn't just a forecast but a performance imperative, from turning AI into your operating system to building decentralized, traceable supply chains to rethinking the workforce for demographic realities.

Taken together, these 11 disruptive movements form the motherboard of reinvention. They define where leaders must calibrate their power settings, between incremental optimization and radical reinvention, fast plays and long-game bets. These are the megatrends, influential, unyielding currents that no enterprise can afford to ignore. They establish the "why now" for transformation.

The global foresight lens is clear: the next decade will be shaped by AI everywhere, synthetic realities, decentralized economies, climate imperatives, and new geopolitics of technology.

But knowing the currents isn't enough. Enterprises need to translate these global forces into actionable systems that deliver speed, resilience, and competitive lift.

And for you and me, this is our opportunity to be a catalyst.

1. Unbanked + Crypto Wallets → Wallets Become Banks

What it is: The "unbanked" are people without access to traditional financial services due to a lack of identification, regulatory restrictions, geographic barriers, or cultural norms.

The World Bank estimates ~1.4 billion adults are unbanked. Mobile-first crypto wallets bypass legacy systems, offering direct access to payments, savings, credit, and commerce.

Why: In places where banks never scaled, wallets become the first, and only, financial identity.

Underlying trends:

- Smartphone adoption in emerging markets is surpassing 70%.
- Stablecoin flows rival traditional remittance channels in key corridors.
- Regulatory sandbox programs enabling wallet licensing.
- Super-app adoption proving bundled finance+commerce works.

Velocity:

- **Faster if**: Stablecoins gain mainstream trust, regulations are clarified, and mobile coverage expands.
- **Slower if**: Governments crack down on crypto rails or telecom access remains patchy.

2. AI-Native Enterprises → Autonomy At Work

What it is: Organizations built (or rebuilt) with AI as the operational backbone. Using AI to plan, produce, sell, and adapt in near real-time.

Why: Automation of cognitive work delivers speed, cost efficiency, and decision quality too compelling to ignore.

Underlying trends:

- Multi-modal AI expanding from language to vision, speech, and planning.
- Enterprise-grade AI agent frameworks are maturing.
- Falling compute costs and inference latency.
- Growth of AI governance and evaluation frameworks.

Velocity:

- **Faster if**: Proven ROI in early adopters drives copycat adoption.
- **Slower if**: High-profile AI failures erode trust, or compliance rules slow integration.

> **TREND VARIABLES**
>
> **Signal-to-Noise**
> Some trends are loud but shallow. Others run quiet yet rewrite industries. Signal-to-noise helps you cut hype and focus on what truly moves the needle.
>
> **Velocity**
> Forces accelerate at different speeds. Velocity shows how fast "next" becomes "now," letting you time bets and responses.
>
> **Sizing Impact**
> Scale matters as much as speed. A slower but massive trend can reshape industries as powerfully as a niche disruptor racing ahead.

3. Decentralized Supply Chains → Traceable by Default

What it is: Supply networks that embed blockchain, IoT, and AI to track every material and component from origin to end use.

Why: Traceability reduces fraud, meets regulations, and appeals to sustainability-minded consumers.

Underlying trends:

3. EU Digital Product Passport mandates.
4. Reputational risk from labor/environment scandals.
5. IoT sensor cost drops and network coverage improvements.
6. Tokenized trade finance pilots proving viability.

Velocity:

- Faster if: Regulations tighten and consumer demand for provenance increases.
- Slower if: Standards fragment, interoperability costs rise.

4. Energy Transition & Climate Tech → Grids Get Smart

What it is: Energy systems that use AI to balance supply and demand, integrate renewables, and optimize storage in real time.

Why: Electrification across industries demands intelligent, adaptive grids.

Underlying trends:

- Rapid growth in renewables' share of generation.
- Falling battery storage costs.
- Carbon border taxes are pushing low-carbon supply chains.
- AI-driven grid balancing showing efficiency gains.

Velocity:

- Faster if: Energy storage tech breakthroughs, policy incentives scale.
- Slower if: Fossil fuel subsidies persist, storage rollout stalls.

5. Synthetic Media & Digital Twins → Reality Goes Programmable

What it is: Digital representations of physical objects, systems, or environments used to simulate and optimize real-world performance, plus AI-generated media for training, marketing, or storytelling.

Why: Virtual testing and creation cut time, cost, and risk in development.

Underlying trends:

- Enterprise digital twin adoption in manufacturing and urban planning.
- Generative media advances in video and spatial modeling.
- Rights management tech maturing.
- Declining rendering costs.

Velocity:

- Faster if: Tooling becomes no-code, rights frameworks stabilize.
- Slower if: IP disputes or data quality issues stall adoption.

6. Next-Gen Biotech & Personalized Medicine → Biology Eats Industry

What it is: Medicine, nutrition, and wellness tailored to individual biology, enabled by genomics, synthetic biology, and AI-assisted drug discovery.

Why: Personalized interventions improve outcomes and reduce waste in health systems.

Underlying trends:

- Sub-$200 genome sequencing.
- AI-driven drug discovery cutting R&D cycles.
- CRISPR approvals scaling.
- Corporate wellness programs integrating biometrics.

Velocity:

- **Faster if:** Insurance covers personalization, and regulatory approvals speed up.
- **Slower if:** Privacy fears or reimbursement delays slow uptake.

7. Autonomous Systems → Hands-Off Operations

What it is: Machines, vehicles, and robots that operate without human input across logistics, manufacturing, agriculture, and infrastructure.

Why: Safety, labor shortages, and cost pressures drive adoption.

Underlying trends:

- Dark warehouse and port automation pilots scaling.
- Agricultural robotics addressing labor gaps.
- Edge AI enabling local decision-making.
- Safety metrics surpass human benchmarks.

Velocity:

- **Faster if**: Safety records improve, insurance costs drop.
- **Slower if**: Regulation lags or public trust erodes.

8. Metaverse & Spatial Computing → Reality, Layered

What it is: Overlaying digital information and interaction on the physical world using AR/VR/XR for design, training, and remote work.

Why: Improves efficiency, collaboration, and engagement in enterprise contexts.

Underlying trends:

- CAD-to-XR workflows maturing.
- Headset cost/weight reductions.
- Industrial AR cutting downtime.
- Retail/real estate using immersive experiences for sales.

Velocity:

- **Faster if**: Hardware becomes mass-affordable, enterprise use cases prove ROI.
- **Slower if**: Consumer hype collapses or interoperability fails.

9. Platform Fragmentation & Walled Gardens 2.0 → Gardens Grow Walls

What it is: Closed digital ecosystems controlling access to data, customers, and monetization, splitting the internet into multiple semi-closed arenas.

Why: Privacy laws, competitive strategy, and geopolitics fragment digital reach.

Underlying trends:

- Death of third-party cookies.
- Data localization laws.
- Platform ad ecosystem concentration.
- App store policy changes.

Velocity:

- **Faster if:** Privacy regulation accelerates, big platforms restrict APIs further.
- **Slower if:** Antitrust action forces more openness.

10. Demographic Shifts & Workforce Automation → Fewer Hands, New Skills

What it is: Aging populations and shrinking workforces in many countries are driving automation and skill transformation.

Why: A reduced labor supply drives the adoption of new work models and technology.

Underlying trends:

- Fertility rates below replacement in 50%+ of countries.
- Tight migration controls.
- AI enabling job redesign.
- Growth in micro-credentialing.

Velocity:

- **Faster if:** Talent shortages intensify, tech adoption accelerates.
- **Slower if:** Migration increases or retirement ages rise significantly.

11. Geopolitical Tech Blocs → The Split Stack

What it is: Competing technology standards, ecosystems, and regulations across major geopolitical spheres, forcing companies to adapt products to regional regimes.

Why: Geopolitical rivalry and national security concerns are re-architecting the tech landscape.

Underlying trends:

- US–China chip and AI rivalry.
- Data sovereignty mandates.
- Alternative payment rails in BRICS+.
- Divergent AI safety/ethics rules.

Velocity:

- **Faster if**: Tensions escalate, standards diverge faster.
- **Slower if**: Global trade pressures push toward interoperability.

How did we arrive at 11? Follow the money — where are folks like AZ16 and Blackrock placing their bets?

What is the pace of innovation in terms of the volume of patents?

Is the government here to help or stand in our way?

Here's a tight, decision-ready scan of each of the 11 future movements, with (1) what it is, (2) a directional 2024 VC pulse, (3) a patent signal, and (4) the regulatory read you should plan against. Sources are cited inline, allowing you to dig deeper quickly.

Notes: Figures vary by methodology; I use reputable rollups (Dealroom, PitchBook/CB Insights, BNEF/PwC, Galaxy, etc.).

Patent "signals" lean on the EPO's 2024 Patent Index and WIPO context.

Treat VC ranges as order-of-magnitude for portfolio planning.

How to use this 11-movement market scan fast (VC | patents | regulation)

- Prioritize by inevitability × readiness. AI platforms, climate/energy, cyber, and supply-chain traceability have both regulatory pull and CAPEX/OPEX budgets already in motion.
- Map patent heat to the moat. Where EPO shows momentum (computer tech/AI; batteries/energy), assume faster feature decay and plan process moats (data rights, distribution, integration). EPO
- Pre-bake compliance. If you handle people or money, assume the AI Act, DSA/OSA, and MiCA rules will apply, and design for audit trails, content/wallet provenance, and rights-respecting defaults. CB Insights Compliance and Risks ESMA

Movement (what it is)	VC pulse (≈2024)
AI platforms & autonomous agents (enterprise AI as an operating layer; agentic workflows)	$110–$132B to AI startups in 2024 (≈one-third of global VC).
Unbanked + crypto wallets (stablecoins/CBDC rails for payments & remittances)	$10–$15B crypto/Web3 VC in 2024 (rebound late-year; Q1'25 $4.8B with one mega-deal).
Decentralized supply chains & product passports (traceability, DPP, tokenized provenance)	Supply-chain tech saw multi-$B quarters in 2024 (e.g., $3.5B in Q4; $2.4B in Q2); annual low-teens $B estimates.
Dark warehouses & autonomous robotics (lights-out fulfillment; mobile/ manipulation)	Robotics startups raised approximately $7–$17 billion in 2024 (methodology varies; $10.9 billion through August; 2024 totals cited ≈at roughly $17.2 billion). The Robot Report, Business Insider
Spatial computing & metaverse (AR/VR/XR and 3D interfaces)	$1.6B XR VC in 2024 (down YoY), with big-tech capex (Meta >$80B cumulatively; on track to >$100B by 2025). Medium Financial Times
Synthetic media & digital twins (genAI content + virtual replicas for design/ops)	Funded inside the AI surge (tens of $B); twins also see industrial budgets vs. pure VC.
Edge AI & on-device (private, low-latency inference; AI chips)	Multi-$B within AI; heavy deep-tech rounds (AI chips) but no single global total; semiconductor VC revived around AI workloads.
Climate tech & energy transition (storage, grid, CCUS, materials)	$30–$56B climate-tech VC in 2024 (down from 2023); energy transition investment across asset classes reached approximately $2.0–$2.1T.
Health AI & precision medicine (diagnostics, discovery, care ops)	~$25B healthtech VC in 2024 (global).
Cybersecurity & digital trust (zero-trust, identity, AI-sec)	High single-digit to low-teens $B in 2024; Crunchbase tracked steady deal flow despite macro.
Data sovereignty & platform fragmentation (privacy, gatekeepers, localization)	Funded via regtech/adtech/privacy tech niches (smaller absolute VC than AI/fintech). (Directional.)

Patent signal	Regulatory read (global)
Strong uptrend. At EPO, "computer technology" (including ML/AI) became the #1 field, with an explicit surge in AI inventions.	The EU AI Act (risk-based, phased in from 2025), NIST AI RMF is widely adopted, and U.S. EO 14028 is shaping federal use; China has GenAI rules. Plan for model transparency, evals, and human-in-the-loop. CB Insights Business Research Company, Semiconductor Engineering News
Moderate. Blockchain/crypto patents steady; more activity clustered in payments & custody (regional variance). (Use EPO "computer tech" as proxy.)	EU MiCA in force (stablecoin rules 2024–26); FATF Travel Rule; region-specific VASP rules (e.g., Nigeria/Philippines). Expect KYC/AML by design.
Rising in data/IoT/ID fields; clean-energy & transport filings also up (relevant to logistics).	EU ESPR/Digital Product Passport, EU Battery Passport, EUDR deforestation due-dates, traceability becomes compliance.
Uptrend. Robotics falls under the category of "computer tech/transport," with AI-robotics filings on the rise.	The EU AI Act will categorize specific machinery /robotics as high-risk, with safety standards remaining a key consideration. Sector-specific rules for drones/AVs vary by region.
Mixed. Patents are active across displays, optics, UI, and embedded in "computer tech," but growth is slower than that of the AI core.	The EU DSA and UK Online Safety Act tighten platform duties & youth protection, with a focus on privacy by design for XR/ biometrics.
Strong within computer tech; twins tie into transport/industrial filings (2024 increases).	EU AI Act transparency rules (synthetic media labeling), sector safety for industrial twins.
Rising: patents in compute architectures & energy-efficient hardware folded into "computer tech."	Data protection regimes (GDPR/DSA/DPDP) favor on-device model governance.
Strong: EPO shows +8.9% in electrical machinery/energy (batteries/clean energy).	SEC/EU climate disclosure, CBAM, national incentives; policy volatility by region, plan scenario-ready capital stacks.
Up: biotech filings +5.4% at EPO; AI/medtech patenting robust (eligibility varies by jurisdiction).	Medical AI faces device-grade oversight (FDA/EMA), data protection, and emerging AI-specific guidance.
Steady-strong across crypto/identity/secure compute patents. (Folded into computer tech at EPO.)	DSA/DMA, data-sovereignty laws, and critical-infrastructure rules tighten security baselines globally.
Ongoing: filings in privacy-preserving ML, identity, and encryption.	The EU DSA/DMA is entirely in force; the UK Online Safety Act has staged enforcement; India's DPDP and China's PIPL are driving localization & consent-centric design.

Introduction to the Decision Scenario Grid

The 2×2 that follows is designed to map how AI and adjacent disruptions unfold across two key dimensions: Value and Transformation Complexity

From Ledger to Action Map

Let's revisit the complexity/value framework from Chapter 3:

- High-value + Low-complexity → Move now (Fast Plays).
- High-value + High-complexity → Explore (Moonshots).
- Low-value + Low-complexity → Opportunistic.
- Low-value + High-complexity → Avoid or monitor.

Overlay the scenario grid with this framework, and you have a Future Action Map, a prioritized portfolio of experiments, investments, and watchlist items.

This grid helps leaders distinguish between where to play now and where to position for the long game, ensuring strategy balances urgency with foresight.

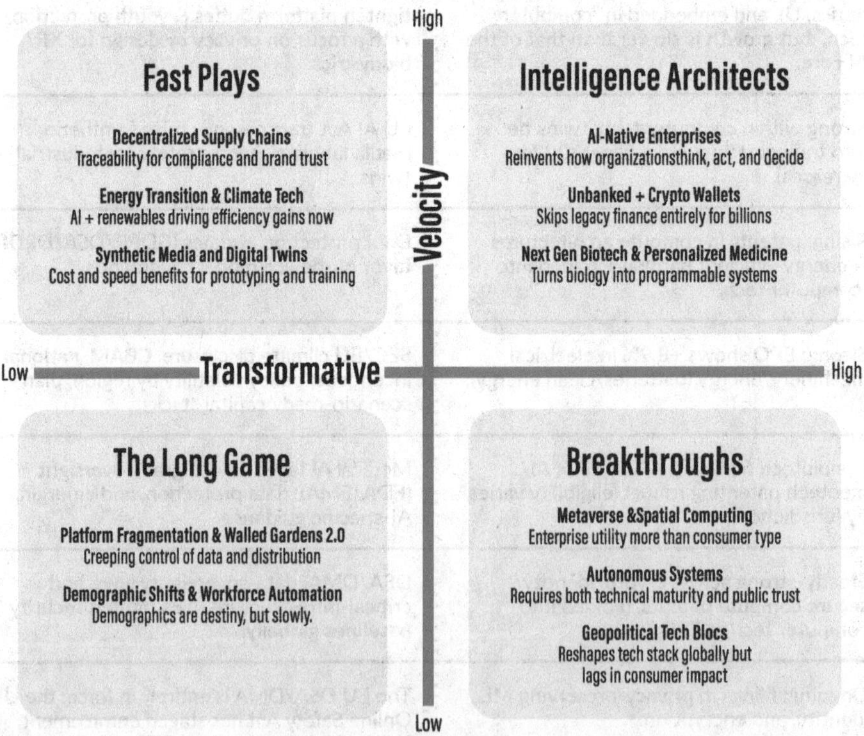

Connecting Signals to Strategic Options

In the future, adapt and edit these trends for your industry and business to monitor the signals, score, and rank opportunities to test.

Remember the *Signal → Prototype → Scale* loop from Chapter 2? Here's how it applies now:

- **Signal**: Identify early evidence (startup activity, patent filings, policy drafts).
- **Prototype**: Test the idea in a low-risk sandbox.
- **Scale**: Integrate into core operations or business models when ROI proves out.

By categorizing the 11 movements into quadrants, you can decide where in the loop to place your bets.

The Personal Dimension

The future-ready organization starts with the future-ready leader. This is where your agency comes in:

- Shift from **control** to orchestration — you can't own every moving part, but you can set the tempo and direct the flow.
- Move from **certainty** to **curiosity** — it's not about knowing the future, it's about asking better questions about it.
- See your **career and legacy** in the context of these movements. What will your leadership be remembered for 10 years from now?

Future Frontier Compass

A directional guide to emerging tech and business model readiness

The Compass isn't about predicting the future perfectly; it's about knowing which horizon you're operating in and tuning your *signals, tools, and behaviors* accordingly. The organizations that thrive are those that move fluidly across stages, instead of getting trapped in firefighting or stuck in endless pilots.

Stage	Signals (What You Notice)	Tools (What You Use)	Behaviors (How You Act)
1. **Firefighting (Reactive)** Short horizon, crisis-driven	· Competitor launches a force reaction · Regulatory shocks · Customer churn spikes	· Basic dashboards · Crisis comms platforms · Manual reporting	· Respond case by case · Patchwork fixes · Wait-and-see posture
2. **Probing (Experimental)** Medium horizon, curiosity-led	· Rising trend chatter (social, VC funding, analyst notes) · Early adopters experimenting · Small customer signals at edges	· Pilots in labs or skunkworks · Hackathons · Startup partnerships	· Launch pilots quickly · Capture learnings systematically · Celebrate experimentation
3. **Shaping (Adaptive)** Longer horizon, opportunity-led	· Clear demand signals in the market · Ecosystem players aligning · Shifts in regulation opening pathways	· Cross-functional foresight teams · APIs & modular cloud · Data-sharing clean rooms · AI for signal clustering	· Orchestrate prototypes across business units · Adapt faster than peers · Integrate customer co-creation
4. **Architecting (Embedded)** Full horizon, system-led	· New categories forming · Tech standards emerging · Customers expect seamless future-state experiences	· Web3 rails, edge computing, autonomous AI agents · Tokenized ecosystems · Next-gen orchestration platforms	· Build frontier business models (participation-based, modular · Institutionalize always-on scanning · Act as ecosystem architect, not just participant

CASE STUDY

KITE Scouting — Building a Muscle for Future-Casting

How enterprises use startup scouting platforms to operationalize foresight.

Enterprises often know they need to "future-proof," but lack a repeatable system to turn noise about emerging startups into actionable opportunities. KITE Scouting has been engaged by global firms such as Campbell's, HP, and Visa to create structured pathways from curiosity → candidate pipeline → pilot engagement.

The Bottleneck

Innovation teams often default to annual reports or one-off events to discover startups. This leads to gaps: too many irrelevant leads, too little signal, and too much lag between discovery and action. By the time a company reacts, competitors have already signed partnerships or pilots.

The Overclock

- Campbell's R&D: KITE delivered "on-demand company recommendations," vetting startups in adjacent food-tech sectors and helping Campbell's focus on the most viable fits rather than scanning the entire ecosystem.
- HP Partnerships: KITE built a taxonomy of 600+ relevant companies in the first month, tagging them by capability, geography, and maturity. This gave HP a living map of potential collaborators rather than a static slide deck.
- Visa Innovation: Supported open innovation recruitment, vetting fintech startups at scale for accelerator-style programs, creating a pipeline aligned with Visa's priorities.

Results

- KITE has delivered over 1,000 custom reports and recruited 10,000+ startups into corporate innovation programs.
- Clients reduced scouting cycles from quarters to weeks by outsourcing the heavy lift of filtering and ranking.
- Engagement shifted from sporadic pilots to systematic scanning, enabling teams to test, learn, and scale with confidence.

What It Means

The KITE example illustrates a broader lesson: future-casting is a muscle, not a moment. Enterprises that treat startup discovery as operational infrastructure, not theater, gain the agility to move from weak signals to market action before competitors.

The Next Horizon

You've now seen the future refracted through seventeen different models, each one a lens into how organizations sense, adapt, and build in an environment where technology accelerates faster than planning cycles. Together, these frameworks form more than diagrams. They are a navigation system for leaders who must run tuned, not default.

Across this journey, a pattern emerges:

- Every maturity model starts in silos and ends in systems.
- Every disruptive movement begins as noise and becomes infrastructure.
- Every Overclocked enterprise moves from reaction to anticipation, not by eliminating uncertainty, but by developing reflexes that thrive within it.

The next frontier isn't just about speed. It's about composure at speed. AI will be your engine, data your telemetry, community your multiplier, and trust your cooling system. However, the decisive factor is not the technology itself; it's the capacity of your organization to learn, adapt, and orchestrate across boundaries more quickly than the competition.

Our next Horizon isn't a destination. It's a discipline of sensing the weak signals, testing bold plays, scaling what works, and discarding what doesn't. It's about repeatedly installing the upgrade until adaptation itself becomes your default operating system.

And here's the truth: the future won't arrive fully formed. It will come as fleeting edge signals, as prototypes on the fringe, as micro-moments of breakthrough. Your challenge is to notice them, act on them, and multiply them before they vanish. Yes, at times you'll misinterpret the signal-to-noise ratio and lean in where you shouldn't. But, because we're taking an incrementalism approach to our GTM, you won't be sprinting in the wrong direction for long. And, as a dual transformation discipline, you didn't sacrifice the core in the process.

Years from now, you'll remember not the models you studied but the choices you made, the experiments you ran, the risks you took, the systems you rewired. The Overclocked Horizon belongs to those who treat foresight as fuel, not theater, and who build futures faster than others can imagine them.

The question is simple, but urgent: will you be a spectator of change, or its architect?

EPILOGUE

The Overclocked Mindset

"The future belongs not to those who predict it, but to those who create it." You've reached the end of Overclocked: Reinvention, but this isn't an ending; it's a new beginning. We've shown that reinvention isn't just about technology, but also about mindset, systems thinking, and rebuilding courage. Leaders adapt, organizations implement innovation processes, and enterprises gain velocity with each test and learn event: operations, logistics, and finance.HR, marketing, product, and sales achieve orchestration through nimble architecture. True transformation happens when you apply these ideas to your context, industry, and challenges.

Small bets create compound effects. Cases like LEGO, P&G, Domino's, and Kraft Heinz started with small bets on big ideas, gaining momentum through experimentation. The overclocked mindset is about spotting opportunities early, testing hypotheses affordably, and scaling successful strategies before competitors catch on.

Choose one framework from this book, focus on the challenge that matters most to you, and test it for 90 days. Build cross-functional teams, run agile sprints, or launch an AI pilot. Committing to systematic experimentation will uncover what works within your organization, among your customers, and in the market.

Successful transformations generate network effects. Each experiment provides insights that help build capabilities for future innovation. People who experience accelerated thinking become advocates for change.

You're not just transforming your organization; you're setting an example for industry, customers, and the community. The ripple effect of bold leadership goes beyond quarterly results.

This is a choice: Will it change shape you, or will you shape change?

Thriving companies won't be those with the most significant budgets, but rather those with a clear vision and the ability to execute it. The future belongs not to those who predict it perfectly but to those who build it consistently.

Your reinvention journey begins today.

Acknowledgments

This book exists through the wisdom and generosity of an extraordinary community who shaped my journey through 25+ years of digital transformation.

Deepest gratitude to peer reviewers Norbert Hudak, Matt Ballesteros, David Wolf, and Todd Piper-Hauswirth for their honest perspectives that strengthened every chapter.

To my clients current and past, who taught me that transformation happens in daily work, not boardrooms, your challenges became my education.

Thanks to the University of Iowa Tippie College of Business for building my foundation and giving me a platform to teach and the University of Chicago Booth School of Business for catalyzing my reinvention.

Special recognition to mentors Jim Wuthrich (Warner Bros) and Hillary Hoffman (Universal Studios) for their enduring guidance.

To the teams who demonstrated innovation in action: **Warner Bros**: Joe Eibert, John Cosley, Cathérine Van den Ostende, Mark Drosos, Patrick Spann, Sharon Braun. **Universal Studios**: Joe Eibert, Tara O'Donnell, Eric Brodsky, Priya Verma, Stephanie Wells, Doug Neal. **Redbox**: Kiera Hynninen, Steve Olson, Susan Parsons, Brett Cherobee, Maria Dabrowski, Kimberlie Christen, Jen Partin, Daisy Yuhas, Jesse Ratliff, Aaron McDowell, Diane Wales, Mike DiMiele, Adriane Lewandowski, Dan Navarro, Tim Bell, Jahi Garrett, Jim Falletti, Maura Gray, Kate Brennan, among many, many others.

Mark Silva, Doug Textor, Chris Dalton, and Matt Schmeltz expanded my perspective beyond corporate transformation to entrepreneurial innovation.

To unnamed colleagues and collaborators who shared insights in boardrooms and coffee conversations, this book synthesizes our collective learning about thriving when velocity is the defining variable.

Finally, heartfelt thanks to my wife Amanda and boys River and Schyler for their enduring support during my reinvention from corporate to consulting, teaching, and authorship. And to my sister Linda, whose enthusiasm always pushes me forward.

Each of you proved that business reinvention is about people willing to challenge convention and build the future while others debate its arrival.

GLOSSARY TERMS

CHAPTER 1 — THE DIGITAL LEADER

Focus: leadership mindset, organizational readiness, customer-centricity

Agility — Organizational capacity to adapt quickly to shifting customer needs, markets, and technologies.

Change Management — Structured approaches for transitioning people and processes toward new ways of working.

Cheat Code — A secret command, usually a sequence of buttons or keystrokes, that a player enters into a video game to gain an advantage, such as unlocking new levels, gaining extra lives, or achieving invincibility.

Customer-Centricity — Placing customer needs and experiences at the heart of strategic decisions.

Digital Culture — Shared values, norms, and practices that encourage digital-first approaches.

Digital Leadership — The ability to guide organizations through transformation by leveraging digital tools, data, and culture.

Digital Mindset — A way of thinking that embraces data-driven insights, experimentation, and adaptability.

Ecosystem Thinking — In a Web3 world is a strategic approach that moves beyond a traditional, company-centric view to focus on building and nurturing a decentralized, interdependent network of participants. In this model, value is co-created and distributed among all stakeholders, rather than being captured by a single, central platform.

Leadership Resilience — The capacity of leaders to adapt, persevere, and inspire during disruption.

Maturity Matrix — A self-assessment tool used by organizations to evaluate their current capability level in a specific area, such as a process, program, or technology, by comparing it against defined stages of maturity. It presents these areas as a table with different levels of development, allowing organizations to identify strengths and weaknesses and create a strategic plan or roadmap to achieve higher levels of performance and meet their objectives.

Organizational Readiness — An assessment of an organization's culture, talent, and infrastructure for digital adoption.

Reskilling — Training employees in new skills required for digital roles and emerging technologies.

Strategic Alignment — Ensuring digital initiatives directly support overall business goals.

Translation Layer — In technology, a translation layer is a software or hardware component that converts information, code, or data from one format or system into another, making them compatible and usable by different systems that were not originally designed to work together.

CHAPTER 2 — STRATEGY REIMAGINED

Focus: frameworks, models, strategic adaptation in the digital era

Behavior Controlled Value Proposition (BCVP) – The concept it describes combines behavioral science principles with traditional value propositions. Instead of simply stating a product's benefits, a BCVP tailors its messaging to influence how customers actually make decisions, focusing on their psychological and emotional drivers.

Blue Ocean Strategy — Strategy for creating uncontested markets and demand rather than competing head-to-head.

Business Model Canvas (BMC) — A framework mapping value proposition, customer segments, channels, and revenue models.

Digital Maturity Model — A staged framework for evaluating organizational progress in digital transformation.

Ecosystem Strategy — Leveraging partnerships and platforms to expand value beyond a single firm.

Horizon Planning — Balancing short-term performance with long-term bets across different time horizons.

Kinetic Strategy Model – A strategic framework that maps organizations along two dimensions, Velocity (speed of sensing and acting) and Adaptability (capacity to pivot and reconfigure). It identifies four archetypes—Defenders, Sprinters, Analysts, and Architects — to emphasize that lasting advantage comes from mastering both dimensions.

Permissionless – In the context of Web3, permissionless refers to a system or network that anyone can join and participate in without needing approval from a central authority. This stands in direct opposition to "permissioned" systems, where gatekeepers control access.

Porter's Five Forces — A tool to analyze industry competition: rivalry, new entrants, substitutes, buyer, and supplier power.

Punctuated Equilibrium – In strategy, punctuated equilibrium describes how a business undergoes long periods of stability (equilibrium), characterized by little change, followed by short, intense bursts of radical, disruptive change (punctuation) in response to a significant event, innovation, or environmental shift.

Strategic Capabilities — Core strengths that enable execution of a digital strategy.

Scenario Planning — A Strategy technique to anticipate and prepare for multiple possible futures.

SWOT Analysis — Evaluation of strengths, weaknesses, opportunities, and threats for strategic clarity.

Value Creation Models — Frameworks that define how organizations generate, deliver, and capture value.

CHAPTER 3 — DIGITAL DISRUPTION & REINVENTION

Focus: disruption theory, adaptation, reinvention cycles

Creative Destruction — An Economic concept where innovation continuously displaces outdated businesses.

Decentralized – In the context of Web3, "decentralized" means that control, data, and decision-making are distributed across a network of users and computers rather than being concentrated in the hands of a single entity, like a corporation or government. This is achieved through technologies like blockchain and smart contracts, enabling users to gain more control over their digital identities, data, and online experiences, fostering greater transparency, security, and user sovereignty.

Digital Disruption — The radical transformation of markets and existing businesses caused by new digital technologies and innovative business models. It involves the use of digital tools like AI and cloud computing to create new ways of operating, which changes customer expectations and fundamentally alters how industries create value, compete, and interact.

Disruption Theory — Christensen's framework explaining how entrants with new models can overtake incumbents.

Dual Transformation — Framework for simultaneously strengthening the core business while launching new growth engines.

Fast Follower Strategy — Adopting proven innovations quickly after pioneers to reduce risk

First-Mover Advantage — Competitive benefit gained by being the first to adopt new technologies or models.

Exponential Technologies — Innovations that scale rapidly, reshaping industries (e.g., AI, blockchain).

Incumbent's Dilemma — When established firms struggle to innovate due to reliance on existing models.

Reinvention — The ongoing adaptation of business models and processes in response to disruption.

Signal vs. Noise — Distinguishing meaningful market shifts from irrelevant data or hype.

Smart Contract — A self-executing computer program, stored on a blockchain, that automatically enforces the terms of a digital contract once predefined conditions are met. It eliminates the need for trusted intermediaries, such as lawyers or banks, because the code itself handles the execution and fulfillment of the contract's promises in a tamper-proof and transparent way.

Strategic Inflection Point — A moment when industry fundamentals shift, requiring a new strategy.

CHAPTER 4 — DIGITAL INFRASTRUCTURE

Focus: technology stack, scalability, security

API (Application Programming Interface) — A set of rules allowing systems to communicate and share data.

Business Owner — In IT governance, a business owner is the individual or business unit accountable for the success of a technology solution from the business side. Unlike an IT manager who handles day-to-day operations, the business owner focuses on the strategic direction, value delivery, and business outcomes achieved through the technology.

Cloud Computing — On-demand access to computing resources via the internet.

Cybersecurity — Practices and technologies for securing systems and data from threats.

Data Lake — A centralized repository for storing large volumes of structured and unstructured data.

Data Lakehouse — A modern data architecture that unifies the benefits of a data lake and a data warehouse, providing a single platform for storing, managing, and analyzing diverse structured and unstructured data. It offers the low-cost, flexible storage of a data lake with the data management features of a data warehouse, such as ACID transactions, schema enforcement, and indexing, all built on open data formats and cloud storage.

Edge Computing — Processing data closer to its source to reduce latency and bandwidth use.

IT governance - A framework, or frameworks, that manages how organizations optimize their use of IT operations to support business objectives.

IaaS (Infrastructure as a Service) — Virtualized computing resources provided over the internet.

Microservices Architecture — Software design where applications are built as a collection of loosely coupled services.

Product Owner — In the context of IT governance, a product manager acts as a strategic and accountable leader for a specific product, balancing the demands of customers with the organization's overarching IT policies.

SaaS (Software as a Service) — Applications delivered over the internet on a subscription basis.

PaaS (Platform as a Service) — Cloud environment enabling developers to build, run, and manage applications.

Zero Trust Security — A model where no user or device is trusted by default, even inside the network.

CHAPTER 5 — DIGITAL BUSINESS MODELS

Focus: value creation, revenue streams, digital-first models

Ad-Supported Model — Revenue from selling advertising placements within a product/service.

As-a-Service Economy — Shift from ownership to pay-per-use models across industries.

Data Monetization — The process of creating tangible economic benefits from a company's data assets, either by selling it directly to third parties or by using it internally to improve operations, develop new products, and enhance customer experiences, ultimately generating revenue or reducing costs.

Disintermediation — Removing intermediaries in the value chain through digital platforms.

Freemium — A model offering basic services free while charging for advanced features.

Gamification — The application of typical elements of game playing (e.g. point scoring, competition with others, rules of play) to other areas of activity, typically as an online marketing technique to encourage engagement with a product or service.

Marketplace Model — A platform connecting buyers and sellers, earning through fees or commissions.

Network Effects — When the value of a product or platform increases as more users join.

Platform Business Model — A model that creates value by connecting two or more interdependent groups (e.g., Uber).

Servitization — Turning products into services by layering ongoing support, subscriptions, or analytics.

Subscription Economy — A Recurring revenue model based on ongoing customer relationships.

Tokenized Model — Digital tokens represent value or ownership, typically based on blockchain technology, and may be either tied to digital or physical assets.

Tokenomics — A business model centered on creating, distributing, and managing digital tokens to align incentives and drive economic activity within a blockchain-based ecosystem. Instead of relying solely on traditional revenue streams like sales or advertising, a token-centric business model leverages the token's programmable utility to create a self-sustaining digital economy.

CHAPTER 6 – DIGITAL-DRIVEN INSIGHTS

Focus: data-driven strategy, analytics, governance

Customer Master – A centralized, accurate, and comprehensive record of a customer's key information, including contact details, purchase history, and preferences, used across an organization. It is important because it provides a single source of truth for customer data, enabling consistent, personalized customer experiences, more efficient operations, improved decision-making, and stronger customer relationships.

Customer Segmentation – Grouping customers based on behavior, demographics, or value.

Dark Data – Dark data is information that organizations and people generate and collect but fail to use or analyze for decision-making, insights, or monetization.

Data Democratization – Making data accessible across the organization for decision-making

Data Governance – Policies and standards ensuring data accuracy, security, and compliance.

Descriptive Analytics – Analyzing past performance to understand "what happened."

Diagnostic Analytics – Focuses on understanding 'why something happened'.

Enterprise Observability – The practice of using comprehensive telemetry (logs, metrics, and traces) to gain deep, contextual insights into the internal state of complex, distributed systems and data platforms within an organization.

Feature Engineering – Creating meaningful input variables for machine learning models.

Identity Management – Identity management provides the foundation for data insights and omnichannel CRM by creating a unified, accurate, and secure view of each customer. Without proper identity management, data remains fragmented across channels, limiting the depth of insights and preventing a truly seamless and personalized customer experience.

KPIs (Key Performance Indicators) – Metrics that measure progress toward business objectives.

Personally Identifiable Information (PII) – Any data that can be used to uniquely identify an individual, whether directly or indirectly. This includes direct identifiers like a name, address, or Social Security number, as well as indirect identifiers such as a date of birth or gender when combined with other information. PII is a prime target for identity theft and data breaches.

Predictive Analytics — Using data to forecast likely outcomes and trends.

Prescriptive Analytics — Suggesting actions based on data insights to achieve desired outcomes.

Real-Time Analytics — Processing data instantly to enable immediate action.

Single Source of Truth (SSOT) — A unified, trusted dataset for consistent decision-making.

CHAPTER 7 — THE DIGITAL CONSUMER

Focus: behavior, expectations, personalization

Behavioral Analytics — Tracking and analyzing user actions to understand and influence behavior.

Customer Acquisition Cost (CAC) — The total expense a business incurred to convince a lead to become a paying customer, including marketing, sales, and other related costs. It is calculated by dividing all sales and marketing expenses by the number of new customers acquired during a specific period.

Customer Journey – The complete experience and set of interactions a person has with a brand, product, or service, from initial awareness and consideration through to purchase and post-purchase engagement and loyalty. This comprehensive path encompasses all touchpoints, both direct (such as customer service interactions) and indirect (like social media or word-of-mouth), enabling businesses to understand customer needs, behaviors, and emotions, thereby optimizing the overall experience.

Customer Journey Mapping — The process of visualizing the stages customers move through, from awareness to loyalty.

CX (Customer Experience) — The total perception of interactions a customer has with a brand.

Experience Economy — Competing on memorable customer experiences, not just products.

Micro-Moments — Small, intent-driven moments when consumers turn to devices for action.

Omnichannel — Delivering seamless experiences across physical and digital touchpoints.

Personalization — Tailoring offerings or content to individual needs using customer data.

Social Proof — Influence created by peer reviews, testimonials, or visible usage trends.

Voice of Customer (VoC) — Collecting and analyzing customer feedback for insights.

ZMOT — The Zero Moment of Truth, is the online research and evaluation stage of the modern customer journey. Coined by Google in 2011, it describes the period after a consumer is exposed to a product or service (the "stimulus," like an advertisement) but before they make a purchase.

Zero-Party Data — Information willingly shared by customers (preferences, intentions).

CHAPTER 8 – THE DIGITAL TRANSFORMATION OF B2B

Focus: ecosystems, platforms, industrial reinvention

AI Native Ecosystem – An AI-native ecosystem is a technological environment designed from the ground up with artificial intelligence as its core, rather than an add-on feature. It's a dynamic, interconnected system where AI enables autonomous, data-driven decision-making and continuous learning to adapt and improve without constant human intervention. Unlike traditional systems, AI is deeply embedded in the architecture, creating an intelligent, adaptive, and context-aware environment that drives new functionalities and business models.

B2B Marketplace — Online platform enabling transactions between businesses.

Co-Creation — Collaboration with partners or customers to design solutions.

Digital Supply Chain — Integrated, data-driven value chain from sourcing to delivery

EDI (Electronic Data Interchange) — Standardized digital exchange of business documents.

Ecosystem Strategy — Building partnerships and networks that extend value creation.

Industry 4.0 — The fourth industrial revolution, driven by IoT, AI, and intelligent automation.

IoT (Internet of Things) — A Network of connected devices that exchange data.

Platformization — Converting products or services into digital platforms.

Procurement Digitization — Modernizing supplier and purchasing processes via digital tools.

Platforms, Marketplaces, and Ecosystems – Platforms provide the underlying infrastructure, marketplaces operate on platforms to facilitate transactions, and ecosystems are the broader networks of interconnected products, services, and participants that grow around a platform or marketplace, creating a more integrated and holistic experience for users. A marketplace can be a component of an ecosystem, with the platform serving as the foundational technology and the ecosystem encompassing all associated services and interactions that extend beyond a single transaction.

CHAPTER 10 – OWNED MEDIA

Focus: building direct, brand-controlled ecosystems

Agentic Marketplace – A decentralized, AI-driven digital marketplace where intelligent agents (software bots) act on behalf of users or businesses to search, negotiate, and transact autonomously.

Content Hub – A centralized digital destination for branded content.

Content Strategy – A plan for how a business will communicate with prospects and customers across digital channels to support their journey and achieve business objectives, such as lead nurturing, sales conversions, and customer loyalty.

CRM (Customer Relationship Management) – Systems for managing customer data, interactions, and relationships.

Customer Data Platform (CDP) – A system that consolidates customer data into unified profiles.

Email Marketing – Owned media channel leveraging newsletters and campaigns to drive engagement

First-Party Data – Customer information collected directly by a company through owned channels.

Omnichannel – A term used in e-commerce and retail to describe a business strategy that aims to provide a seamless shopping experience across all channels.

Owned Media – Digital properties fully controlled by a brand (websites, apps, CRM, email).

Push Notification – A push notification is a message sent from a server to a user's device (like a smartphone or computer) that appears without the user needing to actively open or request it from an app or website.

Retention Marketing — Strategies aimed at engaging and keeping existing customers.

RFM Model — Customer segmentation based on Recency (how recently a customer purchased), Frequency (how often they purchase), and Monetary value (how much they spend). By scoring customers on these three metrics, businesses can identify their most valuable customers and create targeted, personalized marketing campaigns.

SEO (Search Engine Optimization) — Optimizing owned content to rank higher in organic search results.

SMS — Short Message Service, a text messaging service that allows users to send and receive short text-only messages between mobile phones.

User Experience (UX) — The quality of a person's interaction with a company's digital channels.

UI (User Interface) — The visual and interactive elements of a digital product.

CHAPTER 11 — EARNED MEDIA

Focus: trust, advocacy, organic amplification.

Brand Advocacy — When customers voluntarily promote and defend a brand.

Crisis Management — Strategies for protecting brand reputation during negative publicity.

Dark Site — A web presence, either a section of an existing website or a standalone site, that is prepared in advance but kept hidden or "dark" from the public until a crisis occurs. Its purpose is to serve as a central, reliable source of information for media and stakeholders during an emergency or crisis, providing pre-written statements, background details, and updates to control the narrative and build trust when it's needed most.

Earned Media — Unpaid media impressions or mentions from third parties like customers, journalists, and influencers in the form of publicity, customer reviews, social, email pass-along, word of mouth, and user-generated content.

Earned Media Integration — The strategic combination of paid media, owned media, and earned media (unpaid brand mentions from third parties like customers, journalists, and influencers) to maximize brand impact, build trust, and achieve marketing goals. The integration leverages the strengths of each media type, with earned media amplifying the credibility and reach of paid and owned efforts, creating a powerful, coherent marketing system.

Earned Media Value — To value earned media, use the formula Earned Media Value (EMV) = Impressions × CPM × Adjustment Factor, where Impressions are content views, CPM is the cost per thousand impressions for comparable paid media, and the Adjustment Factor accounts for the content's quality or specific campaign goals, like engagement or conversions.

Influencer Marketing — Leveraging creators and thought leaders to drive credibility and reach.

Net Promoter Score (NPS) — A customer loyalty metric that measures how likely customers are to recommend a company's products or services, calculated by subtracting the percentage of "detractors" (those who give a score of 0–6) from the percentage of "promoters" (those who give a score of 9–10) on a 0–10 rating scale. The resulting score, which ranges from –100 to 100, provides a simple way to gauge overall customer satisfaction and loyalty.

Sentiment Analysis — Using AI to evaluate public opinion expressed in online content.

Social Proof — Validation of a brand through testimonials, reviews, or visible endorsements

UGC (User-Generated Content) — Content created by customers that brands amplify.

Virality — Content that spreads rapidly through sharing across digital platforms.

Word of Mouth (WOM) — Organic, peer-to-peer brand advocacy through conversations

CHAPTER 12 — PAID MEDIA

Focus: amplification, advertising, performance marketing

Ad Fraud — Invalid traffic or fake impressions that waste ad spend.

Attribution Modeling — Determining which channels and touchpoints contributed to a conversion.

Clicks — The total number of times your ad was clicked.

CPM (Cost Per Mille/Thousand Impressions) — Pricing model based on ad views per thousand impressions.

Connected TV (CTV) Ads — These ads appear on smart TVs, streaming devices such as Roku, Apple TV, and gaming consoles, delivering video content through apps and services like Netflix, ESPN, and CBS. Unlike traditional linear TV ads that target broad audiences, CTV ads utilize data to reach specific demographics, offering better targeting, measurement, and engagement for advertisers.

Cross Device Ad Tracking — The method advertisers use to identify and follow the same person across multiple devices, such as a phone, laptop, and connected TV, to unify their digital behavior into a single user profile.

Engagement Rate — Measures the level of interaction your ads receive, calculated by dividing total engagements by impressions.

Frequency — The average number of times individuals see the same ad.

Impressions — The number of times your ad was displayed on a platform.

Lookalike Audiences — An Ad targeting technique where algorithms find new users similar to existing customers.

Media Mix Modeling (MMM) — An analytical method for measuring the ROI of different media investments.

Paid Media — Advertising channels where exposure is purchased (search, display, social).

Programmatic Advertising — Automated buying and selling of digital ad inventory using AI.

PPC (Pay-Per-Click) — An advertising model where brands pay each time a user clicks an ad.

Performance Marketing — Paid campaigns optimized for measurable results (e.g., leads, sales).

Quality Score — A rating of the relevance and quality of your ads and landing pages.

Reach — The total number of unique individuals who see your ad at least once within a specific timeframe

Retargeting — Serving ads to users who previously interacted with a brand but didn't convert.

Return on Ad Spend (ROAS) — To calculate ROAS, you divide the total revenue generated by the campaign by the total cost of the campaign: ROAS = Revenue / Advertising Costs.

CHAPTER 13 — ADAPTIVE, INTELLIGENT GO-TO-MARKET (GTM) STRATEGY

Focus: dynamic planning, execution, and market alignment

Affiliate Marketing — A performance-based channel where a business (the merchant) partners with individuals or companies (affiliates) to promote its products or services in exchange for a commission on every sale, lead, or action generated through their unique affiliate link. This strategy extends a brand's reach, leverages the affiliate's audience and content creation skills, and provides a cost-effective way to generate revenue and build credibility by only paying when results are achieved.

Churn Rate — The percentage of customers who stop doing business with a company over a given period

Customer Acquisition Cost (CAC) — The total cost of acquiring a new customer.

Go-to-Market (GTM) Strategy — The tactical plan that outlines how a company delivers its value proposition to customers.

Growth Hacking — Creative, data-driven methods for rapid customer acquisition and scaling.

Ideal Customer Profile (ICP) — A hypothetical description of a customer, whether a company or an individual, that is most likely to benefit from your product or service, remain loyal, and become your most valuable customer

Lifetime Value (LTV) — The predicted net profit attributed to the entire relationship with a customer.

Market Segmentation — Dividing a market into groups of customers with shared characteristics.

Omnichannel GTM — Delivering consistent messaging and sales experiences across multiple channels.

Positioning — Defining how a brand is perceived relative to competitors in the market.

Product-Market Fit — The degree to which a product satisfies strong market demand.

Sales Enablement — Tools, processes, and content provided to help sales teams close deals effectively.

Value Ecosystem — An interconnected network of a company's internal resources, external partners, and users that collectively deliver a comprehensive and seamless experience. The ecosystem creates value for the end-user by providing a holistic, integrated experience that extends beyond any single product or service.

Value Proposition Shift — In the Industrial era, value propositions centered on mass production, efficiency, and scale, with power and ownership concentrated in centralized institutions. In contrast, the Web3 era emphasizes decentralization, user ownership, and equitable value distribution, moving away from corporate intermediaries.

CHAPTER 14 — MEASUREMENT: INTEGRATED ANALYTICS & INTELLIGENCE

Focus: performance tracking, integrated intelligence

Agile Intelligence — Using integrated, real-time analytics to support fast, adaptive decisions.

Attribution Modeling — Identifying which channels and touchpoints drive conversions.

Average Revenue Per User (ARPU) — The total revenue a business generates divided by the average number of users over a specific period, such as monthly or annually. It is a crucial metric for subscription-based and digital service businesses to understand their monetization efficiency, evaluate pricing strategies, and identify opportunities for growth by analyzing trends in revenue generation per customer.

Balanced Scorecard — A framework for measuring performance across financial, customer, internal, and innovation dimensions.

Bounce Rate and Session Length: Tracks how engaging your website is, providing insights into the online customer experience.

Churn Rate: The percentage of customers who stop doing business with you, revealing potential problems with the product or customer experience in either channel.

Cohort Analysis — Studying customer groups over time to identify retention or behavior patterns.

Conversion Rate — Measures the percentage of leads who become paying customers. In a hybrid GTM, this can be tracked at different stages, such as converting a website visitor into an in-store shopper or vice-versa.

Customer Acquisition Cost (CAC) — The total expense (sales and marketing) to acquire a new customer. In a digital-physical GTM, it is crucial to measure CAC across all channels to see which ones are most cost-effective.

Customer Lifetime Value (LTV) – The total revenue a customer is expected to generate over their relationship with your business. This metric shows the long-term value of acquiring customers through both digital and physical channels.

Funnel Velocity – Measures how quickly leads move through each stage of the sales funnel. In a digital-physical strategy, this helps identify friction points in the customer's cross-channel journey.

Media Mix Modeling (MMM) – Evaluating the impact of different media investments on outcomes.

Monthly/Annual Recurring Revenue (MRR/ARR) – The predictable revenue a business expects to receive. In a hybrid GTM, you can track how much of this revenue is driven by online subscriptions versus in-store purchases or contracts.

Retention Rate: The percentage of customers a business retains over a period, indicating how successful the GTM is at building lasting relationships.

CHAPTER 15 – CUSTOMER-CENTRIC INNOVATION

Focus: innovation systems, experimentation, co-creation

Agile – A flexible, iterative framework to implement innovation, transforming creative ideas into valuable products or services by breaking down large challenges into small, manageable tasks, testing hypotheses quickly, and adapting based on constant customer feedback.

Co-Creation – Collaborating directly with customers or partners to design products or services.

Customer-Centric Innovation – Innovation grounded in real customer needs and feedback.

Design Thinking – A problem-solving framework emphasizing empathy, ideation, and iteration.

Disruptive Innovation – Innovations that fundamentally change markets by creating new demand.

Exploit vs. Explore Balance – Balancing optimization of current business with exploration of new opportunities.

Innovation Flight Path Model – A metaphor for a structured process that guides and manages new ideas from initial concept through development and into the market, much like a flight plan guides an aircraft. It provides a repeatable and scalable framework for innovation, helping organizations reduce risk and increase efficiency by evaluating ideas at defined checkpoints, or "gates," before committing more resources.

Innovation Funnel — A process that manages idea generation, evaluation, and scaling.

Lean Experimentation — Testing ideas quickly and cheaply to validate before scaling.

Lean Startup Method — An iterative approach to developing a business or product, focusing on validated learning through a continuous "Build-Measure-Learn" cycle. It involves launching a Minimum Viable Product (MVP) to quickly gather customer feedback, analyzing that data to make decisions, and either improving the product (persevering) or changing direction (pivoting). This process aims to reduce waste, minimize upfront investment, and efficiently develop products that truly meet market needs

MVP (Minimum Viable Product) — A simplified version of a product built to test assumptions with early users.

Open Innovation — Using external ideas and collaborations to drive innovation.

Systems Thinking — When applied to innovation, this involves a holistic approach to problem-solving that recognizes the interconnectedness of all parts within a system. Instead of focusing on isolated elements, it analyzes how these parts interact to influence the whole. For innovators, this means understanding feedback loops, dynamic patterns, and potential long-term consequences to create more sustainable, resilient, and impactful solutions that avoid unintended side effects.

Test-and-Learn — Iterative experimentation with real-world customers to refine solutions.

CHAPTER 16 — AGILE MARKETING

Focus: adaptability, sprint-based marketing, iterative growth

Agile Marketing — Applying agile principles to marketing to emphasize speed, iteration, and adaptability.

Backlog — A prioritized list of marketing ideas, experiments, and tasks awaiting execution.

Cross-Functional Team — A group with diverse skill sets (creative, data, product)

collaborating on marketing.

Kanban — A visual workflow management system that tracks tasks from "to-do" to "done."

MVP Campaign — A minimal marketing campaign designed to quickly test effectiveness before scaling.

Performance System — In the context of agile marketing, this framework encompasses the tools, metrics, and processes used to continuously monitor, measure, and improve marketing efforts. It provides real-time, data-driven insights into the efficiency, effectiveness, and impact of marketing campaigns, enabling teams to adapt quickly to changing market conditions.

Scrum — A framework for agile project management with defined roles (scrum master, product owner).

Sprint — A short, time-boxed cycle in which a marketing team completes a defined set of tasks.

Stand-Up Meeting — A brief daily team meeting to share progress, blockers, and next steps.

Test-and-Learn Culture — Mindset that encourages continuous experimentation and rapid adaptation.

Velocity — A measure of how much work a marketing team can complete in a sprint.

CHAPTER 17 — AI IN MARKETING AND ENTERPRISE

Focus: intelligence at scale, enterprise-wide AI integration

Agentic AI – AI systems composed of "AI agents" that act autonomously to achieve goals, going beyond simple content generation by interacting with tools and environments, making decisions, and executing actions without direct human intervention.

Agentic Marketplace – A platform where autonomous AI agents can be bought, sold, and deployed to perform complex tasks on behalf of users or businesses. These are not simple chatbots but sophisticated AI systems that can proactively reason, plan, and act independently to achieve specific goals, often orchestrating multi-step workflows. This concept is central to agentic commerce, which focuses on AI agents autonomously completing commercial activities.

AI Ethics — Principles to ensure AI is used fairly, responsibly, and transparently.

Artificial Intelligence (AI) — The simulation of human intelligence in machines that learn and adapt.

Computer Vision — AI that enables machines to interpret and analyze visual inputs.

Conversational AI — Chatbots and voice assistants that interact with humans using natural language.

Enterprise AI Operating System — A cross-functional framework embedding AI across all business functions.

Generative AI — AI that can create new content such as text, images, and video.

Large Language Model (LLM) — A type of artificial intelligence that are trained on massive amounts of text data to understand, generate, and manipulate human language. They are used for tasks like generating content, summarizing text, translating languages, writing code, and powering chatbots and virtual assistants.

Machine Learning (ML) — A subset of AI where algorithms learn from data to improve over time.

Model Training — In AI, "model training" is the process of feeding large datasets to a machine learning algorithm so it can learn patterns, relationships, and rules to make accurate predictions or decisions on new, unseen data. It's like teaching a computer by showing it examples, adjusting its internal parameters (weights and biases), and iteratively refining its performance until it achieves a desired level of accuracy and can reliably perform specific tasks.

Natural Language Processing (NLP) — AI techniques enabling machines to interpret and generate human language.

Predictive Analytics — Using AI/ML to forecast customer behaviors or outcomes.

Recommendation Engine — Algorithms that suggest products or content based on user behavior.

CHAPTER 18 — THE FUTURE CASTING

Focus: emerging frontiers, foresight, transformation

Blockchain — A distributed ledger system that records transactions securely and transparently.

DAO (Decentralized Autonomous Organization) — A blockchain-governed entity where rules are executed by code.

Decentralized Finance (DeFi) — Financial services delivered without intermediaries, powered by blockchain.

Digital Twin — A virtual replica of a real-world system used for simulation and optimization.

Future-Readiness — The organizational capability to anticipate, adapt, and thrive in emerging digital landscapes.

Metaverse — A persistent, immersive digital environment blending virtual and physical realities.

Smart Contracts — Self-executing agreements stored and enforced on a blockchain.

Strategic Foresight — Anticipating future disruptions and opportunities through structured scanning.

Tokenization — Turning assets (physical or digital) into blockchain-based tokens

Web3 — The next evolution of the internet based on decentralization, blockchain, and tokenized ownership.

ACADEMIC & FOUNDATIONAL WORKS

Barney, Jay B. 1991. "Firm Resources and Sustained Competitive Advantage." Journal of Management 17 (1): 99–120.

Christensen, Clayton M. 1997. The Innovator's Dilemma. Boston: Harvard Business School Press.

Porter, Michael E. 1980. Competitive Strategy: Techniques for Analyzing Industries and Competitors. New York: Free Press.

Rogers, Everett M. 1962. Diffusion of Innovations. New York: Free Press.

Strategy Frameworks & Models

Baghai, Mehrdad, Stephen Coley, and David White. 1999. The Alchemy of Growth: Practical Insights for Building the Enduring Enterprise. New York: Perseus Publishing.

Osterwalder, Alexander, and Yves Pigneur. 2010. Business Model Generation: A Handbook for Visionaries, Game Changers, and Challengers. Hoboken, NJ: John Wiley & Sons.

Porter, Michael E. 1980. Competitive Strategy: Techniques for Analyzing Industries and Competitors. New York: Free Press.

Barney, Jay B. 1991. "Firm Resources and Sustained Competitive Advantage." Journal of Management 17 (1): 99–120.

Doerr, John. 2018. Measure What Matters: How Google, Bono, and the Gates Foundation Rock the World with OKRs. New York: Portfolio.

Beck, K., et al. (2001). "Manifesto for Agile Software Development." Agile Alliance.
Schwaber, Ken, and Jeff Sutherland. 2020. The Scrum Guide. Scrum.org.

Anderson, David J. 2010. Kanban: Successful Evolutionary Change for Your Technology Business. Sequim, WA: Blue Hole Press.

Industry Reports & Whitepapers

McKinsey & Company. 2023. "The State of AI." McKinsey Global Institute.

Gartner. 2024. Top Strategic Technology Trends. Stamford, CT: Gartner.

Deloitte. 2022. The Future of Work. Deloitte Insights Whitepaper.

Accenture. 2020s. Future of Media & Entertainment Digital Transformation. Accenture Research.

Company Case Studies & Materials

Adobe Systems Incorporated. 2013–2020s. Creative Cloud Transformation. Company reports and investor communications.

Amazon.com, Inc. 1994–2025. Platform ecosystem including AWS, Prime, and logistics network. Annual reports and shareholder letters.

ByteDance Ltd. (TikTok). 2020s. Short-form video platform, consumer attention dynamics. Company materials and industry analyses.

Domino's Pizza, Inc. 2010–2018. Digital ordering and loyalty program transformation. Company filings and investor presentations.

Duolingo, Inc. 2020s. AI-driven gamified language learning platform. Company materials and public statements.

LEGO Group. 2003–2014. Reinvention through digital co-creation and partnerships. Company histories and case materials.

Meta Platforms, Inc. (Facebook/Instagram). 2010s–2020s. Social platforms and the advertising ecosystem. Company materials.

Microsoft Corporation. 2014–2025. Mobile-first, cloud-first strategic transformation; Azure platform growth. Annual reports and executive communications.

Motorola, Inc. 2000s. Mobile device transition and brand decline. Public filings and industry coverage.

Netflix, Inc. 2007–2025. Transition from DVDs to global streaming and studio production. Annual reports and investor letters.

Nike, Inc. 2010s–2020s. Direct-to-consumer ecosystem (apps, community, content). Company communications.

Peloton Interactive, Inc. 2020s. Connected fitness platform evolution. Company filings and public statements.

Procter & Gamble (P&G). 2010s–2020s. AI and digital insights; Oral-B iO connected products. Company communications and case materials.

Red Bull GmbH. 2007–2025. Red Bull Media House and content ecosystem. Company materials and industry coverage.

Salesforce, Inc. 2010s–2020s. CRM and customer data platform evolution. Company materials and analyst reports.

Shopify Inc. 2006–2025. Global commerce operating system; partner ecosystem. Company filings and investor communications.

Spotify AB. 2010s–2020s. Streaming personalization and platform strategy. Annual reports and industry analyses.

The Walt Disney Company. 2019–2025. Disney+ streaming service and media strategy. Company reports and investor communications.

Warner Bros. Entertainment Inc. 2000s–2010s. Digital supply chain and distribution transformation. Company communications and case materials.

Concepts & Methods (Selected Sources)

Court, David, Dave Elzinga, Susan Mulder, and Ole Jørgen Vetvik. 2009. "The Consumer Decision Journey." McKinsey Quarterly.

Lemon, Katherine N., and Peter C. Verhoef. 2016. "Understanding Customer Experience Throughout the Customer Journey." Journal of Marketing 80 (6): 69–96.

Hanssens, Dominique M., and Koen H. Pauwels. 2016. "Demystifying Media Mix Modeling." Applied Marketing Analytics 2 (3): 243–264.

Shaikh, Aastha, and Brett Gordon. 2017. "An Empirical Analysis of Multi-Touch Attribution." Marketing Science 36 (6): 846–867.

ENDNOTES

1 The model was created by Kurt Lewin, a psychologist who studied and applied force field analysis to understand group behavior and organizational change.

2 Kotter, J. P. (2012). Leading change. Harvard Business Review Press.

3 The collapse of the Internet Bubble in 2000, also known as the dot-com bubble burst, occurred when the speculative frenzy surrounding internet-based companies led to soaring stock prices, only for the bubble to pop in March 2000, causing a crash in technology stocks and the failure of many startups that lacked viable business models. This event, driven by excessive venture capital, media hype, and investor overvaluation, led to a market panic, massive sell-offs, and a subsequent recession. However, some tech giants, such as Amazon and eBay, survived and thrived.

4 The ILOVEYOU virus, a destructive email worm, had a significant impact, causing widespread disruption and financial losses globally. It spread rapidly by exploiting user trust and vulnerabilities in email systems, resulting in the infection of millions of computers and causing significant damage to both personal and business systems. Wikipedia

5 Barney, J. B. (1991). Firm Resources and Sustained Competitive Advantage. Journal of Management, 17(1), 99-120.

6 Essentially, "full send" is a mindset of complete commitment and risk-taking, often associated with high-energy activities and a "YOLO" (you only live once) attitude.

7 Tim Berners-Lee's origin for the Semantic Web stems from his initial vision for the World Wide Web (WWW) in the late 1980s and early 1990s, seeing the Web

primarily as a publishing medium for human-readable documents.

8 An NFT (non-fungible token) is a unique digital asset stored on a blockchain that certifies authenticity and ownership of an item, such as digital art, music, or virtual collectibles. Unlike cryptocurrencies like Bitcoin, which are fungible (interchangeable), each NFT is one-of-a-kind and cannot be copied, substituted, or divided. NFTs serve as a digital certificate of authenticity and proof of ownership for digital or, in some cases, physical assets, with their ownership history publicly verified on the blockchain.

9 Decentralized finance (DeFi) is an emerging financial system using blockchain and cryptocurrencies to enable direct transactions between individuals and businesses. By eliminating intermediaries like banks, DeFi aims to reduce costs and speed up processes, although it's currently in its infancy and presents security challenges. Investopedia.

10 "Disruptive Innovation describes a process by which a product or service takes root in simple applications at the bottom of the market, typically by being less expensive and more accessible, and then relentlessly moves upmarket, eventually displacing established competitors." ChristensenInstitute.org

11 Teece's concept of dynamic capabilities essentially says that what matters for business is corporate agility.

12 SOAR analysis was created by Jacqueline Stavros, David Cooperrider, and D. Lynn Kelley in 2003, as a strategic planning tool based on the principles of Appreciative Inquiry

13 MikeCardus.com

14 Edith Penrose, *The Theory of the Growth of the Firm* (1959)

15 Bernard Jaworski and Robert Lurie, "The Organic Growth Playbook: Activate High-Yield Behaviors To Achieve Extraordinary Results — Every Time" American

Marketing Association, 2018.

16 The Origin Of Customer Journey Mapping, Chip Bell, April 2023, CMXToday.com

17 Propensity-based Segmentation relies on dividing your customer base into groups (segments) based on their predicted likelihood (or propensity) to take a specific action such as purchase, churn out, open an email, etc.

18 A value proposition statement that uses principles of behavioral science to clearly articulate the unique benefits a product or service offers, specifically addressing customers' psychological needs and decision-making patterns. It's powerful because it moves beyond traditional benefits by focusing on the "why" behind customer decisions, creating a mental heuristic that makes the product or service offering easy to understand, memorable, and the natural choice when the right moment arises.

19 Rogers, E. M. (1962). Diffusion of innovations. New York, Free Press of Glencoe.

20 Moore, G. A. (1991). *Crossing the Chasm: Marketing and Selling High-Tech Products to Mainstream Customers.* Harper Business.

21 The underlying phenomenon and its challenges were initially observed and documented by Lee James and Warren Schirtzinger in 1989 while working as consultants at Regis McKenna Inc. (RMI).

22 Dial-up is an outdated method of connecting to the internet using a standard telephone line and a modem, requiring a computer, a modem, a phone line, and an Internet Service Provider (ISP) account to function. While it was accessible and served as the initial way to get online for many, its connection speeds (maxing out at 56 kbps) are too slow for today's internet use, making it impractical for streaming, video chat, or playing games. It's also known for its screeching and pinging sound of connecting over telephone lines.

23 The first clickable web banner ad was introduced on October 27, 1994, on the website HotWired.com (now Wired.com). It was a 468x60 pixel banner ad for AT&T. The ad featured the text "Have you ever clicked your mouse right here? You will."

24 The first domain names, including .com, .net, and .org, were introduced in 1985.

25 Amazon launched in July 5, 1994 and was initially named Cadabra. It wouldn't turn a quarterly profit until Q4 2001.

26 The dotcom bubble is also associated with the *NASDAQ Composite index*, which rose by 582% from 751.49 to 5,132.52 from January 1995 to March 2000. The NASDAQ fell by 75% from March 2000 to October 2002, erasing most of the gains since the bubble started building, Corporate Finance Institute.

27 Friendster was founded by Canadian computer programmer Jonathan Abrams in 2002, before MySpace (2003), Hi5 (2004), Wikipedia

28 Cloud computing originated from the 1950s mainframe era's time-sharing concept, which allowed multiple users to share expensive computing resources. The fundamental idea of global computer networking was conceived in the 1960s by J.C.R. Licklider, leading to the development of ARPANET, a precursor to the Internet. The "cloud" metaphor itself emerged in the 1990s, with the term "cloud computing" gaining wider usage in a 1996 Compaq business plan, paving the way for modern cloud infrastructure services, such as those offered by Amazon Web Services, starting in the early 2000s.

29 Federal Reserve Bank of St. Louis.

30 In internet and gaming slang, "NPC" (Non-Player Character) describes a person who lacks individuality, critical thinking, or original thought, essentially acting like a background character in a video game who follows programmed behaviors. It's like a walk-on character in a movie.

31 For Uber, this meant prioritizing driver acquisition over rider acquisition. Drivers are the critical supply side, and attracting them first helps create a network where riders can quickly find a ride.

32 The number of connected Internet of Things (IoT) devices worldwide will jump 12 percent on average annually, from nearly 27 billion in 2017 to 125 billion in 2030, according to new analysis from IHS Markit (Nasdaq: INFO).

33 Meta Platforms Has Spent $46 Billion on the Metaverse Since 2021, Motley Fool.

34 Generative AI is a type of artificial intelligence (AI) that creates new, original content, such as text, images, music, code, and more, by learning patterns from vast datasets and then generating novel outputs in response to user prompts or inputs. Unlike AI that makes predictions, generative AI focuses on creation.

35 The term "Minimum Viable Product" (MVP) originated with Frank Robinson in 2001, and was popularized by Eric Ries in his book, "The Lean Startup". Robinson initially defined it as a product with just enough features to satisfy early customers and gather feedback for future development. Ries later expanded on this concept within the Lean Startup movement.

36 America Online (AOL) began in 1985 as Quantum Computer Services before dominating the dial-up internet market in the 1990s and peaking around 2000. The company capitalized on a user-friendly interface and aggressive mass-marketing tactics to become the gateway to the internet for millions of consumers. 2000: At its peak, AOL had over 20 million subscribers and was one of the world's most valuable companies, with a market cap of $222 billion. I was working at Time Warner, when, at the height of its power, AOL merged with media giant Time Warner in what is often considered one of the most disastrous corporate mergers in history.

37 Gartner.com, 2024.

38 Fitch Ratings, 2021.

39 Capital One Financial had 32 patents in blockchain during Q2 2024. Capital One Financial Corp filed patents in Q2 2024 for systems and methods related to enhancing security in decentralized computing systems, identifying malicious wallet addresses, managing user accounts based on risk values, verifying authenticity of items using blockchain operations, and recovering lost blockchain wallet seed phrases.

40 DePietro, R., Wiarda, E., & Fleischer, M. (1990). *The context of change: An examination of the decision to adopt an innovation.* University of Michigan Press

41 DevSecOps, which stands for Development, Security, and Operations, is a software engineering culture and practice that integrates security into all phases of the software development lifecycle (SDLC). It emphasizes collaboration and shared responsibility among development, security, and operations teams to build secure and resilient software. Instead of treating security as an afterthought, DevSecOps embeds it from the beginning.

42 A generative economy refers to a new economic paradigm driven by generative AI and related technologies, characterized by AI-driven creation and automation that can lower costs, boost productivity, and transform business models across various sectors, including manufacturing, customer service, healthcare, and legal services. This paradigm also encompasses a vision of an economy designed to be socially fair and ecologically sustainable, with different ownership models and a tendency to migrate toward equitable outcomes.

43 An AI agent autonomously performs tasks by designing workflows with available tools. These agents do more than natural language processing; they also involve decision-making, problem-solving, interacting with environments, and performing actions. They handle complex tasks in enterprise applications like software design, IT automation, code generation, and conversational assistance.

44 In Splunk's global research survey of more than 1,300 business and IT

decision makers, 60 percent of respondents reported that half or more of their organization's data is considered dark. A full one-third of respondents reported this amount to be 75 percent or more

45 Peter Weill, et al. 2024. What's Next: Top Performers Are Becoming Real-Time Businesses. MIT Center for Information Systems Research.
Companies operating in the top quartile versus the bottom quartile of "real-timeness" had more than 50 percent higher revenue growth and net margins—a huge premium.

46 The concept of the Zero Moment of Truth (ZMOT) was coined by Google in a 2011 study, "Winning the Zero Moment of Truth," to describe the pre-purchase online research phase in a consumer's decision-making process. This term built upon Procter & Gamble's existing framework of the First Moment of Truth (FMOT), the physical interaction with a product, and introduced a new stage where consumers use the internet to research, compare, and read reviews before making a purchase.

47 Statista, May 2025

48 81% of retail shoppers conduct online research before buying. The overwhelming majority of retail consumers start their journey with online research, GE Capital Retail Bank.

49 And in Q2, we surpassed 185 million 90-day active loyalty users across 60 markets, which is well on our way to our goal of 250 million by 2027. McDonalds.com

50 EDI (Electronic Data Interchange) was developed in the 1960s within the U.S. transportation industry to streamline communication and replace paper-based document exchanges with electronic data. Edward A. Guilbert, known as the "father of EDI," played a crucial role in standardizing these electronic messages. TrueCommerce.

51 Platform Theory in B2B focuses on multi-sided, interconnected organizations

that serve as intermediaries for transactions and value creation between different businesses. Key aspects include network effects, which amplify the value as more users join, digital servitization, integrating digital assets with physical products, and complex governance structures to manage multi-party interactions. B2B platforms differ from B2C in their focus on industrial-scale operations, specialized networks of participants, and the need for strong, tailored relationships to address complex purchase decisions.

52 Caporuscio, A., et al. (2023) Value co-creation: Balancing B2B platform value and potential reverse-value effects. Journal of Business Research.

53 Gartner, 2020.

54 Kirk, Emilia. 2022,The Attention Economy: Standing Out Among The Noise, Forbes,

55 Deloitte, 2025

56 Grand View Research, 2024

57 Recent studies confirm that a large percentage of TV viewers are disengaged during commercials, with many using the time to scroll on their phones. For example, a 2022 Sharethrough study found 66% of viewers did not actively watch TV ads, with 64% citing their phone as the primary distraction. This highlights a significant shift in viewing habits, where commercial breaks are often seen as opportunities to switch to secondary devices rather than a time to focus on the advertisements.

58 Studies from Marketing Week in 2017 found that nearly 70% of consumers distrusted advertising, and a 2023 MediaCat UK survey found 70% find digital ads annoying. A 2017 study also revealed that nearly 70% of consumers distrust advertising.

59 In 2024, 68% of Gen Z consumers discovered new products on social media,

up from 60% in 2023. Nearly 60% went on and made an order, nearly doubling from the previous year. In 2024, more than 53% of Gen Z ordered directly through social media, Entrepreneur. 2025.

60 Salesforce's free online learning platform, Trailhead, uses gamification and hands-on modules to train users, which can indirectly lead to better lead quality and faster sales cycles.

61 The concept of Paid, Owned, and Earned media was first introduced by Nokia in 2008, as a way to categorize and analyze their digital media efforts for marketing and media planning. They used these terms to classify their digital media resources better and determine the best options for developing digital campaigns.

62 CPM – Cost per Thousand impressions is a standard for ad planning and buying.

63 The Context Effect, Sept 2021. AIS & Neuro Science Research Whitepaper

64 PG Lab & Sharethrough: Exploring the Effectiveness Of Native Ads, June, 201

65 First-party data is information a company collects directly from its own audience, such as customers and website visitors, through interactions like website activity, email engagement, and surveys. This data tends to be highly accurate and valuable for creating targeted marketing campaigns and understanding customers at a deeper level, as the company owns and controls it. It's captured via the website visits, email activity, sms response, app downloads and usage, push notifications and in store actions among others.

66 Second-party data is first-party data that another company shares with you directly from their own customers, typically through a trusted, mutually beneficial partnership. It acts as a trusted source of data about an audience you want to reach, providing insights into potential customers you don't have direct relationships with. This type of data is more reliable than third-party data because

it comes from a known and verified source, allowing for more accurate and relevant marketing campaigns.

67 Data collected by companies with no direct relationship to the consumer, often bought from large marketplaces.

68 Marketing automation platforms work by performing actions based on customer behavior and preset rules. A key function is identifying and tracking a user's digital interactions such as website visits, form submissions, and email clicks to trigger timely and relevant follow-up actions.
Key functions often include:

69 Michael Brito — https://www.britopian.com/

70 Agentic AI refers to artificial intelligence systems designed to act autonomously and proactively to achieve user-defined goals by using tools and reasoning to make independent, multi-step decisions and execute complex, goal-oriented workflows with limited human oversight. Key characteristics include autonomy, reasoning, adaptive planning, and the ability to learn from new data to improve performance over time.

71 "Omni-agent fluency" is a term referring to the capabilities of an advanced artificial intelligence (AI) agent that can operate and communicate fluently across all channels, applications, and languages. It is a concept associated with "agentic AI," which describes AI systems that can independently plan and execute complex tasks.

72 The analytics firm DataReportal reported 5.24 billion social media users as of February 2025.

73 https://www.globalmediainsight.com/blog/youtube-users-statistics/

74 Interview with Maria Dabrowski, Dabrowski Digital Connect LLC

75 Social proof is a psychological phenomenon where people look to the actions and behaviors of others to guide their own decisions, especially in situations of uncertainty. In marketing, it's used to build trust and credibility by showcasing evidence of popularity, such as positive reviews, endorsements from experts or celebrities, high follower counts, or certifications. This psychological principle helps influence consumer behavior, leading to increased sales, credibility, and customer engagement.

76 In social media and content strategy, a talk trigger is a specific, intentional operational choice by a business that compels customers to talk about the business with others, generating word-of-mouth marketing. These operational choices must be remarkable, relevant, realistic, and repeatable to be effective, moving beyond mere advertising to become part of the brand's consistent, compelling customer experience.

77 Shoppable social posts originated with the introduction of social commerce features on platforms like Instagram in early 2018, allowing brands to tag products directly in posts and enabling users to click and purchase items without leaving the app. This feature, which creates a seamless, in-app shopping experience, has since expanded and been adopted by other platforms like Pinterest and TikTok, transforming the way consumers discover and buy products.

78 https://contentauthenticity.org/

79 Nobel laureate Herbert A. Simon's 1971 paper, "Designing Organizations for an Information-Rich World", where he first introduced the concept of the "attention economy", was published as a chapter in the book Computers, Communications, and the Public Interest.

80 Ad Effectiveness: TV Plus Digital Significantly Outperforms Digital Only, by Karlene Lukovitz, September 23, 2020, Media Post

81 Eisenmann, Thomas R. *Why Startups Fail: A New Roadmap for Entrepreneurial Success.* Crown Currency, 2021.

82 Bussgang, Jeffrey J. Finding Product-Market Fit in the Age of AI. Damn Gravity Media, 2025

83 An AI OS is an emerging concept that moves beyond traditional operating systems to deeply integrate AI at every level of computing, from the kernel to the user interface.

84 Ecosystem influence modeling uses mathematical and computational techniques to analyze and predict the complex relationships and dynamics within an ecosystem. The purpose of these models is to simulate how various factors, such as human activities, pollution, or climate change, might impact the system and its components over time.

85 Pfeffer, J., & Sutton, R. I. (2006). Evidence-based management. Harvard Business Review, 84(1), 62–74.

86 Real-time value loops are cyclical processes that leverage timely data and user feedback to drive continuous improvement and value creation, often through digital tools and AI, for products, services, or experiences. Key aspects include collecting real-time customer data and user feedback, analyzing this data for insights using AI, then using those insights to make faster, more informed decisions and adjustments within the product or service.

87 Global CVC-backed funding increased by 20% year-over-year (YoY) to $65.9 billion in 2024, but deal count fell to a six-year low. CB Insights

88 Popularized by author Jim Cramer, a Full Fit Flywheel is a customer-centric growth model in product development that goes beyond achieving a basic product-market fit. It emphasizes creating an entire, interconnected system where every component, the product, market, channels, and business model, reinforces the others to build momentum and achieve sustained, long-term growth.

89 A customer data platform (CDP) is software that collects and unifies customer data from multiple sources to create a single, persistent view of

each customer, known as a unified customer profile. This data, which includes behavioral, transactional, and demographic information, is then made accessible to other marketing, sales, and service systems to enable personalized customer experiences and targeted campaigns across all channels.

90 The "working backwards" methodology at Amazon is a customer-centric approach to product and service development, famously paired with the six-page memo culture. Instead of using PowerPoint presentations, teams write detailed, narrative-style six-page memos to outline new ideas, which are then read silently at the start of meetings. This method forces deep thinking, facilitates constructive feedback, and promotes clarity and a data-driven approach to innovation by providing a narrative context for complex initiatives.

91 "Pwned" (pronounced "poned") is internet slang for being compromised, defeated, or taken over, originating from a misspelling of "owned" in online gaming. In the context of cybersecurity, it means a system, network, or online account has been infiltrated and controlled by a hacker..

92 An Agentic Marketplace is a digital platform where users can discover, buy, sell, and deploy specialized, autonomous AI agents to perform tasks on their behalf. Unlike simple AI tools that respond to direct commands, agentic AI can take initiative, reason, plan, and execute multi-step processes autonomously to achieve a goal.

93 Cloaked Identity (n.) An adjustable, user-controlled privacy interface, a spectrum of identity visibility, managed via filters (e.g., anonymized usage, partial location, abstracted preferences). Customers can selectively reveal data tiers, and in exchange receive tangible value (like brand credit, NFT rewards, resale benefits) within a tokenized, bot-mediated ecosystem. 2025, Overclocked:.Business Reinvented *(we said it first)*

94 A Kanban board is a visual project management tool used to manage and track the flow of work, typically divided into columns representing workflow stages (e.g., To Do, In Progress, Done). It helps teams visualize their workload, identify

bottlenecks, and improve overall workflow efficiency.

95 Edelman, David , Heller, Jason, and Spittaels, Steven , Agile marketing: A step-by-step guide, McKinsey, 2016

96 Singla, Alex, Sukharevsky, Alexander, Yee, Lareina, Chui, Michael, Hall, Bryce. The state of AI, How organizations are rewiring to capture value. McKinsey, 2025

97 Embedded intelligence is characterized as the ability of a product, process, or service to reflect on its own operational performance, usage load, or environment. The motivation for this may be to enhance the performance, lifetime, or quality of the product. This self-reflection might be facilitated by information collected via embedded sensors, and processed locally or communicated remotely for processing. Wikipedia.

98 MLOps (Machine Learning Operations) is a discipline that applies DevOps principles to the machine learning (ML) lifecycle, aiming to automate, standardize, and improve the reliability, scalability, and efficiency of building, deploying, and maintaining ML models in production. It involves collaboration between data scientists and operations engineers, automating tasks like experiment tracking, model deployment, monitoring, and retraining to ensure models consistently deliver business value.

99 Retrieval-Augmented Generation (RAG) is an AI framework that enhances a large language model (LLM) by retrieving relevant, external information before generating a response to a user's query. This process allows LLMs to produce more accurate, up-to-date, and contextually relevant answers by grounding them in reliable, external data sources, rather than relying solely on their pre-existing, potentially outdated training data.

100 The NIST AI Risk Management Framework (AI RMF) is a guidance designed to improve the robustness and reliability of artificial intelligence by providing a systematic approach to managing risks. It emphasizes the need for accountability, transparency, and ethical behavior in AI development and deployment.

101 Hyperscalers are large-scale cloud computing providers that offer vast amounts of computing power and storage through a global network of massive data centers. Key examples include Amazon Web Services (AWS), Microsoft Azure, and Google Cloud Platform (GCP). They excel at scaling IT architecture up or down to meet fluctuating demand, providing services like Infrastructure as a Service (IaaS), Platform as a Service (PaaS), and Software as a Service (SaaS).

102 Hyper-personalization uses advanced data analysis and AI to create unique, relevant experiences and offers for individual customers in real-time, transforming mass marketing into a "segment-of-one" approach to drive engagement, loyalty, and conversions.

103 Tokenization is a data security process that replaces sensitive information with non-sensitive equivalent "tokens," which are unique, randomly generated numbers or codes. It is also the process of creating digital tokens on a blockchain to represent real-world assets, such as stocks or real estate, making them tradable and verifiable on a distributed ledger.

104 2025 Tech Trends Report, Future Today Strategy Group (FTSG)

www.ingramcontent.com/pod-product-compliance
Lightning Source LLC
LaVergne TN
LVHW040514210926
848480LV00005BA/1452
* 9 7 9 8 9 9 3 5 9 0 1 2 7 *